# GREEK POPULAR
# MORALITY

# GREEK POPULAR
# MORALITY
## In the time of
## Plato and Aristotle

## K. J. DOVER

## UNIVERSITY OF CALIFORNIA PRESS
Berkeley and Los Angeles, 1974

195883

UNIVERSITY OF CALIFORNIA PRESS
Berkeley and Los Angeles, California

ISBN: 0-520-02721-3
Library of Congress Catalog Card Number: 73-94451

© Basil Blackwell, 1974

Printed in Great Britain

# CONTENTS

# PREFACE

This book is a confluence of streams which have their origins at several times
and places. Many years ago, when I first became interested in Lysias, it seemed
to me that in the study of the Greek orators insufficient attention was paid to
the presuppositions (shared by speaker and jury) without which no argument,
however technically ingenious in form, could have had persuasive effect.
Later, when I came to edit a play of Aristophanes, it occurred to me that it
might be possible to give a reasonably accurate account of the attitudes and
presuppositions which made the Athenians laugh at some things that we too
find funny and at others which we do not. The longer I have worked on
oratory and comic poetry, the more deeply I have been impressed by the
evidence for attitudes and moral principles common to Old Comedy, New
Comedy and the forensic oratory of the fourth century, despite their differences. It happened that in 1970 I was invited by The Council for Philosophical
Studies to take part in a seminar at Colorado Springs on various aspects of
Greek philosophy, and this invitation, for which I remain deeply grateful,
provided me with an opportunity to describe what seemed to me the most
interesting and conspicuous features of the morality (explicit and implicit) of
unphilosophical literature during the lifetimes of Plato and Aristotle. After
the seminar I began to turn my material into a book; it has taken longer than
I expected, and there are many points about which I have changed my mind
since 1970.

I have been very surprised to find how little has been written on this topic.
There are, of course, many books about the history of moral concepts in
early Greek poetry and in Attic tragedy; there are others which follow the
history of these concepts in the historians and philosophers, and some of them
admit Isokrates as an honorary philosopher; others again are concerned with
the legal concepts underlying judicial practice; none, so far as my knowledge
goes, has treated works composed for the persuasion or amusement of large
audiences as the primary evidence for the moral assumptions made by
the average Athenian citizen during the years when Plato was writing the
*Republic* or Aristotle the *Nicomachean Ethics*. I have seldom referred in the

course of my book to Plato or Aristotle, since I judged it prudent to confine myself to a presentation of the data relevant to popular morality, leaving it to philosophers to consider the relation between those data and systematic ethical thought. Partly because popular morality is essentially unsystematic, partly because a speaker in court or a character in a play can at any time use whichever of a pair or range of alternative moral attitudes best serves his purpose, but most of all because some of the material is assembled and classified in this book for the first time, some portions of some chapters inevitably resemble a rampage through an epitome of Stobaeus. I am well aware that a more detailed investigation and a more refined classification are desirable, and, if the topic as a whole is found interesting, I hope that others will pursue it. I must emphasize that I took a quite deliberate decision not to treat Greek terminology and the ancient classification of virtues and vices as my starting-point, but rather to formulate such questions about morality as were prompted by my own moral experience. For this reason it will some-times be found that the same Greek passage is cited in quite different contexts, and often that passages which would have appeared together if I had taken a different starting-point appear in two separate batches.

The bibliography of the subject would have exceeded all reasonable bounds if I had systematically given references even to the principal relevant works whenever I had occasion to mention a particular Greek concept or term. Accordingly, under the heading 'Abbreviations' I have followed a mechanical principle, simply listing those works to which more than one reference is made in the footnotes, and in respect of other works I have been as selective as possible, though it is difficult to be selective without occasionally being arbitrary. Since the book is intended both for readers who know the Greek language and for readers who do not, I have transliterated and translated in the interests of the latter but have also made a few critical observations on individual passages which I hope will interest the former.

Reading, discussion and reflection, over a period of years, on the relations and conflicts between different conceptions of morality in our own society have given considerable impetus to the writing of the book. Belief that the events and utterances reported in the Bible are correctly reported, and with it the belief that God has revealed himself in injunctions which we disobey at our peril, has substantially declined in the course of the last two hundred years, partly through a very great increase in knowledge of how moralities take shape and change in animal groups, in the individual human being from babyhood onwards, and in a wide variety of pre-Christian and non-Christian societies, and partly because so many people find (reasonably, in my view) that the more they know and the more they think about documentation, tradition, religious experience and theological argument, the less inclined they feel to commit themselves to acceptance of the claims of Christianity. These doubts (not confined to agnostics) on the intellectual plane may be offset by a belief (not confined to Christians) that Christianity at least marked a substantial and lasting moral advance on what had preceded it, and that there is still no one moral or religious system so fertile in resources for satisfying the moral needs of man in the twentieth or any other century. Such a belief is sustained sometimes by a crude selectivity in the use of historical evidence (e.g. contrasting the worst pagans with the best Christians) and sometimes by a more subtle selectivity (e.g. taking it for granted that what is generous and selfless in people such as Augustine is more significant than what is cruel and mad in the same people); or again, by pointing out (rightly) that the Gospels supply something valuable which is missing in Plato, without stopping to realize that not many Greeks were Platonists or to wonder whether Greek moralities can supply something valuable which is missing in the Gospels. The history of Christianity from the beginning of the Christian era to this day suggests to me that whether Christian belief makes an individual morally better or morally worse depends on how he interprets ambiguous and enigmatic passages of the New Testament, what criteria he employs as a means of distinguishing between valid and invalid religious experiences, how he applies general injunctions to particular cases, and (above all) the relative importance which he attaches to different elements in Christianity. In taking all these decisions, whether he takes them consciously or not, he is necessarily judging Christianity by standards which are external to it.

I do not for a moment believe that even if the Greeks of the pre-Christian centuries could be shown to have 'believed in' a completely coherent moral system which we might call 'Hellenism', it would be desirable or possible for us now to become 'Hellenists'. Morality is simply not like that; and it might be as well to add that although the average ancient Athenian would have found much to criticize in Christianity (less now than in, say, the seventeenth century), he would have criticized much also in various kinds of liberalism, individualism and totalitarianism, and perhaps most of all in a conscientiously permissive society. I suggest that we use what we can discover about ancient moral attitudes in order to conduct our own criticism and, it is to be hoped, our own modification, of our assumptions and principles, whether individual or collective.

While I was writing this preface my mother died after a very long illness which had the power to destroy her muscles but no power to diminish her self-reliance and the wry humour which somehow communicated itself even when her hand could not write and her speech could not be understood. Every day that I knew her, from my infancy onwards, she showed me by her example how perfectly the unfailing spontaneity of a warm heart can be combined with the passionate objectivity of a truly fair and open mind. It is fitting that I should dedicate to her memory this essay on a sequence in the history of ideas.

*Vecoli,*                                                    K. J. DOVER
*March 1973*

# TRANSLITERATION AND
# TRANSLATION

In transliterating from the Greek alphabet I have represented *v* as *u* in the combinations *au, eu* and *ou*, but otherwise as *y*. I mark long vowels by ‾ above the vowel.

As far as possible, I have avoided transliterating inflected forms of Greek nouns, adjectives and verbs, writing (e.g.) 'to *dikaios* men' or 'to those who are *dikaios*' rather than *tois dikaiois*, and 'I would *polyprāgmonein*' rather than *polyprāgmonoiēn an*. But when a Greek adjective is used as a noun, this procedure becomes too cumbrous, and the following inflected forms should be noted:

(i) Adjectives in -*os*.
  (e.g. *kalos*)
  
  | | |
  |---|---|
  | *kalon* | 'something which is *kalos*' |
  | *kala* | 'things which are *kalos*' |
  | *to kalon* | 'that which is *kalos*', '*kalos*-ness' |
  | *ta kala* | 'those things which are *kalos*' |

(ii) Adjectives in -*ēs*.
  (e.g. *alēthēs*): *alēthes, alēthē, to alēthes, ta alēthē*, as above.
Adverbs mostly end in -*ōs*, e.g. *kalōs, alēthōs*.

It is occasionally necessary also, to avoid cumbrousness, to put nouns into the plural; note that in general the plural of -*a*, -*ā*, -*ē* and -*ēs* is -*ai*, the plural of -*os* is -*oi*, and the plural of -*ma* is -*mata*. Thus: *doxa: doxai, adikiā: adikiai, anankē: anankai, polītes: polītai, nomos: nomoi, adikēma: adikēmata*.

My translations sometimes err on the side of literalness, in order to make their relevance to the argument clear; occasionally the same purpose is served by erring on the side of freedom. In translating a passage isolated from its context, it is sometimes necessary to expand it to make it intelligible; hence I have not hesitated, where necessary. to write (e.g.) 'Philip' or 'my adversary' or 'anyone who does such a thing' instead of 'he'.

# ABBREVIATIONS

*Ancient authors*

| | | | |
|---|---|---|---|
| Aiskh. | = Aiskhylos | Is. | = Isaios |
| And. | = Andokides | Isok. | = Isokrates |
| Ant. | = Antiphon | Lyk. | = Lykourgos |
| Ar. | = Aristophanes | Lys. | = Lysias |
| Arist. | = Aristotle | Men. | = Menander |
| Dein. | = Deinarkhos | Pl. | = Plato |
| Dem. | = Demosthenes | Soph. | = Sophokles |
| Eur. | = Euripides | Theophr. | = Theophrastos |
| Hdt. | = Herodotos | Thuc. | = Thucydides |
| Hom. | = Homer | Xen. | = Xenophon |
| Hyp. | = Hypereides | | |

Abbreviations of the titles of ancient works will be found in the index of Greek passages at the end of the book.

*GVI* = (ed.) W. Peek, *Griechische Versinschriften*, vol. i (Berlin, 1955). Unless otherwise stated, all epitaphs cited from *GVI* are Athenian and datable to the fourth century B.C.

*Modern authors*

Reference will be made to the following works by the author's name only, plus (1), (2), etc., where indicated below.

ADKINS, A. W. H., (1) *Merit and Responsibility: a Study in Greek Values* (Oxford, 1960)

id. (2) *From the Many to the One* (London, 1970)

id. (3) *Moral Values and Political Behaviour from Homer to the End of the Fifth Century* (London, 1972)

BALDRY, H. C., *The Unity of Mankind in Greek Thought* (Cambridge, 1965)

BOLKESTEIN, H., *Wohltätigkeit und Armenpflege im vorchristlichen Altertum* (Utrecht, 1939)

BURFORD, A., *Craftsmen in Greek and Roman Society* (London, 1972)

CONNOR, W. R., *The New Politicians of Fifth-Century Athens* (Princeton, 1971)

DE ROMILLY, J., *La Loi dans la pensée grecque* (Paris, 1971)

DE SAINTE CROIX, G. E. M., *The Origins of the Peloponnesian War* (London, 1972)

DIHLE, A., *Die goldene Regel* (Göttingen, 1962)

DODDS, E. R., *The Greeks and the Irrational* (Berkeley and Los Angeles, 1951)

DOVER, K. J., (1) *Lysias and the Corpus Lysiacum* (Berkeley and Los Angeles, 1968); id. (2) *Aristophanic Comedy* (London, 1972)

EARP, F. R., *The Way of the Greeks* (London, 1929)

EDELSTEIN, L., *The Idea of Progress in Classical Antiquity* (Baltimore, 1967)

EHRENBERG, V., *The People of Aristophanes*, ed. 2 (Oxford, 1951)

FERGUSON, J., *Moral Values in the Ancient World* (London, 1958)

GERLACH, J., *ΑΝΗΡ ΑΓΑΘΟΣ* (Munich, 1932)

GERNET, L., *Recherches sur le développement de la pensée juridique et morale en Grèce* (Paris, 1917)

GLOTZ, G., *La Solidarité de la famille dans le droit criminel en Grèce* (Paris, 1904)

GOMME, A. W., *Essays in Greek History and Literature* (Oxford, 1937)

HANDS, A. R., *Charities and Social Aid in Greece and Rome* (London, 1968)

HARRISON, A. R. W., *The Law of Athens*, 2 vols. (Oxford, 1968–71)

HIRZEL, R., *Themis, Dike und Verwandtes* (Leipzig, 1907)

HUART, P., *Le Vocabulaire de l'analyse psychologique dans l'oeuvre de Thucydide* (Paris, 1968)

JAEGER, W., *Paideia: the Ideals of Greek Culture*, ed. 3, tr. G. Highet, 3 vols. (Oxford, 1946)

JONES, A. H. M., *Athenian Democracy* (Oxford, 1957)

JOST, K., *Das Beispiel und Vorbild der Vorfahren bei den attischen Rednern und Geschichtsschreibern bis Demosthenes* (Paderborn, 1936)

LACEY, W. K., *The Family in Classical Greece* (London, 1968)

LATTE, K., *Heiliges Recht* (Tübingen, 1920; reprinted Aalen, 1964)

LATTIMORE, R., *Themes in Greek and Latin Epitaphs* (Urbana, 1962)

LLOYD-JONES, H., *The Justice of Zeus* (Berkeley and Los Angeles, 1971)

LUDWIG, J., *Quae fuerit vocis ἀρετή vis ac natura ante Demosthenis exitum* (Leipzig, 1906)

MACDOWELL, D. M., *Athenian Homicide Law in the Age of the Orators* (Manchester, 1963)

MARTIN, V., *La Vie internationale dans la Grèce des cités (VIᵉ–IVᵉ siécles av. J.-C.)* (Paris, 1940)

MOSSÉ, C., *The Ancient World at Work*, tr. J. Lloyd (London, 1969)

MÜRI, W., 'Beitrage zum Verständnis des Thukydides', *Museum Helveticum* iv (1947) 251–75

NORTH, H., *Sophrosyne: Self-Knowledge and Self-Restraint in Greek Literature* (Ithaca, N.Y., 1966)

OPSTELTEN, J. C., *Sophocles and Greek Pessimism*, tr. J. A. Ross (Amsterdam, 1952)

PEARSON, L., *Popular Ethics in Ancient Greece* (Stanford, 1962)

POHLENZ, M., *Freedom in Greek Life and Thought*, tr. C. Lofmark (Dordrecht, 1966)

RÄDLE, H., *Untersuchungen zum griechischen Freilassungswesen* (Munich, 1969)

ROHDE, E., *Psyche*, ed. 8, tr. W. B. Hillis (London, 1925)

VOLLGRAFF, W., *L'Oraison funèbre de Gorgias* (Leiden, 1952)

WOLF, E., *Griechisches Rechtsdenken* III.2: *Die Umformung des Rechtsgedanken durch Historik und Rhetorik* (Frankfurt a.M., 1956)

# I

# INTERPRETATION OF THE SOURCES

## I.A. WHAT IS POPULAR MORALITY?

*1. Morality and Moral Philosophy*

It often happens that if I try to do as I wish I necessarily frustrate what some-one else wishes. By the 'morality' of a culture I mean the principles, criteria and values which underlie its reponses to this familiar experience. By 'moral philosophy' or 'ethics' I mean rational, systematic thinking about the rela-tionship between morality and reason; other types of rational thinking about morality I assign to linguistics, psychology and sociology. Very few people indeed in any culture, ancient or modern, are moral philosophers; many pass their whole lives without giving a moment's systematic thought to the prin-ciples underlying the innumerable moral choices which each of us has to make and the innumerable moral judgments which we express in (e.g.) 'That's not fair', 'He's a nice man', 'Honestly, they were fantastic' or 'What a bastard!' A moral philosopher may respect the predominant morality of his own time, place and class to such an extent as to treat it as the least incoherent of all available moral systems; or he may totally reject the values which are funda-mental to it. We cannot know, merely from the study of what he writes, the extent to which he accepts or rejects the actual morality of his own society.

The moral philosophy of the Classical Greek world is dominated for us by Plato and Aristotle, for their work has survived—deservedly, given the artistry of the former and the intellectual penetration of both—while our information on other moral philosophers of the same era is indirect and fragmentary. If we imagined that either Plato's work or Aristotle's represented an intellectual systematization of the principles which were manifested in the moral choices and judgments of the ordinary unphilosophical Greek, it is possible that we might go badly astray.[1] My purpose in this book is to describe the morality—not the moral philosophy—of the period, roughly a century, between the birth of Plato in 428/7 and the death of Aristotle in 322. How far this morality turns out to embody principles and attitudes which resemble any Platonic or Aristotelian axioms, assumptions, hypotheses or findings is a question which I leave entirely to philosophers. Since the literature of the period is practically all written by Athenians or by participants in Athenian culture, nothing of significance for our present enquiry is likely to be discovered about the Greek world outside Athens.[2] And since it is all written by men, we shall learn something about what men believed women to think and portrayed them as thinking, but not necessarily anything about what women actually thought.

The questions which I have attempted to answer are not always or necessarily those which Greeks would have regarded as important or interesting. To understand Greek morality it is certainly necessary to become capable of looking at morality through Greek eyes, but it is necessary also to switch off and become ourselves again whenever we want to know what, if anything, they thought about issues which are important to us. There is no reason why we should not formulate a sort of moral questionnaire equally applicable to all cultures which we may choose to investigate, rather as the field-worker recording unwritten languages often begins with a standard word-list. As in the study of languages, so in the study of moralities we must expect the material itself to force upon our attention much which was not in our minds when we constructed the questionnaire. We may, for example, feel (as I do) that in characterizing the flatterer Theophrastos (*Char.* 2) is dealing with phenomena which are alien to life as we know it. The extent to which Greek values, attitudes and behaviour seem as a whole familiar or unfamiliar to the modern student of the subject will naturally vary greatly between individuals.[3]

---

[1] Cf. Pearson 210–12 on the egregious errors committed by writers who assume Greek morality to be 'epitomised in Plato and Aristotle'; M. I. Finley, 'Athenian Demagogues', *Past and Present* xxi (1962) 3–24 (especially p. 7, on the extent to which Plato was atypical); and Lloyd-Jones 130–7 on the inadequacy (to use no harsher word) of Plato as evidence for the moral thought of intellectuals with whom he disagreed.

[2] Rightly emphasized by Pearson 2, though his enquiry (cf. n. 4 below) is less narrowly focused on Athens than mine is.

[3] Adkins (1) 2 remarks that it is hard to accept the idea 'that there should exist a society so different from our own as to render it impossible to translate "duty" in its Kantian sense into the ethical terminology at all'. But what exactly is 'our own' society? I cannot recall experiencing a temptation to use the word 'duty' in its Kantian sense (except, of course, when talking about Kant) and, at least in the course of the last five or

It must not be imagined that we shall discover the Athenians to have lived, any more than we do, by an internally consistent set of moral principles. If a philosopher builds logical contradictions into a theory, he will lose his reputation as a philosopher; equally, if a man persists in an attempt to live by principles of such a kind that their practical applications are constantly and conspicuously irreconcilable, he is likely to lose his friends and may lose his reason. But it would be quite untrue to say that we *cannot* hold contradictory moral beliefs or apply contradictory principles. We all can, and we all do; and the reasons are simple enough. The first and most important reason is that since a moral attitude ('belief' is usually a misleading term) is a kind of emotional reaction, it is even easier for one person to react differently to the same conduct on different occasions than it is for him to change his beliefs about matters which admit of empirical verification. Favourable valuations are in large measure expressions of what we would like to see existing; they implicitly contrast a hypothetical world with the actual world, and wishes can easily accommodate contradiction. A man may, for example, extol both marital fidelity and promiscuous adultery, because in the world as he would like it to be both types of resultant happiness would be continuously enjoyable by the same person. Secondly, few of us are able to see simultaneously more than one or two aspects of anything, so that our valuation of it varies according to the aspects on which the circumstances of the moment focus our attention. The propositions, 'To forgo revenge is unmanly, and therefore bad' and 'To forgo revenge is charitable, and therefore good', may be equally true in the eyes of anyone who values both manliness and charitableness; which of the two is uttered on a particular occasion depends on the totality of the circumstances which elicit the utterance. Furthermore, many beliefs relevant to morality are of so general a character that a serious attempt to establish their truth or falsity would be totally impracticable, e.g. 'The gods observe and punish sin', 'The sinner goes unpunished', 'A man's bad character comes out in his children', 'Good behaviour depends on upbringing', etc. We therefore tend to justify an assertion of this kind by selecting some of the relevant data and discarding the rest; which data we select depends on the experiences which at any given time make the deepest impression on us. The fact that some of these assertions are unverifiable, e.g. 'The gods punish the sinner after his death' or 'Providence determines events for the best, even if we cannot see the reason', makes it easy for the same person to assert and deny

six years, I do not think I have heard the word so used. Unless I am seriously deceiving myself, I and most of the people I know well find the Greeks of the Classical period easier to understand than Kantians.

the same proposition at different times. A third consideration is that moral judgments and evaluative words are instruments by which we seek to influence the attitudes and behaviour of other people (cf. II.A.2). Since almost any moral judgment and its contrary are equally defensible (for the reasons given above), the judgment which we select as a suitable means to a particular end on one occasion may be irreconcilable with what seems a suitable means to a different end on a different occasion. Our impression of the moral standards of a given culture can only be based on the judgments and assumptions which predominate and on the absence or extreme rarity, so far as our evidence goes, of assertions which our own experience would have led us to expect.

It cannot, of course, be claimed that we can discover much of importance about the extent to which the Greeks actually lived by any of the moral standards which their surviving utterances imply. The sum total of our information about them falls far short of what would be needed for even a diffident generalization on that subject; indeed, we know little more about the realities of their behaviour than a few handfuls of documents and a large collection of newspaper headlines would tell the future about ours. What is needed if we are to build up a lifelike picture of the norms of behaviour in a period of the past is hundreds of private diaries and account-books, parish records and thousands of letters (provided that we are capable of reading between the lines as well as on them). All we can claim in respect of the Athenians is that the available material shows us what moral principles were enunciated or (more often) taken for granted by a certain number of highly articulate men in public utterance. Severe though this limitation may be, we are much better informed about the period 428–322 than about any previous or subsequent period of Greek history.[4] The whole of Attic oratory falls within our period; so do Thucydides, Xenophon, most of the surviving plays of Euripides, some of Sophokles, all those of Aristophanes, and nearly all the citations from Old and Middle Comedy. The circulation of Herodotos's work almost coincided with the birth of Plato, and Menander's career began immediately after the death of Aristotle. When we are tempted, as we often are, to believe that sentiments and concepts which we first encounter in the forensic oratory of the fourth century must represent real differences between

---

[4] Pearson 1 says that we know much more about the Athenians of the *fifth* century 'than about the members of any other ancient Greek community, earlier *or later*' (my italics). It seems to me that most of the questions about morality which we can answer with regard to the fourth century on the basis of firm evidence can be answered with regard to the fifth only by extrapolation; but Pearson's remarks on historiography and tragedy (4f.) show that he and I do not mean quite the same thing by 'the Athenians'.

the outlook of that century and that of the fifth, it is important to remind ourselves that we know nothing at all of oratory and virtually nothing of comedy in the time of Aiskhylos.

## 2. Public Delivery and Private Reading

Although moral philosophy and popular morality are sharply contrasted in respect of reason and reflection, they are not exhaustive alternatives. There still remain the idiosyncratic moralities—which may or may not be reflective and systematic—of abnormal individuals or small categories of people. This fact makes it necessary to consider where, within the whole field of non-philosophical literature, we are to look for a morality which can properly be called popular. The first and most obvious distinction to be made is between (a) what is composed for public delivery, eliciting immediate praise or blame from an audience not of the author's choosing, and (b) what is meant to be read at leisure by such individuals as may be interested, is most likely to be read by those who are (in the broadest sense) in sympathy with the author, and can be put aside at any moment by a reader who does not like it. History, philosophy, science and essays belong to the latter class, oratory and drama to the former. The significance of this differentiation may be illustrated by the fact that Xenophon can refer (Hell. vii 3.4) to the opposing sides in civil strife at Sikyon as 'the best men' and 'the people'; that contrast is inconceivable in a speech addressed to a democratic assembly or jury in Xenophon's own day, but Xenophon's standpoint is close to that of the oligarch Theramenes, whom he represents as contrasting (Hell. ii 3.39) 'opposition to the people' with 'opposition to good men'. Similarly, Thucydides on one occasion (viii 64.5) describes the forcible replacement of democracy by oligarchy as an attainment of 'sensible government'.

Within the category 'composed for public delivery' a further distinction may be drawn according to the issues at stake. From this point of view we may separate four genres or groups of genres: (i) forensic oratory; (ii) political oratory; (iii) drama and epideictic oratory; (iv) epitaphs and dedicatory epigrams.

A speaker in a lawcourt stood to lose money, property, his political rights, even on occasion his life. Since witnesses were not cross-examined and the jury received no objective guidance on points of law, it was of the utmost importance that the speaker should adopt a *persona* which would convey a good impression. He could not afford to express or imply beliefs or principles which were likely to be offensive to the jury;[5] at the same time, it was important that he should impose a discreditable *persona* upon his adversary.[6] For this reason forensic oratory should be treated as our main source of data on popular morality.

A man who contributed to the formation of a political decision by speaking in the assembly did not speak under the threat of immediate penalty, and could therefore take more chances than the forensic speaker in propounding an unorthodox morality; but if he really wanted his advice to be taken—and we may presume that he wanted to go up rather than down on the ladder of social and political status—he was unlikely to risk an argument seriously in conflict with the moral values accepted by a substantial part of his audience.

For the dramatist the issue was different, though not always less momentous. He was competing against rivals for a prize, and his standing as a poet turned upon his success or failure in competition. We are not adequately informed on the extent to which the judges at the dramatic festivals were guided in their voting by applause or hissing from the audience,[7] but the general character of Athenian life would suggest that not many judges would care to display an immovable independence of taste. What is harder to assess, and more important, is the relation between 'the morality of a play' (if I may use an expression which I should not find it easy to define) and the audience's approval of the play. The spectator must on occasion have left the theatre with a feeling, even if he could not translate it into words, that some values had been implicitly commended to him as preferable to some other values. If this commendation had disturbed or disgusted him, the dramatist's status as competitor on future occasions was likely to be adversely affected.

In epideictic oratory explicit commendation was *de rigueur*. The speaker of a funeral oration or panegyric was expected to utter moral sentiments and exhortations appropriate to the occasion. If what seemed to him appropriate seemed less so to his audience, his reputation as an orator might suffer, but he did not have the immediate mortification of being rated below a rival, seeing his political advice rejected, or leaving a lawcourt the poorer by half his estate.

The epitaph or funerary epigram has a *prima facie* claim to be included in

---

[5] The great importance of forensic oratory as evidence for popular moral standards, and the reasons why it is important, are recognized and admirably expounded by Earp 11. Cf. also Dover (1) 76–8.

[6] On ways of doing this cf. W. Voegelin, *Die Diabole bei Lysias* (Basel, 1943).

[7] Cf. Sir Arthur Pickard-Cambridge, *The Dramatic Festivals of Athens* (ed. 2, revised by John Gould and D. M. Lewis, Oxford, 1968), 272–8.

the category of popular composition, since reputation after death was of great importance to most Greeks (cf. V.D.5), and when an epitaph makes a statement about the moral qualities of a dead person it must be remembered that the composer was aware of making this statement to all passers-by for an indefinite period of time. It is a pity that the normal brevity of a Classical epitaph and our lack of independent information about the person praised usually preclude clear understanding of what the composer (commissioned by spouse, parent or child) was trying to communicate. This difficulty is increased by the inclination of the composers of epitaphs to perpetuate traditional formulae and to use resounding Homeric epithets which may have meant different things to different people. Dedicatory epigrams, like epitaphs, were composed in the knowledge that they would be read by visitors to sanctuaries for an indefinite period; if such an epigram includes any proclamation of the dedicator's virtues or achievements, it is likely to be in the terms in which the dedicator wished to be remembered. Both types of epigram, more especially the epitaph, throw some light on the attitudes of the Greeks to their gods.

In addition to speeches, plays and epigrams, three other sources may yield material relevant to popular morality: philosophers' statements about what 'most people' say and think; Plato's and Xenophon's portrayals of unphilosophical men in conversation with Socrates; and the historians' accounts of what was said by the persons who appear in their narratives. In the light of modern philosophers' assertions about what 'we' say, think and feel, I am inclined to treat the first of these three sources with caution.[8] The *faux-naif* strain in Socrates may also mislead; Xenophon (*Oec.* 6.14-.6) portrays him as beginning a search for men who truly deserve the appellation *kalos kāgathos* (cf. I.F.4) by going after those who were *kalos*, 'handsome', but ordinary people who used the expression and held no perverse theories of semantics would not have made that mistake. The philosophers' portrayal of ordinary men is more useful, provided that we bear in mind the possibility that the conflict of standpoint and lack of understanding between Socrates and his interlocutor may have been dramatically sharpened and exaggerated, especially by Plato. As for speeches in historical works, we must, I think, treat

[8] In Pl. *Phaedo* 92D Simmias is represented as saying that the view that the soul is related to the body as the tuning of a lyre to the lyre itself—a sophisticated scientific view—is held by 'most men'. This is hard to believe, unless we take Simmias as meaning that of the two alternatives posed by Socrates, (i) that learning is recollection and (ii) that the soul is a tuning, the latter is more consonant than the former with the attitude implicit in what most people say about the soul, in so far as they permit themselves to theorize about it at all.

Thucydides with suspicion. Even if we allow that he always rendered conscientiously 'the point which the speech as a whole made' (there are respectable reasons for not always allowing that), and that late fifth-century audiences had more of a taste for abstract generalization than their successors, the language of the Thucydidean speeches is so idiosyncratic and their intellectual concentration so formidable that we are not in a position to recover in sufficient detail for our present purpose the sentiments and arguments actually uttered.[9] Speeches in Xenophon, cast in terms of political commonplaces, are a more promising field, but their terminology, so far as we can tell, is Xenophon's own. Anecdotes, particularly when the words used constitute, at least in part, the point of the anecdote (e.g. Thuc. iv 40.2), are more useful than the speeches.

## I.B. SPECIAL CHARACTERISTICS OF ORATORY

### 1. Authenticity

Not all the works ascribed to the Attic orators are forensic or political speeches; not all, in fact, are speeches of any kind, and not all are Attic. Andokides iv is composed as if for an occasion long past,[1] Antiphon ii–iv (the *Tetralogies*) for imaginary cases, Lysias xxxv (incorporated in Plato's Lysias viii was certainly not composed for delivery in a court; Lysias ii and Demosthenes lxi (both 'erotic') for private reading or recitation to friends. Lysias vii was certainly not composed for delivery in a court; Lysias ii and xxxiii, Demosthenes lx and Hypereides vi are epideictic; Lysias xi and xv are rhetorical exercises;[2] 'Demosthenes xii' purports to be a letter from Philip of Macedon; there is room for argument about the nature (though little

---

[9] Paul Shorey's article, 'The Implicit Ethics and Psychology of Thucydides', *Transactions of the American Philological Association* xxiv (1893) 66–88, has an exciting title, but does not succeed in distinguishing between the moral ideas of the historian himself and the moral ideas implied by speakers portrayed in the historian's work.

[1] I have argued (Dover [1] 191f. and in Gomme, Andrewes and Dover, *Historical Commentary on Thucydides* iv [Oxford, 1970] 287f.) that Andokides could very well have been the author of this work. S. Feraboli, 'Lingua e Stile della Orazione "Contro Alcibiade" attribuita ad Andocide', *Studi Italiani di Filologia Classica* xliv (1972) 5–37, has persuaded me that I was wrong. We should probably attribute it to the late fourth century.

[2] Cf. Dover (1) 166f.

room for argument about the date) of Demosthenes xxv and xxvi.[3] Among the works ascribed to Isokrates only xvi–xxi are speeches (all forensic); those of the remainder which have the formal characteristics of a speech were in reality designed for reading.[4]

There is no doubt that by the end of the fourth century B.C. the names of famous orators had been freely attached to speeches which were not in fact their work.[5] Even a few years after the death of Isokrates it was possible to debate (Aristotle fr. 140 Rose) whether or not he had written any forensic speeches. Such a situation is unwelcome to anyone who hopes to recover the views of the techniques of an individual orator; but when our concern is with the morality of a whole society, the more speech-writers are represented in the corpus of work ascribed to the canonical 'Ten Orators', the better. 'Forgery' in the proper sense of the word is not a serious issue, except in the (unimportant) case of Demades.

We do not know, in any given case, the relation between what is available for us to read—the version of the speech circulated in writing—and what was really said in court. Examination of the two great cases of Demosthenes vs. Aiskhines puts it beyond doubt that the written version could be touched up in order to take account of what had been said on the other side, and it is possible that some, perhaps most, of the passages of the familiar type beginning, 'I understand that he will say . . .', were first composed after the trial. The relevance of this to our present enquiry is that it would have been open to the orator to adopt in the written version, which would have been of interest chiefly to educated people, a standpoint different from that which he adopted in addressing the jury. Two considerations, however, suggest that he did not normally change his standpoint to any significant extent. The first is that when Aristophanes in the late fifth century satirizes forensic or political oratory, he obviously has in mind the spoken word, not the written (the circulation of speeches in writing was a practice which had hardly begun at the time of his earlier plays), and yet every element which he satirizes is familiar to us from the written texts of the orators: criticism of the politics

[3] Cf. M. Pohlenz, *Kleine Schriften* ii (Hildesheim, 1965) 314–32 and de Romilly 155–8. From the facts that (i) Dionysios of Halikarnassos denied Demosthenes' authorship of these two speeches on grounds of style alone (Dion. Hal. i p. 192 [Usener-Radermacher]) and (ii) Dionysios was acquainted with Kallimakhos's catalogue of speeches ascribed to Demosthenes (i pp. 311.21–312.1), I infer that Demosthenes xxv and xxvi were listed under the name of Demosthenes by Kallimakhos and identified in the list by their opening words.

[4] Cf. Dover (1) 172–4, 187–93.

[5] Cf. Dover (1) 23–7, 151–5, 159–63.

of an adversary's ancestors (*Knights* 447ff. ~ Ant. fr. 1); comparison of a demagogue to a watchdog (*Knights* 1023ff., *Wasps* 894ff. ~ Dem. xxv 40); the speaker's claim to be speaking with reluctance, under the compulsion of patriotic feeling or intolerable wrong (*Thesm.* 383ff., *Eccl.* 151f. ~ Dem. xxiii 1, xxxix 1); presentation of a defendant's children in tears (*Wasps* 568ff., 976ff. ~ Dem. xxi 186f., al.).[6] Secondly, it is remarkable how often, when in our reading of the orators a passage strikes us as sophisticated, intellectual, artificial or otherwise unusual, the speech in question turns out to belong to one or other of the special categories listed at the beginning of this section.

Ant. iii 8: The law quite rightly and justly provides that those who have killed involuntarily (*i.e. without intending to kill*) shall be punished by involuntary suffering (*i.e. suffering which they do not wish to undergo*).

Dem. xxvi 25: You will find that disobedience of the law performs the works of insanity, incontinence (*akrasiā*) and greed, whereas the laws achieve those of intelligence (*phronēsis*), self-control (*sōphrosynē*) and honesty.

The word *phronēsis* is not to be found elsewhere in the Demosthenic corpus, and nowhere else in the orators is *akrasiā* antithetic to *sōphrosynē*.

Dem. lxi 46: . . . and that Arkhytas, given charge of the city of Taras, administered it with admirable humanity . . . At first held of no account, he owed his great attainment to consorting with Plato . . .

This passage is very strikingly at variance with the view taken of philosophy by speakers in the courts and assembly.

### 2. Attitudes to Philosophy and History

Confronted by a mass audience, an Attic orator shows no regard for the philosophical schools which posterity has treated as one of the glories of the fourth century. The words 'philosopher' (*philosophos*), 'philosophise', and 'philosophy' are used in a laudatory sense only of Solon (Aiskhines iii 108, 257)—whose legislation, moralizing poetry and reputation in folklore as a sage reasonably earned him a name for 'philosophy' in the time of Herodotos (i 30.2) but hardly constituted the same claim in the time of Aristotle—and also of early poets (Aiskhines i 141) and epideictic orators (Hyp. vi 33). Dem. xlviii 49 and Lys. viii 11 use 'philosophise' of dishonest or absurd ingenuity

[6] Cf. A. Burckhardt, *Spuren der athenischen Volksrede in der alten Komödie* (Basel, 1924); Dover (1) 72–4.

in argument; in Lys. xxiv 10 a speaker characterized by humour and sarcasm uses it as a synonym of *phrontizein*, 'think', 'worry', with reference to thinking of ways of obviating a physical handicap. Cf. Xen. *Anab.* ii 1.13, 'You sound like a philosopher!', a jocular comment on a neat riposte. Most revealing is the attack on Lakritos in Dem. xxxv 15, 39–43, as a 'pupil of Isokrates' and a 'wretched sophist' (cf. Lys. xxxiii 3, 'useless sophists'), who has paid fees to Isokrates and now himself professes to educate pupils for a fee.[7] The tone of these passages shows no significant change from that of Aristophanes' *Clouds* (in the days of Demosthenes' grandfather), where Socrates is treated as teaching dishonest men the verbal tricks of 'making wrong appear right'.[8]

This philistine attitude, which even comedy shows some signs of outgrowing by the second half of the fourth century (cf. I.D.2), is matched by the orators' reliance on popular tradition rather than historiography when they refer to the past. Of the only two passages in the oratorical corpus which appear to be based on the work of historians, one is in an epideictic speech (Lys. ii 48–53, a rhetorical elaboration of Thuc. i 105f.); the other, Dem. lix 94–104, plainly relies on Thuc. i 128–33 and ii 2–6 but gives the story of the Theban attack on Plataiai a more patriotic twist, incompatible with Thucydides' account, by alleging (100) that it was the rapid arrival of an Athenian force which made the Thebans withdraw. Other passages of historical content in the orators are considerably wilder.

Aiskhines ii 76: ... the expedition to Sicily, which our ancestors sent to help Leontinoi after the enemy had invaded our territory and Dekeleia was fortified against us ...

The context shows that the speaker is referring to the expedition of 415, nearly two years before the establishment of the Spartan base at Dekeleia—indeed, before Sparta had resumed hostilities against Athens.

And. iii 30: We chose Segesta in preference to Syracuse and chose to send an expedition to Sicily rather than to stay at home and have Syracuse as an ally.

---

[7] In Isokrates 'philosophical' is a complimentary term (e.g. iv 176, ix 78), but he did not mean by it what we mean or what Plato and Aristotle meant.

[8] There are three references to Socrates in Attic forensic oratory: Aiskhines i 173 refers to him as having been executed for his political teaching of Kritias; Hyp. fr. 55 (context unknown) says that he was punished for his *logoi* (i.e. for the arguments which he propounded); Lys. fr. 1.2, much nearer to Socrates in date, refers—in order to explain why the Socratic Aiskhines of Sphettos got financial credit—to Socrates' discussions of honesty and virtue, but it is hard to tell whether the tone of this reference is patronizing, sarcastic or sincere.

Thucydides' account of the events of 415 is not easily reconcilable with the idea that there was a possibility of positive friendship or alliance with Syracuse.

Dem. vii 12: (*In the old days*) Macedonia was under our rule and paid us tribute.

The tribute-lists suffice to prove the falsity of this statement. Only some Greek cities on the fringe of Macedonia were in the Athenian empire.

Dem. xxi 147: Alkibiades mutilated the herms.

We can trace the ancestry of this piece of popular tradition. Alkibiades was not even accused of mutilating the herms in 415—that much is clear from the documents cited in And. i 11–19, to say nothing of Thucydides—but Lys. xiv 42, generalizing about Alkibiades and his family ('some of them have parodied mysteries and mutilated the herms and committed impieties against all the gods'), provides the bridge.

Dem. xxiii 200: Perdikkas ... king of Macedonia, destroyed the Persian forces retreating from Plataiai.

The king of Macedonia at the time of Xerxes' invasion of Greece was not Perdikkas, and Hdt. ix 89 mentions only the Thracians as interfering with the Persian retreat.

Dem. lviii 67: Kritias's faction intended to admit a Spartan force to Eetioneia.

The speaker has moved Kritias's pro-Spartan behaviour back from 404 into the oligarchic revolution of 411, in which Kritias was very far from aligning himself with the pro-Spartan faction.

Isok. xvi 7–9: Alkibiades cleared himself of the charge (*sc. of parodying the mysteries*) so satisfactorily that ... the Athenians elected him general of the force going to Sicily ... Indignant though he was that ... they condemned him in his absence, he did not think it right to go over to the enemy, but was so anxious not to injure Athens that he went to Argos and refrained from action. His enemies, however, ... persuaded you ... to demand him from the Argives ...

Contrast Thuc. vi 28f., 88.9.[9] What is more worthy of remark than any one of these passages is that when Aiskhines in 343 wanted to demonstrate from Athenian history the advantages of making peace-treaties, he did not go to historians for his data, but reproduced with minor changes (ii 172–6) the

---

[9] On another alleged misstatement, that Alkibiades 'belonged on his father's side to the Eupatridai and on the female side to the Alkmeonidai' (Isok. xvi 25), see H. T. Wade-Gery, *Essays in Greek History* (Oxford, 1958) 106ff., and J. K. Davies, *Athenian Propertied Families 600–300 B.C.* (Oxford, 1971) 10ff.

inaccurate survey given by Andokides (iii 3–9) fifty years earlier for a similar argumentative purpose.

The attitudes to philosophy and history which characterize the orators seem to me to justify treating forensic and political oratory as 'popular' in its values and its picture of the world. The undeniable fact that its technical and artistic standards are very high is not an obstacle to this treatment; refined form and crude content are as compatible as the reverse. The treatment of historical events by a speaker scarcely a generation younger than those events (Isok. xvi 7–9, above) raises a further question about the veracity of oratory on matters of fact.

### 3. The Limits of Inference

Only very seldom (And. i vs. Lys. vi, Aiskhines ii vs. Dem. xix, Dem. xviii vs. Aiskhines iii) do we get an idea of what was said on both sides of a case. We do not as a rule know whether the speaker was in the right or in the wrong, nor what the outcome of the case was, nor any of its details except what (if anything) can be inferred from one of the speeches on one side. It is particularly important that a rhetorical case should not be mistaken for a case-history.

Is. ii 6–9: We found . . . that our younger sister, who was married to Menekles, had no children. He . . . spoke very highly of our sister . . . and said . . . it was a poor return for her goodness that she should grow old with him and be left childless. It was quite enough, he said, that he himself should be unfortunate. He asked us therefore . . . to give her in marriage to someone else, with his consent. We told him that he would have to persuade her of this . . . She at first would not hear a word of it, but in the course of time she was, with difficulty, persuaded.

They all sound nice people, and I dare say they were. But the narrative is not good evidence for what any of them actually said or felt; it is only evidence for what the speaker (a) wished the jury to believe and (b) judged that they would not find it hard to believe. Therein lies its importance for the study of Greek morality; if we knew it to be a truthful account of a sequence of negotiations within one particular family, it would actually be less important. Similar considerations apply to general views or standards enunciated or implied by a speaker in court.

Lys. i 14: I thought that my wife had make-up on, although her brother had died less than a month before.

This passage tells us not that no Athenian woman put on make-up for a month after a death in the family, but that the speaker wished (a) to represent himself as a man who took this standard of propriety for granted, and (b) to insinuate into the jurors the idea that they too took it for granted and could therefore draw the conclusion which he wished them to draw.[10]

Dem. lix 122: We have hetairai for pleasure, concubines for our day-to-day physical well-being, and wives in order to beget legitimate children and have trustworthy guardians of our households.

This gives us not, as has been alleged, 'the fourth-century view' of women, but one view which was possible, was judged by the speaker unlikely to offend, and was absolutely necessary for the argument ('Neaira passed herself off as Stephanos's wife') which he is developing in that part of his speech. Orators' generalizations on matters of fact must be treated with great caution. They often tell us (e.g. Is. viii 12) that the extraction of testimony from slaves under torture is of the highest importance in establishing the truth, because (they say) evidence of this category has never been refuted.[11] Yet when such evidence is unfavourable to a speaker, he is quite ready to dismiss it as worthless. Dem. xl 53f. warns the jury to be on their guard against speakers who say, 'Of course, as you all know, . . .'; but it happens to be a trick of which Demosthenes himself is quite fond. Even in so practical a genre of utterance as forensic oratory, the Greek love of imposing artistic form tended towards the development of conventional motifs.

## I.C. SPECIAL CHARACTERISTICS OF TRAGEDY

### 1. Character, Situation and Sentiments

The chief obstacle to the identification of elements of popular morality in drama of any kind is the simple fact that drama consists of the utterances of fictitious persons in fictitious situations. The ancients themselves have set us a very bad example by treating tragic passages and individual verses, isolated

---

[10] Sometimes, perhaps, a speaker overreached himself. It is pertinent to recall that in a recent prosecution of a publisher for publishing an allegedly obscene book counsel asked the jury whether they would 'wish their wives and servants' to read such a book. Few people, I imagine, before the case came into court would have found it possible to believe that such a question could be put to a jury in our own time.

[11] Cf. Harrison ii 147.

from their dramatic contexts, as if they were recommendations given by the poet to his audience. In Euripides' *Hippolytus*, after Phaidra's old nurse has extracted from Hippolytos, under oath, a promise of discretion and has then horrified him by disclosing that Phaidra wants him in her bed, he gives her cause to fear that he may tell his father (612):

My tongue is under oath, my heart unsworn.

The line achieved notoriety;[1] it is turned against Euripides in Ar. *Frogs* 1471, and no doubt there were many in the audience of *Frogs* who relished that. Those who remembered more of *Hippolytus* than the one notorious line and the shocking character of Phaidra (cf. *Frogs* 1043) will have recalled (we hope) that when Hippolytos's first rush of anger has subsided he recognizes (656–60) that an oath spoken by the tongue binds the heart too. This makes no difference to Phaidra herself; overwhelmed by the fear of public shame, she is sure (689–92) that he will not remain silent. But she is wrong; falsely accused by her in a letter she writes before she kills herself, he bears his father's unjust anger and goes into exile keeping his oath. The portrayal of the moods and fears of Hippolytos, Phaidra and the nurse is essentially realistic.

When Hekabe reminds Odysseus of the time when he entered Troy as a spy in disguise and was detected but released by her, he admits (Eur. *Hec.* 249f.) that he made every plea he could think of (literally, 'inventions of many arguments') to save his own life. Similarly, when a tragic poet depicts a person in a predicament which threatens death, suffering or failure, he composes for utterance by that person, with varying degrees of regard for consistency and credibility of character, such arguments as might be usable as a means of self-preservation. Iokaste in Soph. *Oed. Tyr.* 979 declares that it is best to live without worrying about the future; she declares this not as the mouthpiece of Sophokles, but because it is emotionally necessary for her to disbelieve menacing prophecies and to persuade her husband to do likewise. If the play had been lost and line 979 survived only in an anthology, anyone who made use of it for reconstructing Sophokles' 'philosophy of life' would be wide of the mark. So would anyone who made such use of Eur. *Ba.* 283, where we are told that sleep induced by alcohol is the *only* remedy for

---

[1] Arist. *Rhet.* 1416ᵃ29–35 says that a certain Hygiainon, involved in litigation against Euripides on a technical matter of financial liability, 'called him impious because he had written, *commending perjury*, "My tongue . . . etc." '. Aristotle himself affords a striking example of Greek indifference to the context and purpose of memorable passages; in *Rhet.* 1380ᵇ28–30, 'Homer, wishing to put an end to the anger of Achilles against the dead Hektor, says . . .', means 'Homer, portraying Apollo's efforts to persuade Zeus to order Achilles to cease his anger against the dead Hektor, makes Apollo say . . .'.

suffering—an appropriate enough sentiment in a speech of pious devotion to Dionysos, the god who introduced mankind to the cultivation of the vine.

When it is obvious (as it sometimes is) that we are expected to despise or dislike a character, sentiments uttered by that character are likely to differ from what was generally accepted at Athens. There is hardly room for doubt that Sophokles in *Philoctetes* does not intend us to admire the character of Odysseus in those respects in which it is contrasted with that of Neoptolemos. At the other extreme, the sentiments of Theseus in a moralizing and intensely patriotic play such as Euripides' *Suppliants*, notably the sentiments which he utters after he has taken his decision to reclaim the bodies of the fallen heroes for burial, or when he trounces the insolent Theban herald, are likely to be such as would meet with approval at Athens in any social or political context. Yet Theseus is persuaded by his mother Aithra to ask for the bodies; she makes him change his mind, for his original reaction to Adrastos's supplication had been harder-hearted and harder-headed. If his later feeling is right, his earlier feeling was wrong, and the fact that he is a 'good' character does not suffice to prove the acceptability of the principle implied in his advice to Adrastos (248f.):

If you have taken a wrong decision, keep your misfortune to yourself and leave us alone.

A change of heart without the benefit of persuasion by others may be used by a dramatist to heighten effect; in Euripides' *Iphigenia at Aulis*, Iphigeneia at first shrinks from death and begs her father not to sacrifice her, ending her plea with the general sentiment (1250–2):

Nothing is sweeter to mankind than to see the light of day; what lies below is *nothing*. He who declares himself ready to die is insane. Better to live ill than die well.

This is shocking on the lips of a princess, but its dramatic purpose is apparent later in the play, when bloodshed within the Greek camp is averted by Iphigeneia's sudden declaration that she freely chooses after all to die for the cause (1368–1401). Earlier in the same play we have seen Menelaos, at first (303–413) selfish and rancorous, as sometimes elsewhere in Euripides, moved by Agamemnon's tears to abandon his demand for help in the recovery of Helen and to promise every effort to save Iphigeneia (471–503). In this case a 'bad' character has become a 'good' one. When we take adequate account of the fact that the majority of characters in tragedy possess depth and complexity,[2] we realize that all the moral sentiments which they utter deserve to

[2] In our own time the extent to which the Greek tragedians aimed at consistency of characterization has been a matter of controversy, and will no doubt continue to be

be taken seriously as sentiments which some Athenians could accept in some circumstances, but it seems wiser to evaluate characters in the light of their sentiments than to classify sentiments as acceptable or unacceptable on the basis of premature evaluation of the characters.

## 2. Archaism and Anachronism

Tragedy differs from oratory in another respect which is quite distinct from the portrayal of the interaction of fictitious characters. When Euripides' Medeia declares, at the climax (*Med.* 250f.) of her description of the miseries of women,

I would rather stand three times in the battle-line than once give birth,

the audience can treat her devaluation of the citizen-soldier as the kind of thing a person such as Medeia, alien and demonic, might well venture. But when Teiresias in Euripides' *Bacchae* 272–85 treats Demeter and Dionysos as the two principles, 'dry' and 'wet' sustenance, upon which the life of the human body depends, he is propounding a doctrine neither conventional nor shocking, neither specially appropriate nor inappropriate to his own character, neither necessary nor unhelpful to the argument of the scene or the plot of the play, but intellectually interesting in its own right. Tragedy can afford to give an airing to ideas which may be novel to many members of the audience and perhaps may not always be easily grasped; this the audience will accept in a genre in which so much is solemn and impressive, not least the poetic language, which is allowed by tradition to be (in the strict sense of the word) enigmatic. This consideration must be borne in mind also whenever we encounter uncommon moral nuances in tragedy. Even more must it be remembered when we have to deal with an opposed pair of utterances both of which would be acceptable to an anthologist and either of which could be used to 'prove' that Euripides held such-and-such a view or its opposite. A clear example is the highly formalized debate on democracy between Theseus and the Theban herald in *Suppliants* 399–563; a little less obvious, Theseus's castigation of the gods, on the basis of the legends told by poets (Eur. *Her.Fur.* 1314–21), and Herakles' rejection of the legends simply because they portray the gods as immoral. It should be noted that in both cases (cf. change of

so. For our present purpose it is sufficient to notice that whatever their intentions, they did in fact portray many coherent and intelligible characters.

character for the better, discussed above) the second member of the pair expresses the view more congenial to conventional morality.

However much of human complexity a dramatist may put into a heroic character, the dramatist and his audience had been brought up to think of the 'heroic age', the world of the 'half-gods', as different in scale and kind from their own world. Since the gods themselves played so large a part in heroic legend, appearing and speaking to their protégés, questions about divine intervention, reward and punishment do not have in tragedy the hypothetical character that they have in real life, but are necessarily treated as issues of central importance to the dramatic action, resolved before our eyes in the outcome of the action. Further, it is only to be expected that heroic personages, exceptional beings, larger than life and blessed or cursed with spectacular destinies, should sometimes express extreme and uncompromising sentiments and live up to them with a constancy, self-sacrifice, pride or vindictiveness more concentrated and extravagant than we normally achieve, perhaps more than we wish to achieve, in our own lives. The suicide of Ajax is rendered intelligible to Greeks by the universal Greek fear of humiliation (cf. V.B.5), but it is none the less an extreme manifestation of that fear. When Euripides in his *Electra* translates the matricide of Orestes into human terms, there emerges a contrast between his treatment of the story and the 'heroic' treatment of such stories which is more usual in tragedy; Plato's etymologizing (*Cratylus* 394E) of 'Orestes' as showing the 'bestial and savage and wild (*oreinos*) aspect of his nature' may well reflect how an Athenian of the time regarded the story. Tragic poets are not always careful to avoid cultural anachronism, but in certain respects, above all in emphasizing the operation of inherited curses and seldom alluding to the idea of individual punishment after death (cf. V.D.4f.), their legendary material implies religious assumptions rather different from those which were relevant to the morality of their audience.

## I.D. SPECIAL CHARACTERISTICS OF COMEDY

### 1. Moral and Immoral Characters

Aristotle drew a distinction between tragedy and comedy as representing respectively people 'superior' and 'inferior' to 'men as they are now' (*Poetics* 1448ª18). This is a generalization which has many more than one facet, but in respect of the relation between characters and moral values it makes a useful point in that tragic characters may transcend, in pursuit of honour, our limitations and compromises, whereas the comic characters of Aristophanes more often give us vicarious satisfaction by breaking moral and social rules as we too would like to break them if only we dared. Characters such as Dikaiopolis in *Acharnians*, Trygaios in *Peace* and Peisetairos in *Birds* speak and act for 'us' against 'them'—that is to say, against gods, politicians, generals, orators, intellectuals, poets, doctors, scientists, all those who in one way or another are superior to ourselves.[1] These comic heroes get away with trickery, bullying and violence which in real life are restrained by severe legal sanctions; they are characterized also by a brutal sexual opportunism and language uninhibited to a degree which was not tolerated in a serious setting (cf. IV.E.1). In essence the problem of deciding what elements in comedy represent popular morality is as difficult, though for different reasons, as in tragedy. The comic heroes of *Acharnians*, *Peace* and *Birds* triumph unambiguously, and we are invited to identify ourselves with them without serious reservation. But in a comedy such as *Clouds* no one triumphs; everyone is guilty of some degree of immorality or folly. *Wasps* is even more of a problem. There is something endearing about old Philokleon, perhaps because he is always immoderate in everything and somehow or other, even when nominally worsted, he gets the better of sensible and reasonable people, as we all at some time or other wish to do. Yet over and above the violence and selfishness and philistinism which he shares with other Aristophanic characters he is debited with behaviour which is not normally commended in comedy: theft (357, 1200f.), cowardice (358f.), merciless malevolence (*passim*) and—uniquely—a senile groping after incest (607ff.).[2]

It is quite possible that in the majority of comedies known to Aristotle at the time when he wrote the *Poetics* such characters as emerged in the course of a comic plot successful and vindicated won the audience's sympathy essentially by the shrewd, coarse, roguish independence of thought and action which Aristophanes and the poets of Old Comedy had made familiar. Unfortunately, this is the kind of question about Middle Comedy which the surviving citations, numerous as they are, can never answer for us. In the (post-Aristotelian) plays of Menander, the outstanding exponent of New Comedy, the 'happy ending', which gives some characters all that they desire and utterly frustrates the purposes of some others, makes it easier to align

[1] Cf. Dover (2) 31–41 and C. H. Whitman, *Aristophanes and the Comic Hero* (Cambridge, Mass., 1964), chapter II.

[2] Cf. Dover (2) 125–7.

characters with moralities, though Menander's genius for individualization must not be underrated. When moralizing in the course of a persuasive speech uttered by an eventually successful character actually helps to bring about the happy ending, as is the case with Sostratos's speech in *Dyskolos* 797–812 on the right use of money, we can be reasonably sure that the morality of the argument had popular approval.

Some striking and original statements occur among the very numerous citations from lost plays. Since we rarely know who is speaking to whom, or into what rhetorical, argumentative or humorous context the passage fits— and we may on occasion lack assurance that the text is sound or that we are translating it correctly[3]—its relationship to popular morality at the time of the play in question cannot easily be assessed. Let us in particular remember how often old-fashioned, censorious characters appear in comedy, and avoid treating lines which may have been uttered by such characters as if they were reportage, e.g.

Men. fr. 548: What some people nowadays call 'goodness' (*i.e. a kindly and magnanimous disposition*) has given badness a free hand right across the board, for no wrongdoer gets punished.

Often a citation containing an interesting word tells us absolutely nothing about the denotation of the word, e.g. Men. fr. 361, 'My daughter is by nature extremely *philanthrōpos*'.

## 2. Caricature and Parody

Just as tragedy may exaggerate courage and constancy, comedy satirizes and caricatures many ingredients of actual morality and social usage. Consider, for example, the reaction of Sikon the cook to the news that old Knemon has fallen down the well:

Men. *Dysk.* 639–47: There *are* gods, by Dionysos! You won't give a pot to people who're sacrificing, you temple-robber? You begrudge it? Well, you've fallen into

---

[3] Eupolis fr. 208, in which it is said of Kimon that he was 'not a bad man, but drunken and thoughtless' because he would 'go off to Sparta and leave Elpinike to sleep alone' is fully intelligible to us as a sly joke only because we know of the incestuous relationship between Kimon and his sister Elpinike. Antiphanes fr. 247 is more of a puzzle. There the educated man is said to forgo legitimate retaliation when he is wronged and to be moved to compassion in all circumstances. Is this praise or blame? And did Antiphanes really describe education as *alēthes* ('true', 'genuine') or should we emend e.g. to *euēthes* ('simple-minded'), as suggested by Kock? Cf. in general Gomme 96–101 on the

the well, so drink it dry, and then you won't even be able to give anyone water! Now the Nymphs have avenged me on him, and rightly. No one injures a cook and gets away with it; there's something sacred about our art. But you can do what you like to a man who sets the tables.

No doubt many a Greek's faith in divine justice and the existence of gods was boosted when a sudden misfortune struck a man who had injured him (cf. V.D.4), but Sikon's pretentious evaluation of his own profession warns us that even the exclamation, 'There *are* gods!' may be caricature. But of what? Possibly not of self-important cooks, but of attitudes implicit in the reactions of unsophisticated people.[4] In New Comedy, as in Theokritos's or Herodas's representations of countryfolk, housewives and slaves, we may feel that the author is inviting us to laugh *at* such characters, patronizingly, from a superior standpoint. In Old Comedy we are made to feel that we provide in our own behaviour the ingredients which are satirized by exaggeration. Whatever the basis in dramatic technique, the effect is similar in terms of the relationship between comic psychology or theology and the realities of popular belief. In Ar. *Clouds* 1214–21 a creditor whose patience is exhausted comes to demand his money back from Strepsiades. He is embarrassed and uneasy at having to press a fellow-demesman (cf. VI.A.1),[5] but plucks up his courage with grandiloquent illogicality:

Yet never, while I live, will I shame my fatherland! I'll issue a summons to Strepsiades!

Just as in tragedy we must be prepared to encounter archaic attitudes and beliefs judged appropriate by the dramatist to the past age which he is portraying, so in comedy, in so far as it parodies tragedy, we may come up against those same archaic attitudes, as it were, from the opposite direction. It is reasonable to suspect parody of this kind in two passages of Ar. *Knights*: 108, where the slave pours a libation and is suddenly struck by a bright idea,

difficulty of founding arguments on items isolated from their contexts and preserved in anthologies.

[4] It is not impossible in Britain still to find people who believe that a fall off a ladder today is a divinely contrived punishment for yesterday's blasphemy. Sikon's sentiment itself is appropriate to legendary events on a grand scale, and therefore occurs in tragedy in more elaborate and sonorous forms, e.g. Eur. fr. 577, 'When I see the evildoers among mortals laid low, I declare that the gods exist!', Eur. *Supp.* 731f.

[5] It seems evident from Dem. xxxvii 52–4 that those who made a living by lending money at interest were not liked, and represented themselves as kindly souls who were always ready to help out people in trouble. I am now inclined to think (against what I said in my commentary on the play) that Aristophanes intends us to regard the First Creditor in *Clouds* as a money-lender.

and 1203, where the Sausage-seller presents Demos with the hare which the Paphlagonian had brought ready.[6]

108: God of good fortune, yours is the plan, not mine!
1203: The idea was Athena's, but the theft was mine!

In *Wasps* 373ff., the chorus of old jurors, encouraging Philokleon to escape unnoticed by Bdelykleon, proclaim that if Bdelykleon stirs they will strike fear into him,

... that he may learn not to trample underfoot the decrees of the gods.

The old men speak as if their right to spend all their days in sitting on juries were guaranteed by divine ordinance. The concept used is serious (we are reminded of the 'unwritten and unshakable rules of the gods' invoked by Antigone in Soph. *Ant.* 454f.), but its application satirizes men's readiness to treat their own predilections as pious (cf. V.D.2).

Clearly an unthinking collection and acceptance of all comic sentiments and generalizations as 'popular' would lead us to some odd conclusions; every passage needs its own interpretation. In general, the element of literary parody diminishes considerably in comedy towards the end of the fourth century, and satire of social usage and types of temperament increases in importance. At the same time there are indications that the dramatist is writing for a more intellectual audience, or at any rate for an audience containing far fewer people whose attitude to scientific and philosophical speculation was positively impatient and hostile. Understanding of what philosophers were really trying to say is not, perhaps, significantly greater, but some allusions are different in tone from Old Comedy's indiscriminate, knockabout ridicule of philosophy as a whole.[7]

Alexis fr. 93.2–4: Well, you know, Plato says that the good is good everywhere; and what's nice is nice anyway, whether it's here or there.

Amphis fr. 6: What good you're ever going to get through her, master, I can't understand any better than the Good of Plato.

Cf. Philemon fr. 71, on the time spent in vain by philosophers on the problem 'What is *good*?'

[6] Cf. P. Rau, *Paratragodia* (Munich, 1967) 187, 189.

[7] The most striking reference to Plato in comedy is Theopompos fr. 15, which sounds as if the author had some acquaintance with the argument which we encounter in *Phaedo* 96E–97B. The longest extant reference is Epikrates fr. 11, which describes Plato and his pupils discussing botanical taxonomy. It seems a retrograde step into mindless philistinism when Epikouros is treated in later comedy as an advocate of gluttony. On the whole question see T. B. L. Webster, *Studies in Later Greek Comedy* (Manchester, ed. 2, 1969) 50–6, 100–13.

# I.E. ELEMENTS COMMON TO ORATORY AND COMEDY

### 1. Admonition of Juries and Assemblies

It is natural that a speaker in court should express a fear that the jury may be deceived by dishonest arguments on the part of his adversary (e.g. Is. viii 3, Isok. xviii 65, Lys. xix 61); such a fear could be treated as a compliment to the manly simplicity of the jurors. It may, on the other hand, surprise us to find a speaker plainly asserting that juries are commonly deceived into giving unjust verdicts. Occasionally the speaker attributes this view to others and claims not to accept it himself, but it seems to have been practicable to adopt, without serious risk of offence, an admonitory, didactic standpoint *vis-à-vis* the Athenian people as represented by a jury.

Isok. xviii 9f.: Some of my friends . . . advised me to settle my difference with him . . ., saying that things often turn out unexpectedly in the courts and that cases brought before you are decided more by chance than by justice . . . 36: Perhaps he has heard someone say that when you fail to catch the guilty you punish whoever comes your way, but I do not think that you are so inclined . . .

Cf. Dein. i 104; contrast the rather fulsome expression of faith in the jury expressed by Ant. v 8 and Is. ix 35.

Ant. v 91: When on the point of taking an irreparable step, the most careful thought is necessary . . . Some of you before now have repented of giving a capital verdict.

Cf. Dem. xxiii 95, xxxvi 25, xxxvii 20, xl 21, xlvii 3, 39, 46, lviii 70, Lys. xii 38, xx 20.

These are not the terms in which it is nowadays customary to address a jury, and it is even less customary to assert in the terms commonly adopted by an Athenian orator that in a particular case the jury actually was deceived and the verdict was wrong.[1] Here again an apologetic tone could be adopted but was not indispensable.

Dem. xlv 6f.: He put the jury into a frame of mind in which they were not willing to hear a word from me . . . I left the court heavy in heart, treated as outrageously as anyone has ever been . . . But when I think it over, I realise that the jury which decided the case behaved in an entirely forgivable way; for I cannot say that I

---

[1] Athenian law made no provision for appeal against the verdict of a jury.

would have been able to give any different verdict myself if I had known nothing of
the facts but simply heard the evidence given.

Cf. Is. v 8.

Dem. xxxvii 45: I want to tell you by what means he deceived the previous jury
and won his case against Euergos.

Cf. ibid. 48, xlvi 9.

Speakers, especially when prosecuting, attribute the acquittal of the guilty
sometimes to the admission of procedural malpractice (Aiskhines i 178, Lyk.
12), but more often to what they call the slackness, frivolity, emotional
instability or simple-mindedness of juries,

Aiskhines iii 192: What happens nowadays is simply ridiculous. The secretary reads
out the proposal which has been indicted for illegality, and the jurors listen to it as
if it were a spell or something that had nothing to do with them, because their minds
are on something else.

Dem. xxiii 206: You release people who do you (*i.e. the state*) very serious wrong
and are plainly proved guilty, if they say one or two things that tickle your fancy and
advocates elected from their own tribe[2] speak on their behalf.

Cf. Dem. xx 166, xxi 37, xxv 12 ('your usual simple-mindedness'), li 11f.,
15, lviii 63, Lyk. 33, Lys. xix 36, xxvi 2 (criticism of the Council, not of a
jury), xxvii 11.

Since a jury is treated as representing the sovereign people, and may even
be addressed as if it actually were the whole assembled people (cf. VI.B.2), it
is not always easy to separate criticism of juries from criticism of the assembly,
but reference to policy decisions or elections usually suffices to show when the
assembly is meant. The assembly, like a jury, can be treated as the victim of
misleading advice, and its individual decisions can be criticized as the consequence of such deception; cf. Dem. xxiv 161, 'You made a very natural
choice' between the alternatives as Androtion presented them. Yet its
liability to deception can be blamed on its stupidity, laziness or frivolity.
These are not the terms in which a modern politician is prepared to broadcast
to the electorate.

And. iii 35: It is your habit to be suspicious and difficult about what is actually
available to you and to build up the idea that what you do not have is available. If
war is needed, you want peace; and if anyone negotiates a peace for you, you reckon
up all the benefits you have derived from war.

---

[2] The Athenian citizen-body was divided into ten *phŷlai*, membership of one's *phŷlē*
being hereditary on the father's side; 'tribe' is the commonest modern translation of
*phŷlē*.

Dem. xxiii 185: But that isn't enough for the speakers. They propose that Kharidemos should be made a citizen, declared a benefactor ... in return for the bribes he gives them; and the rest of you just sit there, made complete fools, gaping at what is being done.

ibid. 211: Our deliberations are inferior not only to those of our ancestors ... but to those of any nation.

Cf. And. ii 27f., Dein. i 99, Dem. iii 3, 21f., iv 38, vi 34 (when the assembly realizes that it has been cheated, its wrath may fall upon the innocent), 36, viii 30–4 ('You have no idea what to do, but hate being found out'), ix 204, x 7, xiii 13, 36, xvii 13, xviii 133f., 138, 149, 159 ('darkness between your eyes and the truth'), xix 104, xxii 78, xxiii 145, xlviii 24, lix 91, Lys. vi 34. The tactful 'we' of Dem. xxiii 211 is unusual; 'you' is the norm.

To these passages we should add some others in which criticism of the Athenian people is expressed in general terms applicable to conduct of business in the assembly, to the hearing of cases in the courts, or to moral and political attitudes in general: Aiskhines iii 3–5, Dem. xix 228, Lyk. 3. It is common to contrast the Athenians of the speaker's own time with their wiser and more virtuous ancestors: Aiskhines iii 192, Dem. iii 21f., xiii 26, xxii 77f., xxiii 206–11.


## 2. Mistrust of Practised Speakers

It is also common (as in Dem. xxiii 185, cited above) to draw a distinction between the dominated mass of the people and the dominant category of politicians. This distinction is expressed by contrasting 'ordinary people',who have not sought prominent political or administrative roles, with 'politicians' (politeuomenoi), 'speakers' (rhētores) or 'those who speak' (hoi legontes):[3] Aiskhines i 195, Dem. xxiv 142, 155, 198, xxv 40f., 97, lviii 41, Hyp. iv 27, Lys. xxx 24. In a forensic speech the speaker may contrast 'ordinary people', for whom he tries to evoke sympathy, with that skilled orator and hardened politician, his opponent: Aiskhines iii 16, Dem. xx 146, 150, Hyp. v 26. It is one of the ironies and ambivalences of Athenian oratory that a man who is in fact a skilled speaker has to pretend that he is not, and has to try to represent his opponent as a 'formidable speaker' (deinos legein). So Aiskhines calls Demosthenes tekhnītēs logōn (i 170), which strikes halfway between 'artist in words' and 'concocter of arguments' (cf. ibid. 94, 117, 125), and Demosthenes applies almost exactly the same term to Androtion (Dem. xxii 4); cf. id.,

[3] Cf. W. Pilz, Der Rhetor im attischen Staat (Weida, 1934) 31–52; Dover (1) 155–9.

xxiii 5. Speaking against Meidias, Demosthenes knows that Meidias may try
to arouse feeling against him by saying 'Demosthenes is a *rhētōr*', and he
devotes an elaborate *distinguo* (xxi 189–92) to reduction of the damage which
this perfectly true statement may do to him. His cousin Demon, involved in
commercial litigation, also has to try to allay in advance whatever suspicions
might be aroused by his association with his clever kinsman (Dem. xxxii 31),
and Hypereides (i 10, iv 11) explicitly defends as 'democratic' the fact that the
law allows him, *although* he is a well-known speaker, to associate himself
with another man's case. This does not prevent him from using the derogatory term 'speech-writer' against Athenogenes (Hyp. iii 3).⁴ In these connections words for systematic preparation and organization (verb *paraskeuazein*,
noun *paraskeuē*) can be given sinister undertones: Dem. xlviii 36, Is. viii 5,
x 1, fr. 22.2. They are meant to suggest conspiracy and payment for dishonest
services; so Dem. li 2 accuses certain trierarchs, who have neglected their
duties, of 'preparing the speakers' so that they may escape penalty. Allegations
that assemblies and juries are 'misled', and that politicians have habituated
them to 'bad practices', easily pass over into warnings not to allow assembly,
council (Dem. xxii 36f.) or juries (Dem. lviii 61) to come 'into the power of
the speakers'. The analogy of master and servant is used to striking effect by
Demosthenes.

Dem. iii 30f.: In the old days the assembly was master of the politicians and itself
controlled all benefits . . . Now, on the contrary, the politicians control the benefits
. . ., and you, the assembly, enervated and deprived of resources and allies, have
become a sort of servant and appendage of theirs.

Cf. Dem. xiii 31, xxiii 209f., xlii 32.


## 3. Comic Criticism of Speakers

By now any reader who is familiar with Aristophanes will have been struck
by a coincidence of standpoint between Aristophanic comedy and fourth-
century oratory: between the men who actually operated the democratic
system and the poet who is not uncommonly regarded as an upholder of
conservative virtues and a scourge of demagogues. On one point, it must be
granted, there is a difference: the orators, as we have seen, sometimes reproach
jurors for softness, whereas Aristophanes' *Wasps* satirizes them for brutal

---

⁴ In Pl. *Phaedrus* 257CD a man who called Lysias *logographos*, 'speech-writer' is
regarded as having 'abused' or 'vilified' him (*loidorein*).

severity. No doubt Aristophanes speaks for the ordinary man who has avoided litigation and hopes to be able to go on avoiding it, whereas the forensic prosecutor and defendant, men who have not wished or have not been able to avoid it, need a different approach from the outside observer, the prosecutor trying to induce severity by stern admonition (almost, at times, by taunts) and the defendant trying to induce leniency by persuasion and flattery. But one element, a frivolity which produces arbitrary decisions, is common to the comic and the oratorical picture of juries (*Wasps* 566f., 579–87).

The presentation of the Athenian people as master is fundamental to Aristophanes' *Knights*. Demos, the personification of the people, has been hoodwinked by his violent, noisy, corrupt, self-seeking 'Paphlagonian slave' Kleon, whose power over his master is at last broken by the sausage-seller. Demos, restored to his pristine glory (1321–34), hangs his head in shame when the sausage-seller makes him realize that he was cheated by politicians who claimed to be devoted to him (1340–5). But, the sausage-seller assures him,

1356f.: You weren't to blame for all that, don't you worry; those who deceived you were to blame.

Previously old Demos has declared, in a lyric interchange with the chorus, that although he may seem blind and deaf he actually likes to 'maintain one champion at a time', to 'dash him to the ground when he's full', and, by bringing the politicians to trial, make them 'vomit up all that they have stolen' (1121–50).

On similar lines Bdelykleon in *Wasps* manages to persuade the chorus of old jurors that the power which they believe themselves to enjoy is illusory; the real power belongs (654–724) to the politicians who make a parade of devoted patriotism but dishonestly appropriate the wealth which flows into the imperial city (cf. 1101). The jurors, he says, flattered and deluded into thinking that they are the masters, are in fact slaves (682), trained dogs (704f.), of those cheats and bullies.

The word *rhētōr* in Attic Greek denotes any person who speaks in public, whenever and in so far as he speaks, as we can say in English 'the speaker' with reference to a single occasion. But when comedy treats 'the speakers' as a category, '< habitual > speakers', i.e. 'politicians', its references are highly unfavourable. In *Wealth* 30f. 'speakers' appear in a catalogue of villains together with 'temple-robbers' and 'blackmailers'; later in the same play it is assumed (369) that they are always greedy for bribes, and Poverty says (567–70) that so long as 'the speakers' are poor they are good democrats, but once they have become rich by embezzlement they act contrary to the interests of the democracy. Shamelessness is 'their only tutelary deity' (*Knights* 325).

The comic poet and his choruses pose, like the orators, as true champions of the Athenian people against false champions, as honest patriots against self-seeking politicians (cf. *Clouds* 549, *Knights* 511). Like the orator, again, the comic poet treats the people not as malevolent but as deceived (e.g. *Ach.* 125–33, 634–40), and deceived because it is stupid (*Frogs* 734, 'O foolish men!'; cf. Com. anon. fr. 47), fickle (*Knights* 518), impulsive (*Ach.* 632), doomed always to take wrong decisions from which only divine goodwill rescues it at the last minute (*Clouds* 587–9). Earlier generations, the poet assures us, were different: frugal and self-denying in the exercise of their public duties (*Eccl.* 300–10), great fighters, not fancy talkers (*Wasps* 1094–1101); and all would be well if the situation could be restored to how things used to be (*Clouds* 593).[5]

## 4. Comic Abuse of the Audience

We must never forget that comedy is meant to be funny. Comic vilification of politicians is closely akin to ridicule of gods and to the uninhibited violence and sexuality which characterize comic 'heroes'; and comic reproaches against the style of Athenian politics and the people's infirmity of purpose lead easily into vulgar abuse which is evidently intended to make the audience laugh at itself.

Ar. *Peace* 821–3 (*Trygaios has returned to earth from his flight to Olympos*): You were very small from up there. I thought you looked a pretty nasty lot from the sky; but from here, you're much nastier!

id., *Frogs* 274–6 (*Xanthias has run round the lake of the underworld and has rejoined Dionysos*): DIONYSOS: Did you see the parricides and perjurers there (*sc. undergoing punishment*) that Herakles told us about? XANTHIAS: Why, didn't you? DIONYSOS: Indeed I did—(*gesturing towards the audience*) and I see them now!

Cf. *Peace* 55, 'not *your* kind of madness'; *Ach.* 79, only sexual and homosexual prowess earn respect; *Clouds* 1055–102, habitual buggery; ibid., 1172–5, trickery; *Wealth* 340–2, meanness; *Birds* 41, 109, *Clouds* 208, 494–6, 520,

[5] The span of time implied by *arkhaios* ( ~ *arkhē*, 'beginning', 'origin') depends on the context, and is not necessarily very great; to restore a situation *eis to arkhaion*, 'to its original state', could mean turning the clock back only a month or two. On the whole question of Aristophanes' view of the past see W. Kassies, *Aristophanes' Traditionalisme* (Amsterdam, 1963).

*Peace* 505, stock jokes against litigiousness; Plato Comicus fr. 22, 'Our laws are like cobwebs'.

## 5. The Didactic Tradition

The comic poet's assertion of his right to insult his audience, however coarsely or recklessly, can be regarded as a facet of the more general right of the poet, the public speaker and the writer to reproach and admonish as if he were a stern old man entitled to respect as wiser and better than his hearers. The comic chorus in the parabasis declares that it blames or criticizes (*memphesthai*) the audience for its errors and misdeeds: *Ach.* 676, *Clouds* 525, 576, *Thesm.* 830, *Wasps* 1016. It is the business of the chorus to give good advice (*khrēsta parainein*): *Frogs* 686f., *Lys.* 648. In a humorous passage of self-praise Aristophanes represents his 'mission' as vilification:

*Ach.* 647–51: The King of Persia, questioning the envoys from Sparta, asked them first, which side was superior at sea, and secondly, upon which side had our poet heaped abuse; for these, he said, were the better men and would gain by far the upper hand in the war, with our poet as their adviser.

A parabasis is no more a sermon than other ingredients of comedy are, and no less enlivened by imagery and deft conceits.[6] Yet so far as concerns the essential character of the passages to which reference has been made, stripped of their colourful detail, we can observe a striking continuity from the didactic and moralizing tradition of archaic poetry, through the late fifth- and early fourth-century comedy, to the lashings which Demosthenes administers to his fellow-citizens. Even in the earliest extant poetry we find the poet extolling the past and decrying the present, as in Homer's aside (*Il.* xii 447–9 on the great stone lifted by Hektor, 'which two men could not lift . . . such as men are now'. Hesiod presents the history of mankind as a process of degeneration and laments that his fortune has placed him in days of wickedness (*Works and Days* 174–201). Kallinos (fr. 1.1–4) incites his fellow-Ephesians to battle, Solon (fr. 2.3f.) his fellow-Athenians, by taunting them with unmanly sloth. Among the early philosophers, Herakleitos (B1) contrasts

---

[6] The percentage of matter devoted to political issues in the sum total of Aristophanic parabases is not large, unless we stretch the term "political' to cover all aspects of the life of the community. It is less conspicuous, in fact, than the passages in which the poet praises his own talent and denigrates his rivals, and we must also take into account the rich humorous fantasy derived from the role of the chorus as birds, clouds, etc. See G. M. Sifakis, *Parabasis and Animal-Choruses* (London, 1971), especially chapter IV.

himself with other men as if he alone possessed understanding; Parmenides takes an equally uncomplimentary view of his fellows (B1.30, B8.50–2), and Empedokles reinforces the same sentiment with a note of disdainful compassion (B2, B124). The opening sentence of the (in a broad sense) historical work of Hekataios (fr. 1) begins with the announcement that he will relate what he believes to be true, since Greek tradition in general is 'a lot of nonsense'.

Consideration should, I think, be given to the possibility that there existed a traditional role—the role of an angry, minatory moralizer, a lone individual setting himself up against the majority—into which a man addressing an Athenian audience was permitted to step, and that the adoption of this role commonly created a greater distance between strict public attitudes and easy-going private behaviour than might be the case in some other cultures.[7] If this supposition is even partially correct, it has some relevance both to the anti-intellectual, 'pre-sophistic' views of the world which endure to the end in oratory and to the sporadic appearance, in contexts which may slightly surprise us, of values which we should associate with a pre-democratic wealthy class (cf. I.F.).

## 6. Vilification and Ridicule of Individuals

For the student of Athenian society no lacuna in the transmission of Greek literature is more to be deplored than the absence of any complete comedy between the end of Aristophanes' career and the beginning (more than sixty years later) of Menander's. At the same time, the fact that we can so often compare the standpoint, values and techniques of Old Comedy (from *Acharnians* in 425 to *Wealth* in 388) with those of oratory even as late as 325 brings home to us the slow pace at which Athenian society evolved and the essential continuity between the theatrical audiences of Aristophanes and the juries and assemblies addressed by Demosthenes. A striking demonstration of this continuity is to be found in what Demosthenes says about the family of Aiskhines in 343 (speech xix) and 330 (speech xviii).

xix 199f.: The jury all know, don't they, that to start with you read the texts for

---

[7] Thucydides ii 65.8f. remarks that Perikles always spoke his mind fearlessly to the assembly and did not yield to the temptation to tell it what it might have wished to hear. His own representation of Perikles' speeches is in accord with that judgment. But other speakers in Thucydides are just as blunt and admonitory, including Kleon in the debate on Mytilene (iii 37–40).

your mother while she was conducting initiation rites, and knocked around, still only a boy, in congregations of worshippers and drunks?[8] And afterwards, that you were a clerk to magistracies and would do anything[9] for two or three drakhmai? And eventually, in recent times, that you were glad to pick up a living as a third-part actor in performances that other people paid for?[10]

ibid. 237: Perhaps his brothers Philokhares and Aphobetos will speak for him . . . We elected you, Philokhares, when you were painting your toilet-boxes and drums— and Aphobetos and Aiskhines, clerks, little men—to embassies, high commands, the most distinguished positions. Nothing wrong with what you were doing, of course, but hardly the sort of people we want as generals.

ibid. 281: The son of Atrometos the primary-school teacher and Glaukothea who convened the sect . . .

ibid. 287: Timarkhos . . . is ruined, scandalously, and it was Aiskhines . . . who accused him and spoke of (sc. homosexual) prostitution—God almighty! with two relatives of his beside him . . . the disgusting Nikias . . . and the abominable Kyrebion, and there was his brother Aphobetos before his eyes. Well! All the talk about prostitution that day was 'water running uphill'!

xviii 129f.: I don't know what to say first about you. Shall I tell them how your father Tromes was a slave of Elpias, who taught reading and writing by the Theseion . . .? Or how your mother, while she was practising 'daylight marriages' in the brothel by (sc. the shrine of) the hero Kalamites, brought you up as a paragon of manhood, a first-rate third-part actor? Why, everyone knows all that, even if I don't say it. Well, then: how the ship's piper Phormion, the slave of Dion Phrearrios, raised her up from her distinguished profession? . . . Adding a couple of syllables to his father's name, Aiskhines made him 'Atrometos' instead of 'Tromes',[11] and his mother he turned into 'Glaukothea'—an impressive name!—who everyone knows was called 'Empousa' because she could play any part (lit., 'do and undergo everything'; Empousa was a legendary monster who changed her shape at will).

xviii 259–62: When you were a boy you sat in attendance with your father at the school, grinding the ink and washing down the benches and sweeping out the waiting-room; you held the position of a slave, not that of a free boy. When you grew up

[8] Intoxication played a part in some forms of Greek worship. While Greek religion was not closed, in the sense of accepting only a finite number of supernatural beings, nor did it have any developed notion of orthodoxy, the Greeks did not consider that the practices or beliefs of sects and individuals deserved to be treated with respect merely because they were religious.

[9] I interpret these words (literally, 'being bad for two or three drakhmai') as a deliberately ambiguous hint at physical and metaphorical prostitution.

[10] No actor paid for the production of a play in which he appeared; that was the duty of the khorēgos; but Demosthenes is reminding us that Aiskhines, as an actor, did not belong to the category of people who earn honour and admiration by paying for things (cf. IV.B.2, V.B.2).

[11] 'Atrometos' suggests 'not trembling', i.e. 'fearless', and 'Tromes' suggests the noun tromos and adjective tromeros, 'trembling'.

you read out the texts for your mother when she was performing the initiation-rite (*There follows some graphic detail which gives the speaker scope for humorous mimicry*) ... And when you were enrolled in a deme—somehow or other; I'll let that pass, but, anyway—when you were enrolled, you chose such a noble calling, to be a secretary and a servant of minor magistracies! When at last you got out of that ... you hired yourself to the actors Simykas and Socrates, who were called 'the roarers', and played third parts ... There was a truceless war, no quarter given, between you and the audience.

Cf. ibid. 180, 219, 267.

Demosthenes laboured under the disadvantage that Aiskhines' brothers had become very distinguished men (cf. Aiskhines ii 14); he met this unwelcome fact head-on and tried to make something of it, as we see from xix 237. But over an interval of thirteen years he was able to 'improve' considerably on his account of Aiskhines' parents, not in consequence of further prosopographical research, but because he had had longer in which to touch up the story and with the passage of time there were fewer people alive who knew the truth. Similarly, he felt able in 330 to suppress what he could not so easily suppress in 343 (xix 247), that Aiskhines acted in tragedy with Theodoros and Aristo-demos, who were in fact the greatest actors of the time.

The ingredients of these diatribes can be shown to be the common property of comedy and oratory.

(i) One or both of the opponent's parents are of foreign and/or servile birth, and he has improperly become an Athenian citizen.

So Aiskhines alleges (ii 78) that Demosthenes is 'descended on his mother's side from the nomad Scythians' or (iii 172) that he is 'on his mother's side a Greek-speaking Scythian barbarian' (ii 180). So does Deinarkhos i 14; cf. Lys. xxx 2 on Nikomakhos. Compare Kleon as a 'Paphlagonian' in Aristophanes' *Knights*, Kleophon as a 'Thracian' (*Frogs* 678ff., cf. Plato Comicus fr. 60), Hyperbolos as a 'Phrygian' (Polyzelos fr. 5) or 'Lydian' (Plato Comicus fr. 170), and similar accusations of foreign birth against Lykon (Pherekrates fr. 11, Eupolis fr. 53), Arkhedemos (Eupolis fr. 71), Khaireas (Eupolis fr. 80) and Dieitrephes (Plato Comicus fr. 31); this list is only selective.

(ii) The opponent and his kin have followed menial callings, e.g. as clerks, or have made a living by manufacture or retail trade.

Demosthenes in his prosecution of his guardian speaks (xxvii 9) of his own father as having owned two factories, of which the slave component included 32 knife-makers and 20 bed-makers. This makes it possible for Aiskhines to call Demosthenes (ii 93) 'son of the knife-maker'. Compare Kleon the 'tanner' in Aristophanes' *Clouds* 581, the 'leather-seller' in *Knights* 136,

Hyperbolos the 'man from the lamp-market' (*Clouds* 1065) or the 'lamp-maker' (*Peace* 690); Kleophon was remembered in hostile tradition as the 'lyre-maker' (And. i 146, Aiskhines ii 76).[12] Euxitheos, the speaker of Dem. lvii, has to combat the sneer (34) that his mother had been a ribbon-seller and wet-nurse; cf. Eupholis fr. 243, where it is said of someone 'his mother was a Thracian ribbon-seller'. Lysias sneers at Nikomakhos and Teisamenos as 'clerks' (xxx 28); 'Aiskhylos' in Ar. *Frogs* 1083ff. laments that 'our city is full of clerks and demagogic apes who cheat the people'.

(iii) The opponent or his relations have been prostitutes or have at least deviated from conventional norms of sexual behaviour.

Accusations of this type are no longer accepted parliamentary practice, but they were made very freely at Athens. Aiskhines says of Demosthenes: 'There is no part of his body that he has not sold, not even his organ of speech' (ii 23 cf. 88); 'When he was a boy he was called 'Batalos' because of a certain dirty, unnatural practice' (ii 99); 'This young man, who was exceptionally good-looking, stayed a long time in Demosthenes' house; what he was doing, or what was happening to him, is uncertain, and it isn't at all seemly for me to talk about it' (iii 162); 'My brother Aphobetos . . . has begotten legitimate children—he didn't put his own wife out to sleep with Kyrebion, as you did' (ii 149). Compare the generalization in Old Comedy that a boy subjected to much buggery grows into a prominent politician: Ar. *Clouds* 1093f., *Eccl.* 111ff., Plato Comicus fr. 186.5. Allegations of this kind against particular individuals continued in comedy and politics alike into the last years of the fourth century.

Polybios xii 13.1–8: Timaios says that Demokhares (*Demosthenes' nephew*) had prostituted the upper parts of his body, and that he was not a fit person to blow the sacrificial flame . . . But none of this is true; had it been so, it would have been said not only (*sc. as it was*) by the comic poet Arkhedikos but also by many of the friends of Antipatros . . . and many of Demokhares' political opponents, who included Demetrios of Phaleron.

The sexual language of oratory is usually circumspect, sometimes even coy (e.g. Aiskhines i 38, 55, 62), whereas that of comedy is gross and blunt; but the content of sexual accusations can be the same in both genres.

[12] Kleophon 'the lyre-maker', 'the Thracian', now appears not to have been a parvenu, let alone of *barbaros* origin, but the son of the Kleippides who was politically active in the 440's and elected general in 428 (Russell Meiggs and David Lewis, *Greek Historical Inscriptions to the End of the Fifth Century B.C.* [Oxford, 1969] 41f.). Yet it seems to have been acceptable that Aristophanes and other comic poets should make against him the same allegations as might have been less implausible in some other cases.

## I.F. SOCIAL CLASS

### 1. The Jurors

It is remarkable to find Demosthenes, in addressing a mass jury, adopting so supercilious an attitude to schoolmasters, clerks and decorators; even more surprising is the passage in which he contrasts himself as a well-to-do man of leisure with Aiskhines as an unfortunate menial who had to earn a living.

Dem. xviii 265: You taught reading and writing, but I went to school. You initiated, but I was initiated. You were the secretary (*sc. of the assembly*); I was a voting member. You played third parts; I was in the audience. You were kicked out, and I hissed you.

To our way of thinking this comes near to saying, 'You were useful; I was not', but we can hardly believe that Demosthenes, a very experienced speaker by 330, misjudged the effect of his words. There seem, then, to be two possibilities: either the majority of the jurors addressed by the fourth-century orators were fairly prosperous—not rich, for it was possible to exploit their dislike of the really rich (Dem. xxi 98, 213)[1]—and tended to regard the man who can pay for services as better than the man who renders them; or, if they did not belong to the prosperous class, they liked to be treated as if they did, and were willing, at least while performing the role of jurors, to adopt the values of that class. Passages such as Lys. xxviii 3, where 'you', i.e. the jury, are said to be oppressed by capital levies and formerly to have owned substantial family properties, rather point to the former alternative, and are not outweighed by the frequent equation of 'you' with 'the majority (*sc.* of the people)', as in Dem. xxiv 193. It is important to remember that pay for jury service did not rise during the

---

[1] A middle class which attaches the greatest importance to criteria, even of the most trivial kind, which distinguish it from the working-class may also feel acute resentment against the very rich, whom it regards as idle and dissolute people who have not earned and do not deserve their wealth. In that mood the word 'poor' can be used almost with pride. Demosthenes is not joking when (xxi 123) he contrasts the vulnerability of 'the poorest and weakest of you' (*sc.* of the jurors) with 'the filthy rich' (literally, 'the disgusting and having money'). In that same speech he judges it necessary to assure the jury that Straton, whose alleged maltreatment by Meidias is important to his argument, is, although poor, 'not a bad man' (87, 95); it must, however, be noted that since Straton had been charged with misconduct as an arbitrator (87) and disenfranchised, there was a reasonable presumption that he was a very bad man, and also (cf. III.E.1) that a man who needed money was more easily corrupted than a man who did not.

hundred years that followed its establishment at half a drakhme (Ar. *Knights* 255 ~ Arist. Ath. 62.2), while wages and earnings for manual work doubled during the same period.[2] Hence what began as a means of drawing the poor into the administration of the state became an honorarium for people who did not lose by leaving their usual occupation for service on juries—and at the same time a subsistence allowance for those whose earnings were very low indeed. It is a singular fact that payment for attending the assembly, by contrast with payment for jury-service, did rise during the fourth century: beginning at one sixth of a drakhme after the democratic restoration of 403, it was soon raised to half a drakhme, and by the 320's it stood at one and a half drakhmai for each 'principal' meeting and one drakhme for each of the rest. The reason for this disparity is obscure; the poor may or may not have attended the assembly in force,[3] but at any rate a great many of them will have had a motive, increasingly strong with the passage of time, for not seeking to be empanelled as jurors. In 422 Aristophanes suggests (*Wasps* 300ff.) that the characteristic juror is a poor old man to whom half a drakhme makes all the difference, but Philokleon, his juror-hero (or juror-villain) is certainly not a poor man. There is no way of estimating the ratio, in a late fourth-century jury, of prosperous men who expected to be treated as such to virtually destitute men who may have felt flattered at being addressed in the same terms as their prosperous colleagues.

## 2. The Standpoint of Old Comedy

Some interesting passages in Aristophanes express what appears to be a strongly middle-class or even at times upper-class view of political leadership.[4] *Knights* satirizes the style of politics in 424 by constructing a fantasy in which power passes from Kleon to the *ne plus ultra* of uneducated vulgarity,

[2] On this and related matters see Jones 35–7 and 123f.

[3] Cf. Jones 109f. In Ar. *Eccl.* 300ff. (produced in 392) the chorus sing that when the pay for attending the assembly was only a sixth of a drakhme no one came, whereas now that the sum has been raised to half a drakhme they all come. Since the chorus represents women dressed up as men, anxious to pack the assembly at first light and vote for transference of power to the women, and the context is, 'We must hurry and make sure there's no room for all the men who will come from the city', it is necessary for the poet to use the idea, 'The assembly's always overcrowded these days', and hardly possible for us to assess the relation of this idea to reality.

[4] Not oligarchic, for Aristophanes does not suggest that the constitution should be redesigned in such a way as to restrict political power to a section of the citizen-body; de Ste Croix 357 finds Aristophanes' attitude essentially 'paternalistic'.

a sausage-seller. The slave of Demos, the old man who personifies the Athenian people, ascertains that the sausage-seller has the right qualifications.

*Knights* 185–93: SLAVE: You're not by any chance from a good[5] family? SAUSAGE-SELLER: God, no! A very bad one! SLAVE: Congratulations! That's the best thing that could have happened to you for a future in politics. SAUSAGE-SELLER: But—but—I've no education at all except reading and writing, and even that very badly! SLAVE: That's the only thing wrong—that you *can* do it badly! Leadership of the people isn't the job of an educated man any more, or a man of good character; it goes to some filthy oaf.

Later in the play Kleon and the Sausage-seller compete as 'lovers' for the favour of Demos, and the Sausage-seller, who by this point is developing into a critic of precisely the situation which his earlier role was meant to typify, reproaches the old man.

*Knights* 734–40: I've long been in love with you and wanted to do what is best for you, and so have many other good men; but we're not able to, because of *him* (*sc. Kleon*). You're like the boys who have lovers: you don't accept the good ones, but give yourself to lamp-sellers and cobblers and shoemakers and leather-merchants.

An unusual passage of political advice is addressed by the chorus to the city in *Frogs* 718–37.

We have often thought that our city has made the same mistake about those of its citizens who are good as about the old coinage and the new gold. For this . . . the fairest of all currencies . . . we don't use at all, but instead the bad bronze struck only the other day . . . And those citizens whom we know to be well-born and moral men, and honest and good, and brought up in wrestling-schools and dancing and music we spurn, and we use on all occasions the men of bronze, foreigners, red-heads (*implying 'non-Greek'*), bad sons of bad fathers, last-minute arrivals whom the city in the old days would have thought twice about using even as scapegoats.[6] But even at this late hour, senseless people, change your ways and use good men again . . .

Comparable sentiments are expressed in a citation from Eupolis; the lines are evidently spoken by an old man (the leader of a chorus of old men?), but not knowing the context we do not know the degree of caricature or satire.

Eupolis fr. 117: It isn't how we old men used to run the city. Our generals . . . were from the greatest houses, first in wealth and family, and we prayed to them as to

---

[5] Here and at other points in the following passages I have used 'good' to translate the Greek expression *kalos kāgathos*, which will be discussed in section 4 below.

[6] In the technical sense, criminals used in an expiatory ritual.

gods, for that is what they were; and so all that we undertook went well. But nowadays, anything goes when we take the field, and we elect scum as generals.

The alternative possibilities in the interpretation of the upper-class standpoint adopted by comic poets of the late fifth and early fourth centuries are not quite the same as in the interpretation of oratory. Comedies were performed on festival days, on which the opportunities for earning would be greatly restricted; conventions of standpoint can, to a certain extent, be accepted in an artistic genre on the same basis as conventions of form and language; and the most eminent comic poets may well have been, by temperament and upbringing, critical of democratic politics, particularly since the democratic constitution was 'the establishment' and revolution could only come from the right.[7]

But did there exist at Athens a recognizable, definable set of 'working-class' values which never attained expression in oratory and comedy? And if so, how was it possible for speakers and comic poets to suppress it?

### 3. Class Consciousness

For purposes of war service the citizen population of Athens was divided into three classes: cavalry (the highest and smallest class), hoplites (the heavy-armed infantry who provided their own arms and armour), and thetes (who could enlist as rowers in warships or, when required, as light-armed troops). We know the size of the hoplite force at certain points in time during the fifth and fourth centuries, though we could do with more knowledge than we actually have about the upper age-limit for hoplite service. We also encounter the figure 30,000 as the rough popular estimate of the citizen population of Athens in the late fifth century, and there is good evidence that in the late fourth century the actual figure was a little over 20,000, of whom 9,000 owned property valued at 2,000 drakhmai or more; those 9,000 will have been roughly coextensive with the class liable at least for hoplite service and (its upper segment) for cavalry service.[8] There is some reason to think that in 403 it could be plausibly stated that 5,000 citizens owned no land at all.[9]

---

[7] Cf. Connor 168–83 on the reactions of Old Comedy to changes in the style of political leadership—which we must, I think, consider in relation to the standard comic deprecation of change as such, including change in artistic taste and intellectual orientation.

[8] Cf. Jones 76–84.

[9] Dionysios of Halikarnassos *Lys.* 32, referring to the speech of which he quotes a

None of the figures available for the period 450–300 B.C. can be assailed by observing the number of warships manned on important occasions and multiplying by 200 (the complement of a warship) to arrive at a minimum number of thetes, for substantial numbers of men from the Aegean islands and coastal cities came to Athens to enlist as rowers.[10]

How many of the hoplite class possessed property which put them only just above the minimum qualification for that class, and how many thetes possessed property which put them only just below it? If we knew that, we might be in possession of an essential clue to the understanding of the attitudes to social class expressed in Attic literature, for a society in which the median income is coincident with the arithmetic mean income, or even above it, is obviously likely to have a different outlook on class and wealth from a society in which the median is significantly below the mean.[11]

An even more important factor is the relation between capital and labour, and here the Athenian city-state differed fundamentally from modern capitalist societies. Much of the work which is nowadays done by citizens whom other citizens engage, pay and dismiss was done in Athens by slaves who were owned as items of property; it was slaves who manned the factories of Demosthenes' family (Dem. xxvii 9) and Lysias's (Lys. xii 8, 19). Poor men generally, however wretched and insecure their situation, were their own masters, as producers or retailers. So few citizens were regularly employed by other citizens that it was hard for an individual to feel that his own labour was directly enriching someone else; hence polarization of capital and labour could not play any significant part in the political life of the citizen-body.[12] Speeches were designed to persuade a body of citizens, and comedy to amuse a citizen audience; we should not expect either of them ever to look at the economic structure of the community through the eyes of a slave. Class conflict showed itself in resentment against wealthy men who were suspected of believing that by means of gifts and bribes and promises they could escape punishment for arrogant or dishonest behaviour towards

portion (Speech xxxiv in modern editions of Lysias); the datum is presumably drawn from that portion of the speech which he had read but does not quote, and the figure may be no more than a guess on the part of the original speaker.

[10] Cf. A. W. Gomme, *The Population of Athens in the Fifth and Fourth Centuries B.C.* (Oxford, 1933) 12f. and M. Amit, *Athens and the Sea* (Brussels, 1965), 26–49.

[11] Cf. Ehrenberg 80f., 145f., 250–2, 361.

[12] Cf. Connor *passim* (but especially 5–8) on the nature of political alignments and loyalties at Athens in the fifth century. The rivalry of prominent individuals competing for influence over the assembly was characteristic of the Athenian democracy throughout its history, and political groupings were much more fluid than in a state in which conflicting class interests are represented by long-standing parties.

poorer men, or (especially in comedy, e.g. Ar. *Ach.* 595–616, *Peace* 1170–90) against military commanders, ambassadors, and others who rise in status (by election, it should be remembered) in consequence of war and allegedly receive high pay and great honour for doing easy and comfortable jobs while the rank and file suffer. The idea that no decision on national policy should benefit the few while inflicting death and hardship on the many was the cornerstone of democratic theory; it is made explicit by the Syracusan democrat in Thuc. vi 39.2, it underlies the Periklean justification of democracy in Thuc. ii 40.2, and we find reflexes of it in what is said by Hippokrates (*Airs, Waters and Places* 16) about Asiatic despotism and by Dem. ii 16–18, xi 9–12 about the Macedonian monarchy. The rich tended to believe and assert that they suffered more than the poor from war (cf. Ar. *Eccl.* 197f.), taking insufficient account of the fact that having little and losing all of it is a worse blow than having much and losing some of it (cf. Thuc. ii 65.2). Since those who depended wholly or partly on farming land in Attica suffered by enemy invasions which left the urban cobbler or carpenter free to carry on his trade,[13] a polarization of city and country undoubtedly occurred from time to time on issues affecting war and peace: cf. [Xen.] *Ath.* 2.14, Ar. *Peace* 508–11, *Eccl.* loc. cit., Anon. *Hell. Oxy.* 1.3. There were, however, enough other factors to prevent this alignment from becoming as clear and as permanent as is sometimes assumed on the strength of evidence relating to particular military situations.

The very extensive use of slaves for the work now done by unionized wage-earners, combined with the existence at Athens of a very large category of resident aliens who were debarred from participation in the processes of political decision and subject to great legal disabilities, had two distinct and potentially conflicting effects. It allowed even the poorest Athenian citizen to be conscious that he was a member of an élite, a minority of the total number of adult male humans who lived within the boundaries of Attica.[14] Unlike a slave, he could not be struck with impunity; unlike a resident alien, he could vote. In these conditions (and we must allow also for the conventional belief, however vague, in the remote common ancestry of the citizen-body) it is open to question whether a distinctive working-class standpoint and set of values ever took shape within the citizen-body. The extraordinary stability of fourth-century democracy and the apparent absence of any

[13] Cf. Burford 28–36 on the view that craftsmen had less of a 'stake in the country' than those who owned land.

[14] Cf. M. I. Finley, 'Was Greek Civilisation Based on Slave Labour?', *Historia* viii (1959) 145–64.

demand for a significant extension of the state's control over the distribution of land and wealth strongly suggest that the rich, the poor and the economically secure majority between the two extremes did not differ in their values and assumptions to a sufficient degree to warrant a belief that forensic speakers and comic poets must be expressing a minority view when they extol the virtues of inherited wealth and expensive education.[15]

The second important effect of the economic structure of Athens was that to work for another man, to be dependent on him and at the mercy of his approval, was to be *like* a slave.[16] Certainly the free citizen who lived by the kind of tedious specialization of which Xen. *Cyr.* viii 2.5 speaks (with reference to division of labour in shoe-making) must have felt his life-style to be remarkably similar to that of a slave trained to a craft. Given the Athenians' inclination to regard a man's habituation and style of life as having a profound effect on his moral character and the pressures to which he was subjected as limiting his moral capacity (cf. III.B.*1*), it is not surprising if the need to engage in what Dem. lvii 45 calls 'servile and humble activities' (the speaker's tone there is self-defensive) induced shame and diffidence in the poor man himself, embarrassed compassion in his friends and contempt in ill-wishers.

Derisory treatment of '-sellers' and '-makers' in comedy and oratory can be viewed as a special case of contempt for economic dependence, for makers and sellers depend for their living on potential buyers, whom they must please. So in fact did Attic farmers who grew no cereals,[17] but it was perhaps easier for a farmer than for a retailer of lamps to feel that he was self-sufficient and to claim the respect of others on those grounds. Since a buyer usually wishes to pay less than a seller demands, contempt for the seller as economically dependent can be coupled with hostility towards him as avaricious and unreasonable; hence Attic comedy's consistently unfriendly attitude to fish-mongers ('all murderers', Amphis fr. 30.5ff.), slave-traders ('insatiable', Ar. *Wealth* 521), landladies (a subject of broad humour in Ar. *Frogs* 549–78), bread-sellers (cf. Ar. *Wasps* 1388–414) and moneylenders (Dem. xxxvii 52).[18] Dikaiopolis in Ar. *Ach.* 32–6 expresses the resentment of the farmer cooped up in the city at having to pay out money for all his needs, whereas in the country the cry of the hawker is never heard. Inn-keeping, brothel-keeping,

[15] Cf. Jones 35–7.

[16] Cf. Pohlenz 48f. and Mossé 26–8.

[17] Cf. Mossé 54f.

[18] Examples are assembled by Ehrenberg 113–15, 119f., who also (121–3) discusses hostility to sellers in political life but does not relate the phenomena to each other in the way which seems to me plausible.

tax-collecting and gambling are classified by Theophr. *Char.* 6.5, together with working as a herald (cf. the bitter words of Eur. *Hcld.* 292f., *Or.* 895f., *Tro.* 424–6) or as a cook, as callings which a 'desperate' man may follow.

One other consideration should be added. In many Greek states—and in Athens at least until the Long Walls were built—the preservation of the community from destruction by its hostile neighbours depended essentially on the hoplite class. The prestige of such a class, especially in a society in which the rate of tactical innovation is very much slower than artistic and intellectual innovation, is tenacious of life, and the feeling that the hoplites were in the last resort the people upon whom Athens' survival depended, although challenged by the facts and by people who recognized the facts (e.g. Aristophanes' farmer-hero in *Ach.* 162f.), was a force to be reckoned with even in the greatest days of the Athenian navy. In the fourth century it is likely to have regained strength. It was, after all, the sailors who lost the Peloponnesian War; the Athenian hoplites would have lost it long before, had it depended on them, but they were not put to the final test, and the sailors were.

On the extent to which the Greeks regarded wealth not as produced by the ingenious exploitation of other people's labour, but as a matter of luck (or, in religious language, of divine favour), cf. IV.B.1.

## 4. The Expression kalos kāgathos

*Kalos kāgathos* (= . . . *kai ag-*), in comic dialogue *kalos te kāgathos* for metrical reasons (and so occasionally elsewhere), could be analysed as 'both good to look at and manifesting goodness in action'.[19] When Hdt. v 31.1 applies the term to the island of Naxos, he presumably means that it looks beautiful and is also productive. The purely aesthetic element, however, is submerged in the usual moral application of the word, as is clear from the available examples of the abstract noun *kalokāgathiā* and from the addition of 'in < bodily > form' to *kalos kāgathos* to give the sense 'handsome' in Aiskhines i 134.

Aiskhines iii 78: (*Demosthenes did not mourn adequately for his own daughter's death*) A man who is contemptible (*phaulos*) at home can never have been *kalos kāgathos* (*i.e. an honest, patriotic < envoy >*) in Macedonia.

[19] On the history of the expression see Hermann Wankel, '*Kalos kai Agathos*' (Diss. Würzburg, 1961), and J. Jüthner, 'Kalokagathia', in *Charisteria Rzach zum achtzigsten Geburtstag dargebracht* (Reichenberg, 1920) 99–119.

Dem. xviii 93f.: My policy displayed to all mankind the *kalokāgathiā* ('*magnanimity*') of Athens and the treachery (*kakiā*) of Philip; for he, an ally of Byzantion, was seen by everyone to be besieging it, while you, who could very well have made many reasonable complaints against Byzantion for its earlier misconduct towards you, were plainly . . . trying to save it.

ibid. 278: A *kalos kāgathos* citizen should not expect a jury . . . to help him win a private feud, but . . . be relentless . . . when the city's interests are at stake . . . For that is the conduct of a *gennaios* and *agathos* citizen.

ibid. 301–6: The loyal citizen . . . the *kalos kāgathos* citizen . . .

On these last two examples cf. II.B.*3*.

Dem. xxi 218: If you (*sc. the jury*) punish him, you will be regarded as sensible and *kalos kāgathos* and men of probity (*lit.*, '*haters of bad*').

Cf. Dein. iii 18, contrasting 'pretended *kalokāgathiā*' with 'inborn badness', referring to bribery and betrayal.

Dem. xxv 24: Villainy (*ponēriā*) is bold and venturesome and greedy, while *kalokāgathiā*, on the contrary, is peaceable and hesitant and slow and extraordinarily apt to be put at a disadvantage.

Cf. Aiskhines i 31 (contrasted with 'loathsome'), i 69 (sarcastic, coupled with probity and contrasted with shamelessness), Dem. xviii 278, li 19 (implying hostility to shamelessness), liv 14 ('respectable' in behaviour).

Dem. xl 46: You abide by the agreement then made, as *kalos kāgathos* men should.

Cf. Dem. xlix 37f., contrast with willingness to commit perjury, and lii 30.

Dem. xlii 25: *Kalos kāgathos* jurors should give some respite to those who carry out services to the state unstintingly.

Is. iii 20f.: When a man makes a deposition . . . he invites above all the most upright (*epieikēs*) of his fellow-citizens and the best known to you, and . . . we all make our depositions with as many witnesses as we can . . . in order that . . . you may feel confidence in a number of *kalos kāgathos* men all giving the same evidence.

Cf. Dem. xxv 78, 'many of his relatives, *kalos kāgathos* men, will come and plead for him' (sim. Lys. xii 86) ∼ Dem. xxii 40, 'Archias, as being *epieikēs*, will speak for them'. In certain other passages (Aiskhines i 41 [sarcastic], And. i 133, Ant. i 14) the commendation is of the most general kind; cf. Xen. *Oec.* 14.9, 'I enrich good slaves . . . and treat them as *kalos kāgathos*'. In comedy the expression is applied to an oil-flask (Ar. *Frogs* 1236, 'a perfectly good one');[20] to a woman, in citations without contexts (Eupolis fr. 149, Kantharos

---

[20] Ehrenberg 98 (in keeping with his general view of the expression [107, 112]) translates 'a true aristocrat among its kind'; but why?

fr. 5); to a fishmonger from whom the speaker has bought an excellent fish (Nikostratos fr. 6); and, in general, to people whom the speaker is commending to the hearer for reasons which in each case depend on the dramatic situation (Ar. *Clouds* 101, 797, *Knights* 227, *Lys.* 1058f., *Wasps* 1256).

There are, however, certain passages which suggest at first sight that *kalos kāgathos* may also have been used as a 'class label'.

Thuc. viii 48.6: (*Phrynikhos argues that the adherence of the cities of the Athenian Empire to an oligarchy at Athens cannot be secured by promising them the establishment of oligarchies*) They consider that those who are called *kalos kāgathos* would give them as much trouble as the democracy.

Plato, *Rep.* 569A: Suppose the people say . . . that they set up the tyrant . . . so that under his leadership they might be freed from those who are called *kalos kāgathos* . . .

If I am a member of a class of people which believes itself to be better than other classes, I shall naturally tend to denote that class by commendatory terms such as 'decent people', and I may be reluctant to apply the epithet 'decent' to members of other classes except in so far as they display the qualities which I regard as peculiar to my own class.[21] The use of *kalos kāgathos* to denote or imply 'belonging to a high social class' by Greek writers whose views and sentiments are anti-democratic tells us nothing of interest or importance, no matter how numerous the examples; it certainly does not tell us anything about the intentions of a democratic writer when he uses the same term in addressing a mass audience. No word or expression can properly be called a class label unless it is sincerely repudiated by some members of the community, and no one ever says seriously 'I am not *kalos kāgathos*' (on Ar. *Knights* 185f. see below). The passages of Thucydides and Plato cited above would be of no importance if we could take 'called' in both of them to mean 'called *by themselves*'; but that would not be a candid translation of the Greek, and it would be virtually impossible in two passages of Aristotle.

Arist. *Pol.* 1293[b]38–40: Furthermore, the rich are regarded as possessing that for the sake of which wrongdoers do wrong; for that reason they call them (*sc. the rich*) *kalos kāgathos* and *gnōrimos* ('*notable*').

---

[21] I once heard the information, 'He is a member of the Communist Party of Great Britain' conveyed by the words 'He's a *very* nice man', spoken slowly and deliberately by one party member to another. Not all labels of class, party or category involve epithets immediately recognizable as commendatory; cf. 'He fits' or 'He's one of us'. De Ste Croix 373 points out that when *kalos kāgathos* is predicated of individuals we always find that they are 'men of the upper classes', but very few individuals of whom anything at all is predicated in extant Greek literature can be assigned with assurance to the poorer classes.

ibid. 1294ª18: The rich are regarded practically everywhere as holding the position of those who are *kalos kāgathos*.[22]

The implication of these passages taken together is that a certain class's evaluation of itself as *kalos kāgathos* was accepted by an appreciable number of people who did not themselves belong to that class. How large a number, we do not know; but it should be observed that Thucydides, Plato and Aristotle were by no means egalitarians and could well have exaggerated the diffusion of their own attitudes in the general population. Xenophon, who was quite prepared to contrast 'good men' with 'the people', was also prepared to use *kalos (te) kāgathos* with reference to a specific moral virtue.

Xen. *Hell.* vi 1.2: In Pharsalos itself Polydamas was regarded as *kalos te kāgathos* to such an extent that in a time of civil strife the Pharsalians entrusted the akropolis to him, allowing him to receive the revenues . . . and spend them on its administration, including the temples.

Honest administration of money or property entrusted to one's safe-keeping is normally treated as a manifestation—almost the manifestation *par* excellence—of *dikaiosynē* (cf. IV.B.1) and we would have expected Xenophon to describe Polydamas as *dikaios* rather than as *kalos te kāgathos*. Cf. Xen. *Anab.* ii 6.20, where the contrast is with *adikos* ('dishonest'), and ii 6.19, of soldiers who take naturally to good discipline.

In the passages quoted from Aristophanes in F.2, *kalos te kāgathos* is the expression which I translated as 'good': of parentage in *Knights* 185, explicitly contrasted with 'lamp-sellers and cobblers and shoemakers and leather-merchants' in *Knights* 735–8, and coupled with several commendatory adjectives and with 'brought up in wrestling-schools and dancing and music' in *Frogs* 727–9. When the Sausage-seller in *Knights* denies that his parents were *kalos te kāgathos*, he is saying of himself, for the furtherance of the comic fantasy,[23] something which in real life a man might be forced to admit with shame but would be very unlikely to proclaim with pride. In the light of the conventions discussed in E.5, I do not think it can be denied with complete confidence that Aristophanes and the other poets of Old Comedy adopted a

[22] Here and elsewhere Aristotle distinguishes between wealth and *kalokāgathiā*. Cf. especially *Pol.* 1259ᵇ34–1260ª4, 1270ᵇ23–6, 1271ª22–4, where *kalos kāgathos* is synonymous with *agathos* and *kalokāgathiā* with *aretē*; in the second passage 'the *dēmos*' makes sense if it is taken as 'most people' but hardly as 'the poor'. I suppose that for a philosopher a majority cannot be notably good; however good most people are, the standard of goodness justifying the application of the term 'good' must be pitched at a higher point on the scale.

[23] Cf. Dover (2) 59–63.

standpoint generally accepted by the rich and repudiated by the poor;[24] but equally, it cannot be asserted with complete confidence that the poor of Athens refused hereditary wealth and esteem which it claimed, resented its pretensions to political and military leadership, and opposed to its values positive values of their own. Until persuaded otherwise by arguments which I have not yet encountered, I make the assumption that the poor Athenian was normally willing to apply the expression *kalos kāgathos* to any man who had what he himself would have liked to have (wealth, a great name, distinguished ancestors) and was what he himself would have liked to be (educated, cultured, well-dressed and well-groomed, with the physique and poise of a man trained in fighting, wrestling and dancing).[25]

[24] De Ste Croix 359f. points out that Aristophanes does not ridicule the wealthy *as such*. But did anybody?

[25] If the orators always denote courage, honesty, probity and magnanimity when they use *kalos kāgathos*, we can in all cases understand why they use it. If they denote membership of a class characterized by inherited wealth and expensive traditional education, it is not easy to see in each case how their argument is helped by the use of the expression. In And. i 133 *kalos kāgathos* is applied sarcastically to Agyrrhios, but nothing in the context offers any reason to suppose that it differs from the common sarcastic application of *khrēstos* (e.g. Ar. *Clouds* 9, Dem. xxiii 169). Dein. iii 12, 'Philokles, having on three or four occasions commanded the cavalry, *kalos kāgathos* men, and having been elected general by you more than ten times, though unworthy, . . . betrayed the standards of those whom you appoint to commands', is an interesting case; de Ste Croix 375 says that the expression is here 'used beyond question in an essentially social sense'. Certainly the cavalry were all of a high social class; but if Deinarkhos was trying to arouse the jury's indignation against Philokles, how did it help his case to say that Philokles was unworthy to command men of inherited wealth and expensive education?

# II

# THE MORAL VOCABULARY

## II.A. THE USES OF MORAL LANGUAGE

### 1. The Lexical Approach

It might be supposed that if we examined all instances of (e.g.) *dikaios* or *sōphrōn* (and the words cognate with each of them) in comedy and oratory and observed the kinds of character, behaviour and motive to which they are applied, we should eventually be able to make an accurate statement of their denotation in fourth-century popular morality. We certainly have to perform lexical work of this kind at some stage of the enquiry, and we learn much from it. In particular, we learn that Greek and English exhibit nothing like a one-one correspondence in moral vocabulary; *sōphrōn*, for example, requires to be translated in different contexts 'careful', 'intelligent', 'law-abiding', 'sober', 'chaste', 'sensible', 'prudent' or 'wise'. This is not because Greek possesses only a small number of highly generic words and English possesses separate words for all the species of the genus *sōphrōn*, for the reverse is the case; the total Greek moral vocabulary is at least as large as that of English, but the two languages simply seem to classify differently. If, given three virtuous acts, *x*, *y* and *z*, Greek applies *sōphrōn* to *x* and *y* but *dikaios* to *z*, and English applies 'modest' to *x* but 'law-abiding' to *y* and *z*, it is possible that the Greeks discerned a common principle in *x* and *y*—or that they failed to discern, and ought to have discerned, a common principle in *y* and *z*. It is undesirable, however, to make too much of these possibilities; it is always stimulating and salutary to have own's own classifications and principles challenged, and to that extent we can benefit from the study of alien vocabularies, but it should not be supposed that either the Greek moral vocabulary or the English expresses the rational articulation of a moral system. Even if it were true that some degree of reasoning is implicit in morality, it would be contrary to observation to argue that the morality of any given culture at any given time is the product of rational design. And although some kinds of unconscious reasoning are implicit in a child's acquisition of his mother-tongue, we all acquire and use a good range of moral words before we subject our use of them to rational scrutiny.

The lexical approach to the study of morality is limited in certain obvious ways. First, speech communicates more than writing, and may communicate a moral judgment or reaction by emphasis and intonation without using any word which would be recognizable in an index as relevant to morality. Consider, for example, the intonation of 'Has my son done that?' in response to 'I am sorry to say that John has disappeared with the week's takings', contrasted with the same words in response to 'A lot of the boys have seen the careers adviser this week'. Even when evaluative words are used, they may not carry the main weight.[1]

Ar. *Clouds* 1443–51. PHEIDIPPIDES: 'I'll beat up Mother, just as I did you. STREPSIADES: What! What did you say? Worse and worse! (*literally, 'this in-turn < is > another greater bad-thing'*). PHEIDIPPIDES: But suppose, with Wrong on my side, I win the argument and prove that it's all right to beat one's mother? STREPSIADES: Why, if you do that, there'll be no reason why you shouldn't throw yourself into the *barathron*—along with Socrates, and Wrong too!

The words, 'What! What did you say?' can be used in comedy in a variety of situations, and 'Worse and worse!' could be used of a nuisance or incon-venience; the element in this passage which conveys the force of Strepsiades' reaction is his saying to his son, '. . . throw yourself into the *barathron*', the pit into which the bodies of executed criminals were cast. A thorough examination of words which may have a bearing on questions of morality would have to take in *barathron*, and 'avoid', 'pity', 'punish', 'regret', to mention only a few.[2] Even then, if this were our only approach to morality, we should miss the passages of which what is *not* said is the most interesting and significant aspect.[3]

[1] Even when the words are plainly evaluative, order, intonation, vocal punctuation, facial expression and gesture all play a part. Cf. Adkins (3) 7 on the differing implications of 'honest but unsuccessful' and 'unsuccessful but honest'. Each of these can in fact be uttered in at least two ways, so that the speaker who predicates of another person honesty combined with lack of success reveals one or other of at least four different moral standpoints.

[2] Cf. Karl Aschenbrunner, *The Concepts of Value* (Dordrecht, 1971) 11, on the appraisals implicit in (e.g.) 'Do you call that a hat?' or 'They'll always meet you half way'.

[3] This point—like many other simple and but often overlooked points—is made by Earp 11.

The primary evidence for Greek morality is the passages in which some action or category of actions is praised, blamed, urged or deprecated, irrespective of the words used.[4] Passages in which the investigator notices the absence of the praise or blame which his own morality would have led him to expect are of equal importance; so are passages which reveal a speaker's assumptions about the determinants of action and the consequences of action. Investigation of this evidence should precede the use of word-indexes, which serve as a useful check on one part of the original investigation and contribute handsomely to Greek lexicography; that contribution, however, can and should be distinguished from the reconstruction of Greek moral schemata. It would be interesting to make the experiment of taking a number of sample passages at random from oratory and drama, substituting 'X' for every adjective or abstract noun which the speaker claims as applicable to himself or recommends to another, 'Y' for everything which he deprecates or applies to an adversary, and seeing how far a reconstruction of Greek values from the material thus modified would differ from a reconstruction from the same material before modification.

No one needs to be reminded that the denotation of a word varies according to its context; 'induction' means one thing in logic, but other things in connection with electricity, ceremonial or childbirth. Words of evaluation are no exception. 'He's very good' may be said by officers discussing a soldier, lecturers discussing a student, critics discussing a composer, or parents boasting that their baby does not cry at night. The attributes of the soldier which earn him this commendation may have little or nothing in common with the attributes of the student, composer or baby which earn the same commendation; what the occasions of utterance have in common is that the attributes of the person spoken about are welcome to the speaker. Misunderstanding is rare, because most actual utterance has a context; we do not as a rule open a conversation, after a long silence, with words such as 'John's very good' unless we have strong reason to infer from the situation in which we and our hearers find themselves that our unspoken train of thought is known to them. Apart from the situational context of an utterance, which includes the train of utterance leading up to it,[5] difference of phrasing can alter the denotation of a word common to a number of phrases. 'He's pretty bad' is most commonly uttered in discussion of someone's state of health, and means

[4] Cf. Lloyd-Jones 2f.

[5] The words 'Country people are good', divorced from a context, could refer to any of the virtues, skills or proprieties; I actually heard it, from a farm worker in Herefordshire, in the context, 'You can sleep in any of the fields round here, and no one will mind'.

'He is seriously ill'; I would normally take '. . . pretty bad about . . .' to
denote negligence, insensitivity or forgetfulness and '. . . pretty bad at . . .'
lack of skill. The importance of this consideration is that we must not expect
coincidence of denotation between (e.g.) the masculine of the adjective *kalos*,
the neuter of the same adjective, the adverb derived from it, and prepositional
phrases which contain it. Nor have we any right to expect that (e.g.) the
adjective *agathos*, when applied to a person, will denote the same or essentially
similar attributes or capacities irrespective of the total context in which the
word is applied; this has a bearing on the question of observable changes in
moral schemata within the history of Greek civilization. It is perfectly
possible for a word to be derogatory in one context and complimentary in
another, or neutral in one and positive in another; the most extreme and
obvious cases occur in ephemeral slang,[6] but the principle is one which we
must keep in mind whenever there is any possibility (particularly in comedy)
of a shift in linguistic 'register'. We must also be wary of argument from
etymology, as if a stem common to several words always had the same
denotation. After all, 'erring' and 'unerring' are not antonyms, nor can we
always recast an English utterance containing the word 'error' in such a way
as to use 'err'.

In expounding the findings of the present enquiry into Greek popular
morality I have by no means suppressed linguistic information, and I do not
think I have always resisted the temptation to found at least tentative arguments on it. The information is, I hope, of interest for its own sake; and since
we are, after all, concerned with a period whose morality is accessible to us
solely through the written word, it is positively desirable to discuss from time
to time the actual wording of items of evidence upon which the reconstruction of Greek morality depends. If I have on occasion argued from the usage
of individual words in a manner which seems to take insufficient account of
the reservations formulated above, this is because I do not think that the
reservations justify a total and resolute refusal to draw sociological conclusions from linguistic usage in all circumstances. It *may* be significant that the
Greeks commonly used the same words to denote sin, crime and accidental
error, and that the poets extended the denotation of 'illness' to all unwelcome
or undesirable conditions and predicaments. In considering such possibilities,
let us not forget how poor an opinion we should entertain of anyone who

---

[6] A few years ago an Italian couple of my acquaintance were alarmed when their
teenage daughter described a party which she had attended as *bestiale*; but it turned out
that she meant what her English counterpart would have meant by 'fantastic' or our
grandparents by 'ripping'.

argued for 'national mentalities' on the strength of the difference between *I like it* and *es gefällt mir* or the more striking difference between *te quiero* and *ti voglio bene.*

## 2. Description, Reaction and Manipulation

Just as we can discuss with a lawyer whether a contemplated action is legal or illegal, so in ordinary life we can discuss whether an action is right or wrong in terms of general rules or axioms shared by all those participating in the discussion. In the context of such a discussion, words such as 'honest', 'selfish', etc., are just as descriptive as 'legal' and 'illegal'. But occasions for this kind of discussion are few (partly, it may be, because there is so little measure of agreement on moral rules below the highest level of generality), and in what we have defined as popular literature evaluative words hardly ever have a purely descriptive role.

One purpose which they serve most conspicuously in drama is the relaxation of the speaker's tensions. Most of us are familiar with the experience of 'feeling better' when we have found the 'right words' for conversion of our feelings into an articulated sequence of sounds; it is as if we had actually done something to the person whose behaviour has caused our feelings. The relief is comparable in kind, though usually more rapid and intense, to the sensation of bodily well-being which follows from the successful completion of a verbal act of creative artistry or intellectual analysis.

When the speaker's utterance is directed towards another person who is actually present (or apparently present to the speaker's imagination), the expressive aspect of the utterance diminishes in importance by comparison with the relational aspect. To use a moral term is to perform an act of love or hate, affecting the relationship between speaker and hearer. The speaker offers or withdraws affection and respect, and implies the probability of similar offer or withdrawal on the part of others. The power of the utterance to affect the behaviour of the person addressed depends on how the hearer regards the speaker. If an action of mine is called 'shameful' by someone whom I love and whose judgment I respect, the possibility of impairing an affectionate relationship, combined with the possibility that others may turn against me, has a strong deterrent effect. On the other hand, the same reproach from a person I despise may be almost reassuring, especially if he seems agitated.

Furthermore, the use of a moral word is a declaration of alignment; by my judgment on a particular act I associate myself with one category of people and dissociate myself from another. This is of the highest importance when I am trying to secure a decision in my favour. By calling oligarchy 'impious' an Athenian speaker conveys to a jury, 'I am on your side'; equally, he conveys to people of oligarchic sentiments, 'Don't expect anything from me'; and by failing to call oligarchy impious he may make people wonder, 'Whose side is he on?' But by far the most important use of moral words in oratory is the manipulative or persuasive use,[7] in which the speaker tries to bring into being in the minds of the jurors an emotional orientation, favourable or unfavourable, towards particular persons, acts and events. There is a certain affinity between this way of using language and an element familiar in magic, prayer and entreaty, in which we behave as if we thought we could make someone who is despotic or stingy merciful or bountiful by calling him so; the vocative ō gennadā in Ar. *Frogs* 997 and *Knights* 240f. is an example, attempting in the former to instil magnanimity and patience, in the latter courage.[8]

When we reflect on the way in which we actually acquire our moral vocabulary as infants wholly dependent on those who are larger, stronger, more powerful and more intelligent than ourselves, it is not surprising that we apply our most general terms of praise and blame, 'good' and 'bad', together with their equivalents in the slang fashionable at any given time, in three ways: to whatever is for any reason welcome or unwelcome, agreeable or disagreeable, to ourselves (tasty, bitter, inconvenient, reassuring, baffling, enlightening, and so on); to whatever we observe is called good or bad by others or by any individual or institution influential in our upbringing;[9] and

[7] Adkins (1) 38–40 adopts the term 'persuasive definition' for the use of evaluative words in an abnormal sense in order to affect someone else's behaviour, but *definition* is precisely what such usage avoids; the essential principle at work is a behaviouristic stimulus-and-response.

[8] Ferguson 103 says that 'Hermes is described by Aristophanes as "of all the gods the greatest lover of mankind and the greatest giver" ' (*sic*) ' " of gifts" '. In fact, Aristophanes is in no way 'describing' Hermes, but portraying the chorus (of *Peace*) as desperately trying by cajolery, bribes and extravagant promises to persuade Hermes not to prevent them from rescuing Peace.

[9] I once heard a man of exceptional courage and integrity, who devoted his spare time (with great success) to the seduction of women, reply earnestly, when someone questioned the morality of his favourite pursuit, 'Oh yes, it *is* wrong; but it doesn't *matter*'. Reactive and descriptive use of the same word in one short utterance is neatly exemplified by, 'She's no good. She's *good*'. Children seem to acquire an evaluative vocabulary by the same method of trial and error in classification as operates in the rest of their vocabulary; I recall a four-year-old boy saying, 'It was rude of you to crack this cup. It's disappointing to my tongue'; a year later, no doubt, he had learnt more about the difference between rudeness and carelessness and between disappointment and discomfort.

to whatever we assume to be welcome or unwelcome to someone involved, whether as subject or as object, in the situation of which we happen to be speaking. What is true of English is equally true of the common Greek evaluative words, *agathos* and *khrēstos*, 'good', and their antonyms *kakos* and *ponēros*, 'bad'.

Ar. *Clouds* 1458–62 (*Strepsiades has asked the Clouds why they did not warn him off his dishonest course*). CHORUS: That is what we always do, whenever we see a man hankering after evil ways (*literally,* '*ponēros doings*'), until we cast him into misfortune (*lit.,* < *a* > *kakos* < *thing* >), so that he may learn to fear the gods. STREPSIADES: Oh, Clouds! It's bad (*ponēros, i.e.* '*unpleasant for me*'), but just!

Ar. *Wealth* 218–20. KHREMYLOS: And we shall have plenty of others, too, as allies —all the honest men who had nothing to eat; WEALTH: Oh, dear! They're bad (*ponēros*) allies for us! (*i.e. not the strong and resourceful allies we need*).

To moralists the distinction between what is 'good' and what is *hēdys*, 'agreeable', 'welcome', 'pleasant', 'enjoyable', is naturally important,[10] but in ordinary Greek usage *agatha*, 'good things', and *kaka*, 'bad things', often denote respectively material comforts and discomforts.[11] So too Ar. *Eccl.* 893, 'experience something *agathos*' = 'have an enjoyable sexual experience' (an old woman is boasting of her skill), *Frogs* 600, 'if there's anything *khrēstos*' = 'if anything nice turns up', GVI 320.2 (Eretria, s. VI/V) 'He has given few *agatha* to his soul' = 'He worked hard and lived frugally'.

Ar. *Eccl.* 199f.: You're annoyed with the Corinthians, and they with you; now they're *khrēstos*, so it's up to you to be *khrēstos* too.

This passage presents an interesting antithesis between 'be annoying' and 'be good'. Similarly 'good' (*agathos*, *khrēstos* or poetic *esthlos*) may be contrasted with 'painful', 'distressing' (*lȳpēros* [poetic *lȳpros*] or *aniāros*), as in Eur. *Hel.* 1447f., Men. fr. 276.3f ('what will distress you' [*lȳpein*]), fr. 335.7f., fr. 644; Soph. *El.* 646f. contrasts *esthla* (= *agatha*) with *ekhthra*, 'hostile', 'hateful'. With due regard for our ignorance of context, we may note the similarity between Men. fr. 531 'How pleasing (*hēdys*) is good character blended with understanding!' and fr. 535, 'The greatest blessing (*agathon*) is good character accompanied by intelligence!'[12]

---

[10] From a philosophical point of view there may be a great difference between moral and aesthetic values, but psychologically this is not always or necessarily so. The sensation of discovering that one's new neighbour is helpful and generous and the sensation of sinking one's teeth into good bread at the end of a long walk can be remarkably alike; they are both reassurances, as it were, about one's environment.

[11] Cf. Adkins (1) 31.

[12] In Alexis fr. 182.3 the combination '*khrēstos* and *hēdys*', applied to a man, probably

Soph. *Oed. Tyr.* 509–12 (*the Theban chorus sings of Oedipus*): Wise he was seen to be, and, put to the test, welcome to our city (*hēdypolis* = 'hēdys *to the city*'); and for that reason never shall I accuse him in my heart of any fault (*kakiā*).

The identification of patriotism with morality (cf. VI.B.*3*) underlies this passage. There is a highly subjective expression of feeling in Ar. *Thesm.* 869, 'through the *ponēriā* of the ravens' = 'because the ravens, damn them, don't do their job!', *Knights* 547, 'a good (*khrēstos*) Lenaean clamour' = 'a loud clamour, what we'd like to hear at this Lenaia', and *Thesm.* 781, 'This rho is *mokhthēros*!' = 'I didn't make that < letter > rho very well!'

The standpoint of the person addressed or referred to is often adopted, as in Hdt. i 120.3, iii 85.2, 'Have an *agathos* spirit!' = 'Cheer up!', 'Be confident'; GVI 1226, 'Go on < your way > to an *agathos* activity' = '... an activity which, I hope, will prosper' (cf. 'success', 'good times', Hdt. v 31.4, Thuc. iii 82.2). 'Be good to/about/towards ...' means, as in English, 'be kind to ...' (e.g. Hdt. vi 105.2, Soph. *El.* 24), even when the 'goodness' is shown to a bad man and unwelcome to the speaker (Aiskhines i 62), but the same wording in Isok. xiii 6, '*khrēstos* about contractual dealings' means 'honest in ...'. 'Good' or 'bad' followed by an infinitive correspond to our 'good at ...', 'bad at ...', e.g. Thuc. vi 38.2, 'We are *kakos* to take precautions' = 'We are, I am afraid, not very good at taking precautions'. 'Do (*poiein*) well' and 'do badly' = 'treat well' and 'maltreat' are expressions in which the speaker adopts the standpoint of the object;[13] to 'damage' the enemy in a manner highly acceptable to the speaker is literally to 'do him badly' (Isok. xviii 60, Lyk. 72).

## 3. Rhetoric and Hyperbole

It commonly happens that when a speaker wishes to cause in his hearer that degree of hostility towards A which is felt towards people of category B he applies to A the terms appropriate to B. Sometimes, by drawing our attention to what he is doing, he suggests that A and B are more alike than one might have inferred from actual linguistic usage, in that respect which (in his submission) is relevant to the situation and to the action which he requires of his hearers.

denotes a man of integrity who is also agreeable to deal with, but it may be more tautological than that.

[13] Not everyone, apparently, is prepared to take the objective use of evaluative words for granted. A correspondent in *The Times* 5 Jan. 1973 protested that to describe a crime as 'well planned' is 'a prostitution of the word "well"'.

Dem. xxxv 26: In our own city . . . we have been *plundered* of our own property by these men of Phaselis, as if the Phaselites had been granted the right of *plunder* against the Athenians. For when they are not willing to pay back what they received, in what other terns could one describe such behaviour, except that they are taking *by force* what does not belong to them?

The speaker exploits the concept *sȳlē*, the unfriendly seizure of goods or shipping, and an ambiguity of *biāi*, which can mean 'by force' as opposed to verbal persuasion and also 'without consent' or 'contrary to the wishes of . . .'. More blatantly, and with singular lack of persuasive force, Lys. xiii 87 argues that a man who is the ultimate cause of another's death can legitimately be treated as a murderer 'caught in the act'.

Dem. viii 62: How do you suppose it is possible for Philip to do as he likes with you (*hybrizein*, '*assault*', '*insult*', '*outrage*', '*treat as a slave*')—for I don't see what else you can call it . . .

Cf. Dem. xix 220. *Hybris*, behaviour in which a citizen treats a fellow-citizen as if he were dealing with a slave or a foreigner, was an indictable offence under Attic law (Dem. xxi 71f. and Isok. xx 2–11 are important disquisitions on its nature).[14] For practical purposes indictment normally arose from physical maltreatment, but there was nothing to prevent a speaker from using *hybris* and its verb *hybrizein* for emotional effect, whether he was speaking about action by one citizen allegedly contrary to the interests of another or about contemptuous treatment of one state by another. It was easier for him to evoke an abnormally strong reaction against fraud by utilizing an established pattern of response and calling fraud '*hybris*' than by attempting to go against established patterns and to argue 'fraud is worse than *hybris*'.[15]

Dem. xxvii 65: Although they (*sc. my guardians*) received gifts from us to ensure that they exercised an honest guardianship, they have treated us with contempt (*hybrizein*) in the manner which I have described.

The issue here is one of fraud, not of violence.[16] Cf. Aiskhines i 15, Dem. lvi

[14] Cf. Arist. *Rhet.* 1378b10–35; Gernet, 1–33, 184–97, 389–403, 413–24; J. J. Fraenkel, *Hybris* (Utrecht, 1941).

[15] Current rhetorical usage of 'obscene' provides an interesting parallel, e.g. 'The greatest obscenity is that an individual should be prevented from seeing or hearing what he chooses' (Ben Whitaker in *The Times Saturday Review* 11 Dec. 1971).

[16] Apollodoros's curious attempt to indict Phormion for *hybris* on the grounds that Phormion had married Apollodoros's widowed mother (Dem. xlv 3f.) was no doubt

12, Lys. xxx 5. Other words besides *hybris* may be used to stimulate an indignant reaction.

Dem. xxii 4: He will try to cheat you by concocting ... criminal (*kakourgos*) arguments.

In §28 of the same speech *kakourgos* is used in its customary sense, 'malefactor', 'robber'.

Is. viii 39: Having consulted the interpreter of religious law, on his instructions I spent money out of my own pocket and performed the ninth-day rites (*sc. after my grandfather's funeral*) with as good a show as possible, in order to frustrate their sacrilege (*hierosȳliā*).

*Hierosȳliā* is theft of money or valuable objects belonging to a god; the speaker here applies it to his adversaries' alleged attempt to deprive him of the satisfaction and credit (with his acquaintances and with the old man's ghost) of giving his grandfather a good funeral.

Like so much else, hyperbole is caricatured in New Comedy.

Men. *Samia* 508–14. NIKERATOS: I'd be the first to sell the concubine the next day, and disown my son at the same time, so that ... everyone would talk about me and say, 'Nikeratos has been a real man, he's taken the proper steps to prosecute for murder'. MOSKHION: Murder? What do you mean? NIKERATOS: Whenever anyone rebels against authority, I call it murder.

Through Moskhion's incredulous question and Nikeratos's explanation Menander ensures that we understand that it is absurd of Nikeratos to talk in this portentous way of a son's intercourse with his father's concubine, but we cannot always rely on a dramatist to explain his jokes so patiently. There is of course little or no danger of misunderstanding or incorrect inference when, as often happens in comedy, one character is venting his emotion in unrestrained abuse of another. In Ar. *Clouds* 1327–30, for example, when Strepsiades has been assaulted by his son, he calls the young man not only 'vile parricide', which is not so far from the truth, but also 'burglar' and 'tank-arse', which, if taken literally, would denote forms of misbehaviour which his son has not yet committed. 'Tank-arsery' is applied in Eupolis fr. 3513f. to the habit of drinking wine first thing in the morning, as in Ar. fr. 130 a variety of dishes are contemptuously dismissed as 'buggery' compared with a good steak. In Men. *Perik.* 366 Sosias, upbraiding slaves for allowing

an expedient prompted by the temporary suspension of private lawsuits, to which the speaker makes reference; and in any case, it came to nothing.

Glykera to slip out of the house unnoticed, calls them 'temple-robbing animals'.[17] Angry hyperbole in tragedy naturally lacks the coarseness and extravagance of comedy, but when Philoktetes in Soph. *Phil.* 384 refers to Odysseus as (literally) 'worst and from bad', i.e. 'vilest of men and vilely born', we are not really meant to imagine that he entertains a considered opinion on Odysseus's parentage.

Evaluative language can be stretched both ways. Thuc. iii 82.4–7, speaking of the intensification of political faction by war, offers examples not only of derogatory terms applied in contempt to honest men but also of complimentary terms with which a speaker would disguise the villainy of men on his own side.[18] The composers of epitaphs seems sometimes to have selected Homeric epithets (e.g. *iphthīmos*) more for their resounding heroic associations than with any close attention to what they mean when they are used in epic.

### 4. Dramatic Point

Comic hypberbole is closely allied to the conceptual extravagance which has already been noted (I.D.2) as an ingredient of comedy, and it provokes some of the same doubts; its humour may lie either in its inventiveness and piquancy or in its exploitation of vulgar speech. We should probably see humorous invention on the part of the poet, exploiting the humour of incongruity so dear to Old Comedy, when the chorus address Lysistrata (Ar. *Lys.* 1108) as 'bravest of all women', using an adjective (*andreios*) of which the etymology (~ *anēr*, 'man', 'adult male') would seem to preclude a feminine gender. There is more room for doubt in *Thesm.* 421f., where a woman resentfully calls the keys with which husbands lock the store-

---

[17] Cf. the liking of shop stewards and trade union secretaries for the word 'diabolical', which lends itself easily to indignant enunciation.

[18] From the mere fact that a man professes a concern for justice (as Salvatore Giuliano did, repeatedly and passionately) we cannot tell whether he is just or unjust; we need to know which of his acts he calls just. Lloyd-Jones 93 remarks that 'all men, however extreme their views may seem to others, appear moderate to themselves'. This has been generally true of our own culture, and it was generally true of the Greeks, but it is not universally true; Hitler declared publicly 'We are barbarians', and there are people in our universities who would take it amiss if they were accused of moderation. It should be remembered in this connection that the traditional Greek injunction *mēden agān*, ' < Do > nothing in excess', is not a prohibition of absolute integrity, patriotism, justice and piety (cf. Senator Goldwater's dictum, 'Moderation in the pursuit of justice is no virtue'), and *metrios* is applied to the man who behaves as law and honour require, even to the sacrifice of his own life (e.g. Dem. xviii 321).

cupboards *kakoēthēs*, 'of bad character', for although elsewhere in comedy the word is applied only to persons it can be applied in medical literature to injuries and illnesses. Cf. *semnos*, 'august', 'proud', 'majestic', applied by Aristophon fr. 7 to cooked shoulder of tunny.[19]

In Ar. *Peace* 1297 Trygaios calls Kleonymos's young son 'son of a sensible (*sōphrōn*) father'. Kleonymos in Old Comedy is ridiculed for an unforgivable delinquency, cowardice in battle; how, then, can the highly complimentary term *sōphrōn* be applied to him? Since we have *Peace* complete, and do not have to contend with the problem of interpreting a fragment, we can see the point. Two boys are rehearsing songs for Trygaios's wedding party, which is at the same time a celebration of the return of peace. One of them, son of the bellicose Lamakhos, sings of nothing but epic warfare, the inappropriateness of which exasperates Trygaios; the compliment to a coward's son, a recourse to the other extreme, is not without irony ('*You*'re not likely to sing about war!') which turns into outright condemnation once the boy has uttered a couple of verses. The speaker of Alexis fr. 271, who proclaims that the *sōphrōn* man will devote himself to food, drink and sex is presumably an immoralist whose character is itself an object of humour. *Panourgos*, 'capable of anything', is usually a reproach, but it is a compliment when the situation, in the speaker's view, calls for *panourgiā*: Men. *Epitr.* 535 (coupled with *kakoēthēs*, 'of bad character'), *Perinthia* 11f.

There is a further category of passages in comedy in which the normal application of a word seems to be stretched for the sake of the dramatic context.

Ar. *Clouds* 1286–95. STREPSIADES: This 'interest', now, what animal's that? CREDITOR: Why, it's simply that every month and every day the money becomes more and more as time flows by. STREPSIADES: Good. Well, now: do you think that the sea is in any way more now than it used to be? CREDITOR: Why, no, it's the same amount. It isn't right (*dikaios*) that it should be more. STREPSIADES: Then how is it, fool, that while the sea doesn't get any bigger as the rivers run into it, you try to make your money more?

It is not un-Greek to apply *dikaios* to the regularity of the natural order, but a creditor in real life would be more likely to answer, 'Why, you can see it doesn't rise!' It is desirable, however, that he should be made to use a word from which the inference can be drawn that it is unjust or dishonest on his part to expect interest on his money, for Strepsiades' dishonesty in cheating his creditors and his hopes of 'making wrong appear right' are the core of the

---

[19] Cf. however our expression, 'a generous helping'.

whole play. Cf. *Thesm.* 455f., where 'savage (*agrios*) wrongs' is said for the sake of a connection with 'wild (*agrios*) herbs'.

Ar. *Frogs* 736f. (*the concluding words of the parabasis*): And if things go wrong—well, if you have to be hanged, the discerning (*sophos*) will say that it was a fine tree you were hanged from!

The theme of the parabasis would have led us to expect something a little different; but *sophos* (cf. III.F.1) is the word which Aristophanes applies to himself and his plays and to those among the audience and the judges who like his plays (*Clouds* 526, 535, *Wasps* 1049, *Frogs* 1118, *Eccl.* 1155), so that its effect here is deftly to turn attention back from serious political matter to the theatre,[20] perhaps also to suggest, 'I, your best poet, will say . . .'.

Men. *Farmer* 46–8: Kleainetos, on whose farm your son is working, was digging in his vineyard the other day when he cut his leg open well and truly (*khrēstōs*).

*Khrēstōs*, the uncommon adverb of the very common adjective *khrēstos*, may possibly he used here like *epieikōs*, normally 'decently', 'respectably', but often 'quite', 'substantially' (cf. our adverbial 'pretty'). But Daos's speech has a humorous aspect: his narrative will end on a joyful note, and he tells it all in a mood appropriate to the ending, whereas the women to whom he is speaking not unnaturally react with grief to the tale of disaster on which he begins and with some indignation to his manner of telling it. The desire to heighten this humorous contrast of mood may have determined Menander's choice of *khrēstōs*.

## II.B. DEFINITION

### 1. Explicit Definition

Greek philosophical writers sometimes concern themselves with the definition of virtues, asking, for example, as Socrates does in Plato's *Laches*, 'What is courage?' A substantial part of Aristotle's *Nicomachean Ethics* consists of methodical discussion of one virtue after another and investigation of the character of each as a mean between two opposed vices. Theophrastos's

---

[20] Equally, the use of a proverbial phrase, literally 'from worthy wood', which I have expanded and made more explicit, is a characteristic touch of lightness at the end of the parabasis; cf. the humorous introduction of a proverbial motif, 'a nail to drive out a nail', in *Ach.* 717f.

*Characters* is not a philosophical work, but it is the work of a philosopher, and each *Character* begins with a general definition in terms quite unfamiliar, often perhaps unintelligible, to people who are not accustomed to think systematically about morality and psychology. Neither the tentative definitions formulated in the course of a Socratic enquiry nor those adopted in Aristotelian classifications can be treated as contributions to the lexicography of Classical Greek usage, nor are they intended as such; the former are metaphysical explorations, and the latter have a prescriptive function. When, for example, Aristotle says,

Rhet. 1366ᵇ13–15: *Sōphrosynē* is a virtue through which people behave as the law requires them to behave in respect of the bodily pleasures, and *akolasiā* is its opposite,

he is helpfully telling us how he proposes to regard *sōphrosynē* for the purpose of his treatise on rhetoric, and he adopts the same definition in *Eth. Nic.* 1118ᵃ1–3, but he is not making an adequate statement about the denotation of *sōphrosynē* in the language of his own time.[1] Prescriptive and idiosyncratic definition is to be expected in philosophy, for all deliberate analysis and classification requires either the invention of new words or the formulation of special denotations for existing words, but it is not peculiar to philosophy. Anyone who constructed a definition of *anaisthēsiā* ('lack of feeling', 'insensitivity', 'callousness', 'shamelessness') from all the examples of *anaisthētos* in the orators would be greatly surprised when he turned to Theophr. *Char.* 14 and found that absent-mindedness is there treated as the essence of *anaisthēsiā*.[2] Antiphon in the fifth century (fr. 72) said that *sēmeion* meant an item of evidence showing that something had happened in the past, and *tekmērion* an item of evidence from which one inferred what was going to happen in the future, but the orators do not appear to have been influenced by his opinion.

We do not expect to find much in the way of explicit definition of virtues and vices in forensic oratory, let alone in comedy; the nearest we come to them are selective characterizations (e.g.) of the democratic and the oligarchic man (Aiskhines iii 6–8, 168–70, cf. Dem. xxiv 75f.) or of the good citizen, with particular reference to the type of situation which concerns the speaker at the time (Dem. xviii 278f., Hyp. iv 37, Is. vii 40). A characterization of this type is in fact an enumeration of modes of thought and behaviour which the speaker comprehends under a single generic term. The enumeration may be

---

[1] Aristotle himself uses *sōphrōn* in *Eth. Nic.* (e.g. 1123ᵇ5, 1125ᵇ13) in ordinary ways not covered by his prescriptive definition of *sōphrosynē*.

[2] Aristotle suggests *anaisthēsiā* (cf. III.F.1) as the appropriate term for a very rare fault, insensitivity to pleasure (*Eth. Nic.* 1107ᵇ6–8, cf. 1104ᵃ22–4).

detailed (though it is hard to envisage circumstances in which the speaker could claim with confidence that it was exhaustive), or it may consist of items expressed in terms so general that there would be much room for disagreement over the particular cases to which the generalities might be thought to apply. Naturally, since it forms part of a forensic or political argument, it may be tendentious in the extreme; the extent to which it conforms with ordinary usage can only be discovered from the independent evidence for that usage.

Plato sometimes (e.g. *Euthyphro* 5D) represents the interlocutors of Socrates as replying to the question, 'What is *X*?' by naming one or more types of action which have the attribute *x*. As students of Greek philosophical literature we are perhaps a little too ready to smile patronizingly at responses of this kind, forgetting that only the tiniest percentage of the human race has ever defined anything, and that most human achievements—practical, artistic and moral—have owed nothing to the technique of definition. The question, 'How can I be brave unless I know what courage *is*?' is significant only to people who adopt certain religious or metaphysical standpoints, and even for them, let alone for anyone else, a definition of courage in the abstract becomes morally useful only when translated into an enumeration of plausible situations which might call for courage. Accordingly, when Dem. xxiv 25 lists three modes of behaviour which exemplify 'everything which commands admiration and respect and is responsible for the order and preservation of the city' and attaches three highly particular epithets to vice and three opposing epithets to virtue, we should not think of the speaker as a potential butt for a latter-day Socrates but recognize that he is coming as near to explicit definition as we have any right to expect outside philosophical circles (which are, after all, apt to construct problems rather than address themselves to the solution of problems which actually beset us).

## 2. Implicit Definition

In the Melian Dialogue the Melians express the confidence (Thuc. v 104) that if they are attacked by Athens the Spartans will come to their aid, impelled by consciousness of their common ancestry and by fear of the shame which failure to act would incur. The Athenians reply:

Thuc. v 105.4: The Spartans in their dealings with one another and (*sc. in observance of*) the customs of their own country are exceptionally good men (*literally*, '*use* aretē *nost*'); of their behaviour towards other states much could be said, but it could best be summed up by pointing out that, more conspicuously than any people known to us, they treat what is agreeable as honourable and what is advantageous as just.

Two similar but distinct conclusions could be drawn from this passage. One is that *aretē* and 'treating what is agreeable . . .' were commonly believed to be incompatible, as, for instance, timidity and great muscular development are popularly regarded as incompatible. The other conclusion is that when a speaker is concerned with the grant or denial of help to those who claim it, *aretē* is the antonym of whatever word could be defined as 'treating what is agreeable . . .'; which amounts to saying that the passage implies a definition of *aretē* (in the context of a grant or denial of help) as 'doing what is honourable even when it is disagreeable and doing what is just even when it is disadvantageous to oneself', a fairly acceptable definition of moral virtue in many cultures. Which of the two interpretations is correct would have to be decided in the light of further evidence derived from other passages.

The kind of breakdown which affords *prima facie* an implicit definition is particularly important when the word concerned is very rare, e.g. the adjective *anepieikēs* (Thuc. iii 66.2 and—a citation without a context—Ar. fr. 989) and its abstract noun *anepieikeia* (Dem. xxix 3). These might appear to be antonyms of the common adjective *epieikēs* and the abstract *epieikeia*, but etymology is not always a trustworthy guide in semantics. *Akhrēstos*, 'useless', is the antonym of *khrēsimos*, 'useful', not of *khrēstos*, 'good'. *Akakos* and *akakiā*, which stand in the same morphemic relation to *kakos* and *kakiā* as *anepieikēs* and *anepieikeia* to *epieikēs* and *epieikeia*, are not the antonyms of *kakos* and *kakiā* (which seem to be *agathos* and *aretē* or *kalokāgathiā*) but denote guilelessness, the kind of innocence which is easily deceived because it does not practise deceit. Fortunately Demosthenes provides us with a contribution to the implicit definition of *anepieikeia*.

Dem. xxix 2f.: If I exacted from him the satisfaction (*sc. awarded to me in court*) or had been unwilling to come to any reasonable accommodation with him, I would not have been doing him any wrong even in those circumstances, for I would have been exacting from him what had been decided in your court, but none the less it might be said that I had been too cruel and harsh in depriving a kinsman of his whole estate. But as matters stand, it is the other way round . . . and so you would be much more justified in detesting him for what he has done than in treating me as guilty of some *anepieikeia*.

The implication that it is *epieikēs* to be forbearing towards a kinsman, even when one has strict justice on one's side, is fully consistent with our other evidence for *epieikēs* (IV.C.4).

## 3. Synonymy

Synonymy in Greek is most easily demonstrated in closely reasoned argument (e.g. Plato's), where to deny it would be to reduce the argument to a *non sequitur* or even, in cases where three or more synonymous expressions recur in apparently random order, to convict the writer of gibberish. It is highly characteristic of Greek prose literature, even when its subject-matter is scientific or philosophical, to avoid monotony of vocabulary and construction by deliberate variation. The effect is at times strained, but when we become aware of the strain we realize the strength of the writer's inner compulsion to avoid monotony. In forensic oratory the coherence of the argument cannot be used as a test for synonymy as confidently as in philosophy, since the speaker's purpose is not to bring his hearers to a better intellectual understanding of the issues but to induce them to pass the verdict which he desires, and it may sometimes be tactically advisable for him to make them feel, at least temporarily, that two things commonly regarded as distinct are the same. There are, however, circumstances which furnish *prima facie* evidence of the synonymy of two or more words.

(i) 'Ring-form', a characteristically Greek device recognizable from the archaic period onwards, is an exposition introduced by 'Now, this is A' and terminated by 'That, then, is A'.

Dem. xviii 301: What ought the loyal (*eunous*) citizen to have done? . . . 306: That is the way the *kalos kāgathos* citizen should have acted.

Cf. ibid. 278, *kalos kāgathos* ∼ *gennaios* and *agathos*; xix 68f., *ponēros* ∼ *kakos*.

(ii) There are many approximations to ring-form, in which a speaker deliberately resumes an earlier point in his argument, though not in the simple 'now, this . . ./that, then, . . .' form.

Dem. xxxvi 52: Won't you realise that being *khrēstos* is worth more than a great deal of money? At any rate, if what you say is true, you received all that money but, as you say, it's all gone. Yet if you had been *epieikēs* you would never have spent it.

Is. i 26: And they are trying to persuade you to give a verdict contrary to the laws and right and the intention (*gnōmē*) of the deceased . . . 35: and moreover we prove to you that this will is contrary to the law and rights and the intention (*dianoia*) of the deceased.

Here the interchange of singular and plural ('laws and right' ∼ 'law and rights'), as well as the substitution of a different word for 'intention', appears to be motivated by a desire for variation.

(iii) Inevitably a speaker often has to make the same point more than once in a speech; if he uses different words, synonymy is to be presumed unless an examination of the context suggests that what appears at first sight to be a repetition of the same point is in fact designed to make a slightly different point.

Isok. xix 3: She who is laying claim to the property ought not to have attempted to take from me the estate which Thrasylokhos left; she ought to have been good (*khrēstos*) to him and on that basis put in a claim to the estate . . . 16: In order that no one may think that I possess the inheritance for inadequate reasons or that this woman was good (*epieikēs*) to Thrasylokhos and yet is being deprived of the property . . .

The passage does not, of course, prove that *epieikēs* and *khrēstos* are in general synonyms, but only that it was possible for this speaker to use *epieikēs peri* . . . and *khrēstos peri* . . . (cf. Dem. lix 2) synonymously in the sense 'good to . . .', 'kind to . . .', 'dutiful towards . . .'. If both words were rare, we should have to consider the possibility that one of them meant 'kind' (with the implication that kindness was the woman's duty to Thrasylokhos) and the other 'dutiful' (with the implication that the woman's duty to Thrasylokhos was to be kind to him). As it is, passages such as Dem. xxxvi 52 (cited above) illustrate the frequent synonymy of *epieikēs* and *khrēstos*.

(iv) It is in the nature of forensic oratory that similar things should have to be said in different speeches, but they are not always said in the same words. For example, Dem. lviii 62 calls 'good' advisers (in a political context) *agathos*, but Dein. i 76 calls them *spoudaios* (cf. Dem. xx 114). Euripides is 'an *agathos* poet' in Lyk. *Leskr.* 100, Homer 'so *spoudaios* a poet' ibid. 102. One pair of examples would not justify us in inferring from apparent synonymy of AX and BX a general synonymy of A and B, but a whole series of examples gives us something better to go on. A reputation (*doxa*) which is 'good' can be *epieikēs* (Dem. lviii 66), *kalos*[3] (Dem. xx 142) or *khrēstos* (Dem. xxv 82), and if it is 'bad' it can be *aiskhros* (Dem. xx 10), *ponēros* (Dem. xx 50) or *phaulos* (Dem. xxiv 205). 'Good' expectation (*elpis*), i.e. 'hope', is *agathos* in Ar. *Wealth* 212 and Dem. xix 140 but *khrēstos* in Ant. v 33. In poetry *esthlos*, a word not used at all in prose, can replace *agathos* and *khrēstos* in (so far as I can see) any of their denotations; it is used, for example, of good fortune (Soph. *Oed. Col.* 1506), good news (Soph. *Oed. Tyr.* 87, Ar. *Wealth* 632) and the good man who, like the *agathos* citizen in the orators, obeys lawful authority (Soph. *Ajax* 1352). It should also be noted that the comparatives

[3] *Kalos* is a special case; cf. C.3 below.

*ameinōn* and *beltīōn* and the superlatives *aristos* and *beltistos* serve indiscriminately as comparative and superlative of any word meaning 'good'; this is demonstrable from Dem. xx 39, xxi 17, lvii 107, Hdt. ix 27.4. Similarly the comparative *kakīōn* and the superlative *kakistos* correspond indiscriminately to *kakos* and *ponēros* (e.g. Dem. xix 69 [ring-form]).[4]

When two terms are co-ordinated by 'and', it is reasonable to expect that each of them says something that the other does not, but it must be confessed that reasonable expectation is often disappointed. The relationship between the two terms is sometimes hyponymous,[5] e.g. Dem. xxi 160, 'because of his *deiliā* and *anandriā*', i.e. '. . . his uselessness and unmanliness' = 'his cowardice', for *deilos* can be applied not only to a coward but (e.g.) to a slow and stupid slave (Ar. *Birds* 1329, 1336). So too in Dem. xxiii 190, 'a good and patriotic (*philopolis*) man', for patriotism is a species or aspect of goodness. Sometimes the relation is more like hendiadys than hyponymy, e.g. Dem. xxv 54, 'impious and vile' (= 'vilely impious'), Is. v 11, '*hybris* and vileness' (= 'vile hybris'), and at other times it is hard to see anything more than tautology, e.g. Aiskhines i 141, '*khrēstos* and *agathos* poets', Dem. xxxvi 43, '*khrēstos* and just'.

### 4. Antithesis and Antonymy

Antitheses are commonly more satisfactory evidence for antonymy than resumptions of argument or presumed variations are for synonymy, and their abundance is ensured by the strong Greek tendency to antithetical forms of expression. An exposition which explicitly draws attention to antonymy is as rare as are approximations to explicit definition, but valuable when it occurs.

Dem. xx 109: The Thebans are as proud of their cruelty (*ōmotēs*) and villainy (*ponēriā*) as you are of your kindness (*philanthrōpiā*) and rectitude of purpose (*literally, 'wishing what is just'*).

ibid. 165: In the court Leptines is contending against me, but in the mind of each juror kindness (*philanthrōpiā*) is arrayed against grudgingness (*phthonos*), justice (*dikaiosynē*) against injustice (*kakiā*, '*badness*'), and all that is good against all that is worst.

---

[4] In Ant. iv β.4, 'Put into the care of a bad doctor, he died through the doctor's incompetence, not through the blows he had received', both the primary manuscripts have *mokhthēriā* for 'incompetence', but for 'bad' one has *mokhthēros* and the other *ponēros*. In deciding between the variants an editor has to weigh the general tendency of Greek authors to seek variety against a possible tendency of this particular author not to do so.

[5] On 'hyponymy' cf. J. Lyons, *Structural Semantics* (Edinburgh, 1963) 69–71.

Dem. xxiii 75: Everything that is done or said can be qualified in two ways, as honest (*dikaios*) or dishonest (*adikos*). One and the same action or utterance cannot possess both qualifications at the same time ... But each is tested as having one of the two; and if it is revealed as having the qualification 'dishonest', it is judged bad, but if the honest qualification, it is judged good and creditable.

More often the antonymy is implicit but obvious.

Ar. *Clouds* 1019–21: And he will persuade you to think honourable (*kalos*) everything that is disgraceful (*aiskhros*) and < to think > disgraceful what is honourable.

Dem. xxiii 178: You see and understand his villainy (*ponēriā*) and unreliability (*apistiā*), < and > what a lot of nonsense it is. First of all he attacked Kephisodotos ... It's all nonsense, and he did nothing simply (*haplōs*) and honestly (*dikaiōs*).

It is easy to establish many regular pairs of antonyms, notably *agathos* vs. *kakos* (e.g. Lyk. 74, Men. *Epitr.* 727), *kalos* vs. *aiskhros* (e.g. Ar. *Birds* 755f., Aiskhines i 185), *khrēstos* vs. *ponēros* (e.g. Ar. *Frogs* 1455f., Antiphanes fr. 205.3f., Aiskhines i 30),[6] but each member of such a pair appears also with a wide range of antonyms; thus *ponēros* can be contrasted with *agathos* (Lys. ii 77), *epieikēs* (Hyp. i 13f.), *kalos* (Lyk. 111), *kalos kāgathos* (Dem. xxv 24), *sōphrōn* (Ar. *Thesm.* 546), and so on. There are considerable risks in inferring A = C from the occurrence of contrasts both between A and B and between B and C, for hyponymy plays an important part; if A is contrasted with B and B with C, it may be that A is a species of the genus C, or C a species of the genus A, or A and C may both be species of a higher genus.

Dem. xviii 269: I have always been of the opinion that he who has received a benefit should remember it for all time, but he who has conferred it should forget it at once, if the one is to act as a good (*khrēstos*) man should and the other not as a mean (*mikropsȳkhos*, 'small of soul') man would.

Meanness is a species of badness, and we cannot treat 'good' and 'mean' simply as antonyms.

It should be noted that many utterances which are antithetical in form are far from affording us evidence on antonymy.

Ar. *Eccl.* 767f. A: Why, ought a *sōphrōn* man to do what the law says? B: Yes, more than anyone. A: No, only a stupid man (*abelteros*).

[6] Men. *Kolax* 27f. sets a nice problem. The passage is mutilated, but the context suggests 'The gods favour bad (*ponēros*) men, for we who are good do not succeed in anything' (literally, '... do not manage anything *agathos*'). Leo suggested as a supplement in the second line 'We who are *agathos* ...', which would certainly make a rhetorical point, 'Although we *are* good, we don't get good *results*'; but an epithet applied to people and contrasted with *ponēros* is much more likely to be *khrēstos*.

Dem. xlv 48: Nor would anyone be right in thinking that the character he has assumed and the way he walks . . . with a frown are signs of *sōphrosynē* rather than an unfriendly disposition (*mīsanthrōpiā*).

Xen. *Ages.* 11.4: He judged that to deceive the untrusting was clever (*sophos*), but to deceive those who trusted him was unholy (*anosios*).

## II.C. THE ARTICULATION OF VIRTUE

### 1. Encomia

The encomium is a genre of writing in which we may find a useful enumeration of virtues. Xenophon, for example, in his essay on the Spartan king Agesilaos deals in succession with king's piety (3), honesty and uprightness (*dikaiosynē*, 4), temperance and chastity (*sōphrosynē*, 5), courage (6.1–3), intelligence and skill (*sophiā*, 6.4–8), and so on, each virtue being illustrated with examples in sufficient detail to show us precisely what types of behaviour Xenophon would praise by application of the epithets 'pious', 'chaste', etc. The highly formalized and sophistic encomium on Eros which Plato (*Smp.* 194E–197E) puts into the mouth of Agathon is in part devoted to a systematic 'demonstration' that Eros possesses to the highest degree the four virtues *dikaiosynē* (195BC), *sōphrosynē* (195C), courage (195CD), and *sophiā* (196D–197B). We learn from this example nothing of the kind that we learn from Xenophon, but we see that these four virtues are identical with four of the five which head the list in the commendation of Agesilaos; 'piety' is missing for the good reason that Eros is himself a god. The traditional schema[1] of the encomium is used in Demosthenes' expatiation on the Thebans' welcome of an Athenian force within their city in 338.

Dem. xviii 215: On that day the Thebans proclaimed to all mankind three most honourable encomia on you: one on your courage, a second on your *dikaiosynē*, and a third on your *sōphrosynē*. For in choosing to fight on your side rather than against you, they judged that you were better men (*i.e.* braver men) than Philip and had right on your side, and in putting into your keeping what they and all men guard most carefully, their women and children, they displayed their confidence in your *sōphrosynē*.

Absence of any mention of piety in this passage is probably attributable to

[1] On the history of the cardinal virtues see O. Kunsemüller, *Die Herkunft der platonischen Kardinaltugenden* (Erlangen [Diss. Munich], 1935).

the fourth-century tendency to equate virtue and piety, which is reflected commonly in synonymy of 'pious' and 'honest' or antonymy of 'honest' and 'impious'; contrast Aiskh. *Seven* 610, '*sōphrōn*, honest, brave, pious' and Xen. *Mem.* iv 8.11 (on Socrates) 'pious... honest... self-controlled... intelligent', but compare Ar. *Wealth* 89 'honest, wise (*sophos*) and well-behaved (*kosmios*)', ibid. 386f., 'those who are good (*khrēstos*), clever (*dexios*) and *sōphrōn*', Isok. xvi 28 '*sōphrōn*, honest, skilful', Xen. *Hell.* ii 4.40f., 'justice... courage... intelligence (*gnōmē*)'. Of course, it was always possible to draw a distinction between 'piety towards the gods' and 'integrity in dealing with one's fellow-men' (e.g. Isok. xii 204) and to use expressions such as 'in the sight of' (or 'at the hands of') 'both gods and men' (e.g. Ant. i 25, Lys. xiii 3). The equation of piety with virtue will be discussed more fully in V.D.2.

## 2. *Epitaphs*

An epitaph often predicates of the dead person two, three or more virtues.

GVI 887.1 (s. VI/V): *Sōphrōn*, of good understanding, hospitable, reliable, accomplished (*literally, 'knowing the things which are kalos'*).

Sometimes the adjective *agathos* or the corresponding abstract noun *aretē* appears in a list containing words which denote specific virtues, e.g. *dikaiosynē* and *sōphrosynē* (*GVI* 167, 931) or *sōphrosynē* and *sophiā* (*GVI* 81, an epitaph on a woman). In these cases it is to be presumed that *agathos* and *aretē* are equally specific, and where the dead person was an adult male the reference is likely to be to courage; this accords with the expression 'become a good man' = 'fight bravely' (IV.A.*3*) and with the attachment of the epithet 'successful in war' attached to personified Arete in *GVI* 1564, and I accordingly translated *agathos* as 'brave' in Aiskh. *Seven* 610, above. At the same time we should observe that from an early date the pair of epithets *sōphrōn* and *agathos* or the pair of abstracts *sōphrosynē* and *aretē* can be predicated, without mention of any other specific virtues, of people of either sex and any age: *GVI* 54 (s. VI), 98 (s. IV/III), 157 (s. VI), 893 (Rhodes, a woman), 1105 (a young man), 1227 (s. VI), 1535 (s. IV/III), 1698 (a young man apparently of great promise in 'the tragic art'), 1783, *SEG* xxii 79 (s. VI, a Naxian resident at Athens). These examples suggest a tendency to distinguish between 'negative' virtue, which restrains one from doing wrong, and the 'positive' virtue shown in achievement; a similar articulation may underlie the occasional pairing of *aretē* and *sōphrosynē* in literature (e.g. Isok. xiii 20). One striking epitaph warns us against the assumption that pairing of this kind must be tautological, as we might be tempted to assume in Eur. *Alc.* 615f., 'You have lost an *esthlos* and *sōphrōn* wife'.

GVI 890: What is rare for a woman, that the same woman should be manifestly good (*esthlos*) and *sōphrōn*, this Glykera attained.

By the time this epitaph was composed (the middle of the fourth century) *esthlos* had so long been used by poets as a synonym of *agathos* and *khrēstos* that it is hardly credible that the composer intended us to understand (e.g.) 'of noble birth'; he must be saying (truly or falsely, wisely or foolishly) that it is unusual for a woman to display both the modesty expected of a chaste woman and the talents required for the management of a household. The possibility of treating *sōphrosynē* as 'negative' (a term acceptable so long as we recognize that abstention from evil is often much more difficult than performance of good)[2] is supported by Aiskhines i 72f., 22, where *sōphrosynē* is equated with *eukosmiā*, 'obedience to prescribed order and discipline', and by Isok. ix 22f., where Euagoras is said to have exhibited 'beauty, physical strength and *sōphrosynē*' when he was a boy and to have added 'courage, *sophiā* and *dikaiosynē*' when he grew up, as if those virtues differed from *sōphrosynē* in requiring for their exercise a certain capacity not to be expected of a boy.

As we would expect in dealing with unsystematized values, there is more than one way of looking at the same phenomena. Side by side with *aretē* in a highly specific sense and 'positive' *aretē* contrasted with 'negative' *sōphrosynē*, we find the expression *pāsa aretē*, which can be interpreted either as 'every virtue' or 'the whole of virtue'; the latter is on the whole preferable,[3] since the plural *aretai* was used to mean 'occasions or manifestations of valour', and

---

[2] North x is quite right to stress the 'dynamic' nature of *sōphrosynē*, but in her brief discussion of the combination *agathos* + *sōphrōn* (252) she does not give adequate consideration to the possibility that among the majority of people who composed epitaphs (some of which are very rough stuff, considered as art) the combination was a formula originally intended to cover achievement of good and abstention from evil.

[3] Theognis 147f. (= Phokylides fr. 10, treated as a proverb by Arist. *Eth. Nic.* 1129a29), to the effect that 'all virtue' is contained in *dikaiosynē*, cannot have been meant simply to give the name *dikaiosynē* to the sum of all the virtues already recognized (with the implication that it is above all the *dikaios* man who will fight to the death for his fatherland), for the preceding couplet praises honest poverty and deprecates dishonestly acquired wealth; it seems to have been composed by someone whose sense of proportion had been affected by a great injury done to him by a dishonest rogue. Cf. Adkins (1) 78f.

Greek said 'the parts of virtue' (e.g. Isok. viii 32) in cases where we would say 'the virtues'.

*SEG* xxii 73 (s. VI): Alkimakhos, you whom the mound of earth has covered are of good repute, *sōphrōn* and wise, having all virtue.

Cf. *GVI* 335 (a girl).

*GVI* 488: Here the chamber of Persephone possesses Phanagora, who reached the culmination of all virtue.

Cf. ibid. 544 (a young man).


*3. Kalos*

*Kalos* applied to a person, some part of a person, or any artefact or material object, means 'beautiful', 'handsome', 'attractive', and its normal antonym is *aiskhros*, 'ugly' (e.g. Eur. *Hel.* 263, Hdt. vi 60.2). The characteristics by virtue of which a person is *kalos* are usually visual; hence '*khrēstos* appearance' is predicated in Hdt. i 196.2 of those who 'excel in beauty' (*kallisteuein*) or are 'good-looking' (*eueidēs*) or 'shapely' (*eumorphos*), and '*kalos* shape' is contrasted with 'body . . . not of great worth (*spoudaios*) to look upon' in Soph. *Oed. Col.* 576–8. When a distinction is made between body and soul, *kalos* is a possible epithet of the body but not of the soul, e.g. Xenophon on Kyros (*Cyr.* i 2.1), 'in appearance most *kalos*, and in soul most generous . . .', Men. fr. 570, 'beauty (*kallos*) adorned by a *khrēstos* character'. The same is true of other words which may be treated as synonyms of *kalos*, e.g. *euprepēs* (Ar. *Eccl.* 702, ctr. *aiskhros* 705) and *hōraios*[4] (ibid. 616, ctr. *aiskhros* 618; Anaxandrides fr. 52.11, ctr. *aiskhros* 9). These words which denote the attributes by virtue of which their possessor is, if within certain age-limits, sexually attractive (e.g. Ar. *Lys.* 1148, *Eccl.* 625f., Dem. lix 39, Eur. fr. 842) do not necessarily imply any evaluation of such other attributes as may be present.[5] In the case of food, however, what tastes good usually looks good as well, especially to someone who already knows how the dish in question usually tastes, and it should not surprise us that whereas good things to eat are in general *agathos*

---

[4] In Modern Greek this word has taken over many of the functions of ancient *kalos*.

[5] If Eur. fr. 212, 'What is the use of a *kalos* woman, if her mind is not *khrēstos*?', had been corrupted in transmission (with a slight adjustment also of word order, to remove any metrical abnormality) to, 'What is the use of a *khrēstos* woman, if her mind is not *kalos*?', the original could be restored with confidence. On the other hand, in Eur. fr. 548, 'What is the point of shapeliness (*eumorphiā*), if one has not a *kalos* mind?', the metaphor is deliberate: '. . . if one's mind too is not, as it were, beautiful'.

(Anaxandrides fr. 41.35) and can be *khrēstos* (Antiphanes fr. 145.2), fried kidneys (Philippides fr. 5.4) and roast pork (Epikrates fr. 6.4f.) are also *kalos*.

*Kalos* and *aiskhros* are applied very freely indeed by the orators to any action, behaviour or achievement which evokes any kind of favourable reaction and praise or incurs any kind of contempt, hostility or reproach (e.g. Aiskhines i 127, And. ii 17f., Dem. lviii 67, Isok. xix 4, Lyk. 111). *Kalos* thus most often corresponds to our 'admirable', 'creditable, honourable', and *aiskhros* to 'disgraceful', 'shameful', 'scandalous'; they are among the most important tools of manipulative language. Victory being *kalos* and defeat *aiskhros*, to win a lawsuit is to 'contend *kalōs*' (Dem. lvii 2). Anything that 'looks well' because it is honest, just or straightforward is *kalos*; most of us have to change gear morally, as it were, to appreciate Demosthenes' statement (xxix 2) that nothing would have 'looked better' (*kallīon*) for his adversary than to 'prove my claim false by extracting evidence from my slave under torture'. Favourable reactions include unspoken thoughts such as 'I wish I could be like that!' and may in general be subsumed under what the Greeks called *tīmē*, 'honour', 'respect', 'admiration', and unfavourable reactions, including the thoughts (sometimes tinged with compassion) 'I'm glad I'm not like that!' and 'I hope that never happens to me!', are a form of 'dishonour'. Hence wealth and the achievements made possible by wealth are *kalos*, while poverty and the limitations which it imposes are *aiskhros*. This is one reason why *aiskhros* was sometimes applied to behaviour which was not the fault of the agent (cf. V.B.5), and it helps to explain such passages as Hdt. v 6.2, where 'most *kalos*' is opposed to 'most dishonoured (*atīmos*)' and Soph. *Oed. Col.* 43, 'different names (*sc.* for them) are *kalos*' (i.e. 'acceptable', 'sanctioned') 'in different places'.[6]

The application of the adverb *kalōs* and its comparative *kallīon* and superlative *kallista* seems to be somewhat wider than that of the adjective, since they encroach substantially on the field of *eu* (the adverb corresponding to *agathos*) and its degrees of comparison *ameinon* and *arista*.[7] *Kallīon* is used by Aiskhines i 56 and And. ii 5 in the expression 'know better', 'be more familiar with . . .', and Dem. xix 269f. uses both *eu phronein* and *kalōs phronein*

[6] The remarkable glorification of physical beauty in Isok. x 54–60 ('most venerated and precious and divine of all things') is extremely appropriate to its context, an encomium on Helen, but as a factual statement of the extent to which moral and intellectual standards are apt to collapse under the impact of beauty it is marred by a sophistic slither (54), 'and (*sc.* we shall find) that *aretē* owes its good name above all to its being the most *kalos* end that is pursued'.

[7] Cf. Arist. *Eth. Nic.* 1094ᵇ27, 'Each person judges *kalōs* what he knows, and of that he is an *agathos* judge'.

in exact synonymy for 'right thinking' (cf. Eupolis fr. 205.3). A similar extension is observable in prepositional phrases such as *eis kalon*, 'opportunely' (Men. *Dysk.* 773, Soph. *Oed. Tyr.* 78) and *en kalōi*, 'in a good place', *sc.* for seeing and hearing (Ar. *Thesm.* 292f.), 'at a good moment' (Soph. *El.* 384).

It may well be that the extension of the adverb and the use of the prepositional phrases exercised some influence on the adjective. When in Ar. *Lys.* 911 Kinesias, impatient for intercourse with Myrrhine, says 'The cave of Pan is *kalos*', he means that it is suitable or convenient; we might translate 'perfectly all right' or 'quite a good place'. Much more striking is a reference in Menander (fr. 581) to taking silver money to an assayer 'to see if it is *kalos*'; plainly, unless the money were of acceptable appearance there would be no need of an assayer, whose business is to discover whether what looks good really is good. In later Greek *kalos* displaced *agathos* entirely; the scholiast who paraphrased Ar. *Knights* 944 substituted '*kalos* citizen' for '*agathos* citizen' as part of his explanation of the passage.

*Aiskhros*, the antonym of *kalos*, is not so common in extended denotation, nor does the adverb *aiskhrōs* show any sign of displacing *kakōs* as *kalōs* displaces *eu*. Yet in the famous scene of *Lysistrata*, when Myrrhine says (923) that intercourse on a string bed without a mat is *aiskhros*, one may suspect that physical comfort and the resultant mental satisfaction are more to the point than dignity; the word is almost 'nasty', the verbal equivalent of a *moue*. It is possible that the extension of *kalos* and *aiskhros* to cover actions which cause unfavourable responses of various kinds led to a reduction of their application to physical beauty and ugliness. Hence we find comparatively long-winded expressions such as '*kalos kāgathos*[8] in appearance' = 'handsome' in Aiskhines i 134, 'of poor quality in appearance' = 'ugly' in And i 100, and 'horrible to look upon' in Aiskhines i 61.

Although *kalos* and *aiskhros* undoubtedly tended towards synonymy with other common terms of praise and blame, it is synonymy of a special kind, comparable with that which exists between the imperfective and aorist aspects in certain tenses of certain verbs (e.g. *phere* and *enenke*, 'bring me . . .', in comic dialogue) or between a prepositional phrase with the article and the same phrase without the article (e.g. *kata tēn agorān* or *kat' agorān*, 'in the central square'). The speaker may look at the same thing in different ways, and in a great many contexts it does not actually matter which way he chooses.

Dem. xxiii 49: Are you not riding roughshod over all human usage (*sc. by disregarding*

[8] Cf. (I.A.2) Socrates' naïvety in expecting that those who were *kalos kāgathos* would necessarily be *kalos* in the visual sense.

*the difference between deliberate and involuntary wrongdoing*) and setting aside the motivation which makes any given action either *kalos* or *aiskhros*?

Cf. ibid. 75, cited in B.4.

Clearly we can qualify an act either by an epithet suggesting how one reacts to it or by an epithet denoting the attribute by virtue of which one has that reaction. The alternatives are neatly displayed by a passage which Demosthenes adapted from his speech against Androtion for use in his speech against Timokrates.

Dem. xxii 56: His behaviour towards you was so disgraceful (*aiskhrōs*) and self-seeking that he thought it right for his own father, imprisoned for debt . . ., to escape without paying . . . while any other citizen who could not pay . . . should be thrown into prison.

Dem. xxiv 168: Androtion's behaviour towards you was so inequitable (*anisōs*) and self-seeking that he thought it right for his own father (*etc., as above*).

A passage composed in 'ring-form' is instructive, as often.

Hdt. i 196.1: The wisest (*sophōtatos*) of their customs, in my opinion, was the following . . . 196.5: Now, that was the most admirable (*kallistos*) of their customs, but they have not continued to follow it . . . 197.1: Another custom of theirs, (*sc. which I would regard as*) second in *sophiā*, is as follows . . . 199.1: But the most shameful (*aiskhistos*) of the customs of the Babylonians is . . .

When Aiskhines i 180 says that it is *kalos* to imitate the virtues of other states, and Ant. v 71 that it is *agathos* to take time in investigating an alleged crime, they are not saying the same thing about the behaviour which they commend; yet Antiphon could have said that prolonged investigation is *kalos*, i.e. that it causes the investigators to be admired (cf. Dem. lviii 61, where it is said to be *kalos* not to subordinate the law to the speakers), and Aiskhines could have said that imitation of foreign virtues is *agathos*, i.e. that it has consequences welcome to the imitators. One can see the difference of standpoint between And. ii 17, 'generals who achieve something *kalos* for the city' and ibid. 18, 'who confers something *agathos* on his fellow-citizens', but we are getting near to vanishing-point in contrasting Dein. i 8, 'having performed many *kalos* < actions > for you' and ibid. 15, 'he has never yet conferred any benefits (lit., '*agathos* < things >') on you'.

*Kalos* and *kalōs* seem to have a special function as a reinforcement to other words, so that in saying '*x* and *kalos*' I not only communicate the judgment '*x*' but also express, and hope to cause in my hearers, a feeling of admiration, as if I had exclaimed parenthetically, 'How splendid!' Hence: '*kalos* and just', Aiskhines i 121, Dem. xx 98, xxiii 169, xxiv 38, lvii 58; 'just and *kalos*', Ar.

*Clouds* 1340, Dem. xxiii 64; '*kalōs* and democratically', Dem. xxiv 59; 'laboriously and *kalōs*', Isok. xix 11; '*kalos* and legal', Dem. xxiii 70; '*kalos* and *sōphrōn*', Aiskhines i 20; '*khrēstos* and *kalos*', Dem. xxiii 75; 'humanely and *kalōs*', Dem. xxiii 44. Given '*eu* and *khrēstōs*', literally 'well and well', in Ar. *Eccl.* 638, it is doubtful whether '*eu* and *kalōs*' (ibid. 253, cf. Pl. *Smp.* 184A) is anything more than an emphatic (because quadrisyllabic) way of saying 'well' (cf. our 'well and truly', 'good and proper', except that our expressions are less tautological when the denotation of each of their ingredients is looked at more closely). There are, of course, cases in Greek where *kalos* combined with another adjective is something more than a reinforcement, e.g. '*kalos* and great expectations' (Dem. xix 121), 'a *kalos* and just argument' (Aiskhines i 121), for it is possible to entertain great hopes of (e.g.) ill-gotten wealth or to present an argument which is strictly just but reflects little credit on its proponent (cf. IV.C.4).

# III

# DETERMINANTS OF MORAL CAPACITY

## III.A. HUMAN NATURE

### 1. Humans and Animals

The difference between humans and animals lay, in the Greek view, not only in the obvious superiority of human reasoning (Dem. lx 30) but in the extent to which man had used his powers of reasoning to ameliorate his own condition and ensure his survival by growing crops (Isok. iv 28)[1] and by forming communities operating under laws for the restraint of aggression.

Dem. xxv 20: If laws were abolished and each individual were given power to do what he liked, not only does our communal organisation vanish but our very life would be in no way different from that of the animals.

Cf. Xen. *Anab.* v 7.32, equating human lawlessness with the behaviour of beasts.

Communities can be constituted only by people who use language for discussion and mutual persuasion. Isok. iii 5f. treats language as the essential condition of law and art (cf. Eur. *Supp.* 201-204); Xen. *Hiero* 7.3 emphasizes desire for the honour and respect of one's fellows as peculiarly human; all seem to agree in thinking of the individual animal as motivated solely by appetite and impulse. Hence it is 'swinish and bestial' to give precedence to the appetite for food and drink (Xen. *Cyr.* v 2.17), and animals are 'educated' by giving or withholding food (Xen. *Oec.* 13.9); ferocity is inhuman (cf. Eur. *Or.* 1555, '... two lions—for men I cannot call them—...'), and 'beast' (*thērion*) is a normal derogatory term in the orators (e.g. Dem. xxiv 143, xxv 8, lviii 49). This view of animal life does not differ significantly from that of Hesiod, who said (*Op.* 276-80) that Zeus had laid down that

[1] Cf. Baldry 12f., 28f.

beasts and fishes should devour one another, but that men should govern their relationships by law.[2]

In the latter part of the fifth century the realization that a law, custom or usage must have had an origin at a point in time aroused great interest among intellectuals and expressed itself in argument about *physis* ('nature') and *nomos* ('usage', 'custom', 'practice', 'convention', 'law');[3] for example, Demokritos B278 regards it as natural that all creatures should procreate and rear young but a matter of *nomos* that human parents should expect from their offspring some return for their trouble. Ar. *Clouds* 1420–1433 caricatures arguments based on the idea that only what is common to man and beast can properly be called natural: Pheidippides justifies his assault on his father Strepsiades on the grounds that barnyard fowls attack their parents, to which his father replies, 'Why don't you feed on dung, then, and sleep on a perch?'

Human organization creates possibilities of wrongdoing not open to animals, and this fact gave rise to the reflection that we have invented and inflicted upon ourselves more ills than Nature engenders in us and more than she imposes upon animals: Isok. iv 167f., Men. fr. 620. Comic misanthropy expresses itself in Philemon fr. 3 by saying that nothing but our upright position distinguishes us from the animals.

## 2. Humans and Gods

The difference between human nature and divine nature was conceived as greater than that between humans and animals in so far as gods were immortal and capable of action at a distance, but on the moral and emotional plane it was smaller. In comprehension and prescience men fell short of the gods in degree, but not in kind; the theme of most popular contrasts between the human and the divine is our fallibility.

Dem. xix 299f.: The oracle (*cited in 298*) says that we must so act that our enemies do not have cause to rejoice. Zeus, Dione, all the gods, with one voice advise us to

[2] To judge from the pronouncements made throughout human history on the subject of animals, it would seem that ours is the first culture actually to observe animals in their natural state and perhaps the first to care whether what it says about them is true or false. Hesiod treated all non-human creatures as if they constituted a single species. Members of the same species, and to a still greater degree members of the same community within a species, commonly exhibit a *modus vivendi* which makes nonsense of the distinction drawn by Hesiod between *homo sapiens* and the rest.

[3] Cf. F. Heinimann, *Nomos und Physis* (Basel, 1945), M. Pohlenz, 'Nomos und Physis', *Hermes* lxxxi (1953), 418–38; Dodds 182–9, de Romilly 58–114, Adkins (2) 110–26.

punish those who have served our enemies' interests ... Now, one can see *even by human reasoning* that nothing is more inimical and dangerous to us than to allow a man at our head to become close to those whose interests are opposed to the interests of the Athenian people ...

Cf. Alexis fr. 260A (Edmonds), any of us can die at any moment; Antiphanes fr. 227.9f., we cannot know what is in store for anyone else who is close to us; Hdt. iii 65.3, Kambyses' reflection that human nature has not the power to avert misfortune, which the future hides; i 5.4, 207.2, vii 49.3f.; Thuc. iii 45.3, the universality of error, and ii 64.3, the natural tendency of all power to decline; Xen. *Cyr.* i 6.44 (cf. iii 2.15), man's need to choose his courses of action by conjecture, in ignorance of what will succeed or fail; ibid. i 6.23, the importance of asking the gods, through divination, about what we cannot ourselves foresee; Xen. *Mem.* i 1.8, Socrates' belief that the gods have reserved for themselves the most important of all branches of knowledge, knowledge of the future; Xen. *Smp.* 4.47, 'Clearly Greeks and *barbaroi*[4] alike believe that the gods know everything, past, present and future'.

'Most people', according to Xen. *Mem.* i 1.19, believed that there were some things which were hidden even from the gods, a belief which (according to Xenophon) Socrates did not share (cf. III.G.2, on Fate). Isok. xii 64 alludes to a belief that the gods were not entirely *anhamartētos*, an ambiguous word (cf. III.H.3) which covers both freedom from unintentional error and abstention from wrongdoing. Such a belief was firmly founded in the myths related in archaic and classical poetry, which portrayed the gods as subject to rage, spite and lust. 'Even Zeus is worsted by Eros' is suggested by Wrong in Ar. *Clouds* 1080–2 as an excuse which could be offered by an adulterer, and Helen does indeed offer it (cf. III.H.4) in Eur. *Tro.* 948–50 (cf. Eur. fr. 431, Soph. *Ant.* 781–801, fr. 855.14f., Men. *Heros* fr. 2). Although the idea that to be divine entails needing nothing (Xen. *Mem.* i 6.10), and thus desiring nothing, is pre-Platonic (it is expressed by Herakles in Eur. *Her. Fur.* 1345f.), it was commoner to rationalize the traditional procedures of sacrifice and festival by asserting that gods, like men, desire to be honoured (Eur. *Hipp.* 7f., cf. Alexis fr. 245.13). In the story which Plato puts into the mouth of Aristophanes (*Smp.* 190C) Zeus wants to destroy the human race because of its arrogance and ambition but feels that he cannot do so, for whence would the gods then receive the honours which they value?[5] It was commonly

---

[4] *Barbaros*, plural *barbaroi*, = 'non-Greek-speaking'. I have preferred to keep the word in Greek, since 'barbarian' and 'barbarous' have acquired too specific associations in English, and 'foreigner' or 'alien' would be a misleading translation; an Athenian was a foreigner in Sparta or Corinth, but that did not make him a *barbaros*.

[5] It would be fair to say both that the Greeks did not regard their gods as having a

assumed that a god could be hurt by rejection or insult (cf. Kreousa on Apollo, Eur. *Ion* 1311).

It has often been remarked that Greek religion had no Devil. This is certainly much more than a half-truth, but it falls a little short of complete truth. The Greeks did believe in the existence of supernatural beings who were not asked for the blessings which men normally desire but could be invoked magically for disagreeable purposes[6] and otherwise were appeased and averted by ritual acts and formulae (Isok. v 117). Death, under 'Hades' or any other name, was implacable (Soph. fr. 703) and hated (Eur. *Alc.* 61f.), and composers of epitaphs did not hesitate to vilify him as cruel, spiteful, shameless or senseless,[7] but no one thought of him as an adversary of Zeus, tempting men to murder. It was possible to fear, hate and vilify Ares as the personification of war, as it was to adore Peace as kindly (e.g. Ar. *Peace* and Philemon fr. 71.7f.). In so far as sexual desire can lead men to crime, and unrequited desire is one of the great miseries, Aphrodite and Eros could also be feared and hated as a 'sickness' (Eur. fr. 400; cf. III.G.*1*). At a humbler level, people were frightened by apparitions which Hekate (e.g. Eur. *Hel.* 569f., Theophr. *Char.* 16.7; and her character became increasingly sinister in the course of the centuries) sent up from the underworld.

Subjected to apparently undeserved suffering, or witnessing it in others, a Greek felt free to reproach Zeus, any other god, or the gods in general (e.g. Soph. *Phil.* 451f., *Trach.* 1271f.). The scale of human misfortune and the absence of any observable correlation between virtue and prosperity (cf. V.D.*4*) encouraged a belief that a touchy and malevolent jealousy was a conspicuous characteristic of the gods' attitude towards humanity.[8] In a famous anecdote told by Herodotos (i 32.1) Solon, interrogated by Kroisos

special concern for the human race (Lloyd-Jones 3f.), in that the gods would continue to find some way of enjoying themselves even if all humans were exterminated, and also (B. C. Dietrich, *Death, Fate and the Gods* [London, 1965], 6) that the Greeks' view of the universe was anthropocentric, in that so little of their intellectual energy was expended on the investigation of phenomena which do not affect human life. The Greek intellect was capable of a remarkable objectivity in regard to the nature and history of the human race; cf. E. A. Havelock, *The Liberal Temper in Greek Politics* (London, 1957).

[6] On magical procedures in cursing cf. L. H. Jeffery, *Annual of the British School at Athens* 1 (1955) 71–6. The personification of what were felt to be external forces brought to bear on man's mind by the gods (cf. III.G.) may seem to imply a whole regiment of demons, but their functions were limited and subordinate. To treat Hybris as a 'force of nature', as Gernet suggests (208–11, 253f.). is not quite the same as saying that Hybris was a deity who could herself take the initiative in determining human conduct; but Greek personification sets us many problems, on which see III.G.*3*.

[7] Cf. Lattimore 183.

[8] Cf. Opstelten 232–9.

on the subject of good fortune, claims to know that the gods manifest themselves in human affairs as resentful of our successes and destructive of stable prosperity. This view (cf. Hdt. iii 40.2, vii 10 ε, 46.3f.; Xen. *Hell.* vi 4.12), a translation into religious terms of the empirical proposition that we suffer many unforeseen and unmerited disasters (expressed in secular terms by Thuc. iv 62.4, viii 24.5) may have prevailed more widely in the fourth century than literature (let alone philosophy) indicates. Motiveless hostility on the part of Zeus towards mankind, and in particular towards those whom we call good, seems to underlie the blinding of Wealth in Ar. *Wealth* 87–94. The Trojan War was sometimes 'explained' (e.g. Eur. *Hel.* 38–41) by the supposition that Zeus wanted to kill off a lot of people.

The gods as portrayed in legend and poetry were not conspicuously compassionate; since our awareness of our own vulnerability plays a part in arousing our compassion for others, and by human standards the gods were practically invulnerable, we can understand the qualification in Eur. *Her. Fur.* 1115, '< sufferings > at which *even* a god would groan'.[9] The scheme of Eur. *Hipp.* presupposes a divine willingness to treat human beings as pawns played in a fierce game played between deities; Aphrodite does not care how Phaidra suffers, so long as punishment can be contrived for Hippolytos (47–50), and Artemis proposes to hurt Aphrodite in return by killing some mortal of whom she is fond (1420–1422). Similarly, Pasiphae's passion for a bull is implanted in her by Poseidon as means of damaging her husband Minos (Eur. fr. 82 [Austin] 22–8). When a god does take pity on a human being, he does so because that human is a friend, ally or loyal subject who has established by piety and sacrifices a claim on pity and help. Aristophanes satirizes this aspect of the relation between god and man in *Peace* 363–425, where Hermes, at first implacable towards Trygaios and the chorus, is softened by extravagant promises and finally won over by a gift of gold vessels.

> Ah! (*oimoi: he is overcome by emotion*). How compassionate I always feel—to gold plate!

Nevertheless, characters in plays sometimes ask gods for forgiveness and offer excuses which are apparently accepted (Ar. *Clouds* 1476–85, *Peace* 668f.; cf. V.D.4); the Dioskouroi in Eur. *El.* 1327–30, exclaiming in genuine compassion for the miserable and tormented Orestes and Elektra, assert that

---

[9] There is dramatic irony here; the sufferings of Herakles were in fact inflicted on him by a deity.

the gods *do* have pity for human suffering. Lysias ii 40, portraying the sufferings and fears of the Athenians during Xerxes' invasion, asks

What god would not have pitied them for the greatness of their peril?

Thucydides' Nikias (vii 77.4) tells the Athenian troops retreating from Syracuse that even if they aroused divine resentment earlier, their plight now deserves the gods' pity. It sounds from Men. *Epitr.* 855, 874f., as if references to a god's pity were a commonplace in conversation; but cf. IV.D.*1*.

Human affection for benevolent gods was probably a much commoner phenomenon than a reconstruction of the theology implicit in Greek literature might suggest. Euripides has portrayed something of the kind, on the legendary plane, in Hippolytos's love for Artemis and Ion's for Apollo.[10] The adjectives 'dear' and 'dearest' can be attached to a god's name in invocations, e.g. Ar. *Eccl.* 378. The apparent granting of one prayer out of a hundred may well do more to make a man love his gods than the apparent rejection of the other ninety-nine can do to make him hate them, and among men, after all, it is A's doing of what B asks him to do that implants in B affection for A. Even apart from that, it is by no means impossible to live with a belief that men are by and large superior to gods in equanimity, generosity and compassion, any more than it is impossible for a peasant community to endure with cheerful resilience the unpredictability of the weather, the capricious exactions of the local baron and a law which imposes enormous penalties for trivial offences. Undoubtedly a belief in the goodness of the gods is more reassuring, and the Greeks of the classical period showed an increasing tendency to substitute it for mere resilience.

Eur. *Hipp.* 117–20 (*Hippolytos's old slave asks Aphrodite to forgive his master for slighting her*): You ought to forgive him. If a man whose heart is fired with the zeal of youth speaks foolishly of you, imagine that you do not hear him; for gods ought to be more understanding (*sophos*) than mortals.

Cf. Dem. xxv 88f. on sensible old people who 'pretend not to notice' the misbehaviour of the high-spirited younger members of their families.

Eur. *Ba.* 1348 (*Kadmos boldly reproaches Dionysos for the god's terrible revenge*): It is not seemly that gods should be like mortals in temper.

Dem. xxiii 74: I think that they . . ., recognising that, when Orestes admitted that he had killed his mother, he was tried by a jury of gods and acquitted,[11] considered

[10] Cf. A.-J. Festugière, *Personal Religion among the Greeks* (Berkeley and Los Angeles, 1954) 10–16.

[11] Demosthenes is here using a version of the story of Orestes and his trial at Athens different from the version presented in Aiskhylos's *Eumenides*.

that there was such a thing as justifiable homicide; for (*sc. they reckoned that*) the gods would not have given an unjust verdict.

Cf. Dem. xx 126, the undesirability of using religious scruples as a pretext for blameworthy behaviour towards men. Men. fr. 714 asserts that each individual's 'fate' is blameless, for 'the god is in all things good'. Demokritos B175 had declared a century earlier that the gods are the source of all good, so that man is himself responsible for the evils which he suffers.

Belief in gods who were always morally better than men was not easily reconcilable with traditional myths, in which the gods often behaved in ways which would not have been acceptable in an Athenian citizen.[12] In such cases the truth of the myth could simply be denied, as Iphigeneia in Eur. *Iph. Taur.* 380–91 repudiates all myths which represent gods as demanding human sacrifice and asserts 'that no supernatural being is bad'; cf. Isok. xi 38–40, rejecting 'the stories told by the poets' and denying (41) that the gods, who possess all virtue, 'have any part in evil'. Or again, the individual god might be represented as transferring responsibility to a decree of Zeus (this is Dionysos's reply to Kadmos in Eur. *Ba.* 1349), or to divine and immutable laws, such as Artemis invokes in Eur. *Hipp.* 1396 by way of apology for her inability to shed tears over the fate of Hippolytos.[13] Between such 'decrees' or 'laws' and an irrational, inexplicable Fate there is a difference of emphasis, but hardly a difference in kind. Reluctance to attribute cruel and greedy actions to gods manifested itself in a tendency (cf. III.G.2) to put the responsibility for events on to a mechanical, comparatively impersonal 'fate', 'fortune' or 'chance'; this made it easier to think of the gods as good when, and in so far as, a question concerning their character seemed to require an answer.

Although the difference between mortality and immortality is as great a difference as there can be, the Greeks tended in some ways to treat them as opposite ends of a scale rather than totally opposed natures. There were intermediate beings, sometimes 'half-gods', as Hesiod calls the heroes and heroines of legend, children of mixed human and divine parentage (cf. Isok. ix 39, 'no mortal or half-god or immortal'), sometimes *daimones* (a word which could be used either of supernatural beings as a genus or of a species intermediate[14] between man and god), all these recipients of prayer and

[12] Cf. Adkins (1) 62–70.

[13] There is a striking contrast between Artemis's succinctness and Aphrodite's fulsome disavowal of responsibility for the blinding of Teiresias in Kallimakhos, *Hymn* v 97–105.

[14] *Daimōn* is our word 'demon', but Greek *daimones* had more in common with angels than with demons.

sacrifice. Herakles, born of a mortal mother but begotten by Zeus, became a 'full' god on the death of his mortal body; his achievements, of course, from the day when as a new-born infant he strangled the snakes sent by Hera to kill him, had been far above anything to which men could normally aspire, even above those of 'some gods' (Isok. v 114). In historical times a human being of pre-eminent (and therefore super-human, in a strict sense of the word) beauty, strength, skill or achievement could be treated as a hero after his death (people wondered, 'Was his mother perhaps visited by a god?'), as happened (e.g.) to Philippos of Kroton, 'the handsomest man of his time', at Segesta (Hdt. v 47) and in the late fifth century to Diagoras of Rhodes (cf. the Scholia on Pindar, *Ol.* 7). In cases of this kind the community took upon itself election of a new member to the company of the super-natural beings,[15] but theology came a bad second to cult and observance in Greek religion, and probably the community consulted an oracle before 'heroisation' of a dead man.[16] Deification of rulers in the Hellenistic period had very long and deep roots in the practices, concepts and language of earlier times,[17] e.g. Eup. fr. 117.6, where the chorus say of the generals of the previous generation, 'We prayed to them as to gods, *for that is what they were*'. Note also the use of *theios*, the adjective derived from *theos*, 'god', to mean 'prodigious', 'extraordinary', e.g. Men. *Epitr.* 433, 'He has a *theios* hatred for me.'

## 3. Human Society

It will be apparent from what has been said above that however much we humans may regret that compared with deities we are feeble, ignorant, ugly and smelly, we have no reason to feel guilty about being human; on the contrary, each of us can nourish a secret pride in the ability, by and large, to be nicer than deities. No Greek doubted that humans are easily impelled by anger, hatred or appetite (cf. III.F.2) to wrong and disastrous action, from which, as Diodotos observes in Thuc. iii 45.7, they are not deterred even by the provision of the severest penalties; that an individual is very apt to give precedence to his own interest over the interests of others (Is. iii 66, cf.

[15] There is a good measure of continuity between pagan heroization and Christian canonization, as there is between the 'local hero' and the 'local saint'.

[16] Cf. Lattimore 97–101.

[17] Cf. (on different aspects of the transition from human to divine character) Christian Habicht, *Gottmenschtum und griechische Städte* (Munich, 1970), and Dietrich Roloff, *Gottähnlichkeit, Vergöttlichung und Erhöhung zu seligem Leben* (Berlin, 1970).

Isok. xx 11); or that states (Thuc. i 75.2, 76.3, v 89, Dem. iv 5) and individuals (Isok. xvi 38) alike have a natural inclination to aggrandisement when an opportunity presents itself. But it was also observed that a good man could improve on nature.

Dem. viii 72: The city should grow in power step by step with the political careers of its good citizens, and everyone in politics should advocate what is best, not what is easiest. Nature herself will move in the direction of the latter; the good citizen should lead the city on to the former by argument and explanation.

Cf. Isok. ii 45, the natural impulse of most men towards what is pleasurable rather than towards what is healthiest or best for them or most useful; Xen. *Mem.* ii i.23, the path of vice (*kakiā*)[18] 'the easiest and most agreeable way'.

Dem. lx 1: Given that they despised the inborn desire for life which exists in all beings, and chose rather to die honourably than to live and see the Greek world in distress, surely nothing that could be said can exaggerate the virtue for which we remember them?

Cf. Lyk. *Leokr.* 101, the legendary Praxithea put the preservation of her country above the life of her child, 'although all women are disposed by nature to love their children'.

We are *both* competing individuals *and* members of social groups; we are impelled *both* to assert ourselves against others *and* to integrate ourselves with others into society. The Greeks seem to have no difficulty in recognizing as natural the resentments and jealousies of competition (Hdt. iii 80.3, Thuc. vi 16.3) side by side with those forces which make for mutual love and social cohesion.[19]

Dem. xvi 24: We all know that everyone, even when he does not want to do what is right, is up to a point ashamed of not doing it, and openly takes his stand against wrong, especially when someone else is being harmed.

Dem. xviii 275: Suppose that a man, without misdeed or misjudgment, has devoted himself to what appeared to be the common interest, but, in company with everyone else, has failed. It is right not to reproach or vilify such a man, but to sympathise with him. This will not only be seen in our laws; nature herself has prescribed it in unwritten usage[20] and human character.

ibid. 315: What man does not know that all the living have to face a greater or

[18] Literally, 'badness', covering 'inadequacy' and 'uselessness'; the English word 'vice' perhaps has too strong a bite.

[19] I am concerned here with what were regarded as specifically human characteristics, not with natural instincts common to man and beast, e.g. parental love of children (Eur. *Her. Fur.* 633–6).

[20] Cf. V.D.3.

lesser degree of malice, but the dead are not hated any more even by their enemies? This is so by nature; am I then to be considered and judged by comparison with those who have gone before me?

Dem. xlv 65: A man who flatters the fortunate and gives them up when their fortune changes, and . . . considers only means of gain, should surely be hated as an enemy of the human race? (*literally, 'a common enemy of all human nature'*).

Cf. Dem. xxv 35, universal innate reverence for justice ('altars . . . in each man's soul'); Xen. *Mem.* ii 6.21, the instinct to create ties of affection, compassion, gratitude and mutual benefaction, an instinct which is part of human nature. In Dem. xxv 81, where 'compassion, forgiveness and kindness' are treated as part of the 'nature' of all juries, a compliment to Athens rather than to mankind may be intended.

Speakers in Thucydides sometimes discern more subtly conflicting characteristics in human nature: contempt for those who yield and respect for those who stand up for themselves (iii 39.5), or graceful concession to those who voluntarily give way and obdurate resistance to those who are overbearing (iv 19.4).

## III.B. HEREDITY AND ENVIRONMENT

### 1. Nations

Generalizations about human nature admit of exceptions. Xen. *Hiero* 7.3, having observed that men differ from animals in desiring the honour of their fellows, qualifies the observation: there do exist men in whom this desire is lacking. In Xen. *Cyr.* viii 7.13 the fact that not all men are trustworthy is used as evidence that trustworthiness cannot be an ingredient of human nature (cf. the over-confident words of Araspas on sexual love, ibid. v 1.9–12). To bring these two passages together is to be forewarned of the uncertainties which lie below the surface of generalizations about the human race, nations, cultures and individuals.

It was generally taken for granted by the Greeks that Greeks were morally better than *barbaroi*,[1] and it was taken for granted by the Athenians that Athenians were morally better than other Greeks. Isok. xv 293 suggests a ratio, Athenians : other Greeks : : other Greeks : *barbaroi* : : humans :

---

[1] On the general question of Greek attitudes to *barbaroi* see *Entretiens de la Fondation Hardt* viii (1961), *Grecs et Barbares*, and J. Jüthner, *Hellenen und Barbaren* (Leipzig, 1923); cf. Baldry 8–18.

animals.[2] Athenians also attributed specific vices and defects—more rarely, virtues—to different Greek states. It is to be expected that characters in comedy should express these sentiments in crude terms; we also find in the orators expressions of a simple-minded jingoism and xenophobia such as are not now acceptable in public debate. Thus we are told that an Athenian jury is by nature superior to others in intelligence (Aiskhines i 178), that Athenians are not suited by nature to the pursuit of an aggressive policy (Dem. viii 42) and that they are naturally hostile to lack of patriotism (Lyk. *Leokr*. 116); that the policy of the Thessalians has always been by nature untrustworthy to all men (Dem. i 22), the Thebans pride themselves on cruelty and dishonesty even more than the Athenians pride themselves on kindness and honesty (Dem. xx 109), and the Phaselites are exceptionally tricky in commercial dealings (Dem. xxxv 1f.). The Spartans were regarded by others, not only by themselves, as possessing 'inborn (*emphytos*) valour', to which they added the skill derived from intensive training (Lys. xxxiii 7). This last observation is drawn from a speech delivered to a panhellenic audience; at Athens, Spartan perfidy (Ar. *Peace* 1066–68, 1083; Eur. *Andr*. 445–53, *Supp*. 187; cf. Thuc. v 42.2, 45, 105.4) was given more emphasis in popular sentiment.[3]

In general, Greek communities which called themselves 'Dorians' professed a contempt for what they regarded as the martial inadequacies of 'Ionians' (a category which included Athens), and this traditional attitude was exploited by people addressing Dorian assemblies or armies,[4] e.g. Thuc. v 9.1, vi 77.1. 'Natural enmity' could be predicated of the relation between Dorians and Ionians (Thuc. iv 60.1; cf. vi 82.2, '*always* enemies'), but this was not so firmly rooted an assumption that the inevitability of wars between the two 'races' could not be denied (Thuc. iv 61.2f.). We also have to consider—as we shall have to consider again in other connections—that *physis*, 'nature', does not necessarily imply genetic inheritance, but may refer to the way in which a person grows, being his father's son and being subjected from the beginning of his life to the environmental influence of his family and community.[5]

---

[2] Cf. Baldry 69.

[3] Popular ideas about other nations are normally based on an extremely selective attention to very limited data. There are British and American travellers who seem to judge a nation mainly on the efficiency with which it disposes of faeces, and an acquaintance of mine is seriously opposed to British participation in the Common Market since the practice of killing and eating small birds, widespread in France and Italy, proves, in his view, that France and Italy are fundamentally uncivilized countries.

[4] Cf. E. Will, *Doriens et Ioniens* (Strasbourg, 1956).

[5] Cf. Adkins (2) 79–84.

The defeat of Xerxes' invasion early in the fifth century gave an impetus to the Greeks' belief in their own superiority over other nations and tribes. This belief became stronger in the course of the century, and we find many passages in which *barbaros* is used as a derogatory term or it is implied that nothing good can be expected of *barbaroi*: Eur. *Andr.* 173–6, incest and murder of kindred the norm among all *barbaroi*; Eur. *Hcld.* 130f., 'He is dressed like a Greek, but his actions are *barbaros*'; Eur. *Hec.* 328–31, no gratitude or true friendship among *barbaroi*; Eur. *Hel.* 501f., 'No one could be so *barbaros* in heart' as not to pity the shipwrecked Menelaos; Eur. fr. 139, the uselessness of talking rationally to 'a *barbaros* nature'; Men. *Epitr.* 898f., '*barbaros* and pitiless' (a Greek is reproaching himself bitterly); Men. *Farmer* 56, 'slaves and *barbaroi*' (i.e. '*barbaros* slaves'?) callously neglected their injured owner. Conversely, 'Greek' occurs as a complimentary term, like our 'civilized': Alexis fr. 9.8f., Men. *Perik.* 1008f. Cf. also Dem. xxiii 135–38 on the Thracian king Kersebleptes, '*barbaros* and untrustworthy', 'by nature untrustworthy', 'a Thracian person', and Dem. xlv 30 on Phormion, who is called *barbaros* 'in that he hates those whom he should respect'. In Men. fr. 612, where someone declares that if a man is by nature of good character it does not matter 'even if he is an Ethiopian' and that it is absurd to abuse anyone for being a Scythian, it seems that widely accepted beliefs are being attacked.

To ask 'Did the fourth-century Athenian believe that moral qualities, or at least moral capacities, are transmitted genetically?' may seem a hopeless attempt to shift rhetoric and humour on to a scientific plane; none the less, the attempt is justified both by the intrinsic importance of the question and by the availability of some relevant data. Since most children are brought up by their parents, empirical evidence bearing upon the respective roles of nature and nurture is obtainable only when a baby is transferred from its own parents to a different environment. Precisely such an occurrence figures in an amusing passage of Demosthenes.

Dem. xxi 149f.: And who does not know[6] the unutterable story—like a tragic legend[7]—of his birth! . . . His real mother, who bore him, showed better sense than anyone has ever done, while the woman who is regarded as his mother and took him as her own was the stupidest woman of all time. Why? Because his real mother sold him as soon as he was born, and the other woman, who could have got better for the

---

[6] This formula, like 'You all know . . .', commonly introduces a statement which is quite new to the speaker's audience; cf. Dover (1) 80.

[7] Demosthenes has in mind stories of the exposure of infants and their eventual identification; for a similar reference to tragic legend cf. And. i 129.

same price, bought him ... He has found a fatherland ... The (in the true sense) *barbaros* and abominable element in his nature controls him by force and makes it obvious that he treats the society in which he lives as alien to him—which it is!

Demosthenes scores off Meidias and raises a laugh against him by this story; he does not expect us to take it seriously (cf. Men. *Epitr.* 320–33, cited in section 2 below), but he is serious enough about Meidias's behaviour, and the use of which he turns the story implies the racial inheritance of moral character.

The antithesis between *nomos* and *physis* which so interested intellectuals in the late fifth century had a considerable bearing on the question of innate differences between nations. When Pentheus in Eur. *Ba.* 483 denigrates the worship of Dionysos by *barbaroi* on the grounds that 'they have less sense (*phronein*) than Greeks', Dionysos replies (484), 'In *this*, they have more; but their *nomoi* are different', implying that the potentiality of Greeks and *barbaroi* is equal but is realized in different forms. We meet in Antiphon the Sophist B44B.col.2.10–15 an argument to the effect that the differences between Greeks and *barbaroi* are a matter of *nomos*, not of nature.[8] The attempt by the author of the Hippocratic treatise *Airs, Waters and Places* to attribute different physical and psychological types to the operation of climatic and geographical factors[9] implies that although (e.g.) Scythians who have grown up in Scythia since infancy may have general characteristics, owing nothing to *nomos*, which differentiate them from Greeks and Egyptians they would have grown up differently if they had been transferred to Greece or Egypt in infancy. How far argument and speculation of this kind affected popular assumptions about racial and national differences, it is hardly possible to assess, but the orators certainly lay a great deal of emphasis on habituation.

Dem. xiii 25: You have got into the habit of acting in this way not because you are inferior in nature to your ancestors, but because there was pride in their hearts, and of that you have been deprived. I do not think it is ever possible for men whose actions are mean and petty to acquire a great and valiant spirit; for as the practices of men are, so must their spirit necessarily be.

Dem. xxiii 141: Entering those cities, he committed many an outrage, assaulting the sons of citizens and violating women, and doing everything which a man is liable to do when he comes into a position of power after being brought up without laws and the benefits of a political community.

[8] Cf. Baldry 43–5 and G. B. Kerferd, *Proc. Camb. Philol. Soc.* N.S. iv (1956/7) 26–32.
[9] Cf. H. Diller, *Wanderarzt und Aitiologe* = *Philologus* Supplbd. xxvi 3 (1934), particularly 107f. on the question of inherited characteristics.

Cf. ibid. 138f. on mercenary commanders as 'the enemies of civilised communities', since they do not live in cities under codes of law; Dem. xx 123, xxii 51, 57, on the habits (*ethē*) of Athenian political life; Dem. xxiii 56, the friends and enemies of Athens recognizable not by their race (*genos*) but by the record of their behaviour. Cf. also: Alexis fr. 241.1, 'That's not acceptable' (*ennomos*, 'in usage') 'even among the Triballians!'; Hdt. vii 102.1, the valour of Greece not the gift of nature but wrought by *sophiā* (i.e. thought and skill) and strong *nomos*; Thuc. ii 36.4, Perikles' stress on culture and constitutional structure as the source of Athens' strength (cf. ii 61.4);[10] Thuc. vii 21.3, Hermokrates' encouragement to the Syracusans to face the Athenian fleet, on the grounds that the Athenians had only become a naval power because the threat of Persia forced them to it (*sc.* and they were not by nature better sailors than other nations).

An additional factor determining the characteristic behaviour of a nation is its tradition and ancestral example.

Dem. xviii 68: Nor would anyone be so bold as to say that it was inappropriate for Philip, brought up at Pella, a small and inglorious place at that time, to conceive so high a pride in his own worth as to desire to rule the Greek world ...

Dem. xiii 26: Our ancestors erected many honourable trophies on which we still to this day pride ourselves. And you should imagine that they erected these trophies not so that we might look at them in admiration but so that we might imitate the virtues of those who dedicated them.

Cf. Dem. xiii 34, xviii 68, xix 270, xxii 77f.

Lyk. *Leokr.* 110: Leokrates ... shamed the good repute which all the course of time has conferred on our city. If, then, you execute him, you will be regarded by the whole Greek world as abhorring such conduct as his; but if you do not, you will deprive your ancestors of their long-standing reputation, and will do great harm to your fellow-citizens. For those who do not admire your ancestors will try to imitate Leokrates ...

Lys. ii 69: They (*sc. the Athenians killed in this war*) are enviable alike in life and death, for they were educated amid the benefits owed to their ancestors, and when they grew up they both preserved their ancestors' reputation and demonstrated their own valour.

Cf. Dein. i 111 on 'inherited reputation', and Dem. xvii 23, expressing contempt for little cities which do not have traditions like those of Athens.

---

[10] Cf. E. Topitsch, 'Ἀνθρωπεία Φύσις und Ethik bei Thukydides', *Wiener Studien* lxi/lxii (1943–7) 50–67.

## 2. Individuals

It is a matter of observation that, for whatever reasons, children differ greatly in temperament and capability from a very early age, and it often happens that two given individuals differ from each other at forty in the same ways as they differed at four. This is the kind of difference which the Greeks attributed to 'nature'. For Xenophon's Socrates the evidence of a good 'nature' in a boy was his speed of learning and memorization and his intellectual appetite (Xen. *Mem.* iv 1.2). References to an individual's nature (*physis*) or character (*tropos*) are abundant, concerning (e.g.) his ability in public speaking (Aiskhines i 181), his 'inborn vice' (Dein. iii 18), disposition to mourn (Hyp. vi 41), more or less inclination to talk (Philemon fr. 5), honesty (Men. fr. 532), etc.; cf. Xen. *Oec.* 13.9 on slaves who are by nature eager for praise. The extent to which an individual's behaviour is determined by his innate capacity and disposition—as we differ in outward characteristics which are unalterable (Dem. xx 141, xxxvii 56), since they are imposed by 'fortune' (Dem. lxi 8, 14)—and the extent to which it is determined by the environmental forces which have operated on him, including example, precept and habituation, constitute a problem to which it is customary to give extremely confident answers founded on little evidence and even less intellectual effort. 'Nature is everything' and 'upbringing is everything' seem to be equally available clichés, either of which can be elicited by a single occurrence which seems to fit it.

In our sources the dramatic situation or the requirements of an argument in court often decide whether a speaker pronounces in favour of nature or of nurture.

Dem. xxi 186: If Meidias had been so objectionable and aggressive during his past life through complete inability to humble himself, it would be right to modify one's anger somewhat in consideration of his nature and fortune (*i.e. external circumstances*), through which he became the kind of man he is.

This argument is not consistent with ibid. 149f., cited in section *1*, but consistency is not a notable feature of Greek speakers' attacks on their opponents.

Dem. xxiv 133: It was not acceptable to the city that people should be honest for a time and then thieves, but only that, where the property of the community is concerned, they should invariably be honest. For it was felt that a man of that kind (*sc. honest for a time, then dishonest*) had been honest during the earlier period not by nature, but by evil design, in order to be trusted.

Dem. xxv. 15: All human life . . . is governed by nature and by laws. Of these two, nature is outside our control, and each individual's nature is peculiar to him, but the laws are something shared and prescribed and the same for everyone.

Cf. ibid. 93; Dem. xxxvi 43, 'a good man by nature'.

Lys. xix 60: A man could disguise his own character for a short time, but no one could be a bad man and remain undetected for seventy years.

Eur. fr. 810: Nature, it seems, is what matters most, for no one . . . by giving a good upbringing to what is bad can make it good.

Men. fr. 553: It's not white hairs that make a man sensible; some have an old man's character by nature.

Cf. Eur. Or. 126–31, Elektra's bitter comment on Helen's unchanged nature on which experience has had no effect; Eur. fr. 904, the folly of trying to 'overcome nature'; Hyp. i 15 on the alleged impossibility of becoming an adulterer for the first time at the age of fifty; Men. Dysk. 34–6, Myrrhine quite unlike what one would have expected of a girl of her parentage and upbringing; Men. Epitr. 1084–1101, the gods cannot assign each of us a destiny in detail, so they content themselves with giving each man his own character, and this causes our good or bad fortune (the idea goes back to Herakleitos B119); Men. fr. 538, everyone corrupted by his own peculiar defect, as iron by rust and wood by worm; Soph. fr. 739, 'What nature gives to a man, of that you can never rid him'.

On the other hand—

Dein. ii 3: One may perhaps suppress vice by punishment when it is still beginning, but when it is inveterate and has experienced the usual punishments it is, they say, impossible to suppress.

Cf. Aiskhines iii 260 on education as the means by which 'we distinguish between the honourable and the shameful' (note the use of 'education' and 'uneducated' in Aiskhines i 45, ii 113, iii 117, 208, while in Dem. xx 119 'uneducated' and 'stupid' are treated as synonymous); Antiphon the Sophist B60, implanting education in the young is like planting seeds in soil; Demokritos B33, 'Teaching is similar to nature; it changes the tenor of a man and in so doing determines the way he grows (physiopoiein)'; Eur. Supp. 911–15, manliness is teachable and, once acquired, is retained for life; Eur. fr. 1027 (cf. 1067), the importance of good habituation in youth, for otherwise wrongdoing becomes implanted (emphytos, a word which in some contexts we translate as 'innate') and is carried right through to old age; Xen. Apol. 21, education the greatest good in human life.[11]

[11] This is the central theme of Jaeger's Paideia.

There is also very frequent reference to the combination of both factors.

Aiskhines i 11: The legislator considered that if a boy were well brought up he would be useful to the city when he was a man; but when a bad start is imposed on the nature of the individual by his education, he considered that badly brought up boys would become citizens like Timarkhos.

Aiskhines iii 175: Indictment for cowardice is possible. Some of you may be surprised that a man can be indicted for his nature. But he can. Why? So that every one of us may fear the penalties imposed by the law more than he fears the enemy, and thus may be a better fighter in defence of his fatherland.

Alexis fr. 278b (Edmonds): Most slaves are observably like their masters in their ways; their own nature blends with the characters which they serve all the time.

Dem. lxi 4: Every nature becomes better when it has received the appropriate education, and, above all, those natures which were from the beginning better endowed than others.

Eupolis fr. 91 (*Aristeides speaking*): My nature was the main thing, and I zealously collaborated with my nature.

The distinction drawn here is interesting and at first sight unusual, but it accords with the identification of the self with the process of reasoning (III.F.2).

Eur. *Hec.* 592–602: The bad man is never anything but bad, while the good man is good and does not, through misfortune, lose his nature, but is always good ... And yet there is a teaching of virtue in good upbringing.

Eur. *Iph. Aul.* 558–562: Different are the natures of men, and different their characters; what is truly good is always plain to see. But the education in which one is brought up contributes much to *aretē*.

Cf. Xen. *Mem.* iv 1.3f. on how the best natures need most education, for without it they become exceptionally bad people.

In particular, a person's nature is regarded as a disposition which can be, up to a point, forced or suppressed, for better or worse.

Ar. *Wasps* 1457f.: It's hard for anyone to break free of the nature which he has. Yet it's happened to many; through encountering the opinions of others, they have altered their ways.

Eur. fr. 187.5f.: Gone is one's nature when one is worsted by delicious pleasure.

Cf. Hyp. iii 2, the individual's nature worsted by *erōs* (hard to reconcile with Hyp. i 15, cited above).

Soph. *Phil.* 902f.: It is always grievous (*sc. to the man himself*) when a man deserts his own nature and does what is not appropriate to it.

People who breed animals select for breeding on the principle that good parents are more likely than bad parents to produce good offspring. On this analogy, it might be expected that good human parents will produce the best children, and Greeks sometimes asserted that this was so.[12]

Eur. fr. 166: The folly that was his father's sickness[13] is in him; just so, bad men are wont to spring from bad.

Eur. fr. 333: A good man cannot be begotten by a bad father.

Cf. Eur. frr. 215, 1068. (It should be noted in passing that since these passages are citations of which we do not know the dramatic context, they afford no justification whatever for saying that Euripides 'believed in the inheritance of virtues and vices'; each of the passages may have been uttered by a character whose attitude was not vindicated by events.)

The factors which enter into the making of a human being are very much more numerous than are involved in the breeding of horses and dogs, and it could not remain unobserved that (as remarked in general terms by Orestes in Eur. *El.* 369f. and in a particular case by Pl. Com. fr. 64.2f.) children do not necessarily exhibit the same virtues and vices as are conspicuous in their parents. Since most children are brought up by their parents, it is hardly possible to know, when they grow up into good or bad adults, whether their characters are the product of their genetic inheritance, of parental example and training, or of allocation of character on a purely individual basis by destiny, chance, or some other power which lies outside human control. Only the foundling whose true parentage is subsequently discovered (cf. the story of Meidias, in section 1) can offer valid experimental evidence. The legend of the young Kyros (Hdt. i 114f., cf. Isok. v 66) is founded on the assumption that royal blood will assert itself even in a boy who believes himself to be the son of a poor countryman. A similar belief that a foundling may grow up to exhibit noble tastes out of keeping with his servile environment is exploited by Syriskos in Men. *Epitr.* 320–33, but his appeal to the evidence of legend, not to everyday experience, and his reference to 'hunting lions' suggest that we are meant to see the funny side of his using such an argument.[14] Certain passages of oratory afford evidence

---

[12] Cf. Glotz 579.

[13] It must be remembered that *nosos*, 'sickness', is used in poetry of any unwelcome or disadvantageous condition.

[14] F. H. Sandbach in *Entretiens de la Fondation Hardt* xvi (1969) 125f. draws attention to formal elements which give a colouring of tragedy to this comic passage.

from silence that the inheritance of moral qualities was not treated in fourth-century Athens as an important notion.

Dem. lix 50f.: Phano did not know how to live conformably to Phrastor's character; she hankered after her mother's habits (*ethē*) and the immorality prevailing in her mother's house, for that was the licence in which she had been brought up.

The speaker had an opportunity to moralise over the depravity of Neaira as 'coming out' in her daughter Phano, but he did not take that opportunity. Equally surprising, when we reflect what could have been made of the subject, is the absence of any reference to inherited depravity in Lysias xiv. The speech is an attack on the younger Alkibiades, and bitterly hostile to his father.

Lys. xiv 17: When he was still a boy and it was not yet apparent what sort of man he was going to be, he was very nearly handed over to the executioners because of his father's misdeeds (*sc. sacrilege, incurring extirpation of the family*).

To say of children in general that one does not know how good or bad they will be when they are grown men is a rhetorical commonplace (Is. vii 33, Lys. xx 34); Lys. ii 13 applies it, in telling the myth of the Herakleidai, to the sons of Herakles.

We must remind ourselves at this point that *physis* and its cognates do not necessarily carry an implication of genetic inheritance; they may approximate to our words 'essentially' and 'fundamentally', as when in Soph. *Oed. Col.* 270-2 Oedipus declares that the wholly unintentional nature of his crimes shows that he was not 'bad in nature'; cf. Ar. *Frogs* 700, where the audience is called '*sophos* by nature', and especially *Wealth* 118, where the god Wealth is 'wretched by nature' although in fact his wretchedness was not with him from the beginning but inflicted on him by the malice of Zeus.[15]

Dem. xxi 49 (addressed in imagination to slaves): . . . and although there exists by nature a hereditary (*patrikaos*) enmity between you and the Athenians . . .

Lys. vii 35: It would, I think, be extraordinary if . . . when interrogated about their masters, to whom they (*sc. slaves*) are by nature exceedingly ill-disposed, they preferred to endure (*sc. the interrogation under torture*) rather than denounce them and so be released from their pains.

Lysias can hardly mean that slave-infants are born precociously ill-disposed;

---

[15] Cf. O. Thimme, *ΦΥΣΙΣ ΤΡΟΠΟΣ ΗΘΟΣ: semasiologische Untersuchung über die Auffassung des menschlichen Wesens (Charakters) in der älteren griechischen Literatur* (Diss. Göttingen, 1935) 89–91.

he may mean simply that the hatred of slaves for their masters is part of the order of nature. Demosthenes, I think, means simply that slaves are the enemies of their masters by virtue of being their fathers' sons; an enmity maintained by the sons of enemies (cf. Dem. xxv 32, 30, Lys. xiv 2, 40) is normal, but not a necessary part of the order of things.

Emphasis is firmly placed on upbringing in:

Eur. *Hel.* 941–3: If it is said of a man that he was begotten of a good father and imitates his parent's character, there is no fairer fame that he can win.

Eur. fr. 413: I know how to act as a well-born man should ... for I have been educated in the ways of free men.

That it should be necessary, as apparently it was, to argue against popular opinion in defence of the virtues which may be possessed by illegitimate sons, is irreconcilable with a belief in the primacy of genetic inheritance of qualities from the father; it implies the primacy of familial status.

Eur. fr. 168: The bastard is as good in nature as the legitimate child; the only bad thing about him is the name (*sc. of bastard*).

Men. fr. 248: There is no difference between one *genos* (i.e. '< *circumstances of* > birth') and another ... The good man is legitimate, and the bad man a bastard.[16]

Soph. fr. 84: Everything that is good has the *physis* of legitimacy.

Reference to good or bad parentage by use of words such as *eugenēs*, 'well-born', and *dysgenēs*, 'ill-born', rarely, and perhaps never necessarily, reflects a belief in the inheritance of virtues and vices, for to be *eugenēs* is to belong to a family which has earned respect and honour and therefore (normally) to have been brought up with good examples to emulate[17] (this is true even of an orphan, if he knows who his parents were); Eur. fr. 232, 'The *aretē* of those who are *eugenēs* shows in their children' admits of such an interpretation.

And. ii 26: My present conduct is much more characteristic of me than my earlier conduct, and more in keeping with the tradition of my family ... My great-grand-father Leogoras took up arms on the side of the people against the tyrants ...

When Deinarkhos refers (ii 8) to 'good ancestors', he probably has in mind not their membership of a category of 'noble families' conventionally

[16] *Nothos*, 'bastard', is used in Greek in the metaphorical senses 'spurious', 'counterfeit', but not, as in modern colloquial English, in the sense 'disagreeable person'.

[17] Cf. Jost 240f.; D. Loenen, 'De Nobilitate apud Athenienses', *Mnemosyne* N.S. liv (1926) 206–23; W. Haedicke, *Die Gedanken der Griechen über Familienherkunft und Vererbung* (Halle, 1936).

recognized as such but the relationship to the community manifested in the family's conduct. *Eugeneia* in this sense may be made explicit in characterizations of the 'democratic man'.

Aiskhines iii 169: . . . and secondly, his ancestors should have deserved well of the people in some way, or at the very least there should have been no enmity between them (*sc. and the people*), so that he may not attempt to harm the city as redress for his ancestors' misfortunes.

Cf. Is. v 46, 'Perhaps you think you have an advantage over me because your ancestors killed the tyrants'; Isok. xiv 53, shameful to boast of one's ancestors' achievements and yet be seen to act unlike them. Existence of expressions such as 'good/bad and of good/bad family' (literally, '. . . and from good' or '. . . and from bad': And. i 109, Ar. *Frogs* 731, Dem. xviii 10, *GVI* 1458 [Akarnania]; cf. 'a slave and from slaves', Lys. xiii 64) are equally compatible with emphasis on genetic inheritance and with emphasis on parental status and example. In Eur. *El.* 337f. Elektra is confident that Orestes will get the better of Aigisthos, since he is 'young . . . and of a better father'; cf. Eur. *Iph. Taur.* 609f., Orestes faces death bravely as he is 'born of a *eugenēs* root'; Agamemnon was killed when Orestes was a child, but no one could have been more conscious of his own descent than Orestes.

Apart from passages in which the word *eugenēs* refers (as in Attic law) to the qualifications for certain public offices, adjectives from the stem (-)*gen-* are not so very common in forensic oratory: Aiskhines ii 157 applies *eugenēs* to magnanimous behaviour; one of its putative antonyms, *agennēs*, appears in Aiskhines iii 46 to signify 'mean', 'ungenerous', and in Dem. xxi 152 it is applied to a jury which might be overawed and insufficiently concerned to defend the right; only in Aiskhines ii 149 does *agennēs* imply 'low-class', being applied to the humble trades which Demosthenes had ascribed to Aiskhines' brother Philokhares. Occasionally in drama *eugenēs* means simply 'of distinguished family' (and thus with a prima facie claim to be respected): Eur. fr. 336, 'The good man is *eugenēs* in my eyes, and the dishonest man *dysgenēs*'; Eur. *El.* 551, 'Many who are *eugenēs* are bad'; Eur. *Hel.* 1678f., contrasting the *eugenēs* with the 'numberless' masses; Men. *Heros* fr. 3, '*To kalon* ought to be (*sc. treated as*) that which is most *eugenēs*'; cf. Astydamas fr. 8. Most commonly, however, it is a commendatory term of wide moral application: Eur. *El.* 406f., 'If they are *eugenēs*, they will not mind my humble hospitality'; Eur. *Hel.* 950f., 'They say that a *eugenēs* man may shed a tear in misfortune'; Eur. *Her. Fur.* 658–70, contrasting *dysgeneia* (antonym of eugeneia) with those 'who have some *aretē* in them' and equating the contrast with that between bad and good; Eur. *Tro.* 727, literally, 'Grieve at misfortune *eugenōs*', i.e. 'Bear up ...' (cf. Eur. fr. 98, Men. frr. 181, 633); Soph. fr. 76, 'Concealment is bad, and not for a *eugenēs* man'. Antiphanes fr. 176.1 applies *eugenēs* to a hearty eater, and Plato Comicus fr. 46.6f. *agennēs* to playing for mean stakes. The complimentary term *gennadās* is used of unselfish generosity, magnanimity and helpfulness (Ar. *Frogs* 179, 640, 738ff., 997). *Gennaios* is also an extremely general term, rarely referring to lineage (see, however, Hdt. i 146.2, 'those who regard themselves as the most *gennaois* [i.e. 'authentic'] of the Ionians', and Thuc. ii 97.3, 'those of the Odrysians who exercise power and are *gennaios*'): Ar. *Knights* 787, '*gennaios* and democratic'; Ar. *Peace* 773, 'most *gennaios* of poets' = 'best of poets' (cf. *Frogs* 1031); Eur. *Hel.* 728-30, 1640f., of a good slave; Eur. *Supp.* 1178, 'having undergone *gennaia*' = 'having been treated generously'; Herakleides fr. 2, munificence; Nikophon fr. 16.1, 'Be *gennaios*' = 'Do as I beg of you'; Soph. *Phil.* 1068, apparently 'sympathetic', 'compassionate'; Thuc. iii 83.1, 'simplicity of character, which is especially conspicuous in *to gennaion*'; Xen. *Ages.* 4.5, antonymy of *gennaios* and *adikos*; Xen. *Oec.* 15.12, farming makes men '*gennaios* in character'. Cf. *gennikos* as a synonym of *gennaios* and *andreios*, 'brave', 'bold', 'confident', 'robust', in Ar. *Lys.* 1068f. ∼ *Frogs* 372 ∼ 379, Euboulos fr. 36.

## III.C. SEX

### 1. Segregation

Before attempting to formulate any statement whatsoever on that well-known theme, the Greek view of women, it is advisable to remember that every surviving word of Classical Greek was written by a man.[1] In tragedy and comedy female characters are as numerous as male characters, and no less distinctive and memorable, but they are all the creation of male authors, and whatever they say about sexual differentiation—whether in criticism of traditional assumptions or in defence of them (e.g. Klytaimestra in Eur. *El.* 1035, admitting the 'folly' of women)—is all put into their mouths by those authors. Similarly, forensic oratory reports in narrative or constructs in

---

[1] Some poetry, of which a tiny fraction survives, was written by women, and possibly some extant epitaphs were composed by women, but the proportion of the whole is so small as to be negligible.

hypothetical argument the throughts, feelings and utterances of women, but we do not hear the women's own voices.

The Athenians inherited from previous generations the essential structure of a world in which the adult males of separate tribes fight each other in order to keep what they have and, if possible, get more. When the survival of the community depends on hand-to-hand fighting, women, who are on average smaller and weaker than men and are frequently forced into a comparatively inactive role by pregnancy and suckling, tend to be regarded as possessions, like land or herds.[2] Xen. *Oec.* 3.11 has reservations about their responsibility as moral agents: if, he says, there is a fault in a horse or a sheep, we blame the groom or herdsman, and if there is a fault in a woman, *perhaps* it is right to hold her responsible, but there is no doubt about the responsibility of a man. Even in such a world, there is room for much variation, and we find that the Spartans, whose menfolk were incomparable fighters, allowed women far more freedom of movement and activity than Athens or any other Greek state (Xen. *Lac.* 1.3), though not even Sparta allowed women to participate in the process of deliberation and decision on any issue affecting the community or its sub-divisions. The humorous effect of such plays as Aristophanes' *Ecclesiazusae*, *Lysistrata* and *Thesmophoriazusae* lay very largely in their portrayal of women as effectively imitating the procedures of adult male citizens and reversing the accepted role of men and women, even to the extent of deciding on issues of peace and war; cf. the comparable fantasies of Aristophanes' *Birds* and Kratinos's *Beasts*. Ar. *Lys.* 510–15 makes it sound as if a wife's opinions, even her interested questions, were ill-received by her husband, but the portrayal of the marital relationship in comedy may be as stereotyped as the 'My old man . . .' and 'My old woman . . .' stories of the modern comedian or cartoonist, and unable to do justice to the complexity of things as they really are. The effective influence of women on the life of the community was probably exercised through the influence of the individual wife on her husband, and operated by virtue of his unexpressed shame at appearing foolish in his wife's eyes.[3]

Cf. Eur. *Tro.* 655f. (Andromakhe on her wifely virtues) 'I knew when I should prevail over my husband, and when to allow him to prevail in what it was right that he should'; Hdt. i 37.3, 'What sort of man will my new bride think I am?', as a climax to an expression of humiliation; Lyk. *Leokr.*

---

[2] Plato Comicus fr. 98 refers to a woman as the best of possessions (*ktēmata*) if handled firmly, the worst if allowed too much freedom; but against this we must set (e.g.) Eur. fr. 164, 'A sympathetic wife is the best *ktēma*', and, even more important, the use of the verb *ktāsthai*, 'obtain', 'acquire' in a very wide sense, e.g. 'Acquire friends' (Eur. *Or.* 804).

[3] Cf. Lacey 172–6 and Gomme 89–115.

141 (to the jurors), 'Tell your wives and children on your return from court . . .'; Xen. *Cyr.* vi 4.9, 'Zeus, grant that I may be seen to be a worthy husband of Pantheia' (who had demonstrated her own steadfastness) 'and a worthy friend of Kyros!'

The historical reasons for the unusual extent to which the Athenians had come to regard women as objects are a matter for speculation, and irrelevant to the period with which our present enquiry is concerned, a period in which inherited definitions of the respective roles and functions of men and women seem to have been very widely and firmly accepted.[4] Men fought and worked, and men and boys took exercise, while women and girls stayed at home. To call a wife 'industrious and economical' was high praise (e.g. *GVI* 328), but the exertion required of her was not regarded as comparable with what was expected of a man. The women in Ar. *Eccl.* 109, aghast at being told that the safety of Athens depends on them, exclaim, 'But we can't run or row!' Men, says Xen. *Oec.* 7.22, are better able than women to endure the rigours of an outdoor life; cf. the rhetorical indignation of Oedipus in Soph. *Oed. Col.* 337–45 that his sons should stay at home in Thebes while his own survival in exile is the concern of his daughters. Xen. *Oec.* 7.5 alludes to the extreme restrictions on a girl's life and her consequent lack of acquaintance with the world outside; Deianeira in Soph. *Trach.* 144–150 speaks of having been brought up in a life 'freed, by enjoyment, from toil'.

Dramatists were well aware of ways in which a woman could hit back: 'I would rather stand three times in a battle-line than give birth once', says Medeia (Eur. *Med.* 250f.) in the course of a famous speech on the injustice inflicted by society on women, and Klytaimestra, filled with hatred against Agamemnon for his sacrifice of their daughter, observes (Soph. *El.* 532f.) that begetting a daughter is not as painful as bearing her. The pompous sentiment that 'War is no concern of women' (Ar. *Lys.* 626f.) does not impress Lysistrata, for it kills off the sons whom they bore and nourished.

When a girl was given in marriage by her father (or, if he was dead, by the male relative who was legally entitled to dispose of her), a dowry went with her, and ultimately through her to her children; it seems to have been assumed (Dem. lix 8) that, however attractive she was, the dowry was no less so, and Xen. *Hiero* 1.27 seems to suggest that in seeking a bride a man attached primary importance to the wealth and status of her father.[5] Since

[4] On the evidence of comedy, together with evidence drawn from fourth-century prose literature, see Ehrenberg 192–207.

[5] Cf. Lacey 106–9, 162f., on choice of bride. There are some singular marriages in tragic legend, notably Orestes' agreement to marry Hermione (Eur. *Or.* 1672f.), whom he was on the point of murdering in order to spite her father.

there was no effective contraception, and a belief that whatever qualities a son inherits are inherited solely from his father may have prevailed,[6] it was important for a man to ensure that his daughter could not have intercourse with anyone but the man whom he chose as her husband. The best way to ensure this was strict segregation of the sexes; therefore boys and girls were not allowed to mix after an early age, and when a girl married, her husband continued to isolate her, as far as was practicable, from male company.[7]

Lys. iii 6: He came to my house at night, drunk, knocked down the door, and burst into the women's quarters, where my sister and nieces were, ladies who have lived so respectably that they are embarrassed at being seen even by members of the family.

The sentiment that a respectable woman or girl stays indoors is a commonplace in tragedy and comedy, e.g. Eur. Or. 108, Eur. fr. 521, Men. fr. 592. A man's sons could be invited with him to a party, but his womenfolk were not necessarily included in the invitation (Ar. Birds 130–4, Lys. 1060f., cf. Peace 1265–7); the fact of a woman's presence at a men's party could be used as evidence that she was a hetaira (Is. iii 14). Shopping was a man's job, as is clear from Ar. Eccl. 817–22, Wasps 493–9, Theokritos 15.15–20.

Yet below a certain point in the social scale, in families which owned few or no slaves, it simply cannot have been practicable to segregate the women-folk. They would have to go on errands, work in the fields, or sell in the market-place; the bread-woman of Ar. Wasps 1396–8 is unquestionably of citizen status.[8] Whatever the effects of segregation were on patterns of sexual behaviour, attitudes towards women, or beliefs about the moral capacity and responsibility of women, they must have varied between social classes; see further IV.E.3.

## 2. Male and Female Characteristics

Among the characteristics explicitly or implicitly attributed to women in Greek literature it is possible to discern some which were the consequences

---

[6] This view is expressed in Aiskh. Eum. 655; how widely held it was, we do not know.

[7] Perikles' exhortation to women in Thuc. ii 45.4, 'not to be worse than their natures' needs to be compared, for its formal expression, with Arkhidamos's exhortation to his troops in Thuc. ii 11.2 'not to appear worse than your fathers'; cf. III.F.1 n. 7 Perikles' notion (ibid.) that the ideal of feminine virtue was 'to be least spoken of, for good or ill, among men', was not shared by the composers of epitaphs on women or (one presumes) by the families which commissioned the epitaphs.

[8] Cf. Lacey 170f.

of segregation (and even perhaps recognized as such), some which contributed to a rationalization of segregation, and others which fall within both categories. But it is usually up to us to decide, for Athenian writers themselves are normally content to speak as if the different roles of man and woman in their own society were dictated by nature. The sentiment of Agathon fr. 14, that enforced physical idleness makes a woman's intelligence more active, may have been uttered by a female character propounding an idea and preparing the ground for its acceptance. The idea that women are corrupted by the talk of other women (Eur. *Andr.* 943–53) is little more than an example of anti-female moralizing, such as comedy too exploits in all ages (cf. Alexis fr. 302, 'No animal more shameless'; Euboulos fr. 117. 8–15, where a speaker can think of notorious bad women of the past, but runs out of ideas when he tries to think of virtuous women to set against them).

The weakness of women was regarded as manifest not only in their physique but also in inferior intelligence. In Xen. *Smp.* 2.9 a clever girl juggler elicits from a spectator the remark that 'Woman's nature is just as good as man's, though it is deficient in mind (*gnōmē*) and strength', implying that up to a certain point, but not beyond, a woman can be taught to do what a man does (in Eur. *Hel.* 1686f. Helen's 'most noble *gnōmē*, which is not to be found in many women', is rather her steadfast spirit than her intellectual ability). Theseus in Eur. *Supp.* 293f., permits his mother to make a suggestion, since 'Much that is *sophos* comes from the female sex, too'; cf. Eur. *Hel.* 1049 (Helen speaking), '. . . if a woman, too, makes an intelligent proposal'; Eur. *Or.* 1204f., Orestes praises the 'male mind' of Elektra when she thinks of the idea of seizing Hermione as a hostage. Eur. *Iph. Taur.* 1032, 'Women are remarkably fertile in invention' (literally, '. . . formidable to find techniques'), may be influenced by mistrust of women's artfulness (see below).

There is some indication that women were regarded as more credulous and superstitious than men. It takes a lot to convince the chorus in Aiskhylos's *Agamemnon* that Klytaimestra has firm grounds for asserting that Troy is captured (274–7), and they easily revert to the suspicion that a woman's mind 'has no defences' against wild rumour (483–7).[9] In Menander's *Dyskolos* Getas grumbles about the propensity of his mistress to sacrifice to Pan whenever she has had a frightening dream (407–18), and we have the impression that the menfolk of the family take a more philosophical view of dreams. In Aristophanes' *Wealth*, when Khremylos and Karion return from

[9] I interpret the words as, literally, 'Too credulous, the female boundary is encroached upon, quickly passed through'; but the interpretation is controversial.

Epidauros with Wealth healed of his blindness, Karion comes on ahead to tell the story of his wondrous night in the sanctuary to his master's wife, who seems duly impressed (641–748). The element common to all that was said of women by the Greeks is the woman's inability to resist fear, desire, or impulse. A woman, in fact, was thought to have a 'butterfly mind', equally incapable of intelligent, far-sighted deliberation and of foregoing the emotional reaction of the moment in pursuit of distant and impersonal aims (Ar. *Lys.* 1–3, 13–15, 23–5, 137–9, 706–26); and she was a chatterbox (Ar. *Eccl.* 120).

Aiskhylos in *Seven against Thebes* depicts the women of Thebes as prey to panic and despair at the approach of a hostile army, as if defeat and capture were a foregone conclusion. The exceptions to this general picture, the great heroines of legend, prove the rule; in Soph. *El.* 997f. Khrysothemis speaks for ordinary women in declaring to Elektra the impossibility of effective action by the two of them against their father's murderers.

Lys. ii 4: They (*sc. the Amazons*) were looked upon as men, because of their valour, rather than as women, because of their (*sc. bodily*) nature, for they were thought to transcend men in soul more than they fell short of them in appearance.

Cf. Eur. *Hel.* 808, 'unmanly' for Menelaos to save himself by deserting Helen; Eur. *Or.* 786, ignominious death is 'unmanly'. A woman's weakness compels her to act, when she acts in hostility, by guile or poison—means by definition 'unmanly' (Eur. fr. 288)—avoiding a direct trial of strength; cf. Ar. *Eccl.* 238, *Lys.* 12, *Thesm.* 290, on the deceitful tricks of women; Men. frr. 583, 585, 586, 591, their unreliability, untruthfulness, and skill in cajolery. Because a women is weak, she cannot afford to be magnanimous, and least of all in her struggle to retain her value as a sexual object.

Eur. *Med.* 263–66: In all other things a woman is full of fear, and flinches from the sight of battle and weapons; but when she is injured in her love for a man (*literally*, '*wronged in her bed*'), there is no heart more murderous than hers.

Alexis fr. 146.7f.: We men forgive when we are wronged, but women do wrong and then make accusations into the bargain!

Cf. Demokritos B273, 'prompt to devise evil'; Eur. *Andr.* 911f., *Ion* 843–6, on a woman's vindictive jealousy; Eur. *Phoen.* 198–201, malicious gossip; Men. *Epitr.* 564f., the folly of expecting gratitude from a woman.

On the assumption that women lack courage, the chorus in Soph. *Trach.* 898 find it surprising that Deianeira should have dared to kill herself to escape grief and dishonour; cf. Men. fr. 776, a woman's procrastination over suicide, cited by the scholiast on Eur. *Phoen.* 61 to explain why Iokaste (in Euripides' treatment of the legend) lived on after the revelation that she had married her son. In fact, however, the suicide of heroines is commonplace in legend and frequent in Attic tragedy; and cf. Lys. fr. 22, cited in III.F.2.

While it is the part of a man to endure misfortune bravely (Antiphanes fr. 278), women grieve, complain and weep readily: Alexis fr. 146. 10f., 'When there's nothing the matter with them at all, they always say they're sick'; Eur. *Andr.* 93–5, the natural inclination of a woman to express her grief and not contain it within herself; Eur. *Hel.* 991f.; Eur. *Med.* 909, unrestrained anger; ibid. 928, tearfulness; Eur. *Or.* 1022, reproof of Elektra for her 'womanish lamentations'; Soph. *Trach.* 1071–5, Herakles, forced by terrible pain to 'weep like a girl', thus becomes 'female'. In Eur. *Erechtheus* fr. 53 (Austin) 33f. Erechtheus is ashamed to take too fond a farewell of his son, (literally) 'for a woman-hearted spirit is not of a *sophos* man'. On the inability to restrain anger, cf. Aiskhines ii 179 on the 'unmanly and womanish temper' of Demosthenes.

Susceptibility to pity and sympathy is, to our way of thinking, the positive aspect of weakness in resisting the assaults of emotional forces:

Soph. *Ajax* 650–52: For even I, who endured such perils in the past . . . am womanised in tongue, and pity her.

Cf. ibid. 580; Eur. *Her. Fur.* 536 (Megara apologizing to Amphitryon); Eur. *Iph. Taur.* 1054, 'A woman has the capacity to feel pity'.

By contrast with curious beliefs widely propagated in the English-speaking world during the last hundred years or so (conditioned by the presupposition that absence of sexual response is morally praiseworthy), the Greeks were inclined to think that women desired and enjoyed sexual intercourse more than men.[10] Andromakhe in Eur. *Tro.* 665f., refers to a belief ('they say . . .') that one night in bed dissolves a woman's hostility to the man into whose possession she has come; cf. Eur. fr. 323, by bodily contact above all a man 'acquires a woman's soul'.

Anaxandrides fr. 60: To be a slave of pleasure is the behaviour of a licentious woman, not of a man.

Eur. *Hipp.* 967–70: I know young men who are no better than women in defending themselves against the assaults of Aphrodite upon the heart of youth; but they are male, and that helps them.

[10] Hesiod fr. 275 relates a myth in which Teiresias (since he had been both man and woman) was asked by Zeus and Hera to say which sex got more pleasure from intercourse, and his answer was that the woman got nine-tenths, the man one-tenth. The existence of an expression ('white mouse', Philemon fr. 126) for a woman who squeaked and gasped a lot during intercourse may indicate that silent enjoyment was common, but silence is relative.

Isok. x 60: We honour beauty so much that we forgive our own wives when they are overcome by it.

Jason by turns reproaches Medeia and patronizingly excuses her by saying that the bed is the focus of a woman's life (Eur. *Med.* 569–75)—but not if she is *sōphrōn* (1369). Demeas in Menander *Samia* 349f., trying to steel himself to discard his concubine, whom he believes to have been unfaithful to him, says to himself, 'Now you must be a *man*, fall out of love!'

Because of the general contrast between male strength and female weakness, 'be a man' often sufficed as a complimentary or exhortatory expression:[11] Eur. fr. 788.2f., 'We honour them and think them men'; Hdt. iii 134.2, '... that the Persians may learn that they are ruled by a man'; Hdt. viii 88.3 (Xerxes, on seeing the daring of Artemisia at Salamis), 'My men have become women and my women men'; Xen. *Anab.* vii 1.21, 'Now, Xenophon, you have the opportunity to be a man'; Xen. *Hell.* vii 1.24, 'The Arkadians praised Lykomedes to the skies, and thought him alone a man'.[12]

The idea of manliness lent itself to abuse. Menon (Xen. *Anab.* ii 6.25) treated god-fearing and truthful people as 'unmanly'; cf. Euboulos fr. 12, 'We Boeotians are manly (*andrikos*) at eating and drinking and holding out to the end (*sc. at a big meal*)', and IV.C.1.

## III.D.  AGE

### 1. Young and Old

The Athenians viewed progress from infancy to late middle age as a continuous development of rationality. 'Mindless' (*aphrōn*, Hyp. vi 28) at birth, a young man was enrolled at the age of 18 in his father's deme, being by then regarded as beginning to 'have sense' (*phronein*), 'know the law' and 'be capable of telling right from wrong' (Aiskhines i 18, 39, 139; cf. Is. ix 20, Men. fr. 552f.), and thus as a responsible moral agent.[1]

Xen. *Mem.* ii 1.21: ... the age of maturity, at which the young show whether they are going to tread the path of virtue or of vice.

[11] The 'oligarchic man' in Theophr. *Char.* 26.2 grumbles, 'One is enough, but he must be a *man*!'

[12] There is a neat adaptation of this usage in Ar. *Lys.* 124f.: when the Spartan woman finally agrees that a sex-strike to secure peace is worth trying, Lysistrata compliments her as 'the only *woman* among the lot of you!'

[1] Arist. *Eth. Nic.* 1095a2–8 considers the young and the young in heart unfitted, by reason of inexperience and susceptibility to powerful emotion (incompatible with a rational assessment of practical possibilities), to study political theory.

The growing competence of reason in the light of continuously increasing experience seems to be the only feature of moral significance regarded as common to boys and girls, and whatever is said of the young in the rest of this section refers only to young males. The forties are called by Aiskhines i 11, 'the most *sōphrōn* age'; everyone was aware that the ultimate condition of a man who lives long enough may be the moral and intellectual degeneration of senility.

The characteristic behaviour of young manhood was compounded of extravagance, pugnacity, thoughtlessness, drunkenness and sexual excess.

Aiskhines i 24: The legislator was well aware that older men are at their prime in intelligence (*eu phronein*), and audacity (*tolma*) is beginning to desert them because of their practical experience.

Alexis fr. 45: Man and wine are really most alike in their natures. Young wine and a young man have to start by fermenting and working off their violence (*aphybrisai*) ... but when they've gone past all that and had the nonsense (*anoia*) that comes to the surface drawn off, then ... they settle down, and after that they stay agreeable (*hēdys*) to everyone.

Ant. iv γ.2: Young men are much more likely than older men to pick a quarrel and misbehave when drunk. Pride in their youth,[2] their good physical condition and inexperience of drink all incite them to act as their spirit bids them; but older men are chastened by their experience of drunken behaviour, the weakness of old age and the threat offered by the capability of the young.

Cf. Dem. xxv 88, in sensible families the young men try not to obtrude and the old men pretend not to see what in fact they see very well; Dem. liv 14, fights over hetairai normal among young men; ibid. 21; Eur. fr. 149, 'Youth incited me, and boldness which got the better of my sense'; Lys. xx 3; Lys. xxiv 17, *hybris* forgivable in the young but not in their elders; Men. *Perik.* 142f., perhaps implying that youth is characteristically interested in drink and sex; Men. fr. 53, youth in love 'deaf to admonition'; Mnesimakhos fr. 4.18f. *Neānikos*, 'characteristic of youth', and its verb *neānikeuesthai* were sometimes used of 'bold' or 'spirited' action, in a good sense (e.g. Dem. iii 32), but often of violent and outrageous behaviour reckless of the feelings of others: Dem. xix 194, xxi 18, 201, Hyp. iv 27, Isok. xx 17. Amphis fr. 33.9f. joins *neānikos* with *thermos*, 'hot' (metaphorically, 'reckless', 'headstrong').[3]

[2] The text says, literally, 'great-mindedness of their *genos*', which in other contexts would most naturally mean 'pride in their family'; but since the reference is to the young as a whole, whether of distinguished or undistinguished family, I adopt the interpretation of *genos* here as 'generation', 'age-class', 'age-group'.

[3] On the denotation of *neānikos* (with some remarks also on *gennaios*: cf. III.B.2) see

The 'innocence' of childhood was not an Athenian concept, since they did not dissociate morality from reasoning and experience (cf. III.F.*1*), nor did they admire simple and childlike faith. They were, of course, aware that 'naturally' good children could be corrupted by bad adult influence (e.g. Men. *Dysk.* 385ff.), and they accepted the innocence of childhood in the ordinary sense that they did not treat children as blameworthy for doing what would be blamed in an older person, who should know better. A striking story of a child's salutary ability to see an issue in simple terms is told in Hdt. v 51.2, where Kleomenes' small daughter warns him against being beguiled by the promises of Aristagoras, but is it not clear whether Herodotos means us to think that the child was genuinely perceptive or that she hit by accident on a reaction which Kleomenes took virtually as a *klēdōn*, a chance utterance of the kind which a wise man treats as an omen. The generosity of youth (not childhood), a warmth of response not blunted by weariness or cynicism, is invoked by the speaker of Dem. liii 12f. to explain why he had readily impoverished himself to help a friend whose guile he did not suspect. Cf. Hdt. v 19.1, the precipitate anger of Macedonian king's son against the Persians' treatment of Macedonian women, because he was 'young and without experience of evils'.[4]

It may seem striking today that no Greek seems to have been acquainted with the phenomena which we classify under 'youthful idealism'. Gifted young men enjoyed pulling accepted ideas to pieces, an aptitude satirized in Ar. *Clouds* 1171–1213 and 1321–1475, and illustrated by an anecdote (Xen. *Mem.* i 2.40–6) about the young Alkibiades catching out his guardian Perikles in an argument on the nature of law: 'That's just how we used to talk,' exclaims Perikles, 'when I was young!' The mood of this criticism, however, was jaunty and brutally self-confident; the young were not worried by the state of the world or concerned to create a juster society than their parents had done, but excited by the process of intellectual discovery. Isok. xii 26 regards geometry, astronomy and eristic as pursuits in which younger men delight—and a good thing too, thinks Isokrates; it keeps them out of mischief—but which older men would find impossibly tedious and pointless.

It was taken for granted throughout antiquity that young men enjoy and promote war, while old men enjoy and promote peace. 'Sweet is war to the inexperienced', said Pindar (fr. 110); cf. Eur. *Supp.* 232–7, the young have a

G. Björck, 'Das Tragikomische und das Wort νεανικός' in *EPMHNEIA* (*Festchrift Regenbogen*) Heidelberg, 1952) 66–70.

[4] Arist. *Rhet.* 1389ᵇ18–22 represents the old as cynical and suspicious through long experience; 'they "think", but do not "know", and always add "perhaps" and "maybe" '.

reckless desire for war because of the opportunities for honour and gain, and so will fight a war without right on their side (cf. ibid. 160); Soph. *Oed. Col.* 1229–35, on the strife, war and murders arising from the 'light-headed witlessness' of youth; Thuc. i 80.1, the cautionary words of Arkhidamos; ii 8.1, the numerous young men in the population of the Greek states in 432/1 were enthusiastic for war, through inexperience of it; ii 21.2, the younger men at Athens were particularly insistent on a battle against the Peloponnesian invaders; vi 13.1, Nikias assumes that the younger men rather than the older are in favour of the attack on Sicily. Much Greek literature is the work of young men, and there is no reason to suppose any systematic distortion of the facts in this uniform picture of the bellicosity of the young.[5] The strength and agility of the young makes them better at fighting than their elders, and people tend to do most what they do best; moreover, the young can make better use of the opportunities for rape afforded by war, their extravagance and generosity make them glad of loot, they are more strongly excited by praise and cast down by taunts, and their high spirits and optimism play down the risks. Cf. Eur. *Iph. Taur.* 122, 'There is no toil which the young can refuse on any pretext'; Eur. *Phoen.* 994f. (Makareus speaking), 'It is pardonable for my father (*sc. to try to save my life*), for he is an old man, but in me it is not pardonable (*sc. to put my own life above posthumous honour*)'.

Young and old today regard each other as intolerant and censorious (which perhaps means that they tolerate different things), and the old in particular regard 'youthful intolerance' as a facet of 'youthful idealism'. The Greeks regarded the young as more tolerant and forgiving than the old, despite their readier recourse to violence when drunk. The heartless jurors of Aristophanes' *Wasps* are old men, who behave as if revenging themselves on society for their own impotence, and the chorus in Ar. *Peace* 348–52 sing that if peace comes they will no longer be ill-tempered jurors or 'hard in character' but 'tender (*hapalos*) and younger by far', an association of physical suppleness with sensibility.

Eur. *Ba.* 1251f. (*Agaue complaining of Kadmos's lack of enthusiasm*): How ill-tempered (*dyskolos*) old age always is, and frowning in face!

Men. fr. 608: How delightful is a father who is young in character!

Cf. Philetairos fr. 6, on the censoriousness of the old towards sexual

---

[5] In 1938, at the time of the German threat to Czechoslovakia, it was (as I recall) notably students and young people in Britain who wanted to resist Germany even at the cost of war, regarding Chamberlain and his middle-aged or elderly colleagues as hopelessly craven and pacific, and the older generation which preferred the capitulation thinly disguised as the Munich agreement.

behaviour. Perikles in Thuc. ii 44.6, offering consolation to bereaved parents, asserts that honour matters to the old more than material gain; he makes it plain that he is denying what is customarily believed.

## 2. The Example of the Past

What the Greeks thought about their ancestors may not seem at first sight to have any bearing on the ways in which the individual's moral capacity was thought to be limited or affected by circumstances outside his control, but it is relevant in two ways. If we are better than our ancestors, our moral starting-line, as it were, is higher, and we can be blamed, as 'knowing better', or as having more favourable opportunities, for committing misdeeds which were commonplace in their time, whereas, if we are worse than our ancestors, less is expected of us. Secondly, if the process of improvement or deterioration is regarded as continuous, the characteristics of our ancestors will be attributed in some measure to the oldest people alive in our own time.

The Greeks of the classical period considered that mankind had originally progressed from a primitive and bestial condition by the continuous acquisition (through the beneficence of gods or the inventiveness of individual humans) of arts, techniques and laws. Athenians of the fifth century were aware that at least in the arts (notably drama, sculpture and painting) the work of their time attained a higher level of refinement and complexity than appeared to have been attained a hundred years earlier. Some people will also have been aware of the technical advances made in such diverse fields as logic, historiography, the natural sciences and rhetoric. The Corinthian speaker in Thuc. i 71.3, criticizing the Spartans' 'old-fashioned ways' as incapable of dealing with the threat posed by Athenian expansion, remarks, 'The latest developments, as in the case of a technique, must necessarily prevail'.

These are circumstances in which a 'generation gap' tends to appear. When there is no change, every word of advice that a grandfather can give his grandson is of obvious utility; when the rate of change is very great, the grandson has to cope with an environment of which his grandfather had no experience at a comparable age, and nothing that the old man can say seems relevant.[6] By our standards, the rate of change in Athenian culture between

[6] Similarly, people who have passed their childhood and adolescence in a period of inflation will have an attitude to earning, spending and saving totally different from that of those who grew up in a deflationary period.

600 and 300 B.C. was very slow, but it was considerable by the standards of some other ancient cultures, and in the latter part of the fifth century it seemed fast enough to the people experiencing it to cause some of them to use the word *arkhaios*, 'old', 'original', in a contemptuous sense, 'old-fashioned', 'ignorant', 'crude'. In Ar. *Clouds* this usage (e.g. 915, 1357) is characteristic of the sophistic education which is the subject of the play (cf. Eupolis fr. 139).[7]

This tendency was, however, offset by an absence of general agreement that technical progress had been matched by moral progress. Thucydides saw the history of Greece in terms of a gradual diminution of turmoil, robbery and piracy and a corresponding growth in the kind of civilization which is the product of settled conditions,[8] but with most people the idea of a 'golden age' in the remote past may have been much more influential; Hesiod, after all, had described the history of humanity (*Op.* 109–201) in terms of continuous moral degeneration, and no internal contradiction was involved in accepting the Hesiodic picture in essentials and combining it with a belief that in the extremely remote past, before the 'golden age', mankind had been raised from bestial to human conditions by technical inventions.[9] In the case of Athens, the attitude to moral progress or degeneration was complicated by some special factors. The Athenians were highly conscious of the supreme achievements of Athens in 490, when she defeated a Persian invasion of Attica, and in 480, when she made the decisive contribution to the defeat of Xerxes' attempt to subjugate Greece. Old men in comedy were still portrayed as 'the fighters of Marathon' at a time when none of those who had actually fought at Marathon could have been alive. The debates of Right and Wrong and of Pheidippides and Strepsiades in Ar. *Clouds* 889–1104, 1321–1452 respectively and the debate of Aiskhylos with Euripides in Ar. *Frogs* 905–1098, three debates in which some constant motifs in the area 'old vs. new' are discernible, suffice to show that the comparison of contemporary Athenian civilization with what had preceded it was a real issue. Comic characters and comic choruses in general align themselves on the side of the alleged honesty and discipline of the old days against the alleged effeminacy and dishonesty of the young; a call for a

---

[7] In Lys. xxviii 5 the word is derogatory in a different way, referring to the 'bad old days' of false denunciations; the defendant is looking back probably some twenty or thirty years.

[8] Cf. J. de Romilly, 'Thucydide et l'idée de progrès', *Annali della Scuola Normale Superiore di Pisa (Lettere, Storia e Filologia)* xxxv (1966) 143–91.

[9] Cf. Edelstein 1–56 and P. Joos, *ΤΥΧΗ ΦΥΣΙΣ ΤΕΧΝΗ: Studien der Thematik frühgriechischer Lebensbetrachtung* (Winterthur, 1955).

reversion to 'how things used to be' (e.g. Ar. *Eccl.* 214–28) could always reckon on awakening a favourable response. We might expect this response to be particularly strengthened by disappointments and setbacks during the first part of the Peloponnesian War and the really threatening defeats and losses of its last ten years. The war ended with the total defeat and humiliation of Athens and with the loss of the empire upon which her wealth had so greatly depended. We must always reckon with an undercurrent of regret and nostalgia in the utterances of Athenians in the fourth century; they knew that the empire had been created by the generation before Perikles and lost by the generation after him. Whatever else they had to be proud of, there was no escaping the brutal fact that Athens had once dominated half the Greek world, and did so no more.[10]

In those circumstances, it is not surprising that the orators make some use of the theme of ancestral virtue:[11] cf. Aiskhines iii 192f., etc., cited in I.E.*1*; Dem. iii 30f., cited in I.E.*2*; and Dem. ix 36, cited in III.F.*1*. They do not, however suggest (with the possible exception of Dem. ix 36, a melancholy passage) that the spirit of the old days has necessarily gone for good and cannot be recovered; they are inclined rather to exhort on the presumption that, however late the hour, however great the gap, ancestral virtue *can* be imitated if only people will pull themselves together.[12] Aiskhines iii 178–87 makes extensive use of his picture of the past in order to contrast the conduct of Demosthenes with it. Demosthenes retorts (xviii 317), in terms in which some of his own hearers must often have wished to retort to him, that in all ages people have been inclined to think poorly of their contemporaries' standards of achievement and have lauded their ancestors.[13]

[10] Cf. Jost 191 on the importance of the fifth century for Demosthenes' view of ancestral virtue. Edelstein 57–132 discusses the disillusionment of the fourth century (131f., 'licentiousness prevailed', but what conceivable grounds have we for supposing that the contemporaries of Demosthenes were more 'licentious' than the men who repelled the Persians?). It is important to remember that this 'disillusionment' is above all an Athenian phenomenon, and that it was caused by loss of power and wealth; no doubt the Spartans too felt that an era had ended for them when they were defeated by Thebes in a battle on land, but (as Polybios xviii 14 observes), there were many small Greek states which considered that they enjoyed greater freedom under Macedonian hegemony than when they were dominated by one or other of their powerful Greek neighbours.

[11] Cf. Jost 212–15 on the artificial elements in Demosthenes' picture of the past and his lack of concern for what the past was really like.

[12] Cf. Jost 226–31.

[13] Cf. Jost 216.

## III.E. STATUS

*1. Wealth and Poverty*

Confronted with a choice between hunger and crime, a man will be tempted to crime; the Greeks used the words 'compel' (*anankazein*) and 'compulsion' (*anankē*) in speaking of this temptation.

Isok. xvii 18: He covered his face and wept and declared that he had been compelled through destitution to deny (*sc. the misappropriation*), but would try to repay the money within a short time.

Lys. vii 13f.: Anyone who commits such an act does so for the sake of gain, not as *hybris* . . . But my opponent cannot show that I was compelled by poverty to commit such an offence, nor that my land was suffering any ill-effects . . .

Cf. Aiskhines i 88, certain jurors took bribes because 'the unhappy creatures could not combat old age and poverty in combination'; Ar. *Eccl.* 604ff., Praxagora's exposition of how complete community of ownership will remove the motives for crime; Dem. xxi 182, a certain Pyrrhos was executed for serving on a jury when disenfranchised, though he did it 'through want, not *hybris*'; Dem. xxiv 123, a man who illegally draws a salary in two capacities does so 'through poverty'; Dem. xxix 22, including *aporiā*, 'lack of means', as a motive for perjury; Hdt. i 138.1, the Persians have a horror of debt because a debtor is subject to exceptionally strong temptation to lie. Theramenes in Xen. *Hell.* ii 3.48f., is portrayed as treating poverty (he speaks from an anti-democratic standpoint) as a motive for disloyalty ('men who, through destitution, would sell the city for a drachma'). Equally, poverty may drive a man to conduct which, although not necessarily criminal or dishonest, is shameful on some grounds or other (including the grounds discussed in I.F.*3* and IV.B.*1*).

Dem. iii 34: And when he stays at home, he is a better man, freed from the commission of any shameful act under the compulsion of want.

Dem. xxiii 148: Needs which must be met take away a man's rational consideration (*logismos*) of what he should or should not do.

Men. fr. 631: I know that many have become bad through misfortune, though not such by nature.

Cf. Aiskhines i 74, male prostitutes driven to that way of life 'by necessity' show a proper shame; Antiphanes fr. 232b, 'If a rich man behaves shamefully, what would he do if he were poor?'; Antiphanes fr. 294, poverty the 'teacher

of one's character'; Lys. xxxi 11, on forgiveness for those forced into involuntary wrongdoing by poverty or disability; Timokles fr. 4.6, 'They
were poor, so I forgive them'; Xen. *Mem.* iv 2.38, 'I know of some tyrants
who are compelled to do wrong through need (*sc. of what they desire*), like
the most destitute men'; [Xen.] *Ath.* 1.5. The poor man, abject and desperate
by turns, afraid to take a chance (Men. fr. 8) and yet compelled by need to do
so, and at the same time resentful and vindictive (Men. *Dysk.* 296–8), is the
anti-thesis of the self-sufficient, self-reliant character which was admired,
the character of a man who can choose and can afford to forgive.

The recognition that a poor man can nevertheless transcend his limitations
found expression in late fifth-century tragedy, notably in the famous gnomic
speech of Orestes in Eur. *El.* 367–400, which combines the traditional view
that poverty is 'a disease which teaches evil through need' (375f.) with a
puzzled acknowledgement that this is not always or necessarily so: 362,
Elektra's farmer husband is poor but his character is 'not ill-born'; 372, 'a
great heart in an impoverished body'; 394f., 'better a poor host than a rich
one, if he be zealous'. Cf. also Eur. fr. 527, on the birth of an upstanding
(*kalos*)[1] son to poor parents; Soph. fr. 752, on beggars who are morally
upright (*kalōs phronein*). The complementary acknowledgement that bad
man can become wealthy is made in Eur. frr. 20, 95; Men. fr. 84; cf. IV.B.1.
Wealth was called 'blind', as a way of saying that there is no correlation
between possessions and merit.

A conventional contrast between the divergent pressures exerted by
poverty and by wealth[2] is found (where we should expect to find it) in
Aristophanes' *Wealth*.

Ar. *Wealth* 563f.: POVERTY Now I'll go on to speak of good morals (*sōphrosynē*) and
explain to you how orderly behaviour (*kosmiotēs*) dwells with me, but it is characteristic
of wealth to be hybristic. KHREMES (*sarcastically*): Oh yes, it's very well-behaved
(*kosmios*) to steal and burgle!

The besetting sin of the rich was thought to be *hybris*: Dem. xxi 182, Lys. vii
13f. (cited above), where 'need' and '*hybris*' are contrasted motivations; Hdt.
iii 80.3, on the effect of autocratic power; Thuc. iii 45.4 (cf. i 38.6, 84.2),
poverty implants daring through necessity, but high status engenders greed
through *hybris* and pride; Xen. *Cyr.* viii 4.14, the good things of life implant
*hybris* but the bad things *sōphrosynē*. Money was power, the power to buy

---

[1] Possibly simply 'handsome', but I suspect that Euripides means here what a prose
author (cf. Hdt. i 30.4) would have expressed by *kalos kāgathos*.

[2] On the different characteristic temptations of wealth and poverty cf. Bolkestein
187–90.

flattery and support and to bribe witnesses; cf. IV.B.*2* and V.B.*2* on generous expenditure in the pursuit of honour and gratitude.

Dem. xxi 98: But you will find that Meidias's wealth is pretty well the cause of his *hybris*, so that it is more appropriate to deprive him of the resources on which his *hybris* is founded than to acquit him because of them.

ibid. 205: It looks as if excessive good fortune sometimes makes people objectionable.

Cf. Dem. xliv 28, implying that a rich defendant has a great advantage over a poor prosecutor. Like the appetites and passions, wealth can in itself distort an otherwise virtuous character (Men. fr. 616) and replace a sense of shame by over-confidence (Men. fr. 274). Hence there was even a positive advantage in modest means (Men. fr. 401), especially given the propensity of Fortune or the gods to cast down the mighty (cf. III.A.*2*, IV.B.*1*, V.E.*2*.)

A wealthy man was vulnerable to an imputation of *aiskhrokerdeia*, seeking profit or gain in ways, or from sources, which for one reason or another were open to disapproval and reproach.

Dem. xlv 37: There is justification for anger against those who are bad (*poneros*) in prosperity rather than bad in needy circumstances; for the necessity of providing for themselves earns the latter some indulgence on the part of those who reckon in human terms, while those who are bad when wealthy have no justification to offer; it will be obvious that they act through *aiskhrokerdeia*, greed, *hybris* and regarding their own groups of supporters as carrying more weight than the law.

Dem. li 1: If a man is poor and errs through want, is he to be liable to the extreme penalty? And if he is rich and does exactly the same wrong through *aiskhrokerdeia*, is he to be forgiven?

Cf. Xen. *Smp.* 4.35, some who have a lot of money will do anything to get more; Thuc. iv 17.4 is more specific in attributing insatiable desire for more to those who have 'unwontedly' prospered, a sentiment in which (although the passage does not refer to individual wealth; cf. iii 39.4) one seems to hear the familiar complaint of the old rich against the new rich.

A further serious charge against wealth, given substance by Greek superiority in battle to the wealth of the Persian Empire,[3] was the softness engendered by luxury, which made for poor endurance on campaign and cowardice in battle: Ar. *Wealth* 203, 559ff., Eur. *Phoen.* 597, wealth 'fond of life' (a common term for the man who saves his own skin); Eur. fr. 54, wealth 'a bad education for manliness'; Eur. fr. 235, cowardice coupled with

---

[3] On the Greeks' attitudes to Persia and to their victories over Persia cf. W. Kierdorf, *Erlebnis und Darstellung der Perserkriege* (Göttingen, 1966).

'stupidity'; Xen. *Mem*. i 6.9f., ill-equipped to 'be of any use to their friends or their city' on campaigns and sieges. To this extent, the poor man could be regarded as more useful to the community; Isok. ii 2 calls 'taking thought for one's livelihood every day' a better education for ordinary people than comfort. Praise of work and condemnation of idleness (e.g. Xen. *Mem*. ii 7.8) might be thought to imply a high valuation of the usefulness of the poor. Possibly wealthy Greeks considered that they themselves worked very hard and that poverty was often due to idleness (cf. Isok. vii 44, '. . . knowing that want comes about through doing no work,[4] and crime through want', and Xen. *Hiero* 9.8 on the theme 'Satan finds work for idle hands'), but we must remember that usefulness *in war* depended not simply on always having been busy but either on doing the kind of work which makes one physically tough and supple or on acquiring physical aptitude and skill by pursuing the right kinds of sport and exercise in one's leisure time.[5] The reservation 'for ordinary people' (*idiōtai*) in Isok. ii 2 (above) is interesting; the doctrine that security is bad for people—anyway, for some people—has echoed down the ages. A strong middle-class bias, such as is frequently observable in Greek moralizing, appears in Eur. *Supp*. 238–43, where the wealthy are treated as useless and greedy, the poor easily led by a demagogue because of their jealousy, and the solid stratum between the two extremes 'keeps the city safe' because it is law-abiding and disciplined (cf. I.F.3).

Some civic duties which included the custody of temple treasures were restricted to the rich, on the assumption that they would be free of the temptation to steal, but apart from that there is little tendency in popular sources to recognize explicitly that the administration of private wealth could be useful training for public administration; cf. however the Parians' advice to the Milesians in Hdt. v. 29 and the identification of private and public *oikonomiā*, considered as a skill, in Xen. *Mem*. iii 4.12.

## 2. *Town and Country*

It would be interesting to know—but it is an idle speculation, taking us far back beyond the limits of the available evidence—in what circumstances the

[4] *Argiā*, having no work to do, has rather more the colouring of 'idleness' than of 'unemployment'.

[5] Arist. *Rhet*. 1360$^b$39–1361$^a$7 makes industriousness the equivalent in a woman of courage in a man, though even a woman's industriousness, to be a virtue, must be untainted by *aneleutheriā*, 'un-freeness' (cf. section 3 below), i.e. she must not adopt towards work the attitude of someone who *needs* to work in order to make a living.

Athenians came to use *asteios*, etymologically, 'belonging to, or characteristic of, the city' in the senses, 'smart', 'clever', 'witty', 'ingenious', 'elegant' (Alexis fr. 59.3, of silverware), 'sexy' (Anaxilas fr. 21.7), 'tasty' (Alexis fr. 189, Antiphanes fr. 185.2, of pork), and *agroikos*, etymologically, 'living in the country' in the senses 'stupid', 'slow-witted', 'boorish', 'churlish', 'coarse', 'ill-mannered' (coupled with 'servile' in Pl. *Laws* 880A, coupled with the use of obscene [or perhaps, intemperate] language in Ephippos fr. 23, and applied to self-praise in Isok. v 82). In the classical period *agroikiā* is still sometimes associated quite explicitly with the country;[6] Strepsiades in Ar. *Clouds*, abused by Socrates as a 'thick-headed bumpkin' (628; cf. 646f., 655), is acutely conscious that he suffers from the intellectual limitations and narrow ideas of one who lives 'far off in the country' (138f.); cf. Eur. *Iph. Aul.* 266, on the ignorance of country people. In so far as a farmer describes himself in Men. fr. 11 as 'scowling, harsh in temper, parsimonious', the impossibly suspicious and ill-natured Knemon in Men. *Dyskolos* is 'a real Attic farmer' (604), and *asteios* in Men. *Fab. Inc.* 48f. seems to mean 'easygoing', 'good-tempered', the pair of antonyms seems to have retained some relation to popular stereotypes.

For most moralizing purposes, however, the townsman was not contrasted favourably with the countryman;[7] the countryman, blunt and brutal in speech, is honest, upright, a pillar of the traditional values, whereas the townsman has the gift of the gab; a good example is Eur. *Ba.* 717, where it is a man 'well acquainted with the city' who puts forward an apparently bright idea which the countrymen follow with disastrous results. The farmers who work their own land 'alone keep the country safe' (Eur. *Or.* 917–22); in Ar. *Peace* 223f., 254, 508–11, 582–600, it is the farmers who single-mindedly desire to rescue Peace, and succeed, once they are rid of all those who for one reason or another positively impede the operation or cause confusion by not pulling their weight. These same farmers (1172–90) are quite sure that their regimental commanders (self-satisfied, nervous braggarts, as so often in the common soldier's view of his superiors) put the countrymen to a great deal of trouble which the townsmen escape. Xen. *Oec.* 6.6 suggests that if farmers and craftsmen were formed into separate battalions we should soon see the difference, in favour of the farmers, once they faced the enemy; cf. Xen. *Mem.* iv 2.22, where most people engaged in working

---

[6] Theophr. *Char.* 4, portraying the characteristics of *agroikiā*, is clearly (§§ 11f.) thinking of a countryman, not of a boorish townsman.

[7] On presentation of the town/country antithesis in comedy, cf. Ehrenberg 81–94, 315.

metal, wood or leather are dismissed as 'servile'. Conventional attitudes at Athens perhaps exaggerated both the importance of farming to the economy (Xen. *Oec.* 5.17 argues that all the crafts depend ultimately on the good use of land) and the virtues of the farming community (cf. I.F.*3*, IV.B.*1*, and section *1* above). It could be asserted that farming makes men good (Men. fr. 338, Xen. *Oec.* 15.42; cf. Eur. *Supp.* 881-7, 'useful to the city') and particularly so if the land is poor (Men. fr. 57). The sentiment of Men. fr. 560, that 'it is for a *man* to excel in war, since farming is slave's work', was probably uttered by a mercenary soldier.

## 3. Freedom and Slavery

Whatever was said about the moral limitations imposed by poverty could be said *a fortiori* about those imposed by slavery, in so far as poverty was half-way to slavery in respect of social standing, no matter what rights might be guaranteed to the poor man by law; Isok. xiv 48 speaks of people who, in consequence of debt, 'have *(sc. in some cases)* become slaves, others who go to work as hired labourers, others who provide for their daily needs in whatever way they can'. Since slaves were often of foreign birth, captives in war or the children of captives, their 'natural' relation to their individual owners and to the Athenian citizen-body generally was assumed to be enmity and resentment (cf. III.B.*2*). In any case, being denied so many opportunities to *choose* between courses of action, the slave was not expected —as the citizen was expected—to display the virtues of loyalty, good faith and self-sacrifice.

Lys. xiii 18: They were not so foolish or so friendless ... that they brought in Agoratos, a slave and the son of slaves, as if his loyalty could be trusted.

Cf. Eur. fr. 150 (Austin) 6f., the folly of ever trusting a slave.

Men. *Farmer* 55-8: Then, when he needed someone to look after him, the foreign slaves on whom he depends all told him to go to hell *(sc. hoping he would die of his injury).*

The slave could be expected to take the line of least resistance,[8] siding with the winner in any conflict between his betters (Eur. *El.* 633). In comedy, the crude sentiment that food and drink are the best that life can offer is apt

---

[8] We may recall in this connection the single-minded concern of the guard in Soph. *Ant.* 439f., lowly subject of a wilful ruler, for his own safety.

to be uttered by slaves, e.g. Alexis fr. 25.1–5, Men. *Perik.* 98; cf. Xen. *Oec.* 13.9, on 'guiding slaves by their bellies', as one trains animals. This is not to say that no slaves were loyal or could not be loved by their owners. Eur. *Ba.* 1027 portrays one who shows sorrow ('though a slave', he says) for his master's misfortune; cf. Eur. *Hel.* 728–33, discussed in V.A.2; Eur. *Iph. Aul.* 312, the old slave prepared to die in defence of his master's secret, stoutly declaring that such a death confers good repute on a slave.[9] The sentiment that a slave of good character is a better man than free citizens of bad character also found expression:[10] Eur. *Ion* 854–6, 'In every other respect a slave who is good (*esthlos*) is in no way inferior to free men'; Eur. fr. 831 (cf. fr. 511), contrasting the mere 'name' of slave with his 'mind'; Men. fr. 722, 'a mind of free character' can make a slave better than his master. Sage nodding on the part of the audience at such sentiments is hardly more significant than comparable assent a hundred years ago to sentiments of the type, 'Kind hearts are more than coronets . . .'. Nevertheless, criticism of established notions could not abstain indefinitely from the topic of slavery, and Alkidamas, according to Arist. *Rhet.* 1373$^b$18 contributed the observation that 'the gods made all men free, and Nature has enslaved no one';[11] cf. Philemon frr. 22, 95, VI.A.4.

By contrast with the slave, the free men was expected not to be dominated by fear, but to take the path of toil and sacrifice wherever there was a choice between pleasure or safety on the one hand and honour or service to the community on the other; a free man (literally) 'thinks big' (Men. *Heros* fr. 3), i.e. has self-respect, magnanimity and honourable ambitions and is not distracted by short-term pleasure or gain (cf. Men. fr. 534). The mean and illiberal man was called 'un-free' (*aneleutheros*), e.g. Ar. *Wealth* 591; what kind of character expressed the view (Alexis fr. 263) that an awkward and un-dignified gait is a mark of the 'un-free', we do not know, but the point presumably is that the free man should suggest even by his physical move-ments that he is, as it were, in control of the situation. The deceitful Odysseus is reviled by Philoktetes as having (literally), 'a mind in no way healthy (*i.e.* honest) or free' (Soph. *Phil.* 1006), and it is 'an ugly fate for a free man to be called a liar' (Soph. *Trach.* 453f.). The freeman tells the truth because false-hood implies fear or need, and he should not be motivated by either. Dionysios the tyrant of Syracuse, according to Euboulos fr. 25, was hard on

[9] Deianeira in Soph. *Trach.* 61f., pleased at the advice of her slave-nurse, remarks that good ideas may come from those who are 'ill-born', but she makes it sound as if this possibility had not occurred to her before.

[10] Cf. Pohlenz 47.

[11] Cf. Baldry 60.

flatterers but well-disposed to those who made fun of him, 'thinking that such a man alone was free, even if he was (sc. formally) a slave' (cf. Sophilos fr. 9A [Edmonds], 'the tongue of a freeman is free').

As we shall see (IV.B.1, IV.E.2), resisting or submitting to fears or desires which preclude approved behaviour was commonly described in terms of 'mastery' over them or 'enslavement' to them, so that sōphrosynē was held to be characteristic of free men.[12] On the other hand, the free man did not easily bear insult or maltreatment which he felt to be hybristic (Men. fr. 613a; cf. II.A.3), by a perversion similar to that which we have observed (III.C.2) in the case of 'Be a *man*!' and aggressive and self-seeking action could be justified as worthy of a free man (Theophr. Char. 29.4); cf. modern usage such as, 'Who does he think I am?', 'No one's going to push me around', etc.

The contrast between democracy and all forms of constitution in which the distribution of power was restricted could easily be expressed in terms of freedom and slavery; Hdt. v 78 offers the opinion that when the Athenians were ruled by tyrants they fared poorly in war because their hearts were not in the doing of their masters' bidding, but when Athens became a democracy they fought with greater success because each man felt that he was fighting for himself.

## III.F. UNDERSTANDING

### 1. Ends and Means

People are not only of dissimilar temperaments but also of unequal intelligence. Whether we ascribe this inequality to nature or to nurture, the fact remains that of two people whose moral standards are virtually identical and who are are equal in energy, courage and good intention, one may see what should be done in a given situation and the other may misunderstand the situation disastrously; goodwill exercised without intelligence can cause great suffering. But intelligent people and stupid people do not always have equally high moral standards. Most of us have some stupid friends who are better people than some of our intelligent friends. Intelligence is indispensable for choosing the right means to an end, but the intelligent do not always choose good ends; a person of extraordinary ability in the drawing

[12] Cf. Pohlenz 67–71, 81f.

of inferences, with an extraordinarily sharp eye for relevance, may be selfish, cowardly, mean, callous or unreliable, while a halfwit may be helpful and kind and do his utmost to be good, with success so long as the complexities of a situation do not disguise the issue. Christian tradition does not countenance sin as a means to an ostensibly good end, but requires the individual to think first and last of the destiny of his own soul; accordingly, popular literature in Christian cultures has tended to contrast the villainous genius with the simpleton who knows the commands of God and obeys them unflinchingly. Even today popular literature, drama and film often work on the assumption that very high intelligence is incompatible with the warmth for which we love people, presumably because the average reader or spectator wishes to be reassured that he has something to compensate for his lack of high intelligence.[1] Since the Greeks were more inclined to compromise on the relation of means to ends and to judge conduct by its results, they less often contrasted intelligence with goodness, but this is a matter of degree. We are struck by passages which refer to intellectual competence where we would have expected a reference to good will,[2] such as: Dem. xiv 26, if the worst happened, 'who is so silly (*ēlithios*) as not to pay a capital levy?'; Men. fr. 632, the 'folly (*anoia*) of Fortune' (cf. III.G.2); Thuc. i 138.3, on Themistokles' 'natural intelligence'; Thuc. iv 18.5, 'reputation for strength (*iskhȳs*) and intelligence (*synesis*).[3] But the Greeks were by no means totally committed to the 'intellectualization' of virtue.

Eur. *Ion* 834f.: I would rather have as a friend an ordinary man who is good (*khrēstos*) than a bad man who is more able (*sophos*).

Cf. Philemon fr. 228, Soph. *Phil.* 1246.

Eur. *Phoen.* 1680 (*Kreon to Antigone*): There is stout-heartedness (*gennaiotēs*) in you, but (*sc. also*) a certain folly.

Men. fr. 360: Is not intelligence the greatest of blessings (*literally*, '*cause of most goods*') to all men—if it is (*literally*) skilled in the direction of the better?

---

[1] The English phrase 'so-called intellectual', common in controversy, may on occasion be intended to imply that the true intellectual arrives at the same conclusions as the unintellectual traditionalist, while the person who lays claim to an intellectual distinction which he in fact lacks arrives at disturbing conclusions; the phrase is normally used, however, simply as a mode of expressing hostility to the rational use of evidence.

[2] Cf. Opstelten 201–4.

[3] Huart 450 argues from the combination of *aretē* and *synesis* in certain passages of Thucydides that for Thucydides *aretē* always had an intellectual ingredient. The opposite conclusion might be argued; cf. n. 9 below.

Soph. *Ant.* 99 (*Ismene to Antigone*): In going (*sc. to bury him*) you are foolish (*anous*) but rightly loving to those we love.

Soph. *El.* 1023f. (*Elektra's retort to Khrysothemis*): I was (*sc. the same*) in nature then, but inferior in understanding (*nous*) ... 1027: I envy you your understanding (*nous*), but detest you for your cowardice.

Cf. Dem. lxi 23, differentiating 'good (*agathos*) soul' (cf. IV.A.*3*) from 'intelligent mind'; *GVI* 1755, 'soul and outstanding thought (*dianoiai*)'; Men. fr. 595, the greatest pleasure for a father is to see his own son well-behaved (*sōphronein*) and intelligent (*phronein*); Thuc. ii 87.5, encouragement to Peloponnesian sailors to oppose their greater daring to the Athenians' greater skill (while in 89.3 the Athenian sailors are assured that their greater experience makes them the more confident); Thuc. v 9.9, the three elements needed for success in battle are willingness to fight, shame at being seen to falter, and obedience to superior officers (presumably the exercise of intelligence is an additional requirement of a commander).

The Greeks were also well aware that intelligence and skill can be positively exercised in the pursuit of bad ends. This was, after all, precisely what the sophists were accused of doing in the latter part of the fifth century, and Xenophon's Socrates (Xen. *Mem.* iv 1.3f.; cf. III.B.*2*) very clearly recognizes the principle, *corruptio optimi pessima*. Aristophanes in *Clouds* portrays the ability of the intellectual, having demonstrated that beliefs and principles long accepted by most people are mutually contradictory, self-contradictory or founded on factual misapprehension, to conclude (to his own advantage) that the imperatives which those beliefs were supposed to justify should therefore be disobeyed; while direct, simple, law-abiding folk are unable to refute the intellectual's demonstration on the level of rational argument. Since Aristophanes himself was concerned to over-simplify, exaggerate and parody both the new intellectual fashion and the traditionalist reaction to it, he did not do justice to the strength of either case, except in incidental detail (e.g. *Clouds* 1421, 1430f.). The traditionalist's strength is the opportunity he often has—but is seldom able to take—to point out how selective the 'immoralist' is in the evidence which he uses and the axioms which he adopts. It is legitimate, for example, to argue that a community in which people obey the law unquestioningly just because it is the law may be stronger and more enduring, in a world full of predatory enemies, than one in which they are encouraged to believe that they can know better than the law.[4]

Thuc. i 84.3 (*Arkhidamos is speaking for and at Sparta*): We are good soldiers and wise in deliberation (*euboulos*) because of the order in our lives; good soldiers, because a

[4] Cf. de Romilly 212–25.

sense of shame is founded above all on discipline (*sōphrosynē*) and valour (*eupsȳkhiā*) upon fear of reproach; and wise, because we are brought up without intellectual encouragement to look down on our laws (*literally, 'brought up more stupidly than contempt for the laws'*) and under too severe a control ('*more* sōphronōs) to disobey them.

Thuc. iii 37.3f. (*Kleon speaking to the Athenian assembly*): A city which obeys its own laws, even when they are open to criticism, is superior to a city which has good laws but denies them authority; stupidity (*amathiā*) coupled with discipline (*sōphrosynē*) is more useful[5] than cleverness (*dexiotēs*) coupled with licence (*akolasiā*),[6] and as a rule quite ordinary people make a better city than those of high intelligence (*synetos*). The latter want to appear wiser (*sophos*) than the laws ... while the former, mistrusting their own intelligence (*synesis*), do not claim to be as wise as the laws (*literally, 'claim to be stupider than the laws'*).[7]

The terminology of these passages requires some explanation. *Sōphrosynē*, the criterion of which is the overcoming of the impulse to immediate or short-term pleasure or gain (Antiphon the Sophist fr. B58)[8] is here linked with *amathiā* (adjective *amathēs*), which is a common antonym (e.g. Arkhippos fr. 46) of *sophiā* (adjective *sophos*); the impulse to criticize, quibble or demonstrate one's own cleverness must, of course, be included under those impulses which the *sōphrōn* man suppresses. In the archaic and classical periods *sophiā* denoted creative ability, technical skill and inventiveness in poetry and literature (e.g. Antiphanes fr. 274), music (e.g. Theophilos fr. 12.7), medicine (e.g. *GVI* 57), the visual arts (e.g. *GVI* 74.3), and any other field to which specialized knowledge and training are relevant; the list of *sophoi* in Xen. *Mem.* i 4.2f., comprises only poets and painters. Herodotos uses the word (ix 62.3) to describe the superiority of the Greeks to the Persians in the technique of hand-to-hand fighting, and the section of Xenophon's *Agesilaos* devoted to the king's *sophiā* (6.4) concerns only skill in the conduct of war (cf. Eur. *Her. Fur.* 201–3). In Ar. *Frogs* 1515–19 Aiskhylos, departing from the underworld, leaves his throne to Sophokles, whom he judges 'second (*sc. only*) to myself in *sophiā*', i.e. '... in poetic genius'. Scientific and historical enquiry is *sophiā* in Hdt. ii 20.1. Comedy applies *sophos* flatteringly to the audience, to denote its good taste in the arts

---

[5] Cf. VI.C.2.

[6] *Akolasiā*, self-indulgent and immoral extravagance (Aiskhines i 42, 194, Dem. lix 50), is commonly the antonym of *sōphrosynē* in Plato, e.g. *Gorg.* 493D, 507C. Ant. iii β.3 links it with *hybris*, iv α.6 with *paranomiā*, contravention of law and usage. In Lys. xvi 11 it is applied to gambling and implicitly contrasted with *epieikeia*.

[7] Where *x* and *y* are antonyms, 'A is not as *x* as B' is usually expressed is Greek as 'A is more *y* than B'.

[8] Cf. G. J. de Vries, 'Σωφροσύνη en Grec classique', *Mnemosyne* s. III xi (1943) 81–101; North, *passim*.

(Ar. *Eccl.* 1155, *Frogs* 737, *Lys.* 1227, *Wasps* 1195f.), and also to the more down-to-earth techniques of sexual enjoyment (Ar. *Eccl.* 895f.) and cookery (Alexis frr. 110.19f., 213.1f.), whence Amphis fr. 14.1 even applies it to a tasty fish. But we also find *sophos* predicated of a man who is 'wise' in the sense that he understands principles implicit in moral and political situations. It is not difficult to see how such an extension occurred. A forerunner of it is an archaic epitaph from Tanagra (*GVI* 162) which proclaims the dead man to have been '*sophos* in *xeniā* and in horsemanship'. Since *xeniā*, hospitable and generous dealings with guests and visitors from elsewhere, was an aspect of life in which human and divine law were both concerned, *sophiā* in that respect was inevitably moral. In tragedy, especially in Euripides, side by side with passages in which *sophiā* is some kind of expertise or intellectual ability not possessed by most people (e.g. Eur. *Med.* 294–7, where *sophos* is contrasted, incidentally, with *skaios*, 'dull', 'clumsy', 'thick-witted'), it is also freely used of wise, sensitive and virtuous decisions and attitudes in the conduct of life.

Eur. *El.* 294: There is no compassion in stupidity (*amathiā*), but only in those who are perceptive (*sophos*).
ibid. 969–72. ORESTES: Ah! How am I to kill her who bore me and nourished me? ELEKTRA: Just as she killed your father and mine. ORESTES: Apollo, what stupidity there was in your oracular command! ELEKTRA: Where Apollo is dull-witted, who are the wise (*sophos*)?

The *sophos* is strong in bearing misfortune (Alexis fr. 252, Eur. fr. 37), recognizing what cannot be avoided (Eur. fr. 965) and making the best of it (Soph. fr. 861); he mourns only in moderation (Eur. fr. 46) and keeps control over his own nature (Eur. fr. 634). Cf. Eur. *Hcld.* 958f., 'If your enemy is *sophos*, as is to be hoped, and not *skaios*, you will get respect and correct treatment from him'; Eur. *Or.* 415, Menelaos tells Orestes that suicide is not *sophos*; Eur. *Supp.* 219–25, the *sophos* takes care not to bring trouble on himself by offending the gods; ibid. 506–8, *sophoi* should love their children, their parents and their country; Hdt. vii 194.2, 'recognising that he himself had acted hastily rather than *sophōs* . . .'.

This extension of *sophos* was not very greatly favoured by the comic poets and orators, though we may note (e.g.) Alexis fr. 141.14f., 'What is said by most *sophoi*, that it's best not to be born . . .', and Antiphanes fr. 94.4, 'No one who speaks *sophōs* has a good word to say of old age'. On the other hand, neither comedy nor oratory treats the word in a derogatory sense, as 'clever' can so often be used in English (Dem. xlv 18 looks like an exception to this generalization); of course, they could use it sarcastically, but that is true of all other commendatory words, especially *khrēstos*. The orators call great poets *sophos* (e.g. Aiskhines i 142, Homer; Dem. xix 248, Sophokles; cf. Eupolis fr. 357.3), and so too wise legislators (e.g. Aiskhines i 46; cf. Hdt. ii 160.1), for the formulation of laws and constitutions calls for high intelligence and creative imagination (note in this connection that Demosthenes xxv 16 regards every law as originating in 'an agreed decision of intelligent [*phronimos*] men').

Isok. xvi 28 praises Perikles as 'the most *sōphrōn* and *dikaios* and *sophos* of the citizens (*sc. of his time*)'; the phrasing is derived from the articulation of virtue common in encomia (cf. II.C.*1*), but what Isokrates means by the *sophiā* of Perikles must surely have been his ability to understand and handle political situations with foresight. Isokrates still treats *sōphrosynē* and *sophiā* as distinct virtues, as normally in encomia and epitaphs (e.g. *GVI* 492.3).[9] Eur. *Med.* 548f., where Jason tries to justify his discarding of Medeia, appears also to make a firm distinction, 'In the first place *sophos* . . ., and secondly *sōphrōn*', but as we read Jason's speech down to line 567 we find it hard to see which elements in his conduct he regards as *sophos* and which as *sōphrōn*; his formulation of a desirable end and perception of the means to it are presumably *sophos*, and perhaps he thinks himself *sōphrōn* in being able to tear himself away from Medeia's bed for the purpose of a marriage more politically advantageous (cf. III.C.*2* on his criticism of passionate women). The extent to which the same conduct could be called indifferently *sophos* or *sōphrōn* will appear from the following passages.

Aiskhines ii 176 (*referring to the amnesty of 403*): When we returned to a just constitution (*literally*, 'having begun to exercise citizenship sōphronōs', *i.e.* '*when the democracy was restored*') . . . and Arkhinos and Thrasyboulos . . . exacted from us an oath not to revive charges against one another—in consequence of which everyone thought ours the wisest (*sophos*) of cities . . .

And i 140 (*with the same reference*): You (*sc. the Athenians*) are now regarded by the whole Greek world as men of the highest ideals and wisdom (*literally*, '*having become best and most* euboulos'), for you did not address yourselves to vengeance for the acts which had been committed . . . To compose with honour your mutual enmities is quite rightly regarded as the action of good and sensible (*sōphrōn*) men.

It would be incorrect to say that those two passages demonstrate synonymy of *sophos* and *sōphrōn*; but they do show that either term could be applied to

---

[9] It is always hard to decide (cf. II.C.*3*, VI.C.*3*) when the formulation 'A and B' is tautologous and when it implies a distinction between A and B.

the same conduct according to the extent to which it was desired to emphasize its intellectual and imaginative aspects.

And. ii 6: The most fortunate of men are those who err least, but the wisest (*sōphrōn*) are those who most readily change their minds.

Lys. xix 53: They say that the best and wisest (*sophos*) men are the most willing to change their minds.

There is a slightly greater difference between these two passages than might at first appear, since the former relates to change of inclination and behaviour, the latter to rational change of opinion; see below on *gnōmē* and its cognates.

Dem. ii 22: Whoever among you, seeing how fortunate Philip is, considers him to be in this respect a formidable adversary, employs the reasoning (*logismos*, '*calculation*') of a sensible (*sōphrōn*) man.

Cf. Dem. xi 15, almost exactly the same sentence, but with 'foresight' instead of 'calculation'. Here the application of *sōphrosynē* to rational foresight suggests that the *sōphrōn* resists the temptations of wishful thinking just as he resists lust and greed and anger.

And. iii 32: Examples of error in the past are sufficient for *sōphrōn* men, to ensure that they do not err in future.

On 'error' see III.H.*3*; cf. Soph. *Phil.* 304, '*Sōphrōn* men do not sail this way'.

Hdt. vii 104.2: A *sōphrōn* man cannot be expected to reject friendship when it presents itself.

Dem. vi 19: He thinks that because of their greed they will welcome the present turn of events and that because of their dullness (*skaiotēs*) of character they will not foresee what is going to come afterwards. Yet for those with a moderate amount of sense (*sōphronein*) the precedents are perfectly clear to see.

This passage is entirely in keeping with a common use of *sōphronein* (especially in the formula, 'if you are wise'), but the use of *skaios*, so common an antonym of *sophos* in tragedy, is of interest.

Dem. xl 49: He has come to such a degree of boorishness (*amathiā*) . . . that he is going to vilify the man whose son he claims to be—the man in whose defence he ought to resent abuse from anyone else.

Here *amathiā* so often contrasted with *sophiā*, seems a failure to understand what is required by decency and propriety. Cf. *anaisthētos* (abstract *anaisthēsiā*, verb *anaisthētein*), literally 'unperceptive', also 'unfeeling'; it may denote inability to reason (Dem. xviii 120, coupled with *skaios*), lack of self-criticism (ibid. 221), boorishness (Dem. xxi 153) or ruthlessness (Dem. xxii

64, coupled with *ponēriā*); cf. also Aiskhines iii 166, 'O men of iron, how could you bear to listen to him?' ~ Lys. x 20, 'Unless he is made of iron, I think he must be aware that the two words mean the same'.

Isok. xviii 46: At that time everyone thought us the stupidest (*amathēs*) and most unfortunate (*dystykhēs*) of men, but now we are regarded as the most fortunate (*eutykhēs*) and sensible (*sōphrōn*) in the Greek world.

This is a plain enough antonymy of *amathēs* and *sōphrōn*, with chiastic arrangement, in which $A_1 + B_1$ is opposed to $B_2 + A_2$. Compare the antonymy of *anoētos*, 'thoughtless', 'silly', 'foolish', with *sophos* in Ar. *Clouds* 878f., but with *sōphrōn* in Dem. lix 111, Hdt. i 4.2.

In this connection, we must consider the denotational field of *gnōmē*,[10] the abstract noun corresponding to the verb *gignōskein*, 'know', 'recognize', 'judge', 'decide'. When an issue was discussed in the assembly and the question to be answered was the practical one, 'What steps should be taken, given the situation, in the city's interest?', the proposal which a speaker made and supported by argument was his *gnōmē*. A distinction could be drawn, when desired, between intelligent *gnōmē* and courageous spirit (e.g. Dem. lxi 23, cited above); Dem. lx 17 is unusual in making 'understanding' *synesis*) the foundation of goodness (*aretē*), and courage (*andreiā*) the completion without which the foundation is of no use. Both *gnōmē* (e.g. Ant. vi 20) and *dianoia* (e.g. Dem. xxiii 54) can mean 'purpose' or 'intention'; cf. Is. i 26 ~ 35, cited in II.B.3. Neither word, however, is confined to decisions or conclusions which result from intellectual analysis; both could be applied to states or attitudes of mind which we should regard as affirmation of general moral principle or sustained orientation of the will.

And. ii 24: Surely the body is not held to blame for what men do by the mind (*gnōmē*); now, my body is still the same, and has been absolved from blame, but my mind (*gnōmē*) is a different one from what was in me before.

The argument here is sophistically expressed, but sound: Andokides means that the body, which is a spatio-temporal continuum throughout the life of an individual, is the instrument by which the mind effects its intentions, and a person can become 'of another mind' in a sense in which he cannot (in a culture ignorant of cytology) become 'of another body'.

---

[10] In Nikostratos fr. 27, 'If talking were a sign of *phronein*, swallows would be more *sōphrōn*' ('intelligent') 'than men', it has been suggested (by Meineke) that *sōphrōn* should be emended to *emphrōn*, but I doubt whether emendation is justified. Cf. Müri 257–60 on the relation between *gnōmē* and *synesis* in Thucydides; Ernst Meyer, *Erkennen und Wollen bei Thukydides* (Göttingen, 1939).

Dem. ix 36: There was something at that time in the spirit (*gnōmē*) of the Athenian people—and now it is no more—which defeated all the wealth of Persia and led Greece on the path of freedom.

Cf. ibid. 43; and on 'now it is no more' cf. III.D.2.

Dem. xiv 14: The first and most important step to be taken is that you should be disposed in your minds (*gnōmē*) with the intention that every individual shall of his own accord do zealously whatever is needed.

Cf. Dem. xix 270, 'if his judgment (*gignōskein*) is what it should be, he is right-thinking' (*eu phronein*: cf. section 3); Dem. xxi 213, 'preserve this *gnōmē* which you have at present'; Isok. xviii 36, 'disposition', almost 'habit'.

Dem. xlv 69: This is nothing but an outward disguise for his character (*tropos*), and in acting thus he showed the cruelty and harshness of his intentions (*dianoia*) . . . 71: It is right that you should be angry with Phormion . . . now that you have seen the shamelessness of his character (*tropos*) and his ingratitude.

Isok. xviii 32: The greater part of the credit for achievements accomplished in circumstances perilous to the agent can be given to fortune (*tykhē*); but no one could hold anything but our own will (*gnōmē*) responsible for our moderation towards each other.

For a similar distinction between *tykhē* and *gnōmē*, external circumstances and the mind of the person who confronts them, cf. Lys. xxxiv 2.

Isok. xix 22: And what do you imagine my feelings (*gnōmē*) were when my life had undergone such a change of fortune (*sc. the deaths of my mother and sister and my own serious illness*)?

## 2. Reason and the Self

It may happen that I analyse a situation with great acumen and understand what action is required by my own moral standards, and yet find that my wish to perform that action is nullified by fear or desire for some kind of pleasure or gain.

Isok. xv 221: Many men, through *akrasiai* (*i.e. one kind or another of failure to control themselves*) do not abide by (*sc. the outcome of*) their reasonings, but neglect their interests and turn to pleasure.

(On 'interests' cf. V.A.2.) According to Xen. *Mem.* iii 9.4f., Socrates differed from other people (and surprised them considerably) in refusing to draw an ultimate distinction between *sophiā* and *sōphrosynē*, or indeed between *sophiā* and any other virtue. This is a good illustration of the difference between two things which are often thoughtlessly treated as if they were identical, 'the (*sc.* general) Greek view' and 'the Socratic view'.

A political pronouncement by the Thucydidean Perikles is applicable also to 'private' morality.

Thuc. ii 60.6: The man who recognises (*sc. what should be done*) but does not explain it clearly might as well not have thought of it; the man who can do both but is no friend to the city cannot speak as if its interests were his; and if he has the right sentiments but is corruptible (*literally, 'conquered by money'*), that one fault cancels out everything.

Cf. Dem. xv 1, '. . . no difficulty in explaining to you what it is best to do . . . but in making you actually do it'; again, the context is political, but the principle, the gap between assent to a propostion and the wish to put it into effect, is applicable to any level of morality. Dem. xlv 14 lists some emotional conditions which may make one act contrary to one's own best interest: anger, greed of gain, contentiousness, excitement (*paroxysmos*: cf. xlvii 19). He contrasts these emotions with *logismos*, 'reasoning'; cf. Men. fr. 213, 'Nothing in human nature is more important than *logismos*'. The obvious power of anger to distort judgment is a subject of generalization in Ant. v 71f. and Is. i 13 (cf. Thuc. iii 45.4), and needs no comment (Dem. xlviii 6 offers a particular case). Examples of alleged greed are treated in Dem. xxvii 5 and xxxii 12 as similarly distorting right judgment. We must add to the list sexual desire (e.g. Dem. xl 51, Lys. iii 4, 31), falling in love (which deprives us of *nous*, Men. fr. 79), and sexual infatuation (e.g. Hyp. iii 3), a factor acknowledged in testamentary law (Is. ii 19f.). Not only being in love (e.g. Euboulos fr. 41.6), but any state of mind which is unwelcome or may have bad consequences, could be called *nosos*, 'sickness', 'illness', e.g. 'piety towards bad people' (Soph. *Ant.* 732, Kreon speaking) and 'opposing the gods' or 'kicking against the pricks' (Soph. *Trach.* 491f.). This common usage is a link with the absence of distinction between insanity and wrongdoing (cf. section *3*).

In so far as the Greeks spoke of a person as being 'forced', 'conquered', 'worsted', 'overcome' or 'enslaved' by desire or other emotions (Aiskhines i 42, 75, 154, ii 152; Dem. xl 9; Xen. *Oec.* 1.19f., on pleasures which become oppressive masters), they implicitly identified the self with the deliberative element, of which the emotions are the assailants. The same implication is present in such expressions as: Ant. ii γ.3, 'to chastise (*sōphronizein*) the angry (*sc. element*) of his mind (*gnōmē*)'; Ant. iv γ.2, 'to grant the wish of the *thӯmos*', i.e. 'yield to one's (*sc.* aggressive) impulse'; Eur. *Supp.* 581f., 'you will not compel me to make my mind angry'; Lys. fr. 22, 'she committed suicide because she became unable to control her grief'. We might be justified in seeing it also in the use of *paskhein*, 'undergo', 'experience', to denote the relation of an agent to his emotional state.

Ar. *Clouds* 1198: I think that what has happened to them was the same as (*sc. has happened*) to the official tasters

—where we would say 'what they have done . . .', which is in fact a variant reading.

Dem. xix 195: When the guests at the party heard this, there was such applause that Philip was affected (*literally*, '*underwent something*') and granted (*sc. the request*).

Lys. viii 17: Why did I not guard against that? I was too simple-minded (*literally*, '*I underwent something simple-minded*').

Cf. Dem. xix 338, 'undergo something foolish' = 'be misled', 'react foolishly'; Men. *Farmer* 71, 'he underwent something common' = 'he reacted as one often does'. We must however remember that a wide range of expressions in English could be regarded as carrying the same implication, e.g. 'I was struck by a thought', 'I don't know what came over me', etc. The nature of the case is responsible; we cannot, after all, decide to be angry or greedy or lustful, even if we want to be, and when we do not want these emotional conditions we nevertheless become aware that we are in them. Hence the contrast between the self and forces apparently as external to the self as infection or weather. We say, however, 'I restrained myself' as readily as 'I restrained my anger', and so did the Greeks: Aiskhines i 88, Hdt. vi 129. 4, Men. *Sam.* 327, Pl. *Phdr.* 254A (ctr. *Rep.* 554C); cf. Hdt. vii 47.2, 'within myself', i.e. able to suppress my emotional reactions. The Greek language tended to externalization of emotions slightly more than the English language, but not to a degree which would be in itself of great significance (cf. II.A.*1*). The personification of Eros and other emotional forces, the attribution of action to supernatural beings (including Chance), and (perhaps) the wide extension of the word *nosos* are rather more significant.

## 3. Mental Health

The distinction between emotion, thoughtlessness and shamelessness, all of which we tend to think one ought to control, and insanity, which we know one cannot control, was generally treated by the Greeks as quantitative. In this respect popular literature could claim respectable intellectual support; Prodikos (fr. B7) defined *erōs* as 'desire doubled' and '*erōs* doubled' as 'madness' (*maniā*). It may be presumed that the main types of psychotic and neurotic illness known to us were known also to the Greeks, and the total incidence of such illness may have been as great then as now, even if the distribution of types was different. Psychotics who were regarded as dangerous, frightening or offensive could be kept away by stoning (Ar. *Birds* 542f., *Wasps* 1491), and those who had no relatives to shelter them may not have lasted long.[11] A man could be empowered by court order to take over management of the family property if he could show his father to be mentally incapacitated; in Ar. *Clouds* 844f., the eccentricity of Strepsiades' behaviour makes Pheidippides contemplate this possibility (cf. Aiskhines iii 251). Psychotic or neurotic behaviour was described as 'illness' (cf. Ar. *Wasps* 71–7), attributable on occasion to brain injury (e.g. Ar. *Clouds* 1275f.) or to an excess of 'black bile' (e.g. Ar. *Clouds* 832f., *Peace* 65f., Dem. xlviii 56, Men. *Epitr.* 880f.). Socrates in Xen. *Mem.* iii 12.6 speaks of 'forgetfulness, despondency, ill-temper and madness' as arising from a bad condition of the body and invading the mind. *Hygiainein*, 'be in good health', denoted being in one's right mind as well as other kinds of health (e.g. Ar. *Wealth* 364–6).

Dem. xxiv 58: So what possible reason shall we be able to give for making a law which would annul those decisions—unless anyone cares to suggest that we were mad? . . . 74: No one in good health would do this . . .

Hellebore was prescribed as a popular psychiatric medication, e.g. Ar. *Wasps* 1489, Dem. xviii 121, Men. fr. 63.[12]

Greek lacked words which meant 'sane' or 'normal' in the purely clinical sense but did not also denote virtue or intelligence contrasted with vice or stupidity well within the limits of clinical normality.[13] Morally shameless behaviour, carried to an abnormal point, could be treated as evidence of insanity; cf. Hdt. iii 38.1 on Kambyses' 'contempt for sacred things and customary usage' as proof of his madness.

[11] It is not known what, if anything, the homicide laws had to say about the stoning of psychotics.

[12] For an example of 'washing and purification' to cure madness cf. Ar. *Wasps* 118, and on Greek attitudes to madness in general see Dodds, chapter II.

[13] If a contrast is to be drawn between Greek and modern attitudes, 'modern' must be defined carefully. In nineteenth-century fiction and drama psychosis was commonly depicted as a consequence of moral badness. It should also be remembered that even today one often hears 'neurotic' used with a derogatory connotation absent from (e.g.) 'arthritic' and 'diabetic' (cf. V.B.5).

Ant. ii β.5: If, before they had time to strip the bodies, they saw someone coming took fright and ran away, they were sensible (*sōphronein*) and not mad, in attaching more importance to safety than to gain.

Ar. *Birds* 427–30. CHORUS: Is he mad? HOOPOE: You can't imagine how sane (*phronimos*, '*intelligent*')! CHORUS: Has he really got brains? (*Literally*, '*is there anything* sophos *in his mind?*') HOOPOE: As smart as a fox!

Dem. xv 16: If all had gone well with them, I'm not sure that they would ever have been ready to see things straight (*eu phronein*, '*be of good mind*') ... but ... having learned that folly (*anoia*) brings great ills to most people, there is a possibility that they may become more sensible (*sōphrōn*) in the future.

Eur. *Hel.* 97: Was he mad? (*sc. I ask this*,) for who in his right mind (*sōphronein*) would do such a thing?

Is. i 19–21: You should consider that my opponents are alleging exceptional insanity (*paranoia*) on his part. For what madness could be greater than to slight us at the time when he was at odds with Deinias .. ? Who in his right mind (*eu phronein*) would take such a decision about his own property? ... If he was so crazy (*paraphronein*) as to treat us as being of no importance ...

ibid. 43: Remember that Kleonymos cancelled his will when he was in his right mind (*eu phronein*), but disposed of his property when he was angry and not taking proper thought ('*not deliberating rightly*') ... 50: If you believe the arguments of our adversaries you ought ... to convict Kleonymos of insanity (*paranoia*), but if you believe ours, consider that he took proper thought ('*deliberated rightly*') when he wanted to cancel the will.

Cf. Lyk. *Leokr.* 144, antonymy of *paranoia* and *eu phronein*; Xen. *Mem.* i 1.16, antonymy of *sōphrosynē* and *maniā*. A certain degree of synonymy between *sōphrōn* and its derivatives, *phronimos*, *eu phronein* and 'deliberate rightly' can be extended to *noun ekhein*, 'have mind' = 'be intelligent'.

Dem. xix 161: How is it possible for him to escape conviction in a court which is right-thinking (*eu phronein*: '*... which understands the issues*'?) and is prepared to abide by its oath? ... 179: Therefore it is right that he should be convicted, at any rate in an intelligent (*noun ekhein*) court.

Lys. xxix 13: And if you are wise (*eu phronein*), you will now make it clear to everyone that there is no sum of money so great as to deter you from punishing men whom you detect in dishonesty ... 14: If, then, you are wise (*sōphronein*), you will recover what belongs to you.

Cf. Ar. *Wasps* 1405 ∼ 1440, the use of *sōphronein* and *noun ekhein* as formulae of identical function in stories of the same structure; Eur. *Ion* 520f., the question 'Are you in your right mind?' (*eu phronein*) answered by 'I am' (*sōphronein*).

The Greeks used all their words for insanity much more freely in warning, reproach and vilification than we use our corresponding words, and mingled them with words of unambiguous reproach in the same phrase. In Eur. *Ba.* 997–1000 the chorus sing with reference to Pentheus, who has been un-righteous in persecuting the worshippers of Dionysos and has *also*, as a step towards his terrible punishment, been driven out of his wits by the god, (literally) 'unjust mind and temper contrary to law . . . mad heart and crazy spirit' (cf. III.G.*1*). Cf. Aiskhines iii 156, 'Do not convict the Athenian people of insanity' (*sc.* by acquitting Ktesiphon); Lyk. *Leokr.* 63, 'Is it not madness' (i.e. 'inconsequential') 'to say that nothing could have been affected by his action?' Similarly, they said, 'I would be mad to do so' (e.g. Dem. xxxv 40) in circumstances to which we should think '. . . absurd/unreasonable/improper/unwise . . .' more appropriate and 'mad' off-key. The disjunction 'bad *or* mad?' does not seem to have been thought interesting by the Greeks;[14] cf. III.H.*5*.

## 4. Faith and Hope

In the Christian tradition faith and hope have been regarded as virtues, to such an extent that it is easy to find scriptural justification for the extremes of credulity and improvidence, but not to find similar justification for the honest assessment of probabilities.

Faith in other people, whether actuated by loyalty to known persons or by a disposition to trust others in general, will be discussed in connection with magnanimity (IV.C.*4*). The faith which accepts some propositions about the supernatural without adequate evidence or even against available evidence, refusing to take more than a step or two towards treating such propositions (and all the relevant evidence) in exactly the same way as any other propositions, seems to have been on the whole alien to the Greeks.[15] It is probable that for ordinary people participation in cults and festivals and the fulfilment of customary religious observances were the primary

[14] I am not in agreement with those who believe that Aiskhylos was profoundly concerned with the intellectual aspect of the problem of moral responsibility which seems to us to be posed by acceptance of the idea that a god may pervert a human's reasoning processes; see my article, 'Some Neglected Aspects of Agamemnon's Dilemma', *Journal of Hellenic Studies* xciii (1973).

[15] Cf. A. D. Nock, 'Religious Attitudes of the Ancient Greeks', *Proceedings of the American Philosophical Society* lxxxv (1942), 472–82; H. Klees, *Die Eigenart des griechischen Glaubens an Orakel und Seher* (Stuttgart, n.d.) 68–91; W. Fahr, ΘΕΟΥΣ ΝΟΜΙΖΕΙΝ (Hildesheim, 1969).

element in religion, and that rational argument about religious propositions, designed to distinguish between the more probable and the less probable elements in theology and mythology, was not important. The continued existence of the community in a hostile world suggested that the cycle of religious activities which constituted its relation to the supernatural[16] must be, by and large, on the right lines; extremely strong reasons would have been required to justify a deliberate alteration of practices most of which were in any case physically and aesthetically enjoyable. Demosthenes' assertion that Athens is preserved by divine goodwill (xix 256, cf. 297) has none the less something of the character of a declaration of faith.

The legends portrayed in poetry and the visual arts did not have the status of revelation; the Muses inspired poets, but exactly to what extent, no one could say, and it was recognized that they inspired convincing fiction as well as truth.[17] There was no canonical body of myth handed down intact from the early archaic period until it fell victim to higher criticism in the time of the sophists; it was recognized that poets had from the very first told many irreconcilable versions of the same myth, so that mythology in their hands had always been a creative art, not the transmission of a sacrosanct tradition with different embellishments. It was possible for a poet whose standpoint was unreservedly religious to reject some parts of some myths as false on moral or aesthetic grounds, in the light of what he preferred to believe about the character of the gods; the importance of myths for religion was not that some myths were objectionable or that some must be false (because mutually contradictory), but that so many could not be shown to be untrue. 'It is said . . .' or 'There is a story . . .', said with reference to a myth, implies neither scepticism ('It is *said* . . .') nor credulity ('Tradition assures us . . .'). Isokrates' notion (iv 38) that acceptance of a story by many generations serves as evidence in its favour is one way of looking at tradition, in harmony with the Greek tendency (III.D.2) to venerate ancestors. On the other hand, when the chorus in Eur. *El.* 743f., justifies its acceptance of a particular myth ('It is said, and with me it wins credence . . .') on the grounds that 'frightening stories' (*sc.* of divine wrath at human misdeeds) are 'profitable for worship

---

[16] The word 'supernatural' begs a question, and 'superhuman' might often be more appropriate; the distinction between the natural and the supernatural is meaningful in proportion to the extent of our formulation of 'laws of nature' and to the position of our dividing line between the scientifically explicable and the miraculous. If we are concerned with a culture in which a wind is regarded as a person who blows when he wishes and it is believed that the crops will not come up unless a certain ritual is performed, how exactly do we contrast 'natural' with 'supernatural'?

[17] Cf. Dodds 80–2.

of the gods', it is not saying anything which its audience would have thought cynical or even unusually sophisticated.

Herodotos strikes us a religious man, because he often draws our attention to the working of divine justice and the effects of divine propensities on human affairs, and because he accepts the validity in principle of inspired prophecy, but he evidently does not feel himself committed to uncritical belief in every available story of divine intervention. For example, in v 85 he relates (from an Athenian source?) how a party of Athenians sent to remove two statues from Aigina suddenly went mad and killed one another; then (v 87.1f.) he gives the Aiginetan version (less creditable to Athens), in which the Aiginetans, without blatant divine intervention, defeated an Athenian invading force. In vii 189.3, while treating as divine the wind which fell upon the Persian fleet at Artemision, he admits that it is an open question whether this intervention was brought about by the Athenians' prayers. His remark in ix 65.2, 'My opinion is, if an opinion is to be ventured on matters which involve the gods, . . .', does not imply that unquestioning acceptance of traditions about divine intervention is virtuous, but that once the possibility of such intervention is admitted the standards of probability upon which rational opinion about past events is based lose their validity.

The present existence of the gods in general is another matter. Many thoughtful people may have agreed with Protagoras's statement of the agnostic position (B4), 'On the subject of gods, I cannot know either that they exist or that they do not . . .'; it has, after all, the advantage of being true. Thucydides represents the Athenians at Melos as drawing a distinction between what is 'plainly' true of human affairs and what is true, so far as 'opinion' goes, of the gods (v 105.1f.), and as trying to dissuade the Melians from trusting in the supernatural when it is open to them (literally), 'still to be saved humanly', sc. by surrender to the Athenian demands (103.2).[18] The Melians' decision to trust in divine help (104), is partly founded on what an ordinary Greek would have regarded as sound evidence, the fact that Melos had existed for so long (112.2); that is to say, it is not pure faith, but contains a strong element of inference, nor is it allowed to stand alone, but joined (cf. V.A.1) with expectations of help from the Peloponnese (104, 112.2). While the orators freely admit uncertainty about the afterlife (V.C., V.D.5), they do not admit doubts about the existence of the gods. In drama expressions

---

[18] It must be remembered that these demands did not include the submission of the male population to massacre. That was the consequence of a long and desperate siege probably not envisaged by the Athenians as a possibility when they first negotiated with Melos.

of doubt about the character and will of the gods fall very naturally from the lips of people in despair (as presumably in real life), but Eur. *Iph. Aul.* 1034f., 'If there are gods, . . ., but if there are not, . . .' is a little sophisticated, and the speculation of Hekabe (Eur. *Hec.* 799–801) on the possibility that the gods themselves are subordinate to *nomos* (i.e. that we cannot 'know' any more about them than human tradition and custom imply?) may have disturbed some among those members of the audience who comprehended what was being said.

Belief about particular gods must again be distinguished from belief in the existence of the supernatural world as a whole. Xenophon's Socrates is not the man to question the gods' existence or to neglect religious observance, but he does not know whether there are two goddesses 'Aphrodite' or one, only that (i) Zeus, 'regarded as one and the same god, has many different cult-titles', and (ii) cults and sanctuaries of two different Aphroditai exist (Xen. *Smp.* 8.9; cf. Pl. *Smp.* 180D).

As for the virtue of hope, it was commonly realized that in adversity from which we have not yet found an escape it keeps us going, and to that extent it is a good. Moreover, those who embark on an enterprise with high hopes (cf. Dem. xviii 97, cited in IV.A.4), particularly soldiers going into battle, are more likely to succeed than those who are filled with despondency; hence the assertion (Eur. *Her. Fur.* 105f.) that good men trust in hope. Of course, the general Demosthenes, addressing his troops, deprecates rational calculation and requires them to hope, but he goes on to give them reasons justifying such hope (Thuc. iv 10.1–3); cf. the (moral) grounds for hope given in Xen. *Ages.* 1.27. Assessment of probabilities is the mean between optimism and despondency, and since the gap between our hopes and our ability to realize them is often very great—hope may take shape entirely without the consent of reason—there are many circumstances in which the optimist digs a pit for himself,[19] as recognized by Antiphon the Sophist B58, 'Hopes are not in all circumstances a good . . .'. The danger of hope is stressed by speakers in Thucydides (e.g. iii 45.1, the optimism which makes a criminal risk the death penalty; iii 45.6, v 103.1, vi 78.2), and in his narrative it is noticeable that those who trust to luck or to the supernatural are doomed (e.g. the defeated Athenians in Sicily, vii 61.3, 77.1). This theme is, however, distinctively Thucydidean.[20]

We can see for ourselves that religious faith appears to contribute to the goodness and efficiency of some people, and it seems also to contribute towards their happiness, to judge from their reactions when they feel it to be

[19] Cf. Opstelten 204–6.          [20] Cf. Müri 253.

threatened. Moreover, there is no doubt that some individuals of very strong religious faith have performed tasks of extraordinary difficulty and attribute their achievement to their faith. Nevertheless, it is questionable whether Christian faith has been a better moral influence in human history than pagan uncertainty. Clear recognition of the differences between tradition, speculation and evidence is not the least of weapons with which to encounter misfortune and suffering.[21] The history of Christianity can be regarded in many different ways, according to what it is that we are contrasting with Christianity, but no way does justice to the facts if it ignores the perverse insensitivity and cruelty which have been positively fortified by faith based on what the individual believes to be his communication, immediate or through a church, with God.[22] The Greek sense of human fallibility and of the strange turns which events may take,[23] coupled with a tendency to think of superhuman powers as reacting against human success (cf. III.A.2, V.E.2) had the great advantage of tending to discourage in the individual unshakable conviction of his own rightness.

## III.G. DIVINE INTERVENTION

### 1. Mechanisms of Intervention

The gods could intervene most simply and directly in human affairs by causing natural events of kinds recognized as lying entirely outside human control: rain, sunshine and wind (e.g. And. i 137–9, Ar. *Peace* 1143, 1157f., Hdt. i 87.2, Xen. *Hell.* ii 4.14), drought, epidemics, or crop and livestock

---

[21] Cf. Richard Robinson, *An Atheist's Values* (Oxford, 1964) 118–23 for an uncompromising argument that faith is 'not a virtue, but a positive vice', and that to undermine it in others is a 'moral duty'.

[22] Ferguson 242 regards the history of inter-Christian strife as belonging to 'the pathology of religious thought', but does not consider how far that and much other strife has been a product of distinctive features in Christianity, or how far good, useful and agreeable elements in modern Christianity are the product of the strong non-Christian, even anti-Christian, influences to which Christianity has been subjected during the last two centuries.

[23] It is remarkable that Jaeger iii 163 should call Xenophon, as we see him in the *Hipparchicus*, 'a man of simple faith in God' because of his emphasis (9.8) on qualifying statements with the phrase (literally), 'with god'. Xenophon insists on pious observance, since it is to be expected (*eikos*) that the gods will reveal to the pious, through omens and divination, something of the future. This is inference, not faith, and it does not imply that future events themselves will be morally gratifying or reassuring.

diseases (e.g. [Xen.] *Ath.* 2.6). Lyk. *Leokr.* 95ff., tells the story of a miraculous diversion of a lava-stream; Hdt. vi 61.3–5, the story of how Helen, worshipped at Sparta as a heroine, turned a very ugly child into a very beautiful one in answer to a nurse's prayer; miraculous healing was a regular function of certain gods.[1] Our individual characters, in so far as our own ability to form them is limited, could also be treated as god-given; Eur. fr. 156 (Austin) asks why Zeus endows bad men with fluency of speech, while the virtuous are tongue-tied.[2] We may perform the acts required for the procreation of children, but cannot guarantee conception; hence expressions such as 'the sons whom the gods have given me' (Xen. *Cyr.* viii 7.8, cf. *Oec.* 7.12).

Apart from what lay indisputably beyond human control, gods were also thought to determine the outcome of much more complex events, events of which all the constituents are human thoughts, words and acts:[3] a battle (e.g. Xen. *Hell.* vii 5.13, 26), a political turn of events (e.g. Dein. iii 14), or a whole series of military actions combined with diplomatic negotiations (e.g. Dein. i 26, Dem. i 10, xxiv 7). After the fighting over the sanctuary of Demeter at the battle of Plataiai, says Hdt. ix 65.2, it was found that all the Persian dead had somehow fallen on profane ground, outside the sanctuary. Naturally (cf. III.F.4, V.C., V.D.4) there could be room for doubt whether an event was divinely contrived or fortuitous. In a pious man, the decision, 'It *must* be a god's doing' might rest on the premise, 'The outcome was utterly contrary to all rational prediction' (e.g. Xen. *Hell.* iv 4.12). Lys. ii 58 ascribes the Athenian defeat at Aigospotamoi to 'laggard commanders *or* the gods' design', and does not choose between these alternative possibilities; Hdt. ix 91.1 wonders whether it was 'a god's doing' that Leotykhidas asked Hegesistratos for his name at a moment when the utterance of the name was a good omen.

The gods' ability somehow (cf. Men. *Perik.* 49f.) to direct the course of events was presupposed in prayer of all kinds, e.g. Xen. *Cyr.* v 1.29, 'Zeus, grant that I may surpass in benefaction those who do me honour!' So commonly in a speech: Ant. i 13, 'and may Justice steer < the case >'; Hyp. i fr. III, a prayer by the speaker that the gods will help and save him; Aiskhines i 116, Lyk. *Leokr.* 1, his prayer that he may be a worthy accuser. All prayers can be translated out of religious language into statements about one's hopes and fears, and all narrative statements and generalizations about unexpected events can be left as just that, without reference to the supernatural. There

---

[1] Cf. Dodds 111–17.     [2] Cf. Vollgraff 8f. on *entheos aretē*.
[3] Cf. Gernet 316–35; Adkins (1) 116–30.

are times when it is probably correct to treat a Greek utterance about gods as a purely linguistic phenomenon, like the technical term 'act of God' in insurance policies or the religious exclamations which serve believer and unbeliever alike as a means of expressing strong assertion, denial, indignation, and the like. There is at the same time a great deal which would be resistant to translation into secular terms, including, perhaps, the pious convention of attributing success primarily to the gods and in the second place to human agency (e.g. Dem. xxiv 7).

Throughout the classical period Greek states, as well as individuals, consulted oracles (e.g. Dem. xiv 25), and normally expected to receive explicit instruction or prohibition directly from the oracular god; well-known stories about some obscure or ambiguous oracular responses which had disastrous consequences for their recipients[4] should not be taken as typical. Individuals who claimed divine inspiration were also potential media of explicit communication from gods to men; in legend, (e.g.) Kassandra was credited with inspired utterance, but in ordinary life it was hardly possible to establish whose claims were justified, and the prophets who contributed to the Athenian decision to attack Syracuse served their city ill (Thuc. viii 1.1). Since we cannot choose our dreams, and they may make a profound impression on us, the dream was also regarded as a means by which gods could communicate with men.[5] Aiskhines iii 77 ridicules Demosthenes' alleged claim to have learned of Philip's death in a dream, but that is ridicule of an opponent, not of significant dreaming in principle, and a few years later we find the Athenian state sending a delegate to pass the night in a sanctuary in the hope of a god-sent dream (Hyp. iv 14).

Less directly and explicitly, the gods might cause ominous or prodigious events which occasionally spoke for themselves (cf. the Delian earthquake [Hdt. vi 98.1] and Xen. *Anab.* iii 4.12, where the defenders of a city were so frightened by thunder that they lost heart) but usually required interpretation by seers and experts (cf. Xen. *Mem.* i 4.16); this type of intervention particularly affected the process of sacrificing a victim and burning an offering (e.g. Hdt. ix 62.1).

Aiskhines iii 130: Did not the gods tell us in advance, did they not warn us to take care? ... Was not the sign that was revealed at the Mysteries enough, the death of

[4] A punishment for sin; cf. Lyk. *Leokr.* 93.

[5] Cf. Dodds 102–11, 117–21. Theophr. *Char.* 16.11, 25.2 makes the treatment of dreams as portents a characteristic of superstitious and nervous people; his word for 'superstitious', *deisidaimōn*, literally, 'fearful of the supernatural', had by his time become derogatory, but Xenophon, two generations earlier, used it in a complimentary sense, like our 'God-fearing'.

the initiates? Did not Ameiniades warn us that we must proceed very carefully and send to Delphi to ask the god what we should do? ... And did not Demosthenes finally send out our army into obvious peril, when the sacrifices were defective and did not augur well?

Ant. v 82: Moreover, it has often happened that a man present at a sacrifice has been revealed as polluted (*sc. guilty of homicide or impiety*) and as preventing the normal sacrifice from proceeding.

Causation of divine intervention by magic, i.e. by parascientific procedures designed to set in motion a mechanism involving action at a distance, was undoubtedly accepted as a part of life during the classical period, as is attested by some curses which have survived in writing,[6] a few references in literature, and a denial (Men. fr. 210) that a god can be compelled to act by magical means, but the evidence for magic does not become abundant until the Hellenistic age.

Omens, like dreams and the weather, lie outside our control, for we cannot cause (e.g.) two eagles to appear on the left and attack a swan, nor can we decide what shape of liver a bullock will prove to have when it has been slaughtered and cut up. One type of omen, however, is of a rather special kind: the apparently fortuitous utterance of words at a moment which is of great ominous significance to the hearer but is not known to be so by the speaker (e.g. Hdt. ix 91.1, cited above; cf. Xen. *Smp.* 4.8). If a god can cause me to say something at a particular moment, he must intervene directly in my mental processes, and I may not be aware that he is doing so.

Direct manipulation of human thoughts and feelings[7] by gods is taken for granted in Homer, and it is openly postulated in fourth-century oratory; it is in fact the principal mechanism by which a god can determine the outcome of a complex event.

And. i 113f.: My accusers said, if you recall, that the goddesses themselves led me astray, so that I might place the suppliant branch (*sc. in the sanctuary*), their purpose being that I should be punished. But even if we grant that the change brought by my accusers is true, I assert that I have actually been saved by the goddesses. For if I placed the branch there but did not answer (*sc. when the herald demanded, 'Who placed the branch?'*) it follows that I was bringing about my own destruction in placing the branch but was fortunately saved by not answering—plainly, through the goddesses. For if they wished to destroy me, then surely I would have admitted (*i.e. they would have caused me to admit*) placing the branch even if I had not done so.

Dem. iv 42: In my view, a god, ashamed on the city's behalf at the way things are going, has implanted this restless activity in Philip.

[6] Cf. III.A n. 5.        [7] Cf. Dodds 8–18, 186f.

Cf. Aiskhines iii 117, 'a disgusting man, utterly uneducated . . ., and it may be that some supernatural power was leading him'; Dem. ix 54, 'the fear that some supernatural power controls our course'; xiv 39, 'pray that he will fall victim to the same insanity . . .'; xxiv 124, 'outrageous arrogance . . . not . . . spontaneous, but sent upon him by the goddess.'

Dem. xviii 1: I pray . . . that the gods will put it into your minds that you should not treat my opponent as an adviser on how you should hear me . . . 8: I wish to call upon the gods again, and I pray . . . that they may put it into the minds of all of you to give that verdict on this case which will be of benefit . . .

ibid. 324: O gods! May none of you, I pray, give approval to that! Rather may you—best of all—implant even in my opponents a better mind and heart; but if they are past curing, destroy them alone, root and branch, on land and sea, and grant to the rest of us the speediest deliverance from the perils which hang over us.

Lyk. *Leokr.* 92: The very first thing that the gods do is to lead astray the thinking of bad men.

Lys. vi 22: Must it not be that a god destroyed Andokides' judgment, if he thought it better to propose imprisonment for himself than a monetary penalty?

Cf. ibid. 27, 'a god instilled forgetfulness into him'; ibid. 32, 'he has handed himself over . . ., led to this by a compulsion of supernatural origin'. Isok. v 149 suggests that the credit for whatever persuasiveness his argument has should be given to divine inspiration; ibid. 150, the god works by putting ideas into the individual's mind. So often in drama: Eur. *Ba.* 853, 'First drive him (*sc. Pentheus*) out of his wits', so that he may be amenable to the suggestions which will lead him to his death; Eur. *Hyps.* fr. 1.iii.31, 'If a god puts this (*sc. knowledge*) into your thoughts . . .'; Soph. *Oed. Col.* 371-3, (literally) 'From some god or accursed (*alitērios*) mind evil contentiousness entered them'; Soph. *Oed. Tyr.* 1258f., 'Some supernatural being showed him (*sc. the way*), for no man among us who were there (*sc. did so*)'; this last passage gives the reason for supposing divine operation (cf. Xen. *Hell.* iv 4.12, cited above).

Aphrodite and Eros (who, as we have seen [III.A.2], were popularly regarded as irresistible even by other deities, let alone by mortals) are a special and untypical case of divine intervention. When a Greek experienced sexual desire or fell in love, he was fully aware of his condition, and might even describe his own obsessive love as 'madness'. However powerful an assailant Eros might be, at least he was an identifiable adversary, and any slackening of his assault was immediately perceptible. This was true whether Eros acted on his own initiative or at the behest of Aphrodite or was a manifestation of extra-human control in general;[8] cf. Xen. *Smp.* 8.37, 'The gods implanted in you a love for Autolykos'. Again, a man who felt a sudden access of energy and courage might believe that a god had put it into him; cf. the mercenaries who charged with 'god-sent zeal' in Xen. *Hell.* vii 2.21. But a man who acts so thoughtlessly and improvidently as to raise the suspicion that he is *theoblabēs*, 'god-harmed' (Hdt. i 127.2), i.e. rendered insane by divine action on his mind,[9] is in quite a different situation: he thinks that he is master of his own actions, and that they are justified.

## 2. Chance and Fate

Whatever happens without my intending that it should happen I describe as happening by *tykhē*, 'chance', 'luck', 'fortune'; the happening may be, and probably is, intended by someone else (god or man), but it is still, from my standpoint, chance. When acts separately intended by two or more agents coincide or affect each other in some way, their conjunction is chance from the standpoint of all the agents concerned. It is therefore to be expected that events caused by gods should be described as happening by *tykhē*. Note that in the following passages 'god' translates *theos*, an adjective or phrase including the element 'god' translates the adjective *theios*, 'deity' translates *daimōn* (cf. III.A.2), 'supernatural' or a phrase including it translates the adjective *daimonios* or the substantive *to daimonion*, and 'fortune' or 'chance' translates *tykhē*.

Dem. iv 45: Whenever a portion of the citizen-body is included in an expedition, the benevolence of the gods and the (*sc. benevolence? or contribution, working?*) of fortune fight on our side.

Cf. And. i 113f., cited in section *1*; Dem. xiv 36, 'whom fortune (*i.e. the course of events*) and the supernatural reveal as a useless friend'; Dem. xlviii 24, 'in accordance with some fortune and deity'; Lys. xiii 63, 'whom fortune and the deity saved'.

Lys. xxiv 22: Since the deity (*i.e. 'my misfortune'*) deprived me of high honours, the city voted me this payment, considering that good and ill fortune are common to all men.

(Cf. V.E.2).

---

[8] In Men. *Dysk.* 36ff. Pan tells us that he has made Sostratos 'possessed' with love for Myrrhine; the young man chanced to come the right way in hunting, and Myrrhine's beauty was not left to do the job by itself.

[9] On the general question of madness of supernatural origin cf. Dodds 64–81.

At this point we must bring in another concept, 'fate': sometimes *to peprōmenon* or *to heimarmenon*, 'what is fated'; sometimes *moira*, 'allotted portion'; the Fates personified are Moirai, but one can speak also of an individual's *moira* or (indifferently) of his *daimōn*, the supernatural element in his experience which determines what good or ill shall befall him (Eur. *Phoen.* 1595; Men. fr. 714; Philemon fr. 10 [cf. fr. 191] says the same of the individual's *tykhē*), including the time and circumstances of his death, and can thus be vilified as cruel (e.g. Ant. iii γ.4).[10]

All the terms so far mentioned occur in a variety of combinations, and although contrasts can be drawn (e.g. Eur. fr. 901.1f., 'whether chance *or* a deity determines what happens to mortals', Eur. *Hyps.* fr. = Trag. Adesp. fr. 169, '*not* chance *but* the gods'),[11] we find also a certain degree of interchangeability.

Ar. *Peace* 939–45: All that a god wishes and fortune brings to success ... For now plainly a deity is changing (*sc. the situation*) for good.

Dem. ii 1f.: I think that one can on many occasions see the goodwill of the gods towards our city made manifest ... For the fact that there is now a nation prepared to fight Philip ... looks in every way like a supernatural and god-sent benefaction. ... It is shameful ... to disregard ... the allies and opportunities made for us by fortune.

Dem. xviii 192: The conclusion of any event is as the deity wishes ... 193: Do not count it a fault of mine if in the end Philip won the battle; the outcome rested with the god, not with me ... 194: If the owner of a ship, who had done everything ... which he judged necessary for a safe voyage, encountered a storm ... and were blamed for the shipwreck, he would say, 'I was not the pilot, nor had I any control over fortune, but she (*sc. controlled*) everything' ... 195: Consider simply that if it was fated that we, fighting in alliance with Thebes, should fare as we did ...

Dem. lx 19: If, being mortal, he suffered what was fated (*literally, 'he got fate'*), he has undergone what comes about by fortune, and he is not shown inferior in spirit to his adversaries.

Cf. Anaxandrides fr. 4, 'a deity moves the tiller for every man'; cf. also III.F.*1*, on *gnōmē* and *tykhē*.

Consideration of these passages suggests that at one extreme expressions such as 'as the god wishes' (e.g. Dein. ii 3, Dem. iv 7) mean, 'if that is how things go', and that *theos*, *daimōn* and *tykhē* should on occasion be translated as 'the course of events'; cf. Dem. lx 31, 'The deity gave the arms (*sc. of*

---

[10] Cf. Lattimore, 146–51.

[11] For Aristotle, of course, there is a very great difference between *tykhē* and *theiā moira* (*Eth. Nic.* 1099$^{b}$10).

Achilles) to someone else', i.e. 'It came about that the arms were given to someone else'. But in the other direction, there is a tendency (observable as early as Aiskhylos, *Ag.* 664) to personify *tykhē* as Fortune or Chance.[12]

Ant. vi 15: I am not insisting on these details in order to free myself from blame and put it on to someone else—certainly not, except on to Fortune, who, after all, is to blame for the death of many men.

Dem. xviii 207: If you condemn Ktesiphon on the grounds that my policies have not worked to the city's advantage, you will be regarded as having done wrong, not simply as victims of the unkindness[13] of Fortune.

ibid. 306: . . . not to criticise our city or its policy, but to revile Fortune, who decided the outcome of events as she did.

Cf. Ar. *Birds* 410f., 'What fortune brings them . . .?'; *Peace* 359, 'Some good fortune elected you plenipotentiary'; Dem. ix 38, Fortune 'provided an opportunity'; x 38f., she increased the city's revenues; xviii 300, she got the better of an army; xix 55, she was a benefactress; lxi 32, she 'despises inferior men and wishes to stimulate the minds of good men'; Hyp. iii 15, she inflicts diseases; Isok. iv 26, her 'gifts'; Lys. xii 80, she handed over enemies to the city; Thuc. vii 68.1. Menander brings Fortune on stage in *Aspis* 97–148 and puts into her mouth the claim that she 'has the power of decision and management over everything'; cf. Men. frr. 463, 788. In other passages, e.g. Ar. *Wealth* 6f., personification of *tykhē* can be treated more as a grammatical than as a theological phenomenon.

If Fortune is true to her own nature, it is impossible to pray or sacrifice to her, and impossible to explain her behaviour in terms either of human reasoning or of recognizable human emotions, other than malice (*GVI* 899 [Thebes, s. IV/III], 'jealous of the good'; Men. fr. 630). This is equally true of Fate, whose relationship to the will of the personal gods does not seem ever to have been systematically considered by Greek intellectuals. It is possible to equate Fate with the will of Zeus, commonly inscrutable to those whom it affects, or with the operation of a supernatural justice necessarily activated by sin (cf. Hdt. i 91.1). On the other hand, Fate can be regarded as being by her very nature arbitrary and irrational (Alexis fr. 287), and there-

---

[12] Cf. Gernet 336–9, 398; R. S. Radford, *Personification and the Use of Abstract Subjects in the Attic Orators and Thucydides* (Baltimore, 1901) 40f.

[13] *Agnōmosynē*. It is plain from comparing Aiskhines iii 170 with Thuc. ii 60.6 that *eugnōmōn* and *eugnōmosynē* not only denoted good judgment but were used as synonyms of *eunous*, 'loyal', 'well-disposed', and its abstract noun *eunoia*. Their antonyms were not *dysgnōmōn* and *dysgnōmosynē* but (as Xen. *Mem*, ii 8.5f. shows) *agnōmōn* and *agnōmosynē*, which before the fourth century had generally denoted lack of rational judgment.

fore inexplicable (Men. frr. 295, 464), a force more powerful than the gods[14] and deaf to prayer (Moschion fr. 2).

So long as 'chance' is no more than a useful word by which to distinguish the unintended from the intended, and so long as fate is impersonal, neither has any bearing on morality. If one event is fated, then, so far as we can tell, everything is or can be fated, and the use of the word 'fate' is simply a way of talking about what has actually happened. Thus it can be fated not only that I commit a crime but also that I choose to commit it and that I am blamed and punished for it. If, however, some happenings are fated but others are not, or if either Fate or Chance is a supernatural person who designs events and causes them to occur by well-timed intervention in the mental processes of certain unsuspecting agents, it follows that for some of my actions the initiative lies within me and for others it lies with beings more powerful than I. Nikostratos fr. 19 observes that chance governs everything, and forethought is a waste of time (an extension of the banal theme of human fallibility, cf. III.A.2, V.E.2). Characters in New Comedy seem sometimes to have distinguished between what is inflicted on us by fortune and what proceeds from our own characters (Men. fr. 623, Philemon frr. 99.2f., 150), but also to have played down the role of fortune by moralizing on the theme, 'You blame fortune, but the fault lies in your own character': Men. fr. 468, a man who cannot endure what happens to him 'gives the name of Fortune to his own character'; fr. 486, folly a 'misfortune chosen by oneself'; fr. 714, every man's *daimōn* is good at the time of his birth. Long before, Demokritos B119 had observed that 'Men created the image of Fortune to excuse their own lack of thought'.

## 3. Personification

Although it would be extremely misleading to say that Aphrodite is 'only' a personification of sexual desire and Eros 'only' the personification of the experience of falling in love, it is true that Greek writers sometimes speak of them in terms which are reducible in translation to common nouns; Eros may be credited with the characteristics of a person with whom others fall in love (e.g. Pl. *Smp.* 196BC, Agathon's speech) or with those of the lover (e.g. Alexis fr. 245.6–13). On the other hand, the Greeks also say things about sex and love which are not so reducible; for example, the suggestion

[14] Philemon fr. 31 speaks of the gods as slaves of *Anankē*, 'Necessity', a common word which some fifth-century intellectuals had used to denote a cosmic force which had made things to be as they are.

that Iris and Zephyros were the parents of Eros does not mean that looking at rainbows and being blown on by the west wind makes us fall in love, though it may be a riddling way of saying something about the nature of erotic love.

Among all the abstract nouns which denote emotions, forces or conditions, there are some (e.g. Peace, Persuasion) which are very commonly personified, others (e.g. Zeal, Envy) which are personified more rarely; there is not one of which we would dare to affirm that we shall never find it personified in any Greek literature or work of art which may come to light in the future.[15] Some examples which, with varying degrees of infidelity to the original, could be depersonalized in translation are:

Ant. ii γ.1: Misfortune, behind which (*whom?*) he hides his crimes in the hope that his own violence will not be detected, is wronged by him.

Eur. *Phoen.* 782f.: We salute Eulabeia (*Carefulness*), most salutary (*literally, 'useful'*) of deities, and pray to her to bring our city through safely.

Cf. Eur. *Or.* 213f., Orestes on waking apostrophizes Lēthē (Forgetfulness) as a goddess.

GVI 1493: You were archon at Athens, and obtained as your assessor a most august deity, Justice.

GVI 1564: Lady Sōphrosynē, daughter of honourable (*literally, 'great-minded'*) Modesty, he honoured you above all, together with Aretē valiant in war.

Men. *Epitr.* 555f.: Dear Persuasion, be with me as my ally and make my argument succeed!

It would be harder to depersonalize (e.g.) Eur. fr. 403, asking who were the parents of Phthonos (Spiteful Jealousy), 'the greatest of diseases', and where in the body he dwells; [Xen.] *Cyn.* 12.21, a man does not think that he is actually observed by Arete, 'but she is everywhere, for she is immortal', and 'honours' the good man. This last passage explicitly asserts the divinity of an abstraction, and so too:

Eur. *Hel.* 560 (*Helen recognises Menelaos*): O gods!—for recognition of dear ones is a god, too.

Eur. *Iph. Aul.* 392f.: I think that Hope is a goddess, and she, rather than you and your power, brought about (*sc. the swearing of the oath by Helen's suitors*).

Power to affect men seems here to be the criterion of divinity; cf. Men. frr.

---

[15] Cf. T. B. L. Webster, 'Personification as a Mode of Greek Thought', *Journal of the Warburg and Courtauld Institutes* xvii (1954), 10–21; F. W. Hamdorf, *Griechische Kultpersonifikationen der vorhellenistischen Zeit* (Mainz, 1964) is a valuable collection and classification of data.

1.4 (the earth which nourishes us), 249 ('what comes about of its own accord'), 614 (silver and gold), etc.

Personified abstractions also appear as characters on stage, e.g. Lyssa (Raving Madness), 'child of Night' (because a fearful and unwelcome being) in Eur. *Her. Fur.* 822ff., and when she says what she will do (864f.) she is speaking of what she will cause Herakles to do. This type of personification is characteristic of Old Comedy, where we meet not only familiar deities such as Peace (note Ar. *Peace* 211: she was angry because the Greek states went on fighting) but also transformations into visible form of (e.g.) Treaty, Reconciliation, Right and Wrong. Menander in *Perikeiromene* gives a long speech to Agnoia (Ignorance, Misapprehension).

Men. *Perik.* 140–2: ... providing against the possibility that through me, Ignorance, they might let something happen to them (*i.e. though actually siblings, they might fall in love with each other*) without realising what they were doing ... 162–6: And all this was sparked off for the sake of what is to come of it, so that Polemon might go into a rage—I led him on; he's not like that by nature—and start something which will cause everything else to be revealed.

'Through me, Ignorance' could by itself be replaced by 'through ignorance', but if Ignorance caused Polemon to behave contrary to his normal character, she was acting by virtue of her divine power over mortals. Plainly she is not saying that Polemon went into a rage through not knowing the true facts of the situation, for she implies that he acted in a way in which mere ignorance would *not* normally have made him act.

With the exception of Fortune as sometimes seen from the standpoint of the unfortunate, some disagreeable beings who serve, like Lyssa, as the servants of greater deities, and a few 'neutrals' such as Rumour (Aiskhines i 128), it was predominantly revered and welcomed qualities and activities and conditions which were personified.

Dem. xxv 35: There are altars of Justice and Good Order and Modesty throughout mankind, the fairest and holiest in each man's soul and nature, and others built for the community as a whole to honour; but there are no altars of Shamelessness or Blackmail or Perjury or Ingratitude.

Cf. ibid. 11 on Good Order and Justice. As a statement about religious cults, what the speaker says is right; we can pray and sacrifice to Justice, but Injustice is her absence, not her fellow-deity. In certain circumstances, fig-trees and olive-trees are treated as divine,[16] but mud is not. It is interesting

[16] In the document referred to in V.D. n. 7 fruit and vegetable crops are included

that the only oratorical passage (Dem. xxv 52, cited in V.D.5) which personifies disagreeable forces such as Resentment makes explicit reference to the depiction of the underworld by painters.

The presence of the abstract entity in the particular instance, the participation of the particular in the abstract, or whichever way round we should put it, raise metaphysical problems on which popular literature has nothing to say. But the habit of personification, which necessarily means deification—for that which can in any sense be in two places at once is superior to us in power (cf. [Xen.] *Cyn.* 12.21, cited above)—is *prima facie* of great moral importance. It would not be difficult for me, by selecting the right models from here and there in classical Greek literature and concentrating them in a single narrative, to describe a sequence of my own actions entirely in such a way as to make it seem that I was the helpless plaything of supernatural beings.

## III.H. MORAL RESPONSIBILITY

### 1. *General Statements*

Having surveyed the ways in which the Greeks considered the possible range of moral activity on the part of any individual to be limited by circumstances and forces outside his control, we may feel that they posited more numerous and more severe limitations than we are accustomed to posit; in particular, we may be struck by their treatment of sexual desire as an irresistible god, their externalization and personification of emotions, and their readiness to believe that a god may pervert the course of a man's thinking without his necessarily displaying to others any outward sign of insanity. From this we might conclude either that the Greeks were far more tolerant and less punitive than we are, or alternatively that they were unaware that the assignation of responsibility to the individual could be disputable. Neither conclusion would be correct.

Gorgias the sophist, in his 'proof' that Helen cannot be blamed for going to Troy with Paris, appears implicitly to deny moral responsibility altogether.

Gorg. B11.6ff.: She did what she did either through the wish of Fortune and the design of the gods and decrees of Necessity, or because she was carried off by force, or persuaded by argument, or captivated by Love.

among the divine witnesses of the oath; they are divine to the extent that they can be sworn by, if not in any other way.

Clearly a mere mortal (even though Helen was in fact the daughter of Zeus by a mortal mother) cannot resist supernatural power: 'If, therefore, the responsibility is to be put upon Fortune and the god, Helen's name is not to be sullied.' But words and Love, together with fear and madness, also possess irresistible power, as we can all see from our experience (8ff.); cf. Men. fr. 569, Love 'inexorable'.

ibid. 19: She went where she went because she was ensnared by Fortune, not because her mind wished it; she went by the compulsion of Eros, not by calculated design.

The most important aspect of Gorgias's speech is that it is not a philosophical or scientific attempt to discover how far Helen could be held responsible, let alone a philosophical argument about the nature of responsibility in general, but a 'defence', a sophistic attempt to secure the 'acquittal' of a heroine who was often represented in poetry and drama as blameworthy, and it belongs to the sophistic tradition of 'praising and blaming the same thing', i.e. of making a case. In popular literature we do not find, and we should not expect to find, abstract discussion of responsibility cast in hypothetical terms and designed genuinely to solve questions of principle. We find a number of general statements. For example, Dem. xx 140, xxi 43, xxiii 73, xxiv 41, 49, 67 all recognize the distinction between deliberate wrongdoing, which incurs anger and resentment, and unintentional wrongdoing, which deserves indulgence; Dem. xviii 20, 274, xix 98, 101, 185, xxiv 110, recognize that a citizen might advocate wrong policies *either* through ignorance of relevant facts and failure to understand the situation (cf. xviii 172, arguing that patriotism unsupported by intelligent analysis is not enough) *or* with self-seeking, unpatriotic design; Dem. xviii 4, 159, xix 21 argue that responsibility for disastrous policy lies ultimately with those whose conduct has caused it to be followed, not solely with those whose acts constituted the policy; cf. Dem. xxiii 43 on the 'pollution' of the proposer of a decree which might excuse homicide. All these statements, and all those which will be cited below, belong to arguments about particular cases; they are weapons of attack and defence wielded for a purpose, and none of them is intended as a contribution to the solution of a problem in philosophy or jurisprudence.

Aiskhines i 190f.: Do not imagine that wrongdoing originates with the gods rather than with the vileness of men; do not imagine that Furies, as on the tragic stage, harry and punish the impious with blazing torches. No, it is the unbridled pleasures of the flesh, the inability ever to be satisfied, which mans the dens of brigands and fills the pirates' ships; these pleasures are each man's Fury, these incite him to slaughter his fellow-citizens, enslave himself to tyrants, and join in conspiracies against democracy.

The context here shows that by 'punish the impious' Aiskhines means 'cause the impious to commit further acts from which punishment will necessarily follow' (cf. V.D.4). Aiskhines is in fact foregoing a type of argument which we encountered in III.G.1.

Ant. v 91f.: Wrongful acquittal is only an error (*hamartēma*), but wrongful condemnation is an impiety (*asebēma*) ... Errors which are involuntary (*ākousios*) are forgivable, but those which are deliberate (*hekousios*) are not; for the involuntary error proceeds from chance (*tykhē*), but the deliberate from intention (*gnōmē*).

Eur. *Hipp.* 358f.: Those who are *sōphrōn* become enamoured of evils, not with deliberate intent, but none the less.

ibid. 380–3: We know what is good ... but do not carry it out, some through laziness, others preferring some different pleasure to honour.

Eur. fr. 292.4f.: Some sicknesses from which mortals suffer they take upon themselves (*literally, 'are self-chosen'*), while others come from the gods.

Men. fr. 98: It is wrong to maltreat slaves when they err with goodwill and not through bad character ... That is truly disgraceful.

Soph. *Oed. Col.* 252f.: If a god leads, no mortal can escape.

Cf. Men. fr. 358, good or bad fortune given by a god, not caused by 'the error of one's character'.

Thuc. i 69.6: One brings criticism (*aitia*) against friends when they err (*hamartanein*), but an accusation (*katēgoriā*) against enemies when they have committed a wrong (*adikein*).

(This last passage, which Thucydides puts into the mouth of a Corinthian speaker at Sparta, has a sophistic flavour, drawing semantic distinctions which were quite alien to actual usage). Cf. Eur. *Tro.* 886, distinguishing between (literally) 'compulsion of nature *or* mind (*nous*) of mortals'; Lys. xxxi 11f., misdeeds committed by the poor and weak deserve pardon; Men. fr. 359, misfortune happens through *tykhē*, but misdeed (*adikēma*) by choice (*hairesis*); Men. fr. 513, it isn't the amount one drinks that makes one misbehave, but the drinker's own nature; Soph. *Oed. Tyr.* 591, 'If I myself were in power, I would do much even against my will' (because a ruler has to do disagreeable things for his subjects' sake); Thuc. i 32.5.

## 2. Responsibility in Law and in the Courts

Homicide, injury and damage were penalized with comparative leniency in Attic law when it was clear that there had been no intention to do the harm that was actually suffered (Dem. xxi 43, xxiii 71–3), though the penalty of temporary exile for involuntary homicide was in many cases unjust by our standards.[1] A doctor was not penalized if treatment prescribed in good faith killed the patient (Ant. iv γ.5). To rape a woman of citizen status was less heinous than to seduce her (Lys. i 32); conceivably this was (or was sometimes thought to be) a recognition of the power of sexual passion, but more probably it was because rape, an 'involuntary misfortune' to the woman (Men. *Epitr.* 914) was not regarded as alienating her affection for her husband and was therefore less of an injury to him than her seduction (nor, according to Xen. *Hiero* 3.4, did it necessarily damage her reputation).

When a man was accused of *hybris*, the violent or contumacious treatment of a fellow-citizen as if he were a foreigner or a slave, it seems that he might successfully plead drunkenness or an access of anger (Dem. xxi 41, 73f., 180), for the attitude of the aggressor towards his victim was an essential ingredient of *hybris*; civil lawsuits for physical assault existed side by side with indictment for *hybris*. For all we know (and we must remember that we hardly ever know the outcome of the cases for which extant speeches were composed), there may have been many occasions on which a defendant was acquitted because he was thought to have acted under compulsion by circumstances or forces which he could not reasonably be expected to control. We do know, however, that the law itself did not explicitly recognize absence of criminal intent except in respect of death and damage; we hear of very severe penalties inflicted for apparently excusable misdeeds; and a few passages seem to treat with contempt an excuse of *prima facie* validity.

Lys. x 30: I understand that he will have recourse to the argument that he spoke this slander in anger when I had given evidence in support of the testimony of Dionysios. But you must reflect that the legislator has made no allowance for anger, but imposes a penalty on the slanderer unless he demonstrates that what he said is true.

Aiskhines i 87f., speaks of men who as jurors accepted a bribe because they were 'unable to support old age and poverty', and Dem. xxiv 123 refers in general terms to men who are forced into petty administrative dishonesties by poverty; but, says Demosthenes, the offenders are punished just the same, and the old jurors were actually put to death.

Eratosthenes, the defendant against Lys. xii, and the resident aliens prosecuted in Lys. xxii seem to have tried to plead obedience to the orders of superior authority. Eratosthenes cannot have expected much of this plea,

---

[1] On involuntary homicide, and on the law relating to the planning of a murder carried out by someone else, cf. MacDowell 46f., 58–68, 110, 117–25f.

since his superior authority had been the oligarchy of the Thirty Tyrants (Lys. xii 29, 31), but the aliens claimed to be following the guidance of an Athenian magistrate. Lysias tramples swiftly and scornfully on their claim (xxii 5f.). In one other passage Lysias suggests that even a true plea of action under duress should make no difference if the crime is grave enough.

> Lys. xiii 52: Agoratos will perhaps say that he committed crimes of this magnitude against his will (*ākōn*). My opinion is that however much he may be acting against his will, if a man commits great crimes against you, crimes which could not be exceeded, you should not on that account refrain from vengeance on him.

What underlies this argument, I think, is the idea that if a plea of innocent intention is never accepted in the case of a really serious offence, no one can commit such an offence with any expectation of escaping the full measure of punishment by a false plea, and that situation will be to the community's advantage. Lysias does not, however, press his argument, but goes on to ridicule the plea of action under duress in the particular case of Agoratos.

Where the law provided for the possibility of a plea of innocent intent, it was necessary for the defendant to prove an alternative sane intention; what we call 'diminished responsibility' by virtue of insanity does not seem to have been recognized either in theory or in practice. This is much as we would have expected from the Greeks' lack of interest in the distinction 'bad or mad' (III.F.*3*).

> Dem. xix 267: Those men who did that felt no shame ... The acceptance of bribes has such power to make men crazy (*ekphrōn*) and deranged (*paraplēx*).

Here it seems that bad actions make people mad; we would say that yielding to the temptation to commit a shameless act may lastingly impair the sense of shame, but we would not imagine that it could actually cause the peculiar shamelessness manifested in some psychoses. The Greeks would not have considered that madness, however caused, was a justification for keeping a man alive if he did something which normally incurred the death-penalty.

> Dem. xlviii 56: That is the kind of man Olympiodoros is, not only dishonest (*adikos*) but also regarded by all his relatives and friends as mentally sick (*melankholōn*) in the way he lives ... 58: If you do this (*sc. decide the case as I ask*), your verdict will be just and advantageous to all of us, not least to Olympiodoros himself.

The insanity of Olympiodoros lay in his being infatuated with a *hetaira* (52–4) to whose interests he gave precedence (a situation recognized in testamentary law as grounds for disputing a will). The speaker's profession of concern for Olympiodoros rests on his kinship, which causes him embarrassment in bringing the lawsuit.

Dem. lv 30: I think that in walling-in his own ground he is sensible (*sōphronein*), but in bringing a legal action against me he is, in my view, a very bad man (*ponēros*) and adversely affected (*literally, 'corrupted', 'spoiled'*) by sickness.

The adversary here is either bad because he is mad or mad in addition to being bad; legally, it does not matter which.

However clearly it was perceived that an individual's 'nature' circumscribes his moral capacity, the community had a right to deal with its members according to the contribution, for good or ill, which their various natures made.

Dem. xxv 32f.: Do you not see that his nature and his politics are governed neither by reason nor by any sense of decency, but by desperation (*aponoia*),[2] or rather, that his politics as a whole are desperate? Desperation is the greatest of ills for its possessor, formidable and troublesome for everyone else, and for a city, intolerable. For everyone who is desperate has ceased to care about himself and such success as may proceed from reason; if he does succeed, it is only through the unforeseen and unexpected. Who, then, in his senses would bring himself or the interests of his fatherland into association with desperation? Who would not avoid it to the utmost of his ability and put its possessor out of the way (*i.e. kill, outlaw or exile him*), so as never to fall in with it even by mistake?

Cf. Aiskhines i 191, 'Extirpate such natures'; Dem. xx 140, 'Resentment (*phthonos*) is a sign of a vicious nature, and the man who suffers from it cannot on any pretext claim indulgence'.

If a man said of his adversary, 'He has plainly been driven out of his wits by a god', the adversary himself could not hope for too much from the admission that this was indeed so and from a consequent plea that he should be held entirely innocent. No one could demonstrate, nor, probably, could it even be agreed by a pair of adversaries or by those to whose judgment they appealed, that such action on the part of a god was arbitrary and morally meaningless; there was always the possibility that it was a punishment for sin, and no one would be in a hurry to ally himself with someone who had incurred divine anger. In Eur. *Supp.* 504 the Theban herald, justifying the refusal of his city to hand over the bodies of the fallen heroes, says

---

[2] *Aponoia* and the verb *aponoeisthai*, absent from most Attic authors, are not synonymous with *paranoia* and *paranoein* (which denote insanity) but are applied to the desperation which acts without regard for praise, blame or other consequences (e.g. Thuc. i 82.4, vii 67.4, both referring to military forces in hopeless situations). Theophr. *Char.* 6 seems to be describing, under the rubric *aponoia*, the shameless inconsequentiality which on a sufficiently spectacular scale labels the agent a psychopath.

that the divinely-inflicted deaths of Amphiaraos and Kapaneus show Zeus to have been hostile to them, and they should be treated as accursed; the chorus, who want the bodies for burial, retort (511f.) that Zeus's punishment is *enough*, and that the dead heroes deserve no further maltreatment. The attitude of the herald is not fundamentally dissimilar to that of Theseus (ibid. 589–93) when he makes Adrastos stay behind because he does not want a man who has suffered misfortune (to which a certain lack of piety contributed [156]) to imperil, as if by infection, the whole expedition (cf. 223–8). Such concepts could be exploited sophistically; in Ant. iii γ.8 the prosecutor of a young man who has accidentally killed a boy while practising javelin-throwing argues that the young man may have been guilty of an impiety and so, being 'stained', was manoeuvred by the gods into a predicament which would result in his condemnation for accidental homicide; while the defendant argues (iii δ.10) that if it was the divine will that the boy should die, it would be impious to condemn the young man who was the instrument of death (cf. III.G.*1*). Delphi exonerated the priestess Timo for admitting Miltiades to the sanctuary on Paros, since it was destined that he should die there (Hdt. vi 135.3).[3]

### 3. Description of Choice and Error

When it was desired to emphasize that a person not only does things which are unwelcome to the community but does them by deliberate decision, he could be described as 'wishing' (*boulesthai*) to be bad: And. i 95, '. . . who is the most *ponēros* of all men and wishes to be such'; Ant. iii β.1; Ar. *Knights* 1281; cf. Lys. xiv 35, 'Who . . ., if he did not wish to be *ponēros*, would tell the enemy . . .?' In Eur. *Hel.* 998 a similar expression is used of virtue, and the distinction between nature and policy is made explicit: 'I am by nature < such as > to be pious, and I wish to be'. Cf. Pl. *Smp.* 213C, 'Aristophanes or anyone else who is laughable and wishes to be'. *Boulēsis*, 'inclination', is contrasted with proper regard for the law (e.g. Dem. xxv 25f., 75, liv 19) or with the effort to understand by rational thought the nature and consequences of an act (e.g. Dem. iii 19). The English noun 'will' and verb 'to will', as they are used in ethics (or in colloquial language, in expressions such as 'strong

---

[3] 'Fatalism' can predispose to extraordinary magnanimity, as in the case of Abu-Sir (*Arabian Nights* nos. 930–40 [Lane]), who forgives the injury done to him by the unspeakable Abu-Kir: 'May God acquit thee of responsibility and pardon thee! For it was an event predestined from eternity to befall me.'

will' and 'will-power') cannot be translated into Greek except by using words which are also required in translating one or other of 'wish', 'desire', 'have in mind', 'intend', 'plan', 'choose', 'prefer', 'enthusiasm', 'zeal', 'obstinacy', etc. This does not mean that the Greeks were blind to the existence of a distinct factor in thought and action which we call 'will', but that (in common with other highly civilized peoples, modern as well as ancient) they did not find that any useful purpose was served by attempting to distinguish an ingredient other than wishing, choosing and enthusiasm in the directional aspect of thought and action.[4] In this they may well have been wise. Similarly, even if it were true, as has been commonly argued, that the Greeks of the early archaic period had only an imperfect notion of the unity of the personality (since Homer so often speaks of different internal organs as initiating thoughts and feelings), it would not follow from this that they were primitive or perverse; it might rather be said that they understood the disunity of the personality better than their descendants did.[5]

Unlike the noun 'will', it is easy to translate 'choose' and 'choice' into Greek as *haireisthai* and *hairesis*. We all know the difference between the experience which we call 'choosing' and the experiences which we call 'being compelled', 'being driven', 'not stopping to think', etc., whatever the ultimate analysis of these experiences in causal terms may be. The greater the freedom from need or pressure, the more creditable the choice of good was thought to be; cf. Dem. lx 37, on the dead of Khaironeia, making 'the deity' the cause of defeat but the 'choice' of the dead men the justification for the honours paid to them. Aristodemos was honoured for his bravery at the battle of Plataea less than Poseidonios, for he, unlike Poseidonios, was under overwhelming emotional pressure to erase the shame of his surviving the last stand of Leonidas at Thermopylai (Hdt. ix 71.2–4). *Prohairesis*, 'preference', an important term in Aristotelian ethics, is not uncommon in oratory after the middle of the fourth century,[6] and is often translatable as

---

[4] Cf. J. C. Opstelten, *Beschouwingen naar Aanleiding van het Ontbreken van ons ethisch Wilsbegrip in de Oud-Griekse Ethiek* (Amsterdam, 1959).

[5] Any statement to the effect that the early Greeks had *no* notion of the unity of the personality would be adequately refuted by the fact that there is no difficulty in translating 'I wish . . .' or 'I thought . . .' literally into Homeric Greek; for further criticism, see especially Pearson 208–10. Even a judicious contrast between Homeric and later (including 'our') ways of talking about psychology and physiology (Adkins [2] 13–24, 44–8, 60–6) needs to be read with recognition of (i) a certain autonomy of language and thus a possible divergence between the direction of linguistic change and the direction of conceptual change, and (ii) the considerable difference between current views of personality and the less analytic view normally taken by our grandparents.

[6] Cf. Gernet 351f.

'policy', 'plan', '(*sc.* consistent) aim', '(*sc.* preferred) style' (of life: Dem. xxiii 141, xlviii 56, lxi 2). The expressions 'in accordance with *prohairesis*' in Lyk. *Leokr.* 148 and 'out of *prohairesis*' in Dem. vi 16, xxi 44, characterize a series of actions which all confrom to a consistent underlying policy or attitude, but there is no contrast between *prohairesis* and *boulēsis*; Dem. xliv 57 contrasts 'out of *prohairesis* and *boulēsis*' with 'acting under compulsion' (∼ 'having preferred', 59).[7]

We saw in section *1* that it was possible to distinguish between error (*hamartiā, hamartēma,* verb *hamartanein* or *exhamartanein*) on the one hand and crime, wrong-doing (*adikiā, adikēma,* verb *adikein*), sin or impiety (*asebeia, asebēma,* verb *asebein*) on the other. This distinction could also be made in particular cases, e.g. Philippides fr. 26, 'You can't say . . . "I erred", to get my forgiveness . . . The man who does violence to one who is weaker does not "err", but *hybrizei*'. The passages in which the distinction is drawn are, however, in a minority. Not all errors are crimes or sins, but any crime or sin can be called 'error' in Greek.[8]

And. i 29: . . . and that no error towards the goddesses, neither great nor small, can be imputed to me . . . My opponents spoke about others guilty on earlier occasions of error and impiety towards the goddesses < and described > what punishment befell each of them . . . 30: . . . if you were to be angry with me for the errors of others . . . 33: If I have committed no error . . .

Cf. ibid. 67.

Ant. vi 6: Correct verdicts constitute vengeance for him who has been wronged; but that an innocent man should be declared a murderer is error and impiety against the gods and the law.

The contrast between this passage and Ant. v 91f., quoted in section *1*, is striking; it is virtually certain that both speeches are genuine works of Antiphon, both are concerned with verdicts in cases of homicide, and internal evidence suggests that they cannot be more than ten years apart.

Isok. xviii 17: The villainy of the Thirty Tyrants incited many to behave in this way, for the Thirty were so far from punishing those who committed crimes (*adikein*) that they actually enjoined some men to err (*exhamartanein*).

Cf. ibid. 22, 41, 48, 57; Lys. vii 1, xii 4, xx 3, xxix 13, xxxi 27f.

[7] Cf. G. S. Simonetos, 'Die Willensmängel in den Rechtsgeschäften nach altgriechi-schem Recht', in *Wege der Forschung* xlv (1968), 455–82.

[8] Cf. Gernet 304–13, 339–48; he notes a certain shift from *hamart-* towards *adik-* in the later fourth century.

Isok. xx 9: I think that you would become as angry as this case merits if you were to go over in your minds how much greater *hybris* is than other errors (*hamartēmata*), for you will find that other kinds of wrongdoing (*adikiai*) harm only some aspects of the victim's life, whereas *hybris* damages his fortune as a whole . . .

Lys. i 26: You preferred to commit such an error (*hamartēma, exhamartanein, sc. adultery*) against my wife and children . . . 45: Had I not been wronged the greatest of all wrongs (*adikēmata*) . . .

Cf. Thuc. vi 80.2, 'become *kakos*' and *hamartanein* treated as synonyms. It must be emphasized that the *hamart-* group of words was not used simply in referring to alleged misdeeds of one's own, as if hinting at extenuating circumstances, but in direct attack on the misdeeds of a hated adversary; in addition to examples already cited, cf. Dem. xxi 217, Is. iii 27, Lys. xiv *passim* (on the elder and the younger Alkibiades), xxxi 2, 4, 20, 23f. The assumption underlying the usage may have been that if one knew the law and the rules of society and understood both their application to a particular case and the possible consequences, disagreeable to oneself, of breaking them (cf. V.A.*3*), one would not break them. But inference from language to 'underlying assumptions' is dangerous (cf. II.A.*1*), and it is perhaps sufficient to note that just as in war and sport '*hamartanein* the target' is simply to 'miss' it, so in moral action *hamartiā* is 'not attaining' what is desired by oneself or by others.

The possibility of regarding an individual as impelled to wrongdoing by external forces too strong for him to resist encouraged the description of a crime as a 'misfortune' or 'mishap' (*symphorā*) whenever the speaker wished for any reason to evoke sympathy for the wrongdoer.

And. ii 5–7: In my opinion, whoever first said[9] that all men depend on faring well or ill was quite right; error is, surely, a great ill-faring (*dysprāxiā*); they who err least are the most fortunate, and wisest are they who repent soonest . . . My case deserves pity rather than resentment, for I was plunged so deep in ill-fortune (*dysdaimoniā*, '*having a bad* daimōn' [cf. III.G.*2*])—should I say, by youth and folly, or by the ability of those who persuaded me into such a disastrous idea (*literally, 'mishap of the mind'*)?— . . .

Andokides refers here to his participation—at the instigation, he claims, of others—in the mutilation of the herms. Dem. xxiii 70, arguing against a proposal that if a certain alleged friend of Athens were killed every attempt should be made to extradite the killer, points out that the homicide law of Athens does not allow a murderer to be pursued beyond the boundaries of

---

[9] A statement of common Greek type; in drama, 'Wise was he who first said . . .', etc.

Attica; the makers of the law, says Demosthenes, 'did not persecute misfortunes (*atykhēmata*), but alleviated ... mishaps (*symphorai*).' Here murderers are treated as 'unfortunate' because exile is a consequence of the crime; cf. And. i 86, where *symphorai* refers to the exile or disenfranchisement which may have resulted from treasonable activity. When a speaker in Thuc. i 122.4 describes 'lack of understanding, timorousness and neglect' as 'three mishaps', he probably means that to be regarded as guilty of any of those faults is a misfortune to those who incur the reproach, and no psychological externalization is necessarily implied.[10]

## 4. *Attack and Defence*

We can never know the extent of pressure on another person, let alone the extent of supernatural compulsion; hence the attribution of responsibility to such pressures is characteristic of excuse, defence and magnanimity, while its denial is characteristic of attack and reproach. In Eur. *Tro.* Helen (944–54) claims forgiveness for her flight with Paris and tells Hekabe to blame Aphrodite, for even Zeus is 'the slave of Aphrodite'. Hekabe in reply ridicules the story of the Judgment of Paris (969–82) and denies (983–97) that Aphrodite played any part in Helen's flight; Helen's own folly, lust and greed made her desire the beauty of Paris and the wealth of Troy. There is no possibility of their agreeing; Hekabe hates Helen, and Helen has unbearable reproach to fend off. Examples of this kind are numerous in drama. In Euripides' *Cretes* Pasiphae makes a fluent and impassioned defence of her perverted love for a bull, a 'madness inflicted by a god', an ill which grieves her, for it was no choice of hers (Eur. fr. 82 [Austin] 9f., cf. 29f.). Minos in his anger simply ignores her argument (ibid. 44ff.); she might as well not have spoken. Orestes in Eur. *Or.* 596 is in a much stronger position when he says, 'It was Apollo who erred, not I', for the oracle had given him a plain command (cf. Eur. *El.* 1266f.). In Eur. *Tro.* 408–10 Kassandra is grudgingly forgiven by Talthybios for vilifying his superiors, on the grounds that she is obviously in a frenzied state of divine possession. Cf. Eur. *Rhesus* 938–40, Athena (correctly) blamed for what Odysseus and Diomedes did.

Eur. *Hel.* 445f. MENELAOS: Don't push me away by force! OLD WOMAN (*who is*

---

[10] Dem. xiv 32, 'Who is so unfortunate (*dystykhēs*) that he would be willing to sacrifice himself, his parents, his family's tombs, his fatherland, all for brief profit?' means, 'Who is so desperately poor ...?', not, 'Who is so pitiably shameless or demented ...?'.

*obeying her master's orders*): Well, you won't do as I tell you! It's your fault (*sc. if you are pushed*).

Cf. Thuc. iii 55.1, the Plataeans hold the Spartans 'responsible' for Plataiai's fighting on the side of Athens; ibid. 55.4, responsibility belongs to the leader of an alliance, not to the allies who follow.

> Eur. *Hipp.* 476 (*the Nurse to Phaidra*): Be brave, and love! This is a god's will (*i.e.* 'Do not resist Eros').
>
> ibid. 1334f. (*Artemis to Theseus*): Your ignorance (*sc.* of the facts) absolves your error of bad intent.
>
> Ar. *Wasps* 1001f.: Gods, forgive me! I acted unintentionally, and not in my usual character!

Cf. Ar. *Peace* 668f., 'Forgive us—our mind was in our shoes!' (using a proverbial expression for 'We didn't know what we were doing', but also alluding to domination by Kleon 'the tanner'); Eur. *Iph. Taur.* 584–7, a Greek sacrificed by Iphigeneia blamed the *nomos* which she was constrained to follow, not her in person; Eur. *Phoen.* 433f., Polyneikes declares that he has been compelled, against his will, to take up arms against his country; Lys. i 26, 'It is not I who kill you, but the law' (untrue; the law permitted, but did not enjoin, the killing of an adulterer caught in the act); Men. *Epitr.* 1123f., quoting Euripides in a resigned comment on rape, 'Nature willed it, and nature cares nothing for the law'; Philemon fr. 104, 'Wine is the villain'[11] (*sc.* and I am not to blame). In Soph. *Oed. Col.* 521–3, 547f., 693–1002, Oedipus strongly and repeatedly affirms that his ignorance of his parents' identity absolves him from blame for killing his father (under what he regards as provocation fully justifying murder) and marrying his mother; Theseus's attitude throughout the play implies that he (unlike the chorus when Oedipus first reveals his identity) does not feel towards Oedipus in the least as one would feel towards a man who had quite deliberately committed parricide and incest. In Xen. *Cyr.* iii 1.38 a man sentenced to death is so *kalos kāgathos* as to say, 'Don't blame your father for executing me; he is acting in ignorance . . . and what is done in ignorance I count involuntary'.

The same principle applies to many passages of oratory: Dem. lix 58f., 'forced by his sickness' ∼ 'persuaded by his infirmity'; Lys. xviii 19, xxv 34f., excusable that the Athenians should be unforgiving when their anger against the Thirty Tyrants was fresh.

It goes without saying that the defeat of one's own nation in battle is misfortune, not the deserved penalty for cowardice or incompetence, and is

---

[11] *Ho ponēros*; cf. Dem. xix 33, 'Everyone will easily see who is *ho ponēros*'.

encompassed by divine intervention, not by the superior skill or courage of the enemy. This is made explicit in the epitaph on the Athenians killed at Koroneia in 447 (*GVI* 17), where defeat is attributed to the intervention of a hero, 'not the strength of the enemy'.[12]

## 5. Ancient and Modern Presuppositions

Nowadays we are greatly preoccupied with questions of legal responsibility (though we do not talk so much, outside philosophical circles, about moral responsibility). The reasons for this preoccupation are to be sought in three elements of our experience which did not enter into the Greek experience.

The oldest, and perhaps the most influential, of these elements is a distinctive feature of Christianity. Christian doctrine asserts (i) that God is never less than just and has an infinite capacity for mercy, (ii) that every human being without exception will be assigned either to great and eternal happiness or to great and eternal pain, and (iii) that assertions (i) and (ii) are a matter not simply of opinion and speculation, but of revelation by God, who is not pleased by our doubting or rejecting them. Since infinite reward for finite virtue is merciful but not just, and infinite punishment for finite sin is neither just nor such as can be contemplated without disgust by anyone capable of mercy, Christians have been compelled to abandon assertion (iii), or to pretend that certain statements in the Bible do not mean anything at all like what they say, or to sanctify the incompatibility of assertions (i) and (ii) by calling it a 'mystery', or to invent super-laws of super-nature to which we must adjust our erroneous ideas of merit and desert. The third and fourth of these attempts to solve the problem give every encouragement to a belief, commonly voiced without a thought for relevant evidence, or even in defiance of all relevant evidence, that somehow or other the sinner deserves eternal punishment because his sin is his own free choice, for which he is truly responsible.[13] The Greeks, on the other hand, did not expect gods to be merciful, and they were mostly aware that propositions about divine justice were not conclusively demonstrable or refutable. Some of them

---

[12] Ch. the couplet on the Athenian dead at Syracuse, attributed (Plutarch, *Nicias* 17.4) to Euripides, and C. M. Bowra, *Problems in Greek Poetry* (Oxford, 1953), chapter VI.

[13] It is noticeable that when people of sensitivity and intellectual acumen (e.g. the late C. S. Lewis) address themselves to this group of problems they 'change gear', as it were, and accept, or even propound, arguments of a quality which would not impress them if used in any connection other than the defence of Christian eschatology.

thought it was likely that we are judged after death and punished if we have committed any of a certain list of sins; others did not think so. They were therefore free from strong emotional pressures to make generalized assertions about the freedom of the will, and even their philosophers did not think that this was a central problem in ethics.

The second element is new: the fact that during the last hundred years we have discovered (or, in a few cases, rediscovered and described in novel terms) more about the determinants of behaviour and the means of modifying it[14] than in the previous three thousand years. Knowing better why people behave as they do, we find that no cut-and-dried view of responsibility bears any relation to the facts. The gap grows between the pretences which are so often necessary if the instruments of law are to take and enforce decisions and the acknowledgement, which we are completely free to make when we are not functioning as jurors, judges or magistrates,[15] that the more we know about the circumstances of an act and its agent, the more doubtful it becomes that he 'could' have acted otherwise.

The third element is the reason why the second concerns us so much. In Western Europe and America a great many people have become accustomed for a very long time to regard the law and the state as mechanisms for the protection of individual freedoms; this attitude has been reinforced by Christian emphasis on the individual's relation to God. We do not take kindly to the notion that there is no religious, moral or domestic claim on the individual which has precedence over the community's claim on his efforts to promote its security and prosperity *vis-à-vis* other communities. As states grow larger and their structure and way of life increase in complexity at a rate faster than we can adjust to, individuals, associations and areas resist integration even to the point of treating 'I have a right to . . .' as a synonym of 'I would like . . .'. The Greek did not regard himself as having more rights at any given time than the laws of the city into which he was born gave him at that time; these rights could be reduced, for the community was sovereign, and no rights were inalienable. The idea that parents have a

---

[14] This knowledge has naturally not solved problems to which it is not relevant, nor does it prevent evils which are not created by lack of it.

[15] Even then, we have a good measure of freedom, since the factual question, 'Did this man commit that act?', is answerable without reference to what caused him to commit it. In sentencing, it is common for a judge or magistrate to give less consideration to the deserts of the convicted person than to the probable consequences of the sentence for him and for potential lawbreakers in the future. In civil actions involving damages for negligence or slander there is often virtually no point of contact between law and morality.

*right* to educate (or fail to educate) their children in whatever way they please, or that the individual has a *right* to take drugs which may adversely affect his health and so diminish his usefulness, or a *right* to take up the time of doctors and nurses in consequence of not wearing a safety-belt, would have seemed to a Greek too laughable to be discussed.[16] No Greek community would have recognized 'conscientious objection' to war, or to anything else.[17]

From this it followed that the question which a lawsuit or an indictment posed to a Greek jury was not necessarily or always, 'How can we be fair to this individual?', but 'What action in respect of this situation is likely to have the best consequences for the strength of the community?' On some occasions the answer might be forgiveness of a misdeed committed apparently without external pressures on the agent, and on other occasions it might be punishment of a misdeed committed under pressures so great that no member of the jury could be sure he would have resisted them himself. Punishment can have a deterrent effect not only on others who may contemplate the same misdeed in the future, but also on the wrongdoer himself, for even if he could not help doing wrong on the first occasion, memory of punishment is a determinant of his choice, and may prove to be the decisive determinant, on future occasions (cf. Aiskhines i 192, 196).[18] The Greek attitude to the individual (cf. VI.B) and the operation of the law provided no incentive to any attempt at an explicit formulation of a general theory of responsibility.[19] Naturally it matters to an individual whether people think

[16] I do not mean that Greek fathers did not decide how their sons should be educated, nor that the average Greek was so good a man that he always stopped to think whether he was making himself an asset or a liability to other people, but simply that extant Greek literature affords no evidence for a phenomenon comparable with the current extension of 'a right to . . .'; cf. Gerlach 59–61.

[17] When Socrates resisted the pressure of the assembly to put to the vote the proposal that the generals should be tried together after the battle of Arginoussai (Xen. *Hell.* i 7.15), he acted with exemplary courage, but he was not giving precedence to conscience over law; many people at the time, and most people after the event, thought that the proposal was illegal.

[18] Adkins (1) 3f. says, ' "Was the agent responsible for his actions or not?" is the most important question which can be asked of any action to which reward or punishment may be relevant'. Although it is generally more important to us than to the Greeks, some judgments given in the courts of modern democracies (cf. n. 13 above) imply that other considerations are more important. This is not surprising, since the question, however desirable it might be to answer it, is not in fact answerable unless (as is unavoidable in the hearing of court cases) attention is withdrawn from many of the relevant considerations. Any question becomes answerable if evidence is selected with a view to making it so.

[19] J. W. Jones, *The Law and Legal Theory of the Greeks* (Oxford, 1956) 261 describes

better or worse of him, and he therefore does his best to divert blame, reproach and rejection away from himself on to something external to him; but the Greek was aware that he in doing this, and likewise his enemy in ridiculing his attempt, were not offering alternative answers to an answerable question but each rationalizing his own choice of standpoint.

Many of us, if we pause to reflect, have experience of working within systems and organizations which in one important respect resemble a Greek city-state more closely than they resemble a modern nation conceived (by a certain abstraction) as consisting of a code of laws and a large number of individuals. If I am electing a candidate, appointing someone to a job, or considering him for promotion, it does not matter to me so very much whether or not he could 'help' doing the good and bad things that he has done. I do not want to extend the power and authority of someone who may have admirable moral intentions but is constantly prevented from putting them into effect by epilepsy, depression, fatigue, clumsiness, or the repeated bad luck for which no immediate explanation suggests itself. In other words, as soon as I consider a person not simply as a moral agent but in terms of his usefulness for a particular function or purpose, the issue of his moral responsibility recedes into the background. A nation at war turns itself into an organization with a specific and definable purpose, and it deals more severely with negligence and inefficiency than a nation at peace; the more perilous its situation, the less importance is attached to distinctions between incapacity, thoughtlessness and treachery.[20] A totalitarian nation in peacetime, embattled against prospective or imaginary enemies, behaves in ways in which a liberal democracy can imagine itself behaving only under extreme stress; *sabotazh* in Russian has a considerably wider denotation than 'sabotage' in English, and Greek *prodidonai* (abstract noun *prodosiā*) could be applied equally to deliberate betrayal through disloyalty and to failure through inadequate energy and enthusiasm.[21] A Greek democracy, made

the Greeks as having 'long felt unable to delve into men's mental states for the purpose of distinguishing different degrees of guilt', but the absence of a felt need was at least as important as a feeling of inability to meet such a need.

[20] Cf. Hitler's War Directive of 21 Jan. 1945: '. . . I shall impose draconian punishment on any attempt at concealment, whether deliberate or arising from carelessness or oversight'. Russian commanders in the Second World War were sometimes executed for inadequacy which would have meant no more for a British or American general than replacement.

[21] Cf. Thuc. vi 103.4: the Syracusans in 414 replaced their generals, attributing their setbacks to 'either the misfortune or the *prodosiā* of the generals'; Dem. lii 14, 'His eye was letting him down' or '. . . failing him' (*prodidonai*). It must also be remarked in this connection that Greek did not make some distinctions which English makes; *apollynai*

aware by its experience that external enemies threatened the existence of the nation[22] and that the democratic constitution lay under threat of subversion from within as well as without, often talked and behaved in ways which remind us much more of totalitarian states than of parliamentary democracies as we know them. The implication of Dem. xxii 17 is interesting: he argues that no excuses should be accepted for the council's failure to ensure that the annual quota of triremes is constructed, and that if only the assembly will be 'plain and harsh' it will find that the ships will somehow be constructed (§20).

denotes both losing inadvertently and destroying deliberately, i.e. 'being the cause of the non-availability of . . .', and cf. *apoballein*, 'cast away', in the sense 'lose' (Hdt. vi 15.2).

[22] Cf. Adkins (2) 28–32, (3) 13 on the resemblance of a Greek city-state at peace to a modern state at war. We must also remember how many tragedies are about war and the immediate aftermath of war. If I find some of the values implicit in Euripides' *Hecuba* strange (cf. Adkins, 'Moral Values in Euripides' *Hecuba* and *Hercules Furens*', *Classical Quarterly* N.S. vi [1966] 193–219), I can make them seem less so by imagining the scene as somewhere in central Europe, the date 1945, Hekabe the widow of an eminent Nazi, Agamemnon an Allied corps commander, Kassandra the most beautiful of Hekabe's daughters (with whom Agamemnon has made an arrangement agreeable to him and not without advantages for her), and Polymestor a well-to-do Slovak or Croatian who foresaw in good time how things were going to turn out.

# IV

## ONESELF AND OTHERS

### IV.A. DEATH, PAIN AND GRIEF

*1. Danger*

The continued existence of a Greek city-state depended ultimately on the military qualities of its adult male citizens. Defeat in war could result in the physical destruction of the city's walls and buildings and either the forcible transplantation of its population or, at worst, the massacre of its menfolk and the enslavement of its women and children. This fate was inflicted upon Skione and Melos by the Athenians in 422 and 416 respectively, upon Hysiai by the Spartans in 417, upon Plataiai by the Thebans in 373 and upon Thebes by Alexander; and it very nearly befell Athens herself in 404. Although it was not difficult, in poetry and epideictic oratory, to acknowledge and magnify the blessings of peace and the evils of war, the inevitability of frequent warfare was accepted (cf. VI.C.4). In a world so politically fragmented, it could hardly be otherwise; scrupulously pacific policies could have been, and would have been portrayed as being, a stimulant to the appetites of powerful neighbours. It is not surprising, therefore, that an archaic mode of indicating that a man was all that a man should be confined itself to two aspects of his character, his valour on the battlefield and his wisdom in discussion (*sc.* of tactics, organization, and other matters relevant to victory or survival in war). This twofold commendation is found (e.g.) in Hdt. iii 4.1, and in Xen. *Ages.* 10.1 the 'good man' (cf. section *3* below) is defined in terms of 'endurance, valour, and judgment (*gnōmē*) when discussion is called for'. Nor is it surprising that cowardice in battle was severely penalized—Dem. xxiv 103 includes defectors from an expedition in the same list as parricides and hoodlums (cf. ibid. 119 and Aiskhines iii 175f.)—and the sacrifice of one's life for the community was regarded as the supreme virtue.

Hyp. vi 16: They gave their own lives for the freedom of the Greek world,[1] in the belief that they could offer no plainer proof of their will to invest Greece with freedom than to die in battle on her behalf.

Lyk. Leokr. 88: They (sc. the ancient kings of Athens) ... chose to die for their fatherland and to buy the preservation of the community at the price of their own lives.

Cf. Dem. lx 1, cited in III.A.3; GVI 20.11f., cited in V.B.4; Hyp. vi 26, literally, 'They spent life on the good life of others'; ibid. 10, 'He donated his life to his fatherland'; Lys. ii 25, 'not sparing their bodies, nor clinging to life when their aretē was at stake' (cf. V.B.4).

To earn the ultimate praise it was necessary either to win or to die; those killed, whether in victory or in defeat, were given the same credit for having done their best (Dem. xviii 208 ~ 192f.). I cannot prove my willingness to sacrifice my life except by actually sacrificing it; and if I do that I can be forgiven all else. Thucydides' Perikles says, in speaking of the war-dead of 431 (ii 42.2), 'The way in which their lives have ended is, in my view, simultaneously the first revelation and the final confirmation of a man's quality'.

All forms of altruism and generosity earned praise; the acceptance of physical danger has a generic similarity to financial sacrifice, but is commonly and reasonably, rated higher.

Lys. xvi 13: I was put on the list of cavalry by Orthoboulos, but when I saw that everyone thought that the cavalry were bound to be safe and the infantry in danger ... I went to Orthoboulos and asked him to strike me off the list; for I thought it shameful that when the majority were going to be in peril I should take the field in assurance of my own safety ... 18: I have continued throughout to go out with the first and come back with the last.

Cf. Dem. xx 82 on Khabrias, a truly patriotic (philopolis) general, who spared his men casualties but never spared himself dangers;[2] xxi 145, on Alkibiades, who displayed his patriotism 'with his body, not with money or words'; Dem. l 21, '. . . how much money I spent and what dangers I ran in facing bad weather and the enemy'.

The opportunity to risk and sacrifice one's life is naturally commonest

---

[1] In a combination of Greek states against the Macedonians; but praise would have been equally due to the dead if the war had been between one Greek state and another.

[2] This, like 'going out with the first and coming back with the last', is what is expected of junior commanders in any modern army; the nature and scale of military operations now make it harder for a senior commander to observe the same rules as he earned promotion by observing when he was young. To run the risks which the majority run would also have been called 'democratic' by an Athenian.

in war, but its acceptance in other circumstances is equally virtuous. Lys. xiii 60 commends a man who, when threatened by the Thirty Tyrants, preferred to die at their hands rather than betray others. Thuc. ii 51.5 comments that men who 'laid claim to *aretē*' fell easy victims to the plague, because 'they were ashamed to spare themselves' in visiting their infected friends. In Eur. *Alc.* 697 Pheres taunts Admetos as 'worsted by a woman' because he allowed his wife to die in his place. Although brave men can be said to choose death because the prospect of shame or penalty is unbearable to them, the degree of freedom from pressure in choosing to sacrifice oneself could be regarded as relevant to merit, as in the case of the two men, Aristodemos and Poseidonios, who showed extraordinary courage at the battle of Plataiai (Hdt. ix 71.2; cf. p. 151). On the Greek attitude to suicide see pp. 168f.

## 2. Exertion

The good soldier must not only risk his life, but must endure cold, heat, hunger and thirst, and must be able to do without sleep (Xen. *Hell.* v 1.15). What makes these *ponoi* ('exertions', 'labours', 'toils', 'sufferings') virtuous is that they involve neglect of one's own pleasure and comfort for the sake of others.

Hyp. vi 23: No campaign has displayed the *aretē* of the participants more than this recent campaign, in which they had to face the enemy day after day ... and bear with self-discipline exceptional bad weather and deficiencies in their daily needs so frequent and so great ... 24: Leosthenes, who exhorted his fellow-citizens to go through such feats of endurance unhesitatingly ... 26: These men, performing labour after labour ...

That the good things of life, above all manliness and the capacity to earn respect by achievement, can be won only by exertion is one of the commonest Greek maxims: Demokritos B182; Eur. frr. 233, 236, 237, 238 (contrasting 'living pleasurably' with *ponein*), 239 (coupling 'agreeable life' with 'un-manliness'), 240, 1052.7; Soph. *El.* 945; Xen. *Mem.* ii 1.28. Right, as the upholder of the old virtues in Ar. *Clouds*, regards the use of hot water for washing as morally decadent (965, 987, 1044–105.). [Xen]. *Cyneg.* 12.9, 'Exertion removes from the soul and the body all that is shameful and hybristic', enunciates a principle which has had considerable influence on educational practice in more recent times.

Ar. *Clouds* 1048–50: WRONG: Tell me: of the sons of Zeus who do you reckon was the best man in soul and performed most labours (*ponoi*)? RIGHT: I judge no man better than Herakles.

Cf. Lys. ii 16, Herakles the author of great benefits for the rest of mankind through his labours; and on 'best in soul', cf. section 3 below. The speaker of Isok. xix 11 is proud of having nursed his sick friend 'laboriously and well' (*kalōs*: cf. II.C.3) through long months of tuberculosis. When Neoptolemos has proved that he can bear with equanimity the smell of gangrene and the uncontrolled cries of pain from Philoktetes, this, says Philoktetes, is because he is 'of good family' (Soph. *Phil.* 874–6). In Ar. *Frogs* 179, when Xanthias and Dionysos cannot induce a dead man to carry their baggage to the underworld, Xanthias says, 'I'll carry it!', and Dionysos compliments him thankfully, 'You are *khrēstos* and *gennadās*!'

## 3. Terminology

Amphiaraos in Aiskh. *Seven* 610 is called *sōphrōn*, *dikaios*, *agathos* and *eusebēs*, and the word *agathos* must in this instance have a specific denotation, which we can identify, by comparison with other enumerations of virtues (cf. II.C), as 'brave'. So *aretē*, the abstract noun corresponding to *agathos*, was often applied (as we have seen from passages cited above) to that combination of bravery and skill which we look for in a fighter,[3] and the plural *aretai* not to what we would call 'virtues' but to occasions on which, or ways in which, military *aretē* was displayed (e.g. Ar. *Frogs* 1036 ∼ 1039 *agathos*). In Ar. *Peace* 969–72 the members of the chorus are jokingly complimented as *agathos* because they stand their ground when uncomfortably splashed with water. Such a specific application of *agathos* and *aretē* continued throughout the classical period in commendation of men killed in battle. In particular, the exhortation, 'Now be good men!' means 'You must fight bravely' (e.g. Thuc. v 9.9; cf. Xen. *Anab.* iii 2.39), and the formula, 'having become a good man' was applied (e.g. in the ceremonial proclamation of the state's responsibility for war orphans [Aiskhines iii 154])[4] to a man who had died fighting or to a man who had participated in a battle the outcome of which was welcome to the speaker: Dem. lx i, Hdt. v 2.1, Lys. xii 97, xviii 24, 26 ('You thought that those who had died on your behalf were the best of men'),

---

[3] On the application of *aretē* to military virtue cf. Ludwig 12–14, and on its application to fortitude in exertion Ludwig 15, 44–8.

[4] Cf. Gerlach 7–14.

fr. 42b. *Kakos*, as the usual antonym of *agathos*, can therefore mean 'cowardly', e.g. Eur. *Her. Fur.* 494–6, 'It would be enough for you to appear to your enemies even in a dream, for ... they are *kakos*'; Soph. *Phil.* 1306f., '*Kakos* in facing the spear, but bold in talk' (as we might say, 'no good when it comes to a fight').

This special use of 'good man' should not, however, be allowed to obscure the fact that in the majority of cases the same words are applied by virtue of political loyalty (Lys. xii 75, xiii 2), justice (Ant. v 4, Lys. xxv 19), filial dutifulness (Hdt. i 31.4), piety (Hdt. i 87.2), generosity (And. i 118f.)[5] and gratitude ('Lys. xxxv' 234B). While no one who quailed in battle could claim to be an '*agathos* citizen', the expression '*agathos* citizen' is used (e.g. Thuc. vi 14, Dem. viii 72) in non-military contexts. The abstract noun *andragathiā* (e.g. Dem. lix 89)[6] and the verb *andragathizesthai* do not refer to physical courage but to the possession or exhibition of qualities which attract respect and admiration (cf. V.B.*1, 4*). Hdt. i 136.1, on the subject of *andragathiā* among the Persian nobility—i.e. the characteristics by virtue of which a Persian is admired—says that next to the brave in battle the *agathos* is the man who has the most sons.

Nor again is *agathos* the only word of general commendation which could be applied to brave men.

Hdt. v 109.3: Where we have been stationed, there we shall do our best to be *khrēstos*; and you too must ... be *agathos*.

Cf.

Eur. *Tro.* 394–97, if there had been no Trojan War no one would have known how *khrēstos* Hektor was.

Where the context is concerned with the display of courage in battle by adult males, the relation between *aretē* and the usually more specific *andreiā*, 'courage' (derived from the stem *andr-*, 'adult male'), is full of uncertainties.

Lyk. *Leokr.* 104: Your ancestors' disposition to *aretē* was such that they were willing to die not simply for their own fatherland but also for the whole Greek world ... They did not practise their *aretē* only in words, but displayed it in action for all to see. 105: They were such excellent (*spoudaios*) men that when the Spartans, the bravest (*andreios*) of all, were fighting the Messenians ... the god told them to borrow a commander from us ... If the god judged the commanders whom we could provide

---

[5] Cf. D. M. MacDowell, ''Ἀρετή and Generosity', *Mnemosyne* N.S. xvi (1963), 127–34.
[6] Cf. Huart 464.

better (*ameinōn*) than the descendants of Herakles ... must we not regard the *aretē* of our ancestors as unsurpassable? ... 108: Our ancestors made it plain that *andreiā* is superior to wealth and *aretē* to numbers. And the Spartans at Thermopylai ... far exceeded all men in *andreiā*; therefore we can see on their tomb an inscription bearing witness to their *aretē*.

We might be inclined to see mere stylistic variation in the first and last sentences of this passage, but that does not adequately explain the first sentence of 108, with which compare Hyp. vi 19, '... judging that strength is constituted by *aretē* and numbers by *andreiā*, not by a great multitude of bodies'. Lykourgos implies that *andreiā* is a species of *aretē* or a stage on the road to the achievement of *aretē*; the latter accords with Dem. lx 17, 'Understanding is the beginning of *aretē*, *andreiā* is its completion'. Courage to fight to the death when cornered is indeed a virtue, and few Greeks would have predicated *aretē* of a man who lacked it; but the will to take a larger view and risk life in fighting for others, or for a whole of which one feels one's own community to be a part, goes beyond simple *andreiā*.

A reference to the *psȳkhē*, 'soul', of a man could be taken as a specific reference to his courage: Aiskhines ii 181, 'many of those distinguished for their souls in war'; Ar. *Peace* 675, 'best in soul', sarcastically, of the cowardly Kleonymos; Dem. lxi 23, 'good soul', with reference to courage, differentiated from 'intelligent judgment'; *GVI* 1457 (Lemnos), 'good in soul', added to attainment of *sophiā*, in praise of a man killed in battle; Lys. xx 14, 29;[7] Aiskhines iii 170, 'brave in soul', is almost pleonastic. *Eupsȳkhiā*, the state of 'having a good soul', is synonymous with *andreiā*.[8]

Eur. *Suppl.* 159–61. THESEUS: Did you so lightly disregard the divine will? ADRASTOS: Yes, the clamour of young men robbed me of reason. THESEUS: Your heart was more set on *eupsȳkhiā* than on prudence (*eubouliā*, 'goodness in deliberation').

Cf. Eur. *Her. Fur.* 157–64, *eupsȳkhiā* not truly tested by fighting against animals or with bow and arrows; *Hcld.* 569, 597, on the self-sacrifice of Makaria; *Med.* 403, Medeia's own view of the fortitude which she needs to go through with her plan and kill her children.

Lys. ii 14: They judged that it was a mark of freedom to do nothing under constraint, of justice to help those who were wronged, and of *eupsȳkhiā* to die, if need be, fighting in defence of both freedom and justice.

[7] Contrast Lys. xxxiii 12, '... asked him what kind of soul he had', in indignation at a shameful defrauding of orphans.

[8] It does not seem to me that Huart 418–25 makes a satisfactory case for a consistent semantic distinction between *andreiā* and *eupsȳkhiā* in Thucydides.

Naturally words for 'brave' could be applied sarcastically, implying 'shameless' (Dem. lvi 41), and familiarly or humorously (Eupolis fr. 148 is a 'Falstaffian' example). In Ar. *Clouds* 510 the chorus congratulates Strepsiades on his *andreiā* in becoming, at his advanced age, a student in Socrates' school,[9] and in *Frogs* 372–80 the chorus exhorts itself to dance and sing *andreiōs*, 'bravely', and *gennaiōs*, 'stoutly'. We may compare the Platonic passages (e.g. *Rep.* 454B) in which people pursue an argument 'courageously'.

## 4. Endurance of Misfortune

The Greeks were inclined to express grief noisily and extravagantly, weeping when disappointed or humiliated or when asking for clemency. The speaker of Isok. xix 27, who claims to have nursed his friend through a long illness, describes the two of them as shedding tears over their misfortune day after day. When Astyages was ill, says Xen. *Cyr.* i 4.2, Kyros never left his side and never ceased weeping. None the less, the valorous man could refuse to weep or to abase himself by pleading—as Andromakhe, a spirited heroine, refuses when threatened with death by Menelaos in Eur. *Andr.* 458f.

Eur. *Hel.* 947–53 (*Menelāos to Theonoe*): I will not deign to fall about your knees or bathe my eyes in tears; if I played the coward (*deilos*), how more could I diminish the reputation of (*sc. the conquest of*) Troy? They say, I know, that a well-born man sheds a tear in misfortune;[10] but I will not choose this *kalon* (*literally, 'creditable thing'*) —if *kalon* it be—in preference to *eupsȳkhiā*.

Menelaos was, of course, a legendary hero; Herakles, the supreme hero, prided himself on never having wept (Eur. *Her. Fur.* 1354f., Soph. *Trach.* 1071–5, 1199–1201), and Agamemnon in Eur. *Iph. Aul.* 446–53 is ashamed, as commander of an army, to weep. But uncomplaining endurance of misfortune could be an ordinary man's virtue too.

Dem. xviii 97: *Agathos* men should always embark on all honourable enterprises with high hopes as their shield, but should bear stoutly whatever outcome the gods give.

Dem. lx 35 (*consoling the parents of men killed in battle*): Those who have begotten such men and were themselves born to others of the same quality should be seen to bear suffering with more dignity than anyone else and to be unmoved however fortune treats them.

[9] Similarly in *Clouds* 457 the chorus praise the *lēma*, 'spirit', of Strepsiades; the word has strong associations with the portrayal of heroic events in serious poetry.
[10] On sensibility cf. IV.D.1.

Philemon fr. 136: What you are doing now is not *eupsȳkhiā* but unmanliness (*anandriā*), not to be able to endure distress.

That it is unmanly or foolish to lament misfortune (or, in religious language, unkind treatment at the hands of the gods) is a common maxim: Antiphanes frr. 278, 281; Ar. *Thesm.* 198f. (parody of Agathon); Eur. *Her. Fur.* 1227f.; Eur. frr. 572 ('the best man'), 702, 1078 ('just and wise men are not angry with the gods in misfortune'); Lys. iii 4; Men. frr. 632 ('Try to bear bravely the stupidity of Fortune'), 634.1f.; Soph. frr. 296, 861.

It might have been expected that the Athenian attitude to suicide would have been unsympathetic, as to a cowardly flight from suffering. In Eur. *Her. Fur.* 1246–54 Theseus does indeed dissuade Herakles from suicide as an act unworthy of one who has 'endured so much', and Herakles himself 1347–51) comes to acknowledge that suicide would be cowardice (*deiliā*). Euripides may have felt obliged to treat the matter in this way, since he had shown Herakles in a situation to which suicide would have been an appropriate response, but could not turn upside-down a well-established complex of legend. In Eur. *Or.* 1060–4 Orestes proposes to display his 'good birth' by stabbing himself to forestall execution, and he expects Elektra to do the same. They believe that there is no escape for them, but that is not necessarily the case of the hypothetical good wife who (Eur. *Tro.* 1012–14) should kill herself when taken from her husband.

Dem. lx 31 cites Ajax, who 'judged life to be unlivable when he was denied the prize for valour', as an example of heroism which inspired martial courage in the Athenian phyle named after him; the interesting thing here is that the speaker could easily have chosen instead to speak of occasions on which Ajax distinguished himself in fighting at Troy. Aiskhines iii 212 says scornfully that no one need be afraid that Demosthenes will 'go home and do away with himself' if he loses the crown proposed by Ktesiphon. Aiskhines calls this crown *aristeia*, 'prize for valour', to remind us of Ajax, and he sarcastically uses *megalopsȳkhos*, 'great-souled', of Demosthenes. The same word is used in Aiskhines i 145 of Achilles' refusal even to eat or wash until he had avenged the death of Patroklos by killing Hektor, and that too when he knew that by staying to fight at Troy he doomed himself to a short life, while by sailing home and abandoning vengeance he could have attained old age. The Athenians' view of suicide was undoubtedly formed in part by their fear of humiliation (cf. V.B.5), which made 'I would rather die!' and 'Life would not be worth living', come to their lips rather readily, but it was also an aspect of their high regard for the man who faces the instrument of death unflinchingly, no matter whether the hand that wields it is another's or his own.

## 5. Appropriateness of Fear and Aggression

Even the bravest should fear shame, the law, the displeasure of their superiors or their community, or the commission of an offence against the gods.

Philonides fr. 16: No one who fears the law is a coward (*deilos*) ... It is honourable to yield to right.

Cf. Thuc. ii 37.3, Perikles' assertion of the Athenians' obedience to the law 'through fear'. In such connections the Greeks did not seek euphemisms for 'fear' and 'afraid'.[11]

The use of force against an adversary much weaker than oneself is not a manifestation of courage, and was decried as bullying cowardice.

Eur. *Andr.* 454–60 (*Andromakhe's blistering attack on Menelaos and the Spartans*): That was my end, when the unhappy city of the Trojans perished, and with it my glorious husband, who often with his spear turned you from a land-animal into a cowardly sea-creature (*i.e. drove you on to your ships*). But now you appear as a fierce soldier before a woman and threaten to kill me. Kill me, then; I will spare you and your daughter any grovelling words from my tongue.

Cf. Eur. *Tro.* 1188–91, Hekabe's scorn at the Greeks' decision to kill Astyanax: are they afraid of a child?

Eur. *Suppl.* 537–46 (*Theseus reproaches the Theban herald for the Thebans' refusal to surrender the dead heroes for burial*): Do you imagine that you harm Argos by not burying the bodies? No, it affects all Greeks alike if the dead are to be left unburied and robbed of their rights; for if that custom becomes established, it infects the valiant with cowardice (*deiliā*). You came prepared to utter threats against me; and are you Thebans afraid of dead bodies hidden in the earth? Afraid of what? That buried as they are, they may destroy your land? Or may in the darkness of the earth procreate children, from whom vengeance will come?

Cf. Eur. *El.* 326–31, Elektra's bitter allegation that Aigisthos when drunk throws stones at her father's grave.

Isok. xvi 22: They are not ashamed to speak of him, now that he is dead, in abusive terms which they would have been afraid to use of him in his lifetime.

[11] Cf. de Romilly, 'La Crainte dans l'oeuvre de Thucydide', *Classica et Medievalia* xvii (1956), 119–27.

Lys. ii 8: They judged that to chastise a living enemy is the conduct of *agathos* men, but it is for men who have no confidence in themselves to display their *eupsÿkhiā* against the bodies of the dead.

Cf. Thuc. vii 29.5, the bloodthirstiness of the Thracians 'when they feel safe'.

Guile and deception, though often indispensable to victory in warfare (cf. Xen. *Ages.* 1.17), especially to offset numerical weakness, could arouse repugnance (Soph. *Phil.* 90f.) and guilt (Soph. *Trach.* 274–80) if used aggressively against a relatively weak adversary or one whose intentions are innocent; and, of course, those defeated by guile in war would vilify the successful enemy as cowardly (e.g. Eur. *Rhes.* 510f.), although they would not have hesitated to use the same degree of guile if the opportunity had presented itself. Agesilaos in Xen. *Hell.* vi 5.16 declares that he prefers to fight 'honestly and openly' than to run the risk of being attacked in the rear.

## IV.B. MONEY AND PROPERTY

*1. Acquisition*

It has often been thought possible to discuss in the hypothetical terms of economic and political theory whether an individual has a 'natural' right to dispose of any part of the material which exists in his time, and when a society is in process of revolutionary change there is discussion about what rights of possession and disposal shall be given by law to the individual. But most people, including most Greeks, have been born in a society which at that time had stable assumptions about the difference between 'mine' and 'yours'; these assumptions underlie the provisions made by the law for the restraint of any ways in which I may increase what is mine by depriving you, without your consent, of what is yours, and they also underlie the application of words such as 'theft', 'fraud' and 'honesty'.[1]

No investigator of Greek morality could claim credit for making a surprising and original discovery if he collected evidence to show that the Greeks at any given time and place applied the opprobrious word *adikos* to those who tried, by force or deception, to acquire what was regarded, at that time and place, as 'belonging' to someone else, and the complimentary word *dikaios* to those who refrained from such attempts. In that respect

[1] Cf. Gernet 64, 75, and H. Vos, *ΘΕΜΙΣ* (Assen, 1956) 30.

Greek sentiments and laws were like those of other societies, except that (in general) dishonest acquisition of another's belongings by means other than assault was a matter for litigation in which the initiative was not taken by the state. One type of honesty which was felt to be of particular importance is the second half of a provisional definition of *dikaiosynē* suggested by Socrates as a basis for discussion in Pl. *Rep.* 331C: 'Are we to say that *dikaiosynē* is simply truthfulness and rendering what one has received from another?' The verb *apodidonai*, which I have translated 'render', denotes not only giving back what has been borrowed or deposited but also giving when required to do so by the law or by a promise. In the discussion which follows Socrates' lead, the actual examples of 'rendering' concern the return by A to B of property or money which has deposited (*parakatatithesthai*) in A's safe keeping (331E, 332A). Obviously the repayment of a debt or payment in accordance with a promise, contract or recognized obligation is also *dikaios*, and to withhold such payment is *adikos* (e.g. Ar. *Clouds* 1140f.), but to keep honestly, and eventually return to its owner or convey to its proper destination, that which has been entrusted to one's own care, resisting the temptation to deny on oath that one ever received it, affords the true paradigm of *dikaiosynē*.

Ar. *Peace* 877f.: Well, now, who among you is *dikaios*? Who, I wonder? Who'll take over Theoria and keep her safe for the Council?

Cf. Hdt. vi 86, the cautionary tale of the Spartan whose reputation for *dikaiosynē* was such that a Milesian deposited a great sum of money with him; Xen. *Hell.* vi 1.2f., on the Pharsalian Polydamas, who was so *kalos kāgathos* (cf. I.F.5) that in a time of civil strife his fellow-citizens entrusted to him the administration of their akropolis. The solemn associations of 'deposit for safe-keeping' can be discerned in its metaphorical use by the orators, e.g. of entrusting children to teachers (Aiskhines i 9) or to a guardian (Dem. xxviii 15); young soldiers to their commanders (Dein. iii 15); the city, (Aiskhines iii 8), the city's honour (Dem. xxv 11), the laws (Aiskhines i 187, Dem. xxi 177) and a litigant's right's (Is. xi 32) to a jury.

Anyone who, in a situation of great need, preferred to remain poor rather than act in a dishonourable or dishonest way was naturally held up for admiration, e.g. Aiskhines ii 154f., where an impoverished exile is treated as exemplary because he refused a bribe to perjure himself; Dem. xx 13, 1 45, lx 2. *Philokhrēmatein*, 'loving money', is derogatory (e.g. Is. x 17), and a man could be praised as 'superior to money' (e.g. Dem. lviii 29) or blamed as 'worsted by money' or 'enslaved . . .'; Diphilos fr 94A (Edmonds), one who in his eagerness for money omits to consider what is right is 'a slave to money'; Eur. *Supp.* 871–7, Eteoklos did not want his 'character to become a slave to money'; Sannyrion fr. 4, a bad character has an eye solely on gain and is therefore 'easily captured'; Xen. *Mem.* ii 2.64, the dangers of associating with a man who 'is in love (*erōs*) with money-making'; Xen. *Oec.* 14.10, love of honour better than love of gain. The principle could be extended to a contrast of *kerdos*, 'gain', 'profit', in any sense, with honour and self-sacrifice, and could be applied to nations as well as individuals.[2]

Dem. vi 8–10: No one could do anything to persuade you to sacrifice any other Greek people to Philip for your own advantage (*ōpheleia*) . . . This is the greatest compliment paid to you, men of Athens; you have been judged . . . the only people who would not sacrifice the rights of the Greek world for any profit (*kerdos*) or exchange its goodwill for any favour (*kharis*) or advantage (*ōpheleia*).

When motivation by the hope of profit is decried, it is called *aiskhrokerdeia* e.g. Dem. li 10f.; cf. III.E.*1*. As we have seen (I.F.*3*), some ways of making money were open to reproach as *aiskhros*, for a combination of reasons: because they resembled servile work, or because they seemed to make the producer or seller dependent on the favour of others, or because the consumer always thought he had to pay too much. Yet the word *aiskhrokerdeia* is not so much a label for an agreed list of occupations as a means of expressing the speaker's disapproval of (real or putative) material motivation in a particular case.

The refusal to take money even when an apparently respectable opportunity presented itself was also a matter of pride. Dem. xxi 28 declares that he could have brought a private lawsuit against Meidias for assault, but (he says) he rejected that as *pleonexiā*, 'greed', since he would have gained financially by a verdict in his favour, and decided to give priority to the common interest and bring an indictment against Meidias for *hybris*.[3] Xenophon's Socrates, in refusing to take money for teaching, claims that he is 'looking after his freedom' (Xen. *Mem.* i 2.6). The people of Phleious earn Xenophon's very strong commendation as *gennaios* and *alkimos* because they let go a foreigner whom they could have held to ransom (Xen. *Hell.* vii 2.16). Financial gain is naturally apt to be called 'brief' or 'trivial' when it is decried and contrasted with honour (Dem. xiv 32).

People who acquired wealth do not seem to have been admired by the Greeks for commercial acumen, inventiveness, flair for the exploitation of

---

[2] Cf. F. Egermann, *Vom attischen Menschenbild* (Munich, 1952) 52–7.

[3] Curiously enough, Demosthenes compromised and accepted monetary compensation from Meidias, so that the case did not come into court (Aiskhines iii 52).

opportunities, or the single-minded pursuit of profit which causes the self-made millionaire to be an object of admiration in some modern societies. In comedy, some use is made of the assumption that dishonest men become rich and honest men remain poor; this is the theme of Aristophanes' *Wealth*, and cf. Men. *Colax* 43, 'No one gets rich quickly by being honest'.[4] Jealousy enters into this view, fortified by the resentment of injustice which we feel when we compare bad rich people with good poor people, and in the case of the Greeks the comparative absence of innovation in the material conditions of life entailed also an absence of people who could claim to have benefited the population by inventing, producing and marketing something new and useful.

A man who preserved his inheritance intact was admired (e.g. Aiskhines i 30, Dem. ix 30), for a certain level of capital was the basis on which liability for important types of public service was assessed, and its dispersal could be regarded as depriving the state of necessary support; impoverishment could be turned into a boast only if it resulted from support of needy kindred (e.g. Dem. xlv 54) or generosity to the community (see section 2). In Greek literature, the man who is proud to call himself a 'worker' (e.g. Ar. *Ach.* 611, *Peace* 632, cf. Men. fr. 11) is the farmer; it was always respectable to be a good farmer (e.g. Lys. xx 33) who raised the value of his land by hard work, intelligence and frugality. Demosthenes xxii 65 (cf. lix 50) excuses 'the men who work the land and are sparing of expense' a certain inability to meet their public obligations because of their unavoidable private outlays (cf. Dein. i 70). We see here the influence of the middling landowner, not a poor man, but not so rich that he need not get dirty, on the values of Athenian society (cf. III.E.2). There was also a possible contrast between 'work' and 'litigation' or 'blackmail' (Ant. ii β.12; cf. Ar. *Birds* 1430-68, *Wealth* 902-30).

We have an impression at times that the man who made money by trade or finance had to defend his status by emphasizing the benefit which accrued to the community as a whole from his importation of commodities (e.g. Dem. xxxiv 38f., boasting of a most unbusinesslike generosity in the public interest) or from the availability of his capital rating for the performance of public obligations (e.g. Dem. xxxvi 58). Lyk. *Leokr.* 57, however, denies

---

[4] Arist. *Rhet.* 1387ª15 acutely remarks that newly acquired wealth arouses more resentment than hereditary wealth, 'because that which is old is very close to what exists by nature'. The toleration of great unearned wealth in so many countries during the last few centuries, a puzzling phenomenon at first sight, is most easily explained as the product of a widespread inability to distinguish between long-standing but alterable economic structures and the unalterable laws of nature.

(for a rhetorical purpose) that any commercial undertaking can be compared, as a service to the community, with taking up arms and fighting in the ranks. Isok. xix 5–7, describing how a certain Thrasyllos 'acquired great wealth' although he inherited none from his father, certainly presents this process of acquisition in a favourable light, but explains that Thrasyllos was highly regarded by an eminent seer, who left him property and the technical books which subsequently made him a successful seer throughout the Greek world.

There was a strong tendency to regard both wealth and property as matters of luck. *Eudaimoniā*, the condition which indicates the goodwill of a supernatural being, occasionally requires the translation 'happiness', but it was more often applied to material wealth (e.g. Hdt. i 133.1), sometimes to high standing and honour (e.g. Hdt. vii 220.2), and rarely to a state of mind;[5] words from the (-)*tykh-* stem, meaning 'fortunate' and 'unfortunate', similarly require in many cases the translations 'rich' and 'poor'.[6]

Ant. ii γ.8: His payment of levies and service as choregos are sufficient evidence of *eudaimoniā*, but by no means evidence that he is not the murderer; for in fear of being deprived (*sc. by his enemy, in litigation*) of precisely this *eudaimoniā* . . .

ibid. δ.9: On the question of my *eudaimoniā*, they say that I probably committed the murder in fear for it, but the opposite is true. To those who are unfortunate, venturesome action is advantageous . . . but to those who are fortunate, it is advantageous to keep quiet and guard the prosperity which they have.

Dem. i 11: It is much the same, I think, as with the acquisition of money. If a man manages to keep what he has got, he is deeply grateful to fortune . . .

Cf. Dem. x 38f., with reference to public finance; xlii 4, asserting that continuity of good fortune in capital is rare; Eur. *El.* 938–44, a man's wealth may come and go, but his nature abides; Eur. *Phoen.* 555–7, wealth belongs to the gods, we are only the stewards of it, and the gods take it back when they wish (so too Alexis fr. 265); Men. fr. 94.5, 'The stream of fortune is quick to change its course', a warning to the rich that they must not presume on the security of the moment; Philemon fr. 213.7f., the change of fortune which makes today's rich man poor tomorrow; Soph. fr. 588, great wealth disappears in a moment when the gods so decide. Sacrifices were offered to the

---

[5] Eur. *Med.* 598f. envisages a *eudaimōn* life which would be full of worry and distress; obviously 'happy' would be an absurd translation there.

[6] C. de Heer, *ΜΑΚΑΡ—ΕΥΔΑΙΜΟΝ—ΟΛΒΙΟΣ—ΕΥΤΥΧΗΣ* (Amsterdam, 1968) collects and classifies examples down to the end of the fifth century. Eur. *Or.* 540–2 affords an interesting example of synonymy. Tyndareos says, 'I am in all ways *makarios*' (i.e. deserving felicitation) 'except in my daughters; there, I do not *eudaimonein*'. The chorus replies, 'Enviable is he who is *eutykhēs* in his children'.

gods, and prayers addressed to them (cf. Men. fr. 264), on the assumption that they would somehow or other (cf. III.G.1) cause the sacrificer to become wealthy. Men. fr. 177, however, speaks of the gods as providing the opportunity for wealth, which it is 'feeble' not to seize.

Many factors contributed to the formation of the belief that the making and losing of money was a matter of luck: notably, the scale and frequency of loss of crops, orchards, vines, olive plantations and farm buildings in war, and the loss of ships and cargoes through bad weather and piracy; cf. Antiphanes fr. 151, a merchant's goods at the mercy of a wind.[7] Good fortune could certainly be regarded as a sign of divine favour, but the well-known warning, 'Call no man happy until his life is over', served as a warning against inference of divine favour except when a family had remained wealthy for several generations. The practice of trying to keep one's money safe by burying it—with the risk that someone else would come across it and take it all—(cf. Ar. *Birds* 599–602)—also introduced an element of chance into the acquisition and preservation of wealth.


## 2. Expenditure

The distinction between creditable and discreditable expenditure is made clearly and repeatedly in our sources. The good man was expected to sacrifice not only his person but also his money and property; hence, when a speaker in court offered evidence of his own virtue or decried the worth of his opponent, contributions of money in capital levies and the performance of religious, military or administrative functions involving financial outlay were put in the same category as service entailing physical danger.

Dem. xix 281f.: Will you acquit him, a man who has not been in any way useful to the city, neither he himself nor his father nor any of his family? Why, what horse, what trireme, what campaign, what chorus or public service or capital levy, what (*sc. display of*) patriotism or (*sc. acceptance of*) danger has ever, at any time, been seen from them to the city's advantage?

Dem. xxiii 112: What law is so charged with cruel injustice as to deprive of the gratitude due to him a man who has made a gift (*sc. to the state*) from his own pocket and performed an act of kindness and munificence?

Cf. Dem. xxi 159, l 13, 21; Is. vi 60; Lys. xix 9 (cf. 63), a claim to have

[7] Burford 57 compares the ancient attitude to economic problems to 'resignation to bad weather'. This is true enough, but we should never forget how many economic problems for the ancient Greek were actually caused by bad weather.

spent more on the city than on oneself; Lys. xxi 1–11, an enumeration of the speaker's economic services, immediately followed by evidence of his virtues in war.

Although it was permissible on occasion to admit that one might feel these financial obligations a heavy burden and might hope not to incur them (Dem. xxxix 7; cf. Lys. xxix 4), the Athenian citizen did not adopt in public the pose of contemptuous hostility towards the state which nowadays has tended to make tax avoidance respectable. He boasted, if he could, of paying more than he was required to pay (Lyk. *Leokr.* 140), of being the first to give, and of giving with patriotic enthusiasm.

Is. vii 38–40: His father has performed all the required services . . . not standing by the letter of the law, but taking all the trouble he could . . . And Apollodoros himself did not try to grasp what belonged to others while refusing to help the community, but obeyed every charge laid upon him . . . in the belief that he should spend on himself only up to a certain point and keep the rest available for the city . . . Out of this he has discharged every possible obligation . . .

Cf. Dem. xviii 113, 'I drew up no account (*sc. of what I spent on the city*)'; Dem. xxxviii 26, xlix 46; Lys. xxi 16, 'I rejoice in performing public services' (we do not say nowadays, 'I *love* paying my income-tax!'). The speaker might claim that he had gone so far as to impoverish himself and his family: Dem. xxi 189, 'I have spent on you all that I had, except a very little'; Hyp. i 16, 'I have continued to breed horses' (the Athenian cavalry depended on private ownership and maintenance of horses) 'beyond my capacity and on a scale greater than my capital allowed'; Lys. xxi 22, 'I did not care whether I would leave my sons poor' (cf. VI.C.1); Lys. xxvi 22, 'In peacetime our estate was worth eighty talents' (hardly less than a million and a half pounds, by the standard of 1973 prices and wages) 'but during the war it has all been spent in the city's defence'. Dem. xviii 132 cites as a noble example a certain Aristonikos, who presented to the city for military purposes the money which he had laboriously collected for the purpose of paying off a debt and regaining his citizen rights.

We are not in a position to express any opinion on the truth of such claims, and we get an interesting glimpse of the other side of the picture in Ar. *Eccl.* 730–876, where a virtuous citizen, prompt to obey a new law which commands the pooling of all private property, is ridiculed by a cool, shrewd, cynical neighbour, who is quite ready to take such advantage of the new constitution as he can but does not propose to give up anything unless (as he judges most unlikely) universal public acceptance of the law leaves him no

option. Comedy, of course, could kick against the state and the law and the
rules of society to an extent quite impossible for an orator (cf. VI.B.4). So,
no doubt, did individuals when they were not in court; Dem. xxi 153
criticizes Meidias ('disagreeable and insensitive') for his alleged public complaints that the rich are expected to sacrifice their wealth in the national
interest while the people at large make no comparable effort (203).[8]

We have seen from passages already cited that payment of money to the
state and performance of duties prescribed by the state could be called
'kindly' (philanthrōpos: cf. IV.D.2) and contrasted with self-aggrandisement.
The Athenians did not draw a clear distinction between generosity to the
community, channelled through the machinery of state, and charity to
individuals.[9] The ransoming of prisoners of war, provision of dowries for the
daughters of impoverished citizens, payment for other people's funeral
expenses, and a variety of loans and gifts to the needy, were sometimes
treated in the same terms as public service. Demokritos helps to explain this
when he says (B255) that generosity by the rich to the poor produces the
homonoia, 'concord', 'unanimity', that makes a community strong.[10]

Ant. ii β.12: You will see from all that I have done up to now that I am not a man
who has designs on others or an appetite for what does not belong to him, but, on
the contrary, a man who has contributed many substantial capital levies, has several
times been in charge of a trireme, and has paid for choruses which have performed with
distinction. I have made many loans and paid large sums as a guarantor for many
people; I have acquired my property not by litigation but by hard work; I offer
sacrifices to the gods and live as society expects.

Dem. viii 70: Although it would be possible for me to speak of my maintenance of
triremes and payment for choruses and contribution of monetary levies and ransoming
of prisoners of war and many other kindnesses of that kind . . .

Cf. Aiskhines ii 99f.; Ar. Knights 94, 'helping one's friends' in a drunken
dream of wealth; Dem. xviii 268, 'available to all, and kindly and helpful
to those who asked' for ransoms and dowries; Dem. xix 40, 166–70, ransoms;
Dem. xxvii 69, dowries; Dem. xxxvi 58f., kindness and good nature to all
who asked for money; Is. v 43, 'You didn't even ransom anyone', in a reproach against selfish extravagance; Lys. xvi 14, rations for fellow-soldiers
who had come unprovided; Lys. xix 59, dowries, ransoms and funeral
expenses; Lys. xxi 17, help to friends; Lys. xxxi 15 (cf. 19), arms for fellow-

---

[8] Cf. Theophr. Char. 26.6 on the grumbling of the 'oligarchic man' about the oppressive burden of taxation for the benefit of the majority which he hates.

[9] On the enjoyment of giving, cf. Bolkestein 150–2, Hands 29f., 44.

[10] Cf. Connor 18–22 on 'the politics of largesse'.

demesmen; Men. fr. 646, 'This is life, not to live for oneself alone'; Xen. *Cyr.* v 1.1, Kyros speaks of his 'thirst' to give his friends whatever they ask for.

In this type of expense too the speaker could claim to have impoverished himself through an inability to say 'no' (e.g. Dem. liii 6–12); and to ask for repayment of money so spent was criticized as mean (e.g. Lys. xxvi 24). Isok. vii 35 extravagantly speaks of the Athenians' ancestors as so generous that they looked upon borrowers with more pleasure when they borrowed than when they repaid. We may recall the embarrassment of Strepsiades' creditor in Ar. *Clouds* 1215f., when he says that it might have been better in the first place to 'blush it out' and refuse the loan despite the shame of refusing a request from a fellow-demesman. A good man was expected to invite his friends to share his good fortune; the generalization to the contrary in Ar. *Wealth* 340–2, 'It isn't like us!', is an example of the usual comic vilification of the audience (cf. I.E.4), and at variance with the honest man later in the play (829–31) who gave freely to his friends in need. Generosity, being closely related to magnanimity, earned similar commendatory terms. 'You are *gennaios*', says Euripides to Agathon in Ar. *Thesm.* 220, when Agathon has answered his request for a razor with a 'Help yourself!', cf. Agathon's 'I don't begrude it' (ibid. 252), and 'grudging' as a reproach for too small a favour (757). Cf. Eur. fr. 407, if you have money, it is bad to exercise '*ponēros* thrift' and do no good to anyone; Hyp. iv 33, applying *megalopsȳkhos*, 'great of soul', to the man who helps others in need; Men. fr. 507, 'Being well spoken of (*sc. for generosity*) soon brings misfortune (*i.e. poverty, to the over-generous*)'; Soph. fr. 836, a good man's duty to help others in trouble.

The freeing of slaves as a reward for faithful service (Aiskhines iii 41, Aristophon fr. 14, Dem. xxvii 55, Lys. v 5; cf. VI.A.4) was regarded as a generous act, showing a willingness to accept loss in order to be just and return good for good. A slave in Antiphanes fr. 168.5 describes his stingy master as 'the worst man you'd ever find', literally, 'unsurpassable in *ponēriā*', and some of the master's fellow-citizens might have agreed with the sentiment, though not with its hyperbolic expression; Theophr. *Char.* 30.11 includes in his portrayal of *aiskhrokerdeia* a ludicrous stinginess in giving the rations to the household slaves.

It was not impossible for extravagance to earn an implied compliment, as when Apollodoros (Dem. lix 36) says that Neaira could not make a living at Megara as an expensive hetaira because the Megarians are 'illiberal and niggardly'. This passage, however, is most unusual, in keeping with the man-of-the-world element in the *persona* of Apollodoros (cf. I.B.*3*) and exploiting the Athenian principle that any stick is good enough to beat the Megarians with. Since Greek society was slave-owning, it was very easy, if one had a lot of money, to spend it on the acquisition of attractive slaves or on the long-term support of a foreign hetaira; since women of citizen status were segregated to an extent which made a love-affair with someone else's daughter or wife difficult and perilous, expenditure of money on purchasable women was a fairly common type of expenditure; and since the sexual relationship affords the paradigm of all pleasure, it figures very prominently in Greek references to extravagance. Predominant moral sentiment was hostile to expenditure on gambling, good food, sexual enjoyment, or any kind of consumption which only gratified the consumer.

Aiskhines i 42: His father left him a considerable estate, which he has devoured . . . He did this because he is a slave to the most shameful pleasures, gluttony and extravagant dinner-parties and flute-girls and hetairai and gambling and all the other things by which no honourable man should be mastered.

Cf. ibid 75, 'expensive dinners . . . and flute-girls, and the most expensive hetairai, and gambling'; Ar. *Wealth* 242f., 'whores and gambling' as a cause of a fall from wealth to poverty; Dem. xviii 296, 'measuring happiness by his belly and what is most shameful'; Dem. xix 229, 'He went around buying prostitutes and fish'.

Dem. xxxvi 39: Do not pretend that what you have spent disgracefully and immorally from your estate has gone to the city . . . 45: Antimakhos . . . is not complaining if you . . . have ransomed one hetaira and given away another in marriage— and that too when you have a wife!
Lys. xix 9f.: My father, throughout his life, spent more on the city than on himself and his family . . . Do not therefore pass a premature verdict of wrongdoing against a man who spent little on himself and much every year on you, but against those who are accustomed to consume on the most shameful pleasures both their inheritance and anything else that they have received.

Cf. Ar. *Wasps* 1351–9, where Philokleon pretends to be a young man seducing a dancing-girl with the promise that he will ransom her when his skinflint father dies; Is. x 25, 'He has spent all his estate on the pursuit of boys'; Men. fr. 198, 'No one is so parsimonious as not to make some sacrifice of his property to Eros'; Men. *Kithar.* 59–62, 'I was one of those who knew how to make an estate dwindle away . . . He takes after me'; Aiskhines i 30f., 95–7, Dem. xxxviii 27, without specifically sexual reference. The corresponding reproach against a woman seems to have been extravagance in clothing and jewellery; *GVI* 1810 proclaims of a dead wife that she did not 'gape after clothes and gold, but was content to love her husband'; cf. Xen. *Vect.* 4.8.

Expenditure on food, drink and entertainment for other people would be criticized in contexts where the spender-consumer himself was criticized, if it could plausibly be maintained that the beneficiaries were people of the same bad character as himself, but frequent and lavish sacrifices were quite another matter. The more lavish they were, the more could actually be consumed by the human relatives, friends, and fellow-members of deme or phratry whom the sacrificer invited, but since the gods were simultaneously honoured, their goodwill was secured for the community, an invisible but durable return for expenditure. Similarly, expensive dedications were both a lasting beautification of the sanctuary or public place in which they were set and a conciliation of the gods. For a glimmer of criticism of this attitude to religious obligation, cf. V.D.4.

## IV.C. ADVANTAGE

### 1. Friends and Enemies

In the passage of Plato's *Republic* partially cited in IV.B.1 Socrates shifts from 'rendering what one has received from another' to a definition of *dikaiosynē* which he attributes (*Rep.* 331E) to Simonides, 'rendering to each man what is owed' (or 'what is due'), which Polemarkhos amplifies (332A) as owing good to one's friends (*philoi*) and ill to one's enemies (*ekhthroi*)'. The speaker of Lys. ix 20 regards this principle of conduct as 'laid down' or 'prescribed' (i.e. by social usage and approval) and in Eur. *Ion.* 1045–7 it is given precedence over 'piety'. A Greek may apply to any situation or procedure the criterion, 'Does it enable me to harm my enemies and help my friends?' (Ar. *Birds* 420f., Soph. *Ant.* 643f., Xen. *Anab.* i 3.6, *Cyr.* i 4.25, *Hiero* 2.2). Those who excelled in both could be highly commended.

Xen. *Mem.* ii 6.35: You have recognised that the *aretē* of a man is to conquer (*i.e. excel*) his friends in benefaction and his enemies in harm.[1]

Cf. Eur. *Med.* 807–10; Xen. *Anab.* i 9.11, Kyros's prayer that he may live long enough to requite all those who treated him well or ill; Xen. *Cyr.* i

[1] Hdt. iii 140.4 tells a story which illustrates 'surpassing one's friends in benefaction'; Dareios, in power, rewarded with great munificence a man who had done him a comparatively small favour when he was of no consequence.

4.25. A prayer for one's own blessings could include a prayer for one's enemies' misfortunes; cf. Aigisthos's prayer in Eur. *El.* 807. That returning good for good or enforcing such a return (e.g. Ar. *Wealth* 1028f.) should be *dikaios*, and that ingratitude (Dem. xviii 112) or an impudent claim for undeserved help (Dem. xxiii 106, 117) should be *adikos*, is understandable enough; so is the link between 'tit for tat' and 'do as you would be done by' (cf. Lyk. *Leokr.* 88; V.A.1). But while few of us nowadays can expect that no one will ever deliberately do us harm, few of us expect to be involved for long in a relationship deserving the name of enmity, and a man who spoke of 'my enemies' could fairly be suspected of paranoia. Athenians took enmity much more for granted; on their general principle, if I do something for a man, he is likely to think of me as his friend (cf. Thuc. ii 40.4 on the acquisition of friends) and if I do something which he does not like there is a risk that I thereby become his enemy.

Xen. *Anab.* vii 7.46: All men, I think, regard it as right to show goodwill to him from whom one has received gifts.

The creditor who arrives in Ar. *Clouds* to demand his money back from Strepsiades undoubtedly has right on his side, but Strepsiades does not admit it (1137: he calls his own requests for postponement of payment *dikaios*), and the creditor is sure (1218f.) that his own demand will make Strepsiades his 'enemy'. Antiphon the Sophist B44.I.35–II.12 considers that a man necessarily becomes the enemy of anyone for whose adversary he has given evidence in a lawsuit. Dionysos in Ar. *Frogs* 1411f., cannot decide between the rival claims of Aiskhylos and Euripides to the throne of poetry; one of the reasons for his indecision is that both of them are *philos* to him and he does not want to become an enemy of either. Of course, one can change from friend to enemy in respect of the same person (Dem. xxiii 122). If I am his kinsman, I shall be assumed to be *philos* to him unless my hostile conduct turns this classification into a bad joke. In Lys. i 15f., an adulterer becomes an enemy to a woman whom he has seduced, simply because he ceases to visit her; she regards him now as 'wronging' her (*adikein*), and her slave uses this as a justification for betraying him to Euphiletos, whose wife he is currently visiting. *Adikein* in this sense seems to mean little more than acting in a way which the person affected finds disadvantageous; so Dem. xlix 68 says that bankers who become insolvent through the failure of their debtors to repay loans arouse resentment because—although involuntarily—they *adikein* the public at large. Cf. Isok. xviii 63, clear antonymy between *adikein* and *eu poiein*; Lys. vi 15, '*adikein* statues of the gods' = 'damage . . .' (but also, of course, 'act illegally towards . . .'); Thuc. viii 28.4, the Peloponnesians did not *adikein* the Peloponnesian mercenaries who had fought against them under Amorges; Xen. *Hell.* vi 5.12, Agesilaos did not *adikein* (i.e. 'harm') the city of Eutaia, despite its hostile behaviour towards Sparta.

A long-standing feud, year after year of provocation and retaliation, is a conspicuous phenomenon of the upper-class society with which, in the main, extant Attic oratory is concerned (e.g. Dem. xxi *passim*, Is. vii 29), and equally in a fictitious homicide case (Ant. ii *a*.5f.), where it is presumably designed for verisimilitude. Enmity can be inherited (*patrikos*) from the previous generation (e.g. Dem. xix 222, Lys. xxxii 22; cf. Is. ix 20). In such conditions it is not surprising that enmity can be declared, or taken for granted by a defendant, as a prosecutor's motive.

Dem. xxiv 8: I regarded the man who had wrongfully (*adikōs*) put me into such a predicament as an irreconcilable enemy. Seeing him injuring (*adikein*) the city as a whole . . . I proceeded against him, in alliance with Euktemon, in the belief that I had got a suitable opportunity for defending the interests of the city and at the same time obtaining revenge for what had been done to me.

Cf. Dem. liii 2, 15, 18, Lys. vii 20; cf. also V.A.*3* on multiple motives.

It was not the Athenian custom to disguise hatred, and neither party to a case hesitated to declare his adversary deserving of death: Dem. xviii 133, 'You tortured and executed Antiphon, as you should have done to Aiskhines too';[2] Dem. liv 1, 'I would gladly have brought a capital charge', in a case of assault (cf. 22). The attempt to retaliate upon an enemy being justified ('unobjectionable', Dem. lix 15), successful retaliation was a joy, and failure a horror; a man might be respected for attempting revenge and denigrated for making no attempt.[3]

Aiskhines ii 182: What is more pitiable than to look upon the face of an exultant enemy and to hear the sound of his vilifications?

Cf. Eur. *Her. Fur.* 285f., Megara thinks it worse than death that she should give her enemies an opportunity to rejoice over her misfortune; Eur. fr. 460, one's own misfortune should be hidden, for it is 'laughter to one's enemies'; Soph. *Oed. Col.* 902f., Theseus rejects a course which would make him 'laughter' (i.e. 'contemptible') to Kreon. Cf. V.B.*5*.

Thuc. vii 68.1: Let us consider both that it is entirely acceptable (*nomimos*), in dealing with adversaries, to claim satisfaction of the anger in one's heart in vengeance

---

[2] As a citizen, Aiskhines could not have been tortured; this fact intensifies the violence of Demosthenes' words.

[3] Cf. Hirzel 190–2.

upon the aggressor, and also that retaliation upon enemies, which will be possible for us, is proverbially the greatest of pleasures.

Cf. Eur. *El.* 281, Elektra ready to die if she can first spill her mother's blood; Eur. *Her. Fur.* 731–3, Amphitryon goes off to enjoy seeing Lykos being killed; Eur. *Or.* 1163f., Orestes, in exalted mood, willing to die if only he can first murder Helen; Soph. *Phil.* 1040–3, Philoktetes' prayer to the gods to punish Odysseus and the other Greek leaders, since 'if I saw them dead, I should feel that I was cured of my illness'; Xen. *Hiero* 1.34, 'more enjoyable than anything' to take from (*sc. national*) enemies against their will; Xen. *Mem.* iv 5.10, the 'greatest pleasure' as well as advantage, in 'being useful to friends and overcoming enemies'. Athenian homicide law permitted the next of kin of a murdered man to be present at the execution of his murderer (Dem. xxiii 69).

We seem to have come a long way from 'truthfulness', which was the first of the two ingredients of *dikaiosynē* suggested by Socrates in Pl. *Rep.* 331C. The genus of which truthfulness and revenge are two conspicuous species is not, to our way of thinking, easily identified and named, but if we assume that untruth is normally a means of manipulating someone else in pursuit of one's own advantage, it seems that *dikaiosynē* (like courage and generosity) is concerned with the boundary of advantage between oneself and others. If I realize my own wishes in opposition to the wishes of someone who has previously realized his in despite of mine, I am *dikaios* in restoring the boundary; if, acting in my own interest, I deceive, deprive, worry, sadden, insult or injure someone who has not so treated me—and that, after all, means most people—I am *adikos*. A judge, juror or arbitrator is *dikaios* in the sense 'just' if in giving a verdict he has regard solely for the law, and for equity where the law is insufficiently precise, without regard for the advantage which he may gain or lose by the friendship or enmity of either of the parties on trial or in dispute. Dem. xxiii 97 calls goodwill or enmity an '*adikos* reason' for a juror's decision. The Greeks' use of the same word for 'just', 'fair' and 'honest', a trial to translators (especially of such works as Plato's *Republic*) is intelligible in the light of the fact that a decision by A on a dispute between B and C necessarily affected the power and influence of A within the society to which A, B and C belonged.

It was sometimes asserted in self-justification—and it is interesting that it needed to be asserted—that one is bound, short of actual breach of the law, to consider one's own interest: Dem. xxxii 12, on creditors claiming payment; Thuc. vi 83.2, 'No one can be begrudged action in defence of his own well-being'; cf. [Xen.] *Ath.* 2.20. Action taken in requital of a previous wrong was defended by the agent in a similar way.

Dem. lix 15: No one can be begrudged retaliation against him who was the aggressor.

Cf. Ant. iv β.2f., arguing that it is *dikaios* for the striker of the first blow to be killed in retaliation (this notion, which we might call 'a head for an eye', takes account, unlike 'an eye for an eye', of the injured man's feelings as a distinct ingredient of the situation which needs to be rectified); Dem. xxiii 123, *dikaios* to complain of favouritism towards others when you deserve just as much yourself; ibid. 144, *dikaios* to punish those who are ill-disposed towards you and deceive you; Eur. *Ba.* 878–80, 'What fairer privilege is there than to triumph over an enemy?'; Soph. *Oed. Col.* 27–272, Oedipus's insistence that he cannot be blamed by anyone for killing Laios, for 'he was the aggressor, and I retaliated'; Thuc. i 120.3, *agathos* men (i.e. a brave and honourable nation) fight when they are wronged—but make peace as soon as the situation is favourable; Thuc. iii 67.4, we are sorry for those who are treated in a manner which is not fitting, but we are pleased (literally, 'they are rejoiceable-over') when people suffer *dikaiōs*. Xen. *Mem.* iv 8.11 says that Socrates was so *dikaios* as 'never to do anyone the slightest harm, but to confer the greatest benefits on those who had dealings with him', and since he does not credit Socrates with the zeal for retaliation which he seems to find admirable in (e.g.) Kyros, he may mean that Socrates did not retaliate; if so, his use of the word *dikaios* is notable. But in the light of Xen. *Anab.* i 4.8 (cf. V.A.2), it seems that Xenophon was aware that on occasion to ignore a wrong, and to be seen to ignore it, puts one at a great advantage over an adversary.

Retaliation could sometimes be defended not so much on grounds of *dikaiosynē*, as on grounds of 'manliness': Ant. ii α.8; Dem. lix 2, the reproaches uttered (the speaker claims) against Theomnestos as 'unmanly' should he fail to prosecute Stephanos in the interests of his own family; Eur. *Phoen.* 509f., 'unmanliness' to put up with loss; Eur. fr. 1092, 'a man's part' to harm his enemies.


## 2. Law, Custom and Sentiment

We find that while *dikē* is used in prose predominantly in the senses 'lawsuit', 'settlement', 'satisfaction', 'penalty', i.e. the readjustment of a contested balance of gain and loss, *dikaios* and *adikos* and their derivatives express a range of valuations which includes, and at times extends beyond, our 'fair', 'honest', 'justified', 'reasonable', and their antonyms. The respective abstract nouns *dikaiosynē* (in poetry commonly *dikē*, and so almost always when personified [cf. V.D.*3*]) and *adikiā* are similarly extended.

Dem. xxiii 75: There are two possible qualifications of everything that is done or said; and the same action cannot have both at once, nor could the same utterance (for how could the same things be simultaneously *dikaios* and not so?). Everything is tested as having one of the two qualifications; and if it is shown to be *adikos*, it is judged *ponēros*, but if it has the *dikaios* qualification, it is *khrēstos* and *kalos*.

Cf. Aiskhines i 178, 'a most *adikos* habit' of allowing defendants in court to spend time in counter-charges against their prosecutors; Amphis fr. 30.5–7, 'The fishmonger doesn't answer your question, and *dikaiōs*' (i.e. 'that's what you'd expect'), because all fishmongers are cutthroats'; Ar. *Clouds* 25, *adikein* applied to encroaching on another's lane in a race; Ar. *Frogs* 623–37, 'The *logos* is *dikaios*' = 'The suggestion you have made does not give you any advantage which threatens me'; Ar. *Lys.* 403, 'serves you right!' (cf. Men. *Epitr.* 221f., 249); Ar. *Thesm.* 198f. (parody of Agathon), 'It is *dikaios* to support one's misfortunes by going through with them, not by trying ways of escape'; Ar. *Wealth* 89–97, *dikaios* and *khrēstos* treated as synonyms (cf. Soph. *Oed. Tyr.* 609–15); Dein. i 37, '*dikaios* reputation' = 'well-earned...'; Dem. xxiii 137, '*dikaiōs* untrustworthy' = 'distrusted with good reason'; Dem. xlvii 60, 'My neighbour judged it not *dikaios* to enter my house in my absence'; Dem. lviii 25f., not *dikaios* that a jury should have to listen to rambling speeches; *GVI* 748 (Halikarnassos), 'Alas for those who *adikōs* go beneath the earth!', i.e. for those who, we feel, 'ought' not to die so young; Men. fr. 296, 'How *adikos* it is when fortune frustrates the good deeds prompted by one's nature!'; Theophilos fr. 10, 'When you lend money to a bad man, *dikaiōs* the interest you get on it is distress'; Thus. iii 40–3 'sensible' (*sc.* having regard to consequences); Xen. *Eq.* 3.5, a horse with an *adikos* side to its mouth. A convergence of *dikaios* with *eikōs*, 'likely', 'to be expected', 'reasonable', apparent in some of the passages already cited, is obvious in Thuc. ii 74.2, 'Though we have made many *eikōs* demands, they have not been met'.

Since laws are designed to prohibit pursuit of one's own advantage to the detriment of others, the antithesis 'legal'/'illegal' tended to convergence (explicit in Xen. *Mem.* iv 4.12, 6.6) with *dikaios*/*adikos*; and the size, structure and procedures of a democratic city-state being what they were, it was easier than it would be nowadays to regard the law as expressing the collective will and to treat 'legal'/'illegal' as virtually congruent with 'right'/'wrong'.[4]

Dem. xxv 17: There are two reasons for which all laws are made: to prevent anyone from doing anything which is not *dikaios* and to ensure that the punishment of those who transgress these prescriptions makes the rest better men.

Dem. xlii 2: ... as if the law had given him the authority to do whatever he wished and not to act as is *dikaios*.

Cf. ibid. 9; Dein. ii 12, 'the penalties which the laws provide against those who *adikein*'; Dem. xxi 225, 'Regard *adikēmata* of the laws' (i.e. 'injuries done to the laws by the act of disobeying them) 'as (*sc. wrongs committed*) against all of us alike'; Is. vii 16, *ta dikaia* referring to the procedure prescribed by the law of a phratry. In And. i 110 the breaking of 'unwritten law' is *adikiā*.

The expression '*dikaios* citizen' can be used in the sense 'patriot', 'good citizen', as in Dem. viii 72 (where '*agathos* citizen' is also used with exactly the same reference), xv 25, xviii 188 (cf. 180, '*agathos* citizen'), and Hyp. v 17 calls a patriotic and honest politician *dikaios dēmagōgos* (cf. Lys. xxvii 10, *agathos dēmagōgos*, and Dem. iii 21). *Dikaios* can also be applied to conformity with approved social usage: Aiskhines i 136, ii 166, *dikaios erōs* = 'a normal love-affair', or 'a decent ...' (cf. Gorgias B6, applying *nomimos* to the love-affairs which the honoured war-dead enjoyed in life);[5] Dem. xliii 74, 'I named my eldest son after my own father, as is *dikaios*' (he could have said *nomimos*). Synonymy of *dikaios* and *nomimos* is obvious in Xen. *Mem.* iv 4.17, where it is said that one would entrust one's property for safe-keeping to the *nomimos* man above all (cf. IV.B.*1*).

Inevitably, however, a word of so wide an application as *dikaios* expresses a value by which even laws and legality might themselves in some circumstances be judged; that, at least, is the implication of Ar. *Eccl.* 944f., 'It's *dikaios* that this should be done according to the law, if we're a democracy', and it is implied also by the characterization of particular laws as *dikaios* in Dem. xxiv 34 and Hyp. iii 22. It must also be remembered that Athenian law, like any other code of law, was unable to provide for every imaginable contingency, and in such cases the jury was required to exercise 'the most *dikaios* judgement' (Dem. xxxix 40f.),[6] Cf. Dem. xxiv 43, the

---

[4] Cf. Gernet 62–4, 75; E. A. Havelock, 'Dikaiosune: an Essay in Greek Intellectual History', *Phoenix* xxiii (1969) 49–70.

[5] Vollgraff 64–6 takes *erōs* here as metaphorical, but the parallel with Aiskhines seems to me to suggest that it should be taken literally.

[6] Cf. H. Meyer-Laurin, *Gesetz und Billigkeit im attischen Prozess* (Weimar, 1965).

legislator thought it *dikaios* that a law should not be valid until it is inscribed; Lys. xvi 6f., to discover who served in the cavalry it is more *dikaios* (i.e. a better guide to the facts, and therefore fairer to an innocent defendant) to look at the accounts than to look at the nominal roll only.

Dem. xliv 8: If they prove to you that the laws grant them what they have declared on oath, then give the verdict that the inheritance should be theirs; and if their claim is not substantiated by the law, but it is clear to you that their case is *dikaios* and *philanthrōpos* (*i.e. such as to win sympathy; cf. IV.D.2*), then, if that is so, we concur in their claim.

From this distinction it is a short step to contrasting what is *dikaios* with what is strictly prescribed or permitted by law, as in Isok. xix 16, 'not only in accordance with the law, but also *dikaiōs*'.


## 3. Litigation

Disputes and litigation within the family, where mutual toleration was expected (Dem. xxv 87–9, Lys. xxxi 22), earned opprobrium: Dem. xlviii 3, 8; Is. v 30; Lys. xxii 1 ('most disgraceful'); cf. VI.A.1. Even without reference to the restraint imposed by the family tie, to call a man 'litigious' (*philodikos:* Dem. xl 32) or 'quarrelsome' (*philoloidoros:* Dem. xviii 126) was a serious reproach. It was thought better to seek reconciliation, even at a disadvantage, than to press a claim with the intention of seeking complete satisfaction; it might also be better, if a claim were to be made at all, to aim lower than the letter of the law would seem to permit.

Dem. xli 1: If I had not made every effort and exertion to reach a settlement and entrust the issue to our friends' judgment, I would blame myself for preferring to have all the trouble of a law-suit rather than to put up with a settlement somewhat to my disadvantage.

Dem. liv 24: If we chose not to bring an action under the laws concerning violence, that can reasonably be regarded as showing that we are *aprāgmōn* and *metrios*. but not as showing him in any better a light.

(On the terms used here, see below).

Dem. lvi 14: We agreed to this, not because we were unaware of our rights under the contract, but because we thought we should accept a disadvantageous settlement in order not to be thought *philodikos*.

Lys. x 2: Nor would I have proceeded against him if he had said anything else actionable about me, because I regard prosecution for slander as not befitting a free man and as excessively *philodikos*.

Cf. Isok. xv 27, on settling a dispute through mutual friends rather than going to court. A blackmailer and trouble-maker is told by Peisetairos in Ar. *Birds* 1433–5 that there are many *sōphrōn* ways of making a living in accordance with what is *dikaios*, preferable to 'legal machinations' (*dikorraphein*, etymologically, 'stitching lawsuits'; the word is contemptuous also in Ar. *Clouds* 1483, where Strepsiades takes the manlier course of setting fire to Socrates' school). The speaker of Dem. xlvii 70, who consulted the experts in religious procedure to see whether he should prosecute the men who had caused the death of an old woman, formerly his slave but later freed, was advised that to do so might excite resentment, since she was neither a relation of his nor any longer his slave at the time of the incident.

The man who was not prompt to litigate or to insist on his rights, not anxious for *prāgmata*, 'doings', 'business',' trouble', was called *aprāgmōn* (e.g. Dem. xxxvi 53, xl 32, Lys. fr. 32, cf. Ar. *Birds* 39–44).[7] The word is coupled with *metrios* (e.g. Dem. liv 24, cited above, and xlii 12) and *akakos*, 'guileless' (Dem. xlvii 82), and the abstract noun *aprāgmosynē* with *askholiā*, 'lack of leisure' (Dem. xxi 141), which implies full engagement in honest work. *Polyprāgmosynē*, interfering in other people's business (e.g. Lys. i 16; in Ar. *Frogs* 749 it is used by a slave of doing what a slave has no business to do) and preventing them from doing what they wish to do has something in common with litigiousness; it is associated in Lys. xxiv 24 with the bold relish of enmities, and the verb *polyprāgmonein* is applied in Ar. *Wealth* 913 to the man who claims always to be ready to prosecute in the city's interests.[8] But *philoprāgmōn* (abstract noun *philoprāgmosynē*) is the normal antonym of *aprāgmōn*; it is applied to the man who is determined to keep the initiative in dominating those whose interests he regards as conflicting with his (Dem. xxi 137), has recourse to litigation on trivial grounds (disclaimed by the speaker of Dem. xxxix 1), or presses ruthlessly for satisfaction (Is. iv 30). Similarly Trygaios, announcing himself to Hermes in Ar. *Peace* 191, proclaims that he is a good vine-farmer and no blackmailer or 'lover of *prāgmata*'.

Lyk. *Leokr.* 3: Now it has come to such a pass that a man who takes the risk on himself and incurs enmity through his defence of the common interest is regarded not as

[7] Cf. W. Nestle, ''Ἀπραγμοσύνη', *Philologus* lxxxi (1926) 129–40 and K. Dienelt, ''Ἀπραγμοσύνη', *Wiener Studien* lxvi (1953) 94–104, both with particular reference to the political application of *aprāgmosynē* in Thuc. ii 63.

[8] On the application of this concept to interstate politics cf. V. Ehrenberg, 'Polypragmosyne: a Study in Greek Politics', *Journal of Hellenic Studies* lxvii (1947) 46–67.

patriotic (*philopolis*) but as *philoprāgmon*. . . . 5f.: I have brought this indictment not through any enmity . . . but because I thought it shameful to see how Leokrates . . . has become a reproach to our fatherland . . . For a good (*dikaios*) citizen ought not to bring to trial, through his own enmities, men who have done the city no wrong, but to regard as his own enemies those who transgress against our fatherland.

In this passage the speaker's need to disclaim motivation by personal enmity explains why a man who insisted that the prosecutions which he initiated were disinterested should have been mistrusted as *philoprāgmon*.

Inexperience of legal procedures, characteristic of the man who is *aprāgmōn* and *hēsykhios*, 'quiet' (Ant. iii β.1), could be treated as a positive commendation, and was on occasion claimed even when (as in Dem. xxiv 6) the claim was patently false.

Lys. vii 1: I always used to think that anyone who wished, if he kept to himself (*literally*, '*if he led* hēsykhiā'), need have no litigation or troubles.

Cf. Ant. i 1–5, Is. fr. 4 (in both, the speaker stresses his own youth and inexperience); Ar. *Wealth* 900–2, where being *hēsykhios* is contrasted with the habits of the blackmailer who threatened wealthy people with prosecution; Dem. xxvii 2; Lys. fr. 78.4; in Ar. *Eccl.* 151f., a similar disclaimer refers to speaking in the assembly. The adversary, by contrast, was represented as highly experienced in the courts: Dem. xli 2, 24, Hyp. i 19. In Lys. xxvi 3–5 *ta heautou prāttein*, literally, 'carrying on his own things', i.e. 'attending exclusively to his own concerns', is called *hēsykhiotēs*; being treated there as characteristic of the *sōphrōn* man, it covers absence of covetousness as well as general reluctance to interfere with others.

*Aprāgmosynē* might, of course, lead to violation of the law through ignorance (Dem. lviii 24). A litigious man, on the other hand, needed to know the law well, and the less honest he was, the more attention he was likely to pay to the operation of legal traps; this is the implication of *kyrbis* (an archaic type of inscribed law) as a term of abuse in Ar. *Clouds* 448; cf. the patronizing, jocular, 'You're ignorant and not *polyprāgmōn*, and you don't know your Aesop' of Ar. *Birds* 471. In consequence (I am speaking of psychological, not logical, consequence) knowledge of the law could itself be suspect: Dem. xx 93, contrasting *idiōtai* with 'those who know the laws'; Dem. lvii 5, 'He knows the law better than he ought to'; Men. fr. 545, 'The man who has a detailed knowledge of the law is revealed as a blackmailer'. A litigant might actually apologize for displaying his understanding of legal detail (Dem. liv 17f., '*compelled* to find out . . . by my opponent') or for going into his adversary's conduct too closely and precisely (Dem. lviii 19); cf. Dem xlix 5, where a banker explains that he recalls the details because bankers have to keep records. Even a detached intellectual interest in legal proceedings could be disclaimed: Is. i 1, Lys. xix 55. In Antiphon's second *Tetralogy* (Ant. iii β.1f., δ.2, cf. γ.3) *akrībeia*, 'subtlety' or 'precision' in argumentation, is treated as being in itself suspect and antipathetic, as if the litigant who employs it must be trying by means of sophistry to get the better of his honest, plain-spoken opponent. Cf. also I.E.2 on 'professionalism' in the assembly and the courts.

## 4. Magnanimity

Even though *dikaiosynē* afforded a standard by which law could on occasion be judged, it could itself be judged by the standards of the behaviour which we find attractive and reassuring in our fellow-men.[9] Dramatic treatment of the legends of the house of Atreus provided the opportunity for expressing the important distinction between 'It is *dikaios* on the part of A to hurt B' and 'It is *dikaios* that B should be hurt'.

Eur. *El.* 1051f. (*Chorus to Klytaimestra*): Your plea has been *dikaios*, but the *dikē* is shameful, for a wife should agree with her husband in everything.

ibid. 1244 (*Dioskouroi to Orestes*): What has happened to Klytaimestra is *dikaios* (*i.e. she has her deserts*), but what you have done (*sc. killing her, your mother*) is not.

Soph. *El.* 558–60 (*Elektra to Klytaimestra*): You admit that you killed my father. What plea could be more shameful than that, whether (*sc. you killed him*) *dikaiōs* or not?

In Soph. *El.* 1042, 'There are circumstances in which justice (*dikē*) brings harm', the warning seems prudential rather than the expression of a moral reaction on the emotional plane, and the same is true of Thuc. iii 46.4, where Diodotos argues that it is not in the interests of the assembly to be 'strict judges' since it can be more advantageous to accept injury than justly to destroy those who have injured us; but if we make this distinction, we must not press it too hard, since the modern predilection for ignoring consequences (cf. V.A.3) is not necessarily preferable to the Greeks' refusal to ignore them. Is. ii 30 mentions a case in which an arbitrator suggested a solution 'advan-

---

[9] Dicta to the effect that *dikaiosynē* is 'the whole of virtue' (cf. Theognis 147f., cited in II.C n. 3) or (e.g.) that 'health and *dikaiosynē* are the best things in life' (*GVI* 1213 [Eretria, s. III]), are expressed in terms of the easily defined and labelled virtues and goods. In any case, a superstructure of niceness can only be erected—unless it is mere hypocrisy—on a foundation of honesty and fairness.

tageous to both parties' in preference to a strictly just solution which would create lasting ill-feeling.

The fictitious defendant of Ant. ii β.13 claims that he will act *'epieikōs* rather than *dikaiōs'* in refraining from speaking of the wrongdoing of the murdered man and his associates; that is to say, with kindness, decency and magnanimity, foregoing a possible advantage.[10] The distinction is made by Gorgias B6, 'giving preference to kindly (*prāos*) magnanimity (*to epieikes*) over obstinate insistence on justice (*to dikaion*)', and in the debate on Mytilene (Thuc. iii 40.3, 48.1) *epieikeia* clearly denotes the waiving of a right to just retaliation. Cf. Eur. fr. 645.5f., the gods forgive perjury to save one's life, 'for they put what is *epieikēs* above *dikē*'; Hdt. iii 53.4, 'Many prefer what is *epieikēs* to what is *dikaios*'. The Athenian speaker at Sparta in Thuc. i 76.4 claims *epieikeia* for the Athenian empire on the grounds that it is administered with regard for justice even in circumstances where superior force would make it easy for Athens to impose her will unjustly. This is rather like the speaker of Dem. xlvii 81, who regards himself as *prāos*, 'mild', 'moderate', because he observes proper procedure and does not claim more than his due. In ancient times, says Isok. vii 33, simultaneously exploiting the motif of ancestral virtue and the motif of careless contemporary juries (cf. I.E.*1*), they judged cases with strict regard for the law, not for *epieikeia*; and it is, I imagine, an old-fashioned character who grumbles in Men. fr. 548 that 'what some nowadays call *khrēstotēs*', i.e. 'goodness', 'kindness'. has had the bad effect that 'no one who does wrong gets punished'.

Dem. xl 40: Although in dealing with other people it is not *epieikēs* to insist on the validity of arbitrations, in dealing with this adversary of mine it was entirely *dikaios*.

The passage means: normally, insistence on the validity of an arbitration elicits the reproach, 'You are not *epieikēs*', whereas in dealing with this adversary there can be no question of *epieikeia*, and one can only act so as not to incur the reproach, 'You are not *dikaios*'.

Greek frankness in admitting that revenge is enjoyable, the obvious contrast between careful justice and Christian love, and the tendency in modern study of Greek morality to concentrate either on the evidence of early periods (for which oratory and comedy are not available) or on what Plato treats as *dikaiosynē*, have all combined to exaggerate the cold or fierce aspects of Greek morality and to play down the credit which the Greeks

[10] Cf. Vollgraff 12–14; P. Stoffels, *Billijkheid in het Oud-Griekse Recht* (Amsterdam, 1954).

gave to diffidence, trustfulness, peaceableness and magnanimity.[11] Against cases in which enmity between a speaker and his adversary is admitted we must set those in which it is denied (Dem. xxiii 1, Lys. xxxi 2) or even denounced as a discreditable motive for prosecution.

Dem. xviii 278: A good citizen ought not to expect a jury, which has come into court to decide issues affecting the whole community, to validate his own anger or enmity or anything of that kind, nor should he come before you in pursuit of such satisfaction. It is preferable that he should be by nature incapable of these emotions; if that is impossible, they should be governed by decency and restraint.

Cf. Eur. *Med.* 463f. (Jason to Medeia, admittedly at a point when he still has nothing to complain about), 'Even if you hate me, I can never be ill-disposed to you'; Isok. xviii 38, 'Think them bad (*kakos*) men if they claim satisfaction on an exceptional scale' (cf. V.E.2); Lyk. *Leokr.* 6; Lys. ix 7; Thuc. iv 19.2, one should put an end to a great enmity by coming to an agreement on moderate terms, not pressing one's own advantage but 'outdoing one's adversary in *aretē* also, looking to *to epieikes*'.

It is natural enough that a man should claim that he has lived in such a way that no one has ever prosecuted him (Lys. xvi 10, xxi 19); he might in addition claim that he himself had never prosecuted anyone else. Lysias boasts that he and his family had no enemies and had never, down to the time of the Thirty Tyrants, been either prosecutors or defendants in a lawsuit (xii 4, 20); so too the speakers of Dem. xxxiv 1 and Is. x 1. Aiskhines i 1 claims never before to have brought an indictment (though he says nothing there of private lawsuits), and the *hēsykhiā* which Dem. xviii 308 praises and regards as characteristic of the majority of Athenian citizens appears from the context to be an indifference to such advantages as might be gained by exploiting public circumstances to pursue a private feud. Returning positive good for ill, an important stage beyond mere refraining from requiting ill, does not seem to be exemplified in the available literature; Demosthenes' prayer (xviii 324) that the gods may *either* put sense into his opponents *or*, if they are incurable, destroy them, hardly comes into the category of loving one's enemies, for even without the expressed alternative the divine 'cure' is requested for the city's sake, not the patients'. Simple forgiveness was often regarded as the product of compassion, empathy and a pleasing emotional vulnerability, and as such it will be discussed in part D. It might, however, be the expression of a magnanimous disposition, a feeling

---

[11] Cf. Dihle 41–60 on the emergence of magnanimity. G. H. Macurdy, *The Quality of Mercy* (New Haven, 1940) pays insufficient attention to the orators.

that if things have turned out all right in the end it is wrong to bear ill will (e.g. Men. *Perik.* 1023), or a feeling that revenge for small offences is undignified. 'Take it lightly and give it no more thought', says Achilles when Klytaimestra is overcome with shame (Eur. *Iph. Aul.* 850). Dionysos is admiringly called *gennadās* by the slave of Pluto in Ar. *Frogs* 738–42 since he did not punish Xanthias for the tricks which Xanthias had played on him; precisely that word is used earlier in the play (640) by Aiakos to Xanthias as commendation of his fair (*dikaios*) acceptance of a painful test—an interesting example of the application of the same laudatory term to equity and to magnanimity. The related word *gennaios* is used by Xanthias (615) of his own lordly, almost extravagant, willingness to be put to death if the evidence of his 'slave', extracted under torture, should prove him guilty of the theft of Kerberos; the point here is that his robust confidence in his own innocence makes it incompatible with his moral dignity to haggle over procedural details even in so dangerous a predicament.[12] Just as greed, aggression and fraud are all aspects of *pleonexiā*, 'trying to get more', so an anxiety to avoid any imputation of *pleonexiā* is a strong inducment to accept less than one's due. A speaker who has plenty of sticks with which to beat his adversary may embellish his own *persona* by suggesting that there is much which he waives; cf. Ar. *Thesm.* 418, 'All that is forgivable; but ...' (i.e. 'None of that really matters; but ...'). Cf. Demokritos B46, treating the easy tolerance of an offence against oneself as 'greatness of soul'; Men. fr. 95, on 'knowing how to be wronged *enkratōs*', i.e. '... without losing one's composure'.

After the restoration of the democracy in 403 the citizen body took a far-reaching oath of amnesty for offences committed before or during the reign of the Thirty Tyrants, and the democrats' decision to rate the well-being of the city above the pleasure of just retaliation was subsequently a source of great pride: And. i 140, Lys. ii 64, *Mē mnēsikakein*, literally, 'not to recall ills', i.e. 'to bear no grudges', is described by Aiskhines iii 208 (with reference to the events of 403) as 'the noblest words which civilisation can utter'. Demosthenes treats Athenian support for Sparta against Thebes after the battle of Leuktra as an example of magnanimity deserving imitation in his own time (xviii 98–101); he also advises against *mnēsikakein* in dealing with Rhodes (xv 16), and flatters the Athenians by telling them that it is not in their character to remember past injuries (vi 30)—though it is, of course, highly creditable to remember benefits received (xxiv 182); cf. Xen. *Hell.* vi 5.48, *gennaios* to remember the good done by Sparta and to show

[12] There are, of course, many layers of humour in this splendid scene, from which it is difficult to isolate one element without misrepresentation.

gratitude for that, forgetting past injuries. When facing the hypothetical criticism—obviously damaging—that it is *mnēsikakein* to mistrust the Thracian king Kersebleptes because of his past hostility to Athens (Dem. xxiii 192f.), Demosthenes distinguishes between *mnēsikakein* as a pretext for aggression (cf. Lys. xxx 9, *adikōs mnēsikakein* = 'bear a grudge with intent to do harm') from a sensible caution in one's own vital interest. The most illuminating exploitation of the concept is his treatment of the Athenian intervention at Byzantion, in a passage (Dem. xviii 93f.) cited in I.F.*4* (the *kalokāgathiā* of Athens . . . unwilling to *mnēsikakein* . . .). Cf. ibid. 269; Aiskhines iii 85, it is not *dikaios* to recall former grounds of anger against someone who now trusts you.

To be magnanimous is necessarily to liberate oneself from the oppressive fear of being deceived and—which is more important, for an intelligent man who chooses to be magnanimous may know very well what is going on—from the fear of being seen or thought to be deceived. To trust a friend with money, instead of leaving it with a banker, was *megaloprepēs*, the act of a proud man who wanted to be seen to rate friendship above security (Dem. lii 24). To be genuinely deceived is a mark of a character which is itself unable to deceive and therefore trustworthy (cf. Xen. *Anab.* vii 6.21, shameful to be deceived by an enemy, but more shameful to deceive a friend than to be deceived by a friend), and to detect deceit in others may be an index of one's own capacity to deceive (Ar. *Eccl.* 237f.). A suspicious disposition was not well regarded (Dem. lix 81, 83), nor was readiness to believe slander (Men. fr. 541). The parasite worms his way into a guileless (*akakos*) man and 'devours him from the inside' (Anaxilas fr. 33).

The messenger in Eur. *Hipp.* 1250–4 declares that he would not believe the written accusation against Hippolytos which Phaidra left when she killed herself 'even if the whole female sex hanged itself and filled a forest of tablets with writing'. As the chorus and the audience know, but Theseus does not yet know, the messenger's opinion is justified; in the actual situation, it is intelligent of him to treat Hippolytos's known character as strong evidence, but in the situation which he depicts in such hyperbolic terms he imagines himself as faithful against all reason. The story told in Dem. xiii 116f., reflects the opposite attitude to trustfulness; a certain Philokrates would not accept any 'pledge' from the Spartans short of a situation in which they were unable to do him harm—for, he said, that they would harm him if they could he took for granted. This story is told as an argument to make Athens distrust people who had shown themselves her enemies. Similarly, Eur. *Hel.* 1617f., 'Nothing is more useful than *sōphrōn apistiā*', i.e. '. . . a wise scepticism', is uttered in a dramatic situation in which overt and declared enmity is an ingredient.

## IV.D. SENSIBILITY

*1. Compassion*

We have seen that a misdeed could be thought to deserve forgiveness if it was committed without malicious intent (III.H.*1*), and that it could also be forgiven if the offended person enjoyed, or wished to display, the emotional security which predisposes to magnanimity (IV.C.*4*). A further motive for forgiveness, however, was compassion, the sensitivity which makes us identify ourselves with a sufferer and advance his interests even to the detriment of our own. It was common practice for a defendant on a serious charge to bring his children and other relatives into court (Pl. *Apol.* 34D, 35B) in the hope that pity for the predicament in which they would be left by his condemnation would induce the jury to acquit him or at least to reduce his penalty.

Ar. *Wasps* 568–74 (*Philokleon, boasting of the jurors' life*): And if we're not persuaded by that, straight away he hauls up his kids by the hand, daughters and sons, and I listen, and they put their heads down and bleat. Then their father beseeches me, trembling, as if I were a god, to let him off his examination. 'If you take pleasure in the voice of a lamb, take pity on the voice of a child!' Or, if I take pleasure in piglets,[1] to do what I'm asked by his daughter's voice. Then we slacken off just a bit of our anger against him.

In the famous trial of the dog later in the play, Bdelykleon's impassioned plea for the defendant, including the display of the whimpering puppies (975–8), actually wrings a tear out of the fierce old man (982–4). Fourth-century oratory provides us with many references (some of them a hundred years later than the *Wasps*) to the presentation of a defendant's children or aged parents as a means of arousing the jury's compassion, e.g. Dem. xxxi 99, 186, liii 29, Hyp. iv 41.

It must be conceded that words denoting pity (*eleos*, verb *eleein*, and *oiktos*, verb *oiktīrein*, together with their cognates) do not always or necessarily denote a feeling or state of mind;[2] the stronger 'pities' the weaker, i.e.

---

[1] There is a joke here, depending on a secondary sexual meaning.

[2] Throughout this section I am conscious of a debt to the Rev. Alfred Bingham, with whom I spent many hours in discussing the extent to which different ingredients can be

shows pity, behaves as if compassionate, when he does what the weaker has asked him to do—rather as *thaumazein*, 'admire', or *philein*, 'love', can be used of outward manifestations without regard to inward feelings.

Lys. xviii 1: We claim that we should be pitied by you and receive our rights.

Lys. xix 53: If you think that our plea is justified and that the evidence we adduce is adequate, then, I beg of you, pity us.

Cf. Ant. iii α.2, γ.3, pity for the plaintiff shown by a verdict against the defendant; Is. ii 44, where 'pity' is tantamount to 'a just verdict in accordance with the evidence';[3] Soph. *Oed. Tyr.* 671f. (Oedipus to the chorus, which has interceded on behalf of Kreon), 'Your utterance moves compassion, and I take pity on it.' Explicit separation of pity as a sentiment from the manifestation of pity in action is sophistic (Ant. ii δ.6, 'I ask you to acquit me and congratulate me' [*sc.* on my acquittal], 'not to condemn me and pity me' [*sc.* on my condemnation]), though in practice it may not have been uncommon to punish severely, for the future good of the community, while feeling very sorry for those punished. Such passages as Lys. xix 53, however, remind us that however easy it may be in theory and definition to separate pity from justice, in practice it is often hard. We tend to pity people in proportion to their desert rather than to their suffering, and Lysias's speaker, in asking for pity if his case is proved, implies that he is the victim of injustice; cf. Dem. lvii 3 (~ 44), 'most pitiable' if we were penalized, for it would be unjust and illegal; Is. x 22, pity earned by death in battle; Lys. ii 14, 'pitying the victims of wrong and detesting those who outraged them'. Bdelykleon in Ar. *Wasps* 967–72 asks Philokleon to 'pity' the dog Labes because he is a good dog (cf. 952) and his prosecutor a bad dog; and the indignation which the chorus in Ar. *Knights* 526–36 expresses in reproaching the audience for its lack of pity for old Kratinos is essentially indignation at ingratitude towards a man who had deserved well of Athens as a comic poet. We may compare the pathos of Dem. xix 310, which turns not simply on the sufferings of the Olynthians but upon Athens' debt to them; cf. Eur. *Her. Fur.* 1236–8, Theseus pities Herakles in return for what Herakles had once done for him.

There is an obvious relationship between such passages and those in which pity is earned by objectively judged merit. (Cf. VI.A.2).[4]

distinguished in passages of early Greek poetry which portray appeals for pity or describe acts of pity.

[3] Cf. Adkins (1) 203f.

[4] Arist. *Eth. Nic.* 1114a25–8 considers that while it would be right to pity a man blinded by an accident it would be appropriate to reproach, not to pity, a man who had gone blind through alcoholism.

Soph. *Phil.* 1318–20: When men are involved in ills that they have brought upon themselves, as you are, it is not *dikaios* that they should be forgiven or that anyone should express pity for them.

Cf. Antiphanes fr. 258, pity for 'being poor *kalōs*', i.e. in a manner which evokes favourable response, not distaste; *GVI* 217 (Pharsalos, s. V in.), 'Let everyone pity a good man and pass on'; Philippides fr. 9, pity aroused for free men who are destitute while slaves of bad character live comfortably; Isok. xviii 62, Lys. iii 47f., xii 20, xx 35f., xxii 21. In many cases it is hardly possible to discern whether merit enters into consideration or not, e.g. Ar. *Lys.* 961, the old men's sympathy with the sex-starved Kinesias.

A similar phenomenon is the fact that misfortune was commonly felt to be more pitiable if it contrasted strongly with previous good fortune or with what the status of the sufferer would have led him to expect. Moskhion fr. 9 generalizes to that effect, and Menelaos in Eur. *Hel.* 417–19 (a hero acutely conscious of his status and indignant at what has befallen him) declares that misfortune which is unaccustomed to the sufferer is even worse than that of the man who has always been unfortunate. Cf. Ar. *Frogs* 1063f., the presentation of a legendary king in rags on the tragic stage evokes the audience's pity; Eur. *Hel.* 944f., the chorus's compassion for Helen; Hdt. iii 14.10, Psammetikhos's pity for a man fallen in old age from wealth to beggary; Isok. v 67, the pitiable exposure of the noble infant Kyros; Isok. xvi 48 combines two aspects of pity in suggesting that it should be proportionate both to the desert of the sufferer and to the extent of his fall.

A further reservation which should be made in analysis of Greek concepts of pity is that *eleein* and *oiktīrein* in epitaphs refer in some cases, and may refer in many more cases, less to sentiment than to formal acts or utterances which maintain the approved relationship between the world of the living and that of the dead:[5] 'Pause and pity ...' (*GVI* 1224, 1225.1, cf. 1223.2 [all s. VI]), 'Pity ... and pass on' (*GVI* 1226.2 [s. VI]), 'Whoever was not at my funeral, let him lament me now' (*GVI* 1228 [Thasos, *c.* 500]). So Talthybios in Eur. *Tro.* 735f. tells Andromakhe that if her words anger the Greeks her child, who is in any case to be dashed to pieces, 'will not receive burial or pity', i.e. '... the formal acts of pity for the dead'. Nevertheless, there are epitaphs which clearly presuppose the arousal of compassionate feeling in the passer-by: *GVI* 1913 (s. III in.), 'No one is so insensitive as not to pity this dead woman'; *GVI* 1985, 'Who does not pity your fate? You died through longing for your dead son'. Cf. Eur. *El.* 545, Elektra's suggestion

[5] Cf. Lattimore 234f.

that some stranger was moved by pity to put an offering on Agamemnon's tomb.

Is there such a thing as 'pure' pity? If A and B suffer the same blow—that is to say, if there is at least one grief-provoking element common to their two predicaments—each of them suffers it in a context which includes his own memories, associations, expectations, apprehensions and personal relationships, and it cannot be the same experience for both of them. If, knowing both of them well, we try to persuade ourselves that we pity both of them equally, solely by virtue of the 'same blow' which has fallen upon them, we put ourselves in the foolish position of pretending not to know what in fact we do know; by trying to identify ourselves with them in respect of a single aspect of their experience, without entering into the other aspects which combine to make up the actual experience (including, for example, a sense of injustice) we are treating them as if they were hypothetical cases instead of real people. But if we know little or nothing about them, and identify ourselves with them by virtue of the only thing we do know, the fact that they are suffering, and do not excuse ourselves by imagining that their suffering is deserved, or that they are accustomed to it, we can fairly claim to be motivated by 'pure' compassion. *A fortiori*, we can make this claim if we know well that their suffering is deserved, or that they have done us great harm in the past, and yet find that spontaneous compassion overrides such considerations.

Greek forensic practice assumes that pity can motivate decisions contrary to justice.

Dem. xxxviii 20: Anyone sued for his administration of so large an estate would have paid up three talents to buy off the danger which threatened him and the advantages which naturally belonged to his wards. They were young, and orphans, and no one knew what sort of people they were. Everyone says that factors of this kind are much more important in court than a strong case in law.

Lys. xx 34: We see that if a man brings forward his own children in court and weeps and laments, you are moved to pity at the idea that they should be deprived of their rights as citizens because of him, and you forgive the wrongdoing of the fathers for the sake of the children, although you do not yet know whether those children will be good men or bad when they are grown up.

Cf. Is. v 35, a warning to the jury (on the assumption that it needed to be warned) not to pity the speaker's adversary for his misfortunes and poverty. One implication of these passages is that pity for the children would not operate if the jury knew that it would one day prove not to have been in the city's interests; but since that could not be known, the fact that the jury liked to be told that their compassion did on occasion override justice is a much more important implication. It is not hard to find passages in which there seems to be no rationalization of pity or measurement of pity in proportion to desert.

Dem. xxxiii 34: If . . . the disaster (*sc. the loss of his wife and children in an earthquake*) had happened to the man before the announcement of the result of the arbitration, no litigant or arbitrator would have been so cruel as not to put off the announcement until the man should be back in Athens.

Cf. Aiskhines ii 179, where Aiskhines could have exploited the theme that his brothers had deserved well of Athens, but does not (ctr. 147, where an element of this kind does enter into his pathetic description of his 94-year-old father); Ar. *Clouds* 1253, where Strepsiades says patronizingly to the creditor whom he has frustrated, 'Mind you, I don't *want* you to come off so badly!'

Dem. xxv 83f.: The men towards whom Aristogeiton behaved so cruelly and harshly were quite rightly acquitted by juries . . . But his harshness, bloodthirstiness and cruelty were exposed for all to see. Some defendants brought into court their children and aged mothers; he saw them, but he had no pity on them.

Cf. Dem. x 43, the cruelty of not pitying old age and poverty;[6] Dem. xxvii 68, where 'unexpected misfortune' as well as victimization is a ground of pity; Dem. lvii 45; Eur. *Hec.* 566, pity for Polyxene aroused in the man whose job it is to kill her (but regret that the young and beautiful and noble should die?); Eur. *Ion* 43–9, the Delphian priestess was angry when she first saw the baby Ion deposited in the sanctuary, but 'through pity discarded her anger'; ibid. 923f., a store of ills 'at which anyone would shed a tear'; Eur. *Iph. Aul.* 477–84, Menelaos, after at first insisting on the sacrifice of Iphigeneia, relents through pity at his brother's tears (but see VI.A.*1*); Eur. *Iph. Taur.* 584, the Greek who pitied Iphigeneia even though (or because) she was required to sacrifice him; Eur. *Phoen.* 418, Iokaste exclaims in compassion as soon as she hears the words 'another man, an exile', before knowing anything about him; Eur. *Supp.* 95f., 287f., Theseus's pity for the suppliants (but here it is not so easy to disentangle pity from the respect due to suppliants and commanded by the gods);[7] Eur. *Tro.* 786–9, Talthybios complains that the message he has been ordered to transmit should have been entrusted to someone who is 'pitiless and a greater friend to shamelessness than my heart is'; Eur. fr. 33, 'Who, on hearing this, would not shed a tear?';

[6] Cf. Bolkestein 112–14.    [7] Cf. Pearson 136f. on pity for suppliants.

Eur. fr. 127, Perseus pities Andromeda at first sight; Eur. fr. 407, it shows lack of education not to shed a tear at what is pitiable; Hdt. v 92. γ.3, the men who went to kill Labda's baby flinched, one after another, when the baby smiled, and could not kill him; Lys. xxiv 7 ('pitiable even to one's enemies'), xxxi 19, xxxii 19; Men. *Perik.* 356ff., Sosias's pity for his master Polemon, who is so *kakodaimōn*; Men. fr. 641, the supreme value to the unfortunate man of having others to come and share his grief; Soph. *El.* 920 (Elektra to Khrysothemis), 'O, how I have long pitied you for your folly!'; Soph. *Oed. Col.* 109f., 241–53, Oedipus and Antigone claim the pity of the Athenian chorus by virtue of their suffering; Soph. *Oed. Tyr.* 12f., 'Immune to pain I would be, if I did not take pity on you who sit before me'; ibid. 402f. (Oedipus to Teiresias), 'If you were not an old man, you would (*sc. be made to*) realise, by the punishment inflicted on you, the nature of your intention'; ibid. 1178f., Polybos's slave pitied the infant Oedipus and gave him to a Theban shepherd instead of ensuring his death; Soph. *Phil. passim* (especially 169–90, 965f.), the pity which Philoktetes' suffering arouses in Neoptolemos and the chorus; Soph. *Trach.* 298–302, Deianeira's immediate pity for the captive women (but 464–7, especially for Iole, because of her beauty and nobility of bearing); Soph. fr. 598.8f., even a pitiless man would be moved to pity by the shorn mare; Thuc. iii 36.4, the Athenians reopened the question of Mytilene because they felt that their precipitate decision had been cruel.

Dem. xxiv 171 calls it an Athenian characteristic to 'pity the weak', and in xxvii 65 he alleges that when the estate of an indicted and condemned defendant is confiscated the jury is moved by pity not to confiscate everything but to leave a little for his unhappy wife and children. These statements may be untrue, but what matters is the speaker's judgment of what the jury liked to be told about itself. When a prosecutor or a speaker in the assembly reproaches and upbraids his fellow-citizens, it is not for their harshness but for their leniency, kindness and compassion, which, he argues (cf. I.E.1), misleads them into taking decisions contrary to the city's interests.

Lyk. *Leokr.* 33: Whom does he think it is possible to seduce by argument? Whose character is so pliant that he thinks he can bring it round to compassion by tears? The jurors', of course!

Dem. xiii 17 unusually (the speech is deliberative, not forensic) tells the Athenians that they should be frightening under arms but kindly (*philan-thrōpos*: cf. section 2) in the courts. Cf. Ar. *Peace* 349–52, cited in III.D.1. In this connection we should note Dem. xxiii 69 on the democratic principle observed in Athenian law ('mildness' towards those charged) and Perikles' boast (Thuc. ii 37.2f.) of Athenian social tolerance. Both tolerance and compassion, of course, are relative. Not even Athenian society, let alone that of other Greek states, was tolerant by our standards, and in certain important respects we may judge the Athenians lacking in compassion, notably in the individual's reluctance to involve himself in the (perhaps divinely caused) misfortunes of others ('Go your own way!' says Strepsiades apotropaically to the creditor who announces himself as *kakodaimōn* [Ar. *Clouds* 1263]),[8] or the brutal jokes against skin- or eye-diseases from which one eminent figure or other happened to suffer (Ar. *Birds* 150f., *Eccl.* 400f., *Wealth* 665f., 716–25); see further VI.A.*3.*

## 2. *Friendliness*

In a pair of passages in Demosthenes' speech against Meidias (xxi 101 and 185), one of which appears to be a rewriting of the other, *eleēmōn* 'compassionate', and *pollous eleōn*, 'pitying many', are coupled with *philanthrōpos* (etymologically, 'fond of human beings').[9] The close relation between the two is indicated by the fact that in Dem. xxii 57, 'pity and forgiveness' are treated as characteristics of the Athenian legal code, while in Dem. xxv 81 (cf. 76) these two are joined with *philanthrōpiā* as 'what each member of the jury brings with him to court from home', and *philanthrōpiā* may denote that element in constitutional democracy and its laws which reassures and conciliates the ordinary citizen and the same time predisposes jurors to leniency: Dem. xix 104, xxi 184, xxii 51, xxiv 120, 163, 193; Hyp. v 25, with *prāotēs*, 'leniency'. Cf. Dem. xviii 132 (undemocratic to treat the unfortunate arrogantly) and xxi 12.

Excess of *philanthrōpiā* is reproached as servile by Dem. lxi 18, 21 (cf. 13f., on *prāotēs*), but without those passages (and the speech is epideictic) we would not have suspected from oratory or comedy that an excess of *philanthrōpiā* was possible.[10] Indeed, the word encroaches upon other value-terms

[8] This principle is made quite explicit in Eur. *Supp.* 223–8. Cf. Ehrenberg 242–6. A British business executive made 'redundant' in 1971 remarked, 'Your men friends tend to avoid you; they seem to think this sort of failure is catching' (*Daily Telegraph* 14 July 1971, p. 9).

[9] Since *philanthrōpiā* is not a conspicuous virtue in Plato and Aristotle, little has been written about it; see however Ferguson 102–17, who considers (228) that of all Greek moral concepts *philanthrōpiā* comes nearest to providing a basis for a universal morality. Some of its limitations will be considered in VI.A.

[10] *Eirōneiā*, 'playing down', pretending innocence and ignorance (cf. Arist. *Eth. Nic.*

in such a way as to suggest recognition of the fact that love of one's fellow-men is that orientation of personality which distinguishes the giver from the taker and expresses itself in honesty and self-sacrifice as well as in compassion.

Dem. xxi 128: Now if Meidias had behaved in other respects as a *sōphrōn* and *metrios* man ... and had been objectionable and violent towards me alone, I should in the first place regard this as a misfortune of my own; secondly, I should be afraid that by pointing to the rest of his life as being *metrios* and *philanthrōpos* he might escape any penalty for his outrage against me.

Here there seems to be an interesting convergence of *philanthrōpiā* and *sōphrosynē*. Cf. Aiskhines ii 39f., Dem. xviii 298, of friendly and conciliatory conversation; Dem. xviii 5, of the community's goodwill towards an individual citizen; Dem. xix 99, of the citizen who comes forward to help the community;[11] Dem. xxv 52, of kindness, courtesy and compassion in personal relations;[12] ibid. 86f., of *epieikēs* men who are ready to act as guarantors for others; Men. *Aspis* 394–6, contrasting *philanthrōpōs*, 'unselfishly', with 'to my own advantage'; Men. fr. 19, of the kindly generosity of a wealthy man. The same word was used of relations between states, denoting the sacrifice of self-interest: Dem. xvi 16, xix 39, xxiii 13, 131.

Like the commoner word *kharis*, *philanthrōpiā* can denote either end of a two-term relationship, the manifestation of affection or the quality which evokes such a manifestation in others:[13] Aiskhines ii 15, 'the *philanthrōpiā* of the (*sc. dramatic*) art'; Dem. vi 1, of attractive arguments; Dem. xix 95, of a plea for peace; ibid. 220, of generous and agreeable proposals; Dem. xliv 8, of a plea which, although not based on strict law, strikes a jury as fair; Dem. xlv 4, of a mother's entreaty of her son to drop a lawsuit against his stepfather. In Dem. xxiv 24 '*philanthrōpōs* and democratically' is opposed to 'cruelly and violently and oligarchically'. Just as *philanthrōpos* extends its denotation to a wide range of virtues, so *ōmos*, 'cruel', extends to a comparable range of vices, from gross savagery (Dem. xxv 63, biting off another man's nose in a brawl) and indiscriminate execution (Thuc. iii 36.4, cited in section 1) to the defrauding of orphans (Dem. xxvii 26, 68), ruthless unfairness towards an opponent (Aiskhines ii 1), unwillingness to forgive (Dem. xviii 274f.), and ingratitude (Hyp. iii 32). *Mīsanthrōpiā*, etymologically, 'hating

1127ª13–1127ᵇ32), could also, I imagine, be taken as a manifestation of *philanthrōpiā*, but it is interesting that Theophr. *Char.* 1 sees much deceit and hypocrisy in it.
[11] Cf. Bolkestein 108–11.          [12] Cf. Bolkestein 122–6.
[13] Cf. Hands 35f.

humans', can also be applied to ingratitude (Dem. xviii 112). 'Cruelty', however, merges into severity and unbending single-mindedness. In Soph. *Ant.* 471f., Antigone, '*ōmos* child of an *ōmos* father, does not know how to give way before (*sc. the threat of*) ills', i.e. she is unbending, and Xen. *Anab.* ii 6.12 describes Klearkhos, a formidable commander of troops, as 'entirely without charm, always harsh and *ōmos*'; Agesilaos, a commander of a different stamp, was mild towards ordinary soldiers but hard on officers (Xen. *Ages.* 11.5), in consequence of which his men loved and obeyed him (ibid. 6.4).

In connection with cruelty, it is striking that the Athenians were apparently unable to think of punishments worse than death (Lys. i 31, xii 37, 82f., Thuc. iii 45.3f.); even a great hatred expresses itself in a wish that one's enemy might die many times (Alkmene to Eurystheus, Eur. *Hcld.* 959f.). Rhesos's threat of impalement (Eur. *Rhes.* 512–17) is the threat of a *barbaros*, and later cultures have had little difficulty in devising punishments which make the sufferer pray for death as a release from pain; we must, however, remember that an Athenian citizen enjoyed some immunities which were denied to foreigners and slaves (VI.A.*3f.*).

An epitaph often proclaims that the dead person gave no *lȳpē*, 'pain', 'distress', 'grief', 'trouble', to anyone: *GVI* 342.2 (a midwife), 'To no one *lȳperos*, and missed in death by all'; *GVI* 540, 'pleasing all'; *GVI* 931, 'friend to all, distressing no one'; *GVI* 1533.2, 'enemy to no one'; *GVI* 1689, 'I so lived that no one had any complaint against me' (a link with the boast of avoiding litigation: IV.C.*3*); *GVI* 2016, 'having given no distress to anyone'. This group of expressions is known also from literary sources. It is claimed by Lysias (fr. I 6.II [Albini]) that he 'never yet gave pain to any Athenian'. Cf. Aiskhines ii 181, 'I have behaved in a way that caused no pain to them'; Ar. *Peace* 764, 'having given little pain and much pleasure'; Eur. *Hyps.* fr. 1.i.9f. (Bond), 'We shall give no trouble to this house'; Isok. xii 5, 'trying to live without wrong-doing and without giving pain to others'; Men. fr. 416, a good death if you 'depart enemy to no one'.

Soph. *Trach.* 330–2 (*Deianeira, with reference to Iole*): And may no distress be inflicted on her by me, to add to the ills she has; her present distress is enough.

Despite the natural need for sympathy in misfortune, the principle 'Enough's enough' could be invoked as a reason for not inflicting one's own troubles on others. Cf. Eur. *Alc.* 1041 (Admetos to Herakles, explaining why he said nothing of his wife's death), 'It was enough for me to weep for my own suffering'; Her. *Fur.* 277f.; *Iph. Aul.* 981f. (Klytaimestra to Achilles), 'I am ashamed to impose *my* troubles upon *you*'; Hdt. i 42.1, not right for a man in misfortune to associate with the fortunate.

Good temper and an equable manner (*eukoliā*) could also be regarded as both a private (e.g. *GVI* 1498) and a public virtue, since in Ar. *Frogs* 359 the man who is '*eukolos* to his fellow-citizens' is the antithesis of the man who stirs up civil strife. To be *ēpios*, 'mild', 'gentle', 'merciful' (a virtue of kings in Homer) is also commended, as by Erekhtheus in Eur. fr. 53.6 (Austin), and Athena commends the '*ēpios* temper' of Poseidon in Eur. *Tro.* 53; cf. Eur. *Ba.* 641, 'A *sophos* man cultivates a *sōphrōn* good temper'.[14]

The high regard in which magnanimity, forgiveness, compassion and sympathy were held illustrates one respect in which we can discern a popular foundation for the Aristotelian concept of the virtuous response to any given situation as the right point on a scale between the inappropriate responses dictated by one or the other of two opposing vices. So many of the virtues which we have examined are the virtues of a soul which has fortified itself by reason against the assaults of fear, greed, desire and impulse. Life in a society in which no one ever yielded to an impulse would be a life not worth living, and there is no doubt that some Greeks who thought too hard and too narrowly about morality exaggerated the virtues of self-sufficiency and invulnerability. Xen. *Cyr.* viii 1.42 makes no adverse comment on Kyros's requirement that Persians should not be seen to spit, blow their noses, or 'turn aside to look at anything', since it should appear that 'nothing excites their wonder'. Nor does Hdt. iii 14.10 comment on the odd behaviour of Amasis, who formally severed his friendship with Polykrates of Samos because he was sure that Polykrates would come to grief and he did not want to be distressed by the misfortunes of a friend. Cf. Eur. *Hipp.* 250–66 on the unwisdom of loving too much, for it leads to suffering when those whom one loves are afflicted. These, however, are unusual sentiments. Falling in love, regarded by Lys. iii 44 as characteristic of the *euēthēs* (etymologically, 'good in character', but in actual usage normally 'simple-minded', 'guileless'), seems to Aiskhines i 131 as something which happens to those who are *philanthrōpos* and well-disposed to others. Again, the Greek saying (e.g. Hdt. iii 52.5) 'Better envied than pitied', sounds a little harsh to modern ears, but perhaps only because it is true, and we do not always like the truth; it does

---

[14] Greek is rich in words for the types of behaviour motivated by goodwill. In Ar. *Lys.* 1109 *aganos*, a poetic word, is contrasted with *semnos*, 'august', 'reverend' (applied to people who think a lot of themselves). Xen. *Mem.* ii 8.6 advises 'avoiding those who are *philaitios*' (i.e. fond of finding fault with others) and 'going after those who are *eugnōmōn*'; cf. III.C n. 13.

not, after all, say, 'Better envious than compassionate', and no Greek known to us, historical or fictional, said such a thing or would have wanted to say it.

## IV.E. SEXUAL BEHAVIOUR

### 1. Inhibition

It is easy to see that certain types of behaviour motivated by sexual desire—notably rape, alienation of affection, and seduction under false pretences—are particular cases of self-advancement without regard for the interests of others, and can therefore be subsumed under the same moral category as theft, cowardice, cruelty and avarice. It is not too difficult to observe or construct cases in which people who believe their sexual conduct to be free from any moral objection would not continue to believe this if they reflected a little longer and a little more efficiently. There remains, however, a very considerable range of sexual behaviour, by no means confined to marriage or even to heterosexual or one-to-one relationships, which is exempt from the charge of 'self-advancement without regard for the interests of others'.[1] At first glance many aspects of Athenian life might appear to justify the belief, favoured by some popular writers in our own day, that the Greeks lived in a rosy haze of uninhibited sexuality, untroubled by the fear, guilt and shame which later cultures were to invent. The Greeks did, after all, treat sexual enjoyment as the province of a goddess, Aphrodite (in the same way as they regarded other activities as the provinces of other deities), calling it 'what belongs to Aphrodite' (ta aphrodisia, verb aphrodisiazein; 'Aphrodite' in the same sense, Antiphon the Sophist B17). In the Dionysiac festivals at Athens giant models of the erect penis were taken in procession, to the accompaniment of suitably happy songs; a minor but affectionately regarded deity, Phales, seems to have been the personification of the erect penis (Ar. Ach. 263–79). The poets represented the gods themselves as enjoying adultery, fornication and sodomy, and the vase-painters of the late archaic and early classical periods often depicted sexual intercourse, masturbation and fellatio. Xenophon's Socrates, although hostile to the body on such issues as appeared to involve a clear body/mind antithesis, lists among the blessings conferred on mankind by beneficent providence

---

[1] This is denied by apologists from some religious systems, but I have not yet encountered a denial which was not founded on idiosyncratic definitions (e.g. of 'exploitation'), ill-considered analogies (cf. n. 15 below) or psychological propositions which seem, so far as the evidence goes, to be untrue.

(Xen. *Mem.* i 4.12) the fact that we, unlike so many animals, can be sexually active at all seasons.

We must remember, however, that when vase-painters show what may seem to be two or more couples having intercourse in the same room or out of doors in close proximity, pictorial conventions play a part; the author of the *Dissoi Logoi* remarks (2.4) that it is thought honourable for a woman and her husband to have intercourse in the privacy of their home, but it is *aiskhros* for them to do so out of doors where they can be seen. Xenophon's troops were shocked (Xen. *Anab.* v 4.34) by a tribe in Asia Minor 'the most *barbaros* and remote from Greek usage', to whom privacy in sexual behaviour meant nothing.[2] However much some of the gods and goddesses enjoyed sex, human sexual intercourse in temples and sanctuaries was forbidden (Hdt. ii 64), people were required to wash (to become 'pure', *hagnos*) before entering a sanctuary after intercourse (Ar. *Lys.* 912f.), and chastity was required in many religious connections (e.g. Eur. *Ion* 150).[3]

It may come as a further surprise to us to observe the sexual inhibition which operated with increasing strength throughout the classical period. The beginning and end of this historical process are summed up by the contrast between *Iliad* xxiv 129–31, where the goddess Thetis says to her son Achilles, 'How long . . . will you eat your heart out, with no thought for food or bed? It is good to lie with a woman in love', and the Alexandrian rejection of the passage as an interpolation on the grounds that 'It is unseemly for a mother to say this to her son' or 'it is inappropriate to a hero and a goddess'. Totally uninhibited language was the norm in Aristophanic comedy; by the late fourth century it was seldom heard on the comic stage.[4] Aristotle, remarking on this fact (*Eth. Nic.* 1128ᵃ22–4), calls direct sexual language *aiskhrologiā*, etymologically, 'speaking what is shameful' (or '. . . ugly'). The serious literature of the period tended to be circumspect, even coy, in expression, although not reticent in content.

Dem. xix 309: Philokrates . . . brought back here, to treat as he pleased, Olynthian women of citizen status; and the disgusting way in which he has lived is so well

---

[2] In Ar. *Frogs* 542–8 Dionysos imagines himself as a slave masturbating in the corner while his master makes good progress with a flute-girl on a couch, but possibly when a Greek said, 'There's no one here' he meant '. . . except slaves'.

[3] Cf. E. Fehrle, *Die kultische Keuschheit im Altertum* (Giessen, 1910), especially 25–38.

[4] The same is true of references to excretion. In Men. *Phasma* 39–43 a slave says to his young master, 'The trouble with you is—well, it makes me think of something rather vulgar, I hope you don't mind, but everything's so perfect, as they say, you've nowhere to shit'. A slave character in comedy fifty years earlier would probably not have apologized for using the word 'shit'.

known that I need not say anything ugly or unpleasant about him now; if I simply say that Philokrates brought back some women,[5] you all know, and so does the crowd round the court, what followed.

Xen. *Hiero* 1.4: We take pleasure or pain in sights through the eyes, in sounds through the ears, in smells through the nose, in food and drink through the mouth, and the (*sc. pleasure*) of Aphrodite through—we all know what.

Cf. Aiskhines i 38, 52, 55, iii 162, Dem. liv 9, 17. The increasingly rigorous confinement of unhibited sexual expression to 'privileged' compartments of progressively narrowed artistic, literary and ritual practice must reflect a growing feeling of shame and fear towards sexual activity *per se*.[6]

As we shall see, there were strong reasons—some of them valid for many cultures, others the product of Greek social structures in particular—why the moral character of people who seemed to attach great importance to their own sexual satisfaction should have been treated with suspicion, and many ways in which it was impossible for an Athenian to achieve satisfaction without clearly and indisputably breaking laws and rules of a much more general application. But it must be emphasized that at Athens, as in our own culture until very recent times, chastity differed from other virtues in that whereas a precise and detailed description of an offence against (e.g.) financial probity could be interesting or boring and could arouse amusement or indignation, an equally precise description, in the same ambience, of an offence against chastity was impermissible. The real problem lies outside the period with which we are concerned, for it is: what enabled the Greeks of the late archaic and early classical periods to achieve a considerable rupture of the inhibitions which are manifested in so many cultures and were operative in the early archaic period? Despite his acceptance of the fornication as one of the good things of life. Homer, who delights in precise descriptions of cooking meat or stabbing through a chink in an adversary's armour, never gives a comparable description of sexual contact. The latter half of the classical period seems to have returned to the spirit of Homeric inhibition and patched up a breach which had been opened in the intervening period.[7]

[5] But he does not 'simply' say that; he has already said that Philokrates brought them back 'for *hybris*', i.e. 'to treat as he pleased', and *hybris* very commonly implies sexual use under constraint. An orator sometimes denies saying what he has in fact said or has deliberately conveyed by innuendo.

[6] On Greek sexual behaviour in general cf. Ehrenberg 173, 177–80, and my article 'Classical Greek Attitudes to Sexual Behaviour', *Arethusa* vi (1973) 69–73.

[7] We must not always expect the difference between sexual and non-sexual reference to be apparent. When Moskhion in Men. *Samia* 47–50 says, 'I hesitate to tell you the

## 2. Resistance to Desire

The Greeks tended to speak of sexual desire as an external force acting upon the soul (cf. III.A.2, III.F.2), since one does not choose to desire but becomes aware of the fact that one desires. In this respect sexual desire is like hunger and fatigue, and the Greeks admired those whose pride, courage, sense of honour or rational principles gave them the power to resist. Xenophon treats the chastity of Agesilaos (*Ages.* 5.1–4) as an aspect of his *sōphrosynē* (5.7; cf. 5.4) together with his ability to abstain from food and drink when hungry and thirsty, to sleep little ('He treated sleep not as the master of his activity, but as its servant') and to endure extremes of hot and cold weather. Association of chastity with abstemiousness, endurance, industrious energy and the like is found also in Xen. *Mem.* i 2.1, ii 1.1, ii 6.1, iv 5.9, *Oec.* 12.11–14. Its link with the qualities required of a soldier is obvious (cf. IV.A.2), and the common contrast between masculine endurance and feminine weakness is also relevant (cf. III.C.2). Desire for pleasure plays at least as large a part as fear and greed in preventing us from putting the interests of others above our own; if we yield to any of these forces, it can be said that we are 'worsted', 'mastered' or 'enslaved' by them.

Lys. xxi 19: Do not only remember my services to the state, but think also of my private conduct, reflecting that this is the most laborious of all services, to be law-abiding and self-controlled and neither to be worsted by pleasure nor incited by prospect of gain, but to behave (*sc. as I have done*) in such a way that not one of my fellow-citizens has ever found fault with me or gone so far as to call me into court.

Cf. Lys. i 26, 'By transgressing the law you put it below your own pleasures' (adultery, in the case in question) and Dem. xl 9, 'not so completely conquered by his desire' for his mistress; Xen. *Ap.* 16 ('a slave to the desires of the body'), *Hell.* iv 8.22, vi 1.16, *Mem.* iv 5.3, *Oec.* 1.19f. Xenophon represents Socrates as warning him that by one kiss he can 'straightway become a slave and no longer free' (*Mem.* i 3.11). Similar expressions are used of greed for food (Eur. fr. 282.6) and addiction to wine (Philemon fr. 104); cf. III.F.2. There is, of course, a tendentious element in judgments of this kind, for we can be 'enslaved' to ambitions, fantasies and conventions of many kinds (as remarked by Philemon fr. 93.8–10; cf. Men. fr. 620), but it is

rest . . . The girl got pregnant. In saying that, I'm telling you what went before it', he is displaying an embarrassment which would be equally appropriate to cheating or injustice.

understandable that the individual who was known to value his own sexual satisfaction highly was regarded with suspicion as a potential lawbreaker and an unreliable friend.

## 3. Effects of Segregation

In connection with what were regarded by the Greeks as the natural differences between men and women, we have seen (III.C.1) that segregation of the sexes was strict at Athens, with the result that a young man might have little say in the choice of bride made for him, and she none. His opportunities for a love-affair with a neighbour's daughter (or wife) were very restricted. Women and girls did, however, take part in processions (cf. Dikaiopolis's daughter in Ar. Ach. 242–58), funerals and family celebrations, and as spectators at festivals; although they may have kept in pairs or groups as far as possible, with female slaves in attendance, on such an occasion a sighting was possible from which an intrigue might begin, with a faithful slave as go-between (e.g. Lys. i 8, cf. Theokritos ii 66–80), and on the periphery of a women's festival, especially if it went on at night and there was plenty to drink, a girl could be seduced or raped (Eur. Ion 545–54; Men. Epitr. 477–90, Sam. 38–50).

Such, at least, is the predominant impression we get from the literary sources, but the varying practicability of continuous and effective segregation and supervision implies a difference between social classes and between town and country (cf. III.C.1). In poorer families there was more opportunity for boys and girls to carry on love-affairs; the song sung by the girl in Ar. Eccl., while she awaits a lover, says provocatively (912), 'I'm left all alone here; my mother's away'. The kind of family about which we hear in forensic oratory is normally well-to-do, part of a society which made it difficult for a youth to establish contact with the daughter of another citizen; and even if he overcame all the obstacles he might put himself in a position of considerable danger. It was moikheiā, 'adultery', to seduce the wife, widowed mother, unmarried daughter, sister or niece of a citizen; that much is clear from the law cited by Dem. xxiii 53–5.[8] The adulterer could be killed, if caught in the act, by the offended head of the household (Lys. i concerns just such a case); or he could be held until he agreed to pay compensation (Dem. lix 64, Lys. i 25; cf. Kallias fr. 1); or he could be prosecuted (Lys. frr. 18–22) or maltreated and injured (Ar. Clouds 1083); and, whatever else happened, he

[8] Cf. Harrison i 32–8.

was shamed as having wronged a fellow-citizen (cf. *Dissoi Logoi* 2.5).[9] It is obvious that a man of conspicuous enthusiasm for women would be suspect as a potential adulterer (Pl. *Smp.* 191D); that is to say, as a potential wrong-doer.

No danger attended the sexual use of women of servile or foreign status, whether they were prostitutes owned by a brothel-keeper, hetairai who were looking for long-term dependence on agreeable and well-to-do men, concubines owned by the user himself or lent by a relative or friend, or dancers, singers or musicians whose presence at men's drinking-parties exposed them to importuning, mauling, kidnapping (an occasion for fighting between rival males), temporary hire, or straightforward seduction enjoyed by both partners. In Ar. *Thesm.* 1176–211 Euripides, disguised as an old woman, makes use of a dancing-girl to distract the attention of a policeman. Thoroughly aroused, the policeman asks, 'Can I sleep with her?', and the 'old woman', after a perfunctory refusal, agrees that he can, for a drakhme; and off he goes with the girl, who has neither been asked whether she wants to sleep with him nor given any say in the price (despite which she is apparently [1210f.] a loving partner).

We saw, however, in IV.B.2 reasons why expenditure of money on sexual pleasure was treated as discreditable; Xen. *Oec.* 1.13 indicates a belief that it was also bad for one's health, which no one, presumably, would have alleged of the same amount of legitimate marital intercourse. Isok. iii 40 regards it as *kakiā* to insult a loyal wife by pursuing pleasure outside the home. Moreover, purchased sexual relations do not give a man the satisfaction of being accepted and welcomed for his own sake; he wants to love and be loved (cf. Xen. *Hiero* 1.30–33),[10] and even an enduring relationship with a hetaira has an economic basis that makes it difficult for a lover to be quite sure that he is loved in return (the sort of hetaira who 'remembers only her last lover' is denigrated in Ar. *Eccl.* 1161f.). One consequence of the dis-approval incurred, on different grounds, by attempts to satisfy heterosexual desire was diversion of strong sexual emotion into homosexuality (cf. section 4). Another consequence was the common treatment of falling in love as a misfortune, since it was so commonly a love which could not be consummated without danger, disgrace or financial ruin. Eros is a 'sickness', a 'madness' (Eur. fr. 161), a cruel god who robs us of our wits (Men. fr. 79).[11]

[9] Cf. Lacey 113–16.

[10] The context refers to homosexual love, but that does not affect the point.

[11] Cf. Arist. *Eth. Nic.* 1116ᵃ12f., 'To die (*sc. by one's own hand*) as an escape from poverty or eros or something painful is not brave, but cowardly'.

The youth and the girl in Ar. *Eccl.* 956–9, 966–8, singing outside the girl's window, do not sing, 'How wonderful to be in love!' but 'Eros, I implore you, *let me go!*', by which they mean, 'Allow me, by repeated consummation of my desire, to be rid of the torment you inflict on me'. Beautiful women were not, as we say, 'easy on the eye', but 'a pain to the eyes' (Hdt. v. 18.4), because they arouse a desire which cannot easily be satisfied. A husband and wife in love with one another, like Nikeratos and his wife (Xen. *Smp.* 8.3, using the verb *erān*), and many a young couple in New Comedy, were the most fortunate of people. There were no doubt many more of them than we are encouraged to suppose by the view commonly taken nowadays of the Greek tendency to treat marriage as a mechanism for the inheritance of property. Although there is much inconsequentiality in the plot of *Lysistrata*, as in all Aristophanic comedy, the whole idea of the play (it is, after all, a strike not of women as such, but of citizen's wives only) could hardly have taken shape except in a society in which the marital relationship was central to sexuality, and the development of the plot in detail makes this more explicit. Recalling the fact that strict segregation was possible only to the well-to-do, and recognizing that preoccupation with the transmission of property and the acquisition of influential and distinguished political connections is naturally strongest among those who already have property and influence, we may suspect that in the middle and lower classes young men and girls knew more about each other, had definite ideas about whom they wanted to marry, and had a habit of getting their own way (often with their mothers as pertinacious allies) despite the formal authority of their fathers. If that is so, the love-match was more commonly than has generally been imagined, and even in the upper strata of society there is a further factor which must not be left out of account. The negative attitude to sexual response so characteristic of Greek philosophy, an attitude which Christianity in some respects exaggerated,[12] has given rise to a belief that sexual desire is intended by God to be a product, and its satisfaction an expression, of love. In fact, however, sexual desire is a normal response to sensory stimuli; other factors are needed to generate love,[13] and one of its most effective generators is the

[12] Christian apologists who presuppose that (i) God is good, (ii) a positive and constructive sexual morality is good, (iii) Jesus was divine, and (iv) the utterances of Jesus are correctly reported in the Gospels, have little option but to persuade themselves that the sexual doctrines of Matthew 5.27–32 and 19.1–12 are positive and constructive. Abstention from considering the passages in relation to their contexts makes this easier, but I see no real solution of the difficulty except discarding any one of the four presuppositions; it is not necessary to discard more than one.

[13] Of the speakers in Plato's *Symposium*, only Aristophanes treats eros as a search by

fulfilment of mutual desire—a fact long known to societies in which arranged marriages are frequent, and presumably taken for granted by the Greeks (cf. III.C.2, and Ar. *Lys. passim*). Eros was normally regarded by the Greeks as an exceptionally strong response to stimuli, i.e. a very strong and obsessive desire, distinguishable from the ordinary level of desire which could be satisfied by any one of a wide range of partners.[14] The Greek term for love—the affection, strong or weak, which can be felt for a sexual partner, a child, an old man, a friend or colleague—was *philiā* (verb *philein*). The question, 'Do you love me?' requires *philein*, whether the question is put by a young man to a girl whom he is kissing (Xen. *Smp.* 9.6) or by a father wanting an assurance of filial obedience from his son (Ar. *Clouds* 82; cf. ibid. 1488, master to slave). This is the relationship between a man and a woman accustomed to mutual enjoyment of intercourse (Ar. *Eccl.* 1161f., *Lys.* 870f., 905f.; Dem. lix 21, 35, 64).

A further disagreeable consequence of Greek restrictions on heterosexual relationships was a depersonalization of women, such as we have noticed (IV.B.2) in the classification of women, fish and wine as if they were commodities of the same kind (cf. Demokritos B235 on the brevity of the pleasure to be derived from food, drink and sex).[15] A woman becomes, in the eyes of the moralist, a temptation, an assault on the integrity of the disciplined and fortified soul, and (if hire or purchase is in question) an expensive luxury with which the self-sufficient man can dispense. Xenophon's Antisthenes (Xen. *Smp.* 4.38) thinks that the good and wise man does not have intercourse, or even give it a thought, until he is troubled by genital tension, whereupon he satisfies himself as easily and cheaply as possible, in

---

any given individual for the person who is his 'other half', i.e. his true complement. I have discussed this matter more fully in 'Aristophanes' Speech in Plato's *Symposium*', *Journal of Hellenic Studies* lxxxvi (1966), 47–50. Plato gives 'Aristophanes' a good run for his money, while rejecting his view of eros (*Smp.* 205DE, cf. 212C). Plato is, however, aware that, so far from falling in love with people because of their sensory characteristics, we may come to admire the sensory characteristics of those with whom we have fallen in love.

[14] Prodikos B7 defined eros as 'desire doubled', and 'eros doubled' as 'madness'. Lys. iii 44 speaks of falling in love as characteristic of those who are most *euēthēs*', etymologically 'of good character', but normally with the overtones 'soft-hearted', 'guileless', 'simple', 'simple-minded'.

[15] Analogies between sex and food are sometimes drawn by modern Christian apologists, who appear to think that a night with a person of the opposite sex is the same sort of experience, leaving the same sort of memories and having the same sort of effect on the personality, as eating a plateful of mushrooms. It is no doubt hard to make people chaste, but they are not likely to be made so by arguments of which the folly is either immediately discernible or discovered by subsequent experience.

order not to commit his soul; and Xenophon's Socrates (*Mem.* i 3.14) and Prodikos (*Mem.* ii 1.30) adopt what is fundamentally the same view.[16]

## 4. Homosexuality

Homosexual relations provided a youth, for whom marriage lay some years ahead, with the opportunity for the seduction of a partner on the same social plane as himself, an opportunity of the kind which exists in modern heterosexual societies which neither own slaves nor segregate the sexes. At least from the sixth century onwards, the Greeks regarded homosexual desire by a man or youth for a boy, or by a man for a youth, as natural. Hiero in Xen. *Hiero* 1.33 says that he is in love with the young Dailokhos and wants 'what perhaps human nature compels us to want from the beautiful'.[17] An Athenian who said, 'I am in love' would not have taken it amiss if asked, 'With a boy or a woman?' (cf. Ar. *Frogs* 55–7, Herakles' response to Dionysos; Theokritos ii 44, 150, a girl's uncertainty whether her absent lover has deserted her for a male or a female alternative). Robust and roguish Aristophanic characters, whose sexual ethos is characterized by the seizure of opportunities, are not averse to occasional homosexual experiences with good-looking boys (Ar. *Birds* 131–45, *Knights* 1384–6, *Thesm.* 35, *Wasps* 578). When Xenophon wishes to illustrate the remarkable chastity of Agesilaos, he chooses an example of homosexual temptation (Xen. *Ages.* 5.4). The speaker of Lys. iii, who has to admit to an affair with a handsome youth, betrays a measure of embarrassment (3f.), but he reminds the jury, 'There is desire in all men', and his embarrassment is no different in kind from that which may attend the pursuit of a hetaira by a man who is expected to have attained years of discretion (Dem. lix 22, 30, Is. vi 21). Although Aphrodite, the deity who presides over sexual enjoyment, is female, her province includes homosexual relations, which are covered by the term *aphrodisia* (Xen. *Oec.* 12.14, *Smp.* 8.21). The reasons for the great scale of homosexual activity and sentiment among the Greeks must be sought long before the period with which we are concerned, and comparison with other

[16] Diogenes the Cynic simplified his sex-life even further by merely masturbating when his penis erected itself (cf. Plutarch, *De Stoicorum Repugnantiis* 1044B). Philosophical hostility to sex is apparent also in the doctrine of Musonius Rufus (p. 63.17ff. Hense) that sexual intercourse was morally permissible only for the procreation of children within marriage.

[17] It is not clear whether this 'perhaps' indicates a reservation about the structure of human nature or about the propriety of 'compel'.

cultures in which women are segregated suggests that segregation by itself is not an adequate explanation; anyway, the Athenian adolescent growing up in Plato's time took homosexuality for granted because his father's and grandfather's generations took it for granted, and he was not taught that he was 'unnatural' or 'effeminate' if he experienced homosexual desire for younger boys.[18] He would certainly not have regarded homosexual activity in adolescence as incompatible with the enjoyment of women or with his eventual prospect of a harmonious marriage.

What is said about homosexuality in Aiskhines i or in Plato should not mislead us into thinking that homosexual relations were what has come to be called 'platonic', even though Xenophon claims (*Smp.* 8.30) that Zeus desired the soul of Ganymede, not his body (Pindar [*Ol.*1. 41–5] knew better) and denies (*Smp.* 8.31) that there was a physical relationship between Achilles and Patroklos (Homer would have agreed with the denial, but Aiskhylos [cf. Pl. *Smp.* 180A] thought otherwise). The language used is euphemistic ('grant a favour to . . .', 'serve the wishes of . . .', etc.) in much the same way as the language of heterosexual relationships was euphemistic in European literature until quite recent times, and although homosexual courting and importuning is a very common subject in vase-painting, portrayal of the consummation of homosexual desire—by contrast with numerous scenes of heterosexual coitus—is very rare indeed. Reality breaks through in remarks such as that of Xenophon's *Hieron* (cited above) and in Xen. *Mem.* i 2.30, where Socrates compares Kritias's desire for Euthydemos to a pig's desire to rub its itching back on a rock. The speech attributed to Lysias in Plato's *Phaedrus* ('Lysias xxxv') is an argument, formulated as if addressed to a boy, to the effect that it is better for a boy to 'yield to a non-lover' i.e. to a man who wants a physical relationship but will not lose his head over any particular boy. 'Lovers', says the writer (234B) 'are admonished by their friends, who tell them that being in love is not a good way to live, but those who do not fall in love had never yet been reproached by anyone as having failed to consider their own best interests'.

Since a boy grows up to be a youth, and a youth grows into a man, the object of homosexual affection can model himself on his lover, who in turn must try to excel in the boy's eyes ([Xen.] *Cyn.* 12.30), for there is no way, except by attracting and earning hero-worship, in which he can win the boy's love and admiration and so attain his object. For this reason it was possible for a deep and complex mutual devotion, not without an educational

[18] On psychological and sociological aspects of the question cf. G. Devereux, 'Greek Pseudo-homosexuality and the "Greek Miracle" ', *Symbolae Osloenses* xlii (1967) 70–92.

aspect, to grow out of the original homosexual stimulus, and presumably a physical relationship could also arise out of what began as admiration and mutual interest; homosexual love, like heterosexual love, is *philiā* (Aiskhines i 132, Lys. iii 5). At the same time, since a male becomes a different category of being in his appearance and social role when his beard grows, whereas there is little significant change in appearance involved in the transition from girlhood to womanhood, and even marriage and motherhood do not alter the essential social dependence of the female on the male in Greek society, homosexual relationships were sterile in more than the literal sense, and may well have deepened philosophical contempt for the realm of Aphrodite as transitory.

Public attitudes to the lover and his boy in fourth-century Athens seem to have been remarkably similar (Pl. *Smp.* 182A–185C) to modern attitudes to pre-marital heterosexual relationships.[19] While the homosexual lover had no need to conceal his desire,[20] and it was possible for him to boast to his friends of its attainment (Pl. *Phdr.* 232A), the boy whom he pursued was expected to resist seduction and had to bear reproaches if it was known that his resistance was overcome. It seems to have been felt that the boy who yielded had assimilated himself to a hetaira (Aiskhines i 111, 131, 167, 185), detracting from his future role as a citizen-warrior, and that he had been worsted in a contest with his seducer. It would not have been permissible for him to admit that he wanted to attract a lover,[21] still less to behave in a way which seemed to invite the attention of potential lovers (cf. Ar. *Clouds* 979); such behaviour labelled him effeminate, and (so far as the literary evidence goes)[22] men seem to have fallen in love not with effeminate-looking boys but with boys of well-developed masculine physique, distinguished for their success in athletics.

If a man was proved to have prostituted himself for money, as a boy or at any subsequent time in his life, he lost his citizen-rights in perpetuity, to the same degree as a man who was unable to pay off a financial debt to the state.

[19] I have discussed this matter more fully in 'Eros and Nomos', *Bulletin of the Institute of Classical Studies* x (1964) 31–42.

[20] A man of abnormal enthusiasm for boys was suspect as a potential lawbreaker, for much the same reasons as a man of abnormal heterosexual enthusiasm, and was called *agrios* ('wild', 'savage') or 'hairy' (Ar. *Clouds* 348–50; Aiskhines i 52), to assimilate him to the hybristic centaurs (Ar., loc. cit.) or the ungovernable and insatiable satyrs.

[21] When Alkibiades in Pl. *Smp.* 219BC tells the story of how he tried, as an adolescent, to seduce Socrates, he is looking back some twenty-five years, and in any case the attempt had been unsuccessful.

[22] The vase-painters do not help us here, since any given painter tends to make all the adolescents he portrays conform to the same physical type.

Presumably it was felt that a male prostitute had deliberately identified himself with the category of female prostitutes, who were predominantly not of citizen status; cf. I.F.*3* on the consequences of doing work of a type usually done by slaves. Since some element of prostitution—that is to say, submission to another person's desires as a means to an end distinguishable from the sexual relationship itself—*can* enter into any kind of sexual activity (even marriage), it was difficult for a boy who was known to have submitted to his lover to rebut an ill-wisher's allegation of prostitution; we may compare the way in which 'prostitute' is sometimes applied nowadays to a girl who enjoys extra-marital sex, even when there is no reason to suppose she seeks any end but the sexual relationship itself.

Ar. *Wealth* 153–9 KARION: And they say that boys do the same too, not for their lovers' sake but for money. KHREMYLOS: Not the good ones, only the whores; the good ones don't ask for money. KARION: What, then? KHREMYLOS: One of them asks for a good horse, another for hunting-dogs. KARION: Maybe that's because they're ashamed to ask for money, so they wrap up their vice under a different word.

No legal penalty was imposed on a boy against whom prostitution could not be plausibly alleged; nor, of course, on a boy who openly advertised himself as a prostitute but was not of citizen status in the first place (Aiskhines i 74, 119f., 123, 195).[23]

---

[23] Discussion of Greek homosexuality in works of the last hundred years, being too much influenced by modern European law, has in general failed to see that Greek laws did not penalize an unnatural act *per se* but were concerned with the civic status of the participants and with the relationships of which the act was an ingredient.

# V

## SANCTIONS

### V.A. TYPES OF ARGUMENT

#### 1. Consistency

People do not commonly ask the explicit questions, 'Why should I?'and 'Why shouldn't I?' with the serious intention of staying for an answer, but whenever we recommend or deprecate an action one of those questions is implicit in the situation. In most cases—and this applies as much to Greek oratory and drama as to ordinary life—the use of evaluative words serves in itself as an answer to the question. These words carry with them a promise of the speaker's affection and respect or a threat of his hostility and contempt; they may also carry by implication a promise or threat of similar reactions on the part of other people in general. This is essentially an argument from consequences: '*If* you perform this act which I deprecate, the consequences will be unwelcome to you'. If the speaker has any claim to authority *vis-à-vis* the hearer, his use of an evaluative word may carry the implication that he has perceived a matter of moral fact more acutely, by virtue of superior intelligence or longer experience. Whether this too is an argument from consequences is a problem which will be explored in more detail below. In all such cases the moral judgment bears within itself, as it were, the argument for its own truth. We could put the matter another way by saying that the evaluative word carries a charge which may be powerful enough to impel or deter the hearer.

It is not powerful enough to affect the man who has deliberately withdrawn from consideration of the moral aspect of his act; Kreon in Soph. *Oed. Col.* 883, in reply to the Chorus's indignant, 'But this is *hybris*!', says grimly, 'Yes, it is, but you'll have to put up with it', a striking contrast to the interchange of more normal type in 831f., 'What you are doing is not right!' —'It *is* right!'—'How *can* it be right?' Nor, again, can evaluative words touch the man who follows up the question, 'Why should I do this?' with such supplementary questions as, 'Why should I be honest?', 'Why should I be rational?', 'Why should I be reconciled to God?', or even (like the sophistically-educated young man caricatured in Aristophanes' *Clouds*) offers reasons why he 'should' be dishonest. In such cases, an answer can be offered only in terms of the probability of consequences welcome or unwelcome to the agent, e.g., 'Because you will lie awake at night', 'Because you will go to Hell', etc. There is always the risk that in any given case the estimate of probability may turn out to be false, so far as concerns this life, and the case for an afterlife is not very strong. The question, 'Why should I want to be happy?', may be left out of account as senseless, on the assumption that happiness is the state of being what one wants to be, doing what one wants to do and having what one wants to have.

If I know that a man who asks me, 'Why should I do this?', values honesty, I may try to demonstrate that the contemplated act is a particular case to which the rule, 'Be honest', is applicable. This is a normal situation, for within the same society, especially within a small society undergoing a comparatively slow rate of change, most people's evaluations agree much of the time. So Lyk. *Leokr.* 94 subsumes filial devotion under the principle that our lives are of lower value than 'those from whom we have received the beginning (*arkhē*) of life', and Is. viii 32 represents the necessity of supporting one's grandparents as depending on the fact that 'they are the beginning (*arkhē*) of the family, and what was theirs is handed on to their descendants'. Neither speaker considers the question, 'Why should I subordinate myself to my *arkhē*?', and both perhaps exploit the inclusion of 'command' and 'rule' within the semantic field of *arkhē*, thus profiting from general acceptance of the rule, 'Obey the officers and magistrates whom the community has appointed'.

A particular case may be brought under a general rule by representing it as analogous to some other type of case which is readily admitted to fall under the rule. Dem. xxi 184f., assimilates a defendant's claim on a jury's mercy to the claim which we establish on our friends' financial resources by our own generosity in making loans (cf. Eur. *Supp.* 267–70, 'as a wounded beast flees to the rocks, and a fugitive slave to an altar . . .'; Hyp. ii 7, Lyk. *Leokr.* 143). Dem. xxiii 56 justifies the killing of an adulterer on the grounds that an adulterer identifies himself with the enemies against whom we wage war in order to save our wives and children from the sexual outrage consequent on captivity. On the assumption that devotion to one's parents is virtuous, patriotism can be justified by treatment of our own land as a parent:[1] Dem. lx 5, Attica 'the mother of our ancestors', since it bore the crops on which they lived; Lyk. *Leokr.* 53, 'What should be done to a man who does not repay his fatherland for bringing him up?', Lys. ii 70, 'They died . . . having repaid their fatherland for their upbringing'; Soph. *Oed. Col.* 759f., Thebes' claim on Oedipus as his 'nurse'. Isok. iv 24 exploits the belief that the Athenians were autochthonous in order to argue that Attica is literally their mother, father and nurse. In general, analogies between the relation of an individual to his community and his relation to his family and friends are an obvious and productive type of argument: Dem. x 41–3 argues for economic protection of the old as 'parents of the community', and Lys. xiii 92f., suggests that a benefactor of the community as a whole deserves to be treated as a friend by each individual within the community; cf. Alexis fr. 280, paying back to one's son the debt contracted to one's father.

The argument, 'But suppose *everyone* did it?', was occasionally used, but it was made to turn upon consequences rather than upon moral logic: Dem. xxv 20, 'If everyone were given the power to do as he wished . . . our life would be indistinguishable from that of the beasts'; Lyk. *Leokr.* 59, if everyone behaved like Leokrates and went abroad in times of trouble Attica would become uninhabited. This type of argument is not very effective against a wrongdoer who is not interested in remotely hypothetical situations. Appeal to consistency, on the other hand, was much more favoured.

Dem. xx 135: Are you not, then, ashamed to risk being seen to commit a wrong for which, if others should do it, you have prescribed the death penalty?

Dem. xxiii 143: You would surely be shown to have behaved in a shameful (*aiskhros*) and extraordinary way if everyone knew that you honoured those Athenians who performed such an act as I have described and yet you have decreed that men of similar patriotic intentions towards their own countries should be outlawed.

These two passages make use of an implicit threat of humiliation (note 'being seen' and 'be shown'), the shame of being regarded by others as inconsistent to the point of irrationality (cf. III.F.3 on the relation between irrationality, insanity and shamelessness). The threat is equally clear in Dem. xxiii 124, 'What case can we make if we are seen . . .?', and 140, 'shameful to complain . . .', but it is not invariably made explicit.

Lyk. *Leokr.* 140: I do not imagine that anyone . . . is so foolish (*anoētos*) as to serve the city patriotically but support Leokrates, by whom the work of the patriot above all was undone.

Cf. Hdt. i 159.4, a reproach uttered against Apollo; Dem. xxiii 168, the

[1] Cf. de Romilly 130f.

'illogicality' of taking two decisions of which the implications are irreconcilable; Dem. xxiv 197.

## 2. Conscience

When we say of a man that he 'has a bad conscience' we are commonly referring to his fear of detection and of the punishment or humiliation which may be inflicted on him by others (human or divine). If he firmly believes in a judgment after death which will consign him either to eternal bliss or eternal agony, it is hardly possible to decide whether any element other than hope of good consequences for himself or fear of bad enters into any experience which he may call 'conscience'. There are, however, people who, regarding an afterlife as improbable, set themselves standards and are happy or unhappy according to the distance of their actual behaviour from the ideal which their moral experience has led them to construct. In so far as the prospect of future satisfaction or dissatisfaction with oneself is a determinant of moral action—and, of course, no one can know that he will forget what he has done, nor can he compel himself to forget it—such a prospect is classifiable in the genus 'hope and fear of consequences for oneself', but it is none the less distinct, as an experience, from the hope or fear of reward or punishment by others. Conscience in this sense is often passed over in silence in Greek passages where we might have expected it to be mentioned: Aiskhines i 50, '. . . to see if Misgolas, through fear of the gods and shame before those who know the facts . . ., may be willing to tell the truth'; ibid. 67, 'in contempt of the gods, in disregard of the law, and insensitive to all shame'; Dem. lvi 2, 'unless the borrower is honest in character and also either afraid of the courts or ashamed before the lender'. Those Greek expressions which, when translated into English, require the word 'conscience', e.g. enthȳmios, 'on the conscience', literally 'in the spirit',[2] and syneidenai heautōi . . ., literally, 'share in one's own knowledge that . . .', usually refer to fear of punishment by others, not to the guilt or shame[3]

---

[2] In archaic Greek thȳmos denotes the seat of thought and emotion; in Attic prose of the Classical period it is confined to some inherited phrases, but the element (-)thȳm- appears in many derived words.

[3] The difference between 'guilt-cultures' and 'shame-cultures' (cf. Dodds 28–50) seems to me a difference more in the way people talk than in the way they feel; if 'guilt' means 'fear of the gods' and 'shame' means 'fear of the hostility and ridicule of other people', Greek culture contained both elements (cf. Lloyd-Jones 24–6), and so does ours.

resulting from the recognition that one has fallen below one's own standards. Isok. xviii 43, 'those who have even a trivial misdeed on their consciences' refers, as the context shows, to calculation of the good or harm that one's reputation will do to oneself in the courts, and 'those who are aware that they have committed some trivial misdeed' would be a valid translation. Aiskhines i 47 speaks of 'men who err against themselves' by giving false evidence, but the use of the same expression with reference to young men who marry *hetairai* (Is. iii 17) suggests that Aiskhines has in mind social and legal consequences. Ant. vi 5, 'If a man committed impiety and transgressed against the gods, he would deprive himself of hope itself, the greatest good in human life', alludes to the possibility of divine punishment, as appears from Ant. v 93, 'If a man (*sc. accused*) has an unrighteous act on his conscience . . . he believes that punishment for his impieties has fallen upon him', and Dem. xix 240, where a juror's 'good hopes' for himself and his children are made to depend on the gods' awareness that he has given a just verdict. Similarly, Ant. ii δ.10, 'The dead man will be on your conscience (*enthȳmios*)' must be understood in terms of the gods' interest in the unavenged dead (cf. V.C.). In Ar. *Wealth* 354 ∼ 358 it seems clear that 'repentance' is the product of fear.

There are none the less some passages which seem to carry a suggestion (perhaps in some cases illusory) that self-respect and the prospect of self-contempt are genuine motives.[4]

Ant. v 41: In the end he (*sc. the slave under torture*) lamented the unjust fate inflicted upon me and upon himself, not out of any love for me—how could that be, seeing that he had (*sc. earlier*) accused me falsely?—but compelled by the truth.

Cf. 33, 'When he knew that he was going to die, he told the truth'.

ibid. 49f.: The free man has not yet said anything against me, although subjected to the same torture . . . He preferred, with truth on his side, to endure whatever might befall him.

ibid., 91: When the verdict is irreversible, repentance and recognition of error make matters worse (*sc. for the jury*).

(By implanting fear of the consequences of an unrighteous verdict, as suggested earlier in the context? Or because we 'kick ourselves' for being wrong?)

ibid. 93: Though my flesh is weak, my soul has helped to revive my strength, willing to suffer because it has a clear conscience.

Ant. vi 1: It is most welcome to a man . . . if he is in unavoidable peril, that he

[4] Cf. Gernet 346.

should at least—and this, in my view, is the most important thing in a case of this kind—be conscious that he has done no wrong, and that any misfortune which befalls him should be without bad character (*kakotēs*) or shame, and inflicted by chance, not wrongdoing.

ibid. 23: I told them . . . to put the free men to the test as it is right to test free men, who would give a true account of the facts for their own sake and for the sake of right.

These passages of Antiphon may be compared with a striking statement of his contemporary Demokritos: B264, on the need to *aiskhȳnesthai* oneself rather than other people (the word denotes feeling and/or showing shame, respect, submissiveness or awareness of inferiority); cf. B262, if a man has given an unjust verdict of acquittal, it must 'remain in his heart'. A similar view of self-respect reappears in New Comedy, Diphilos fr. 92: the first requisite for virtue is that a man should *aiskhȳnesthai* himself when he knows that he has done wrong. Cf. Xen. *Mem.* ii 1.31, '. . . missing the most agreeable of all sights, for you have never seen anything that has been well done by yourself'. The most striking use of the idea of conscience occurs in a story told of the younger Kyros by Xen. *Anab.* i 4.8: he allowed two men who had wronged him to go free, though their families were in his power, saying, 'Let them go in the knowledge that they were not as good men in their dealings with me as I have been in mine with them'.

Dem. xix 208: The truth is strong, and their awareness that they have sold our interests is their weakness . . . 210: And so his mind could not bring itself to make the accusation, but wriggled away, for conscience had a grip on it.

Despite a superficial resemblance to the passages of Antiphon cited above, the context as a whole suggests that his adversaries' fear of detection and punishment is very much in the speaker's mind.

Lys. xix 59: He (*sc. my father*) did all this in the belief that a good man should help his friends even if no one was going to know of it.

The speaker's point here is that his father behaved generously not in order to attract public notice and cut a good figure in the courts (cf. 56); those who received help would know of it, and a nexus of affection and loyalty would be the reward of generosity. Only the preservation of anonymity in the conferment of favours, coupled with a highly sceptical view of religion, can be considered prima facie evidence for the operation of 'conscience' in the strictest sense.

Eur. *Hel.* 728–33: Though I am a servant, I pray that I may be numbered among honest slaves; I am not called free, but my mind is free; for this is better than that one man should suffer two ills, to have a bad mind and also to be a slave at another's beck and call.

A loyal slave cannot exclude from his mind the prospect of happiness resulting from the recognition of his loyalty by his owner and by others, but the speaker surely means to suggest that vice is its own punishment.

## 3. Consequences

Although we know from experience (*pace* Dem. ii 10) that some misdeeds remain undetected and some good deeds unappreciated, I cannot possibly be certain that a given act of mine will never be known; I may boast of it when drunk, or confess it in a mood of repentance or depression, or talk of it in my sleep, or simply yield to the common human urge to share confidences, and even if I know that I am dying with my secret I cannot know that I shall not be called to account in an afterlife. Action in the absolute certainty of 'escaping the notice of gods and men' (Pl. *Rep.* 366E)[5] is not just an experience which rarely comes our way, but a purely hypothetical experience which we cannot have. Plato's Socrates, attempting to demonstrate that virtue is better than vice for its possessor, irrespective of the consequences of his being recognized by others as virtuous or vicious, succeeds only in demonstrating that good men will earn honour, and bad men contempt, from those whose psychological and philosophical standpoint is Socratic. He suggests reasons for which a good man, though persecuted, may sometimes be happier than bad men who enjoy power and success, but he cannot show that this must necessarily be the case; one single tyrant dying in old age well content with a lifetime of oppression and self-indulgence would be enough to refute such a contention. Not surprisingly, the *Republic* ends with a story about reward and punishment of the soul after death. It would be interesting to know on what lines Demokritos defended his own dictum (B45) that 'the wrongdoer is more unfortunate (*kakodaimōn*) than he who is wronged', but not impossible to guess; another of his dicta (B103), 'I think that he who loves no one is loved by no one', suggests that he understood the demand which our nature as social creatures makes upon us (cf. III.A.*3*) and saw an honest regard for likely consequences as the least infirm foundation of a cohesive society. Cf. Dem. xlv 14, on the effect of impulse and emotion in 'taking away a man's calculation of his own interests', and Isok.

[5] Cf. Vollgraff 32-9.

xv 221, on 'calculation' overcome by 'incontinence' and so turned from the 'advantageous' to the 'pleasurable'. (III.F.2).[6]

Inasmuch as everything that we do, say, think or feel has consequences—that is to say, it contributes to the formation of subsequent events—it is hardly possible for us so completely to withdraw our attention from the putative consequences of our actions as to be absolutely free (if we wished to be free) from any imputation of self-regard. A state of such unawareness is no easier for us to imagine than total and lifelong blindness or deafness can be imagined by those who have not been born blind or deaf.[7] We can only try to recall[8] the relative prominence of different considerations in our conscious minds at the time of moral choice and entertain provisional opinions, subject to revision without limit, on the kind and degree of self-regard which has played a part. It is seldom possible to form a worthwhile opinion on (say) how far someone else's generous and loving actions are determined by his awareness that they may normally be expected to generate affection and respect in the beneficiaries.[9] The contrast between selfish and unselfish acts is not significantly altered, either for the agent for others concerned, by recognition that they cannot be placed in one or the other of two compartments but only represented by points in a multidimensional field.

[6] That a really good man 'wishes to *be* good, not to be *thought* good' (Philemon fr. 94.7f.) is of little interest, for none of us would call 'good' a bad man who does his best to get a false reputation for virtue, but it is not just a truism, given the considerations discussed in V.B.4.

[7] Perhaps the nearest we can come to imagining it is by concentrating on the absence, in some kinds of dream, of all causal connection, and its replacement by a simple temporal succession which can be recalled but not explained.

[8] I say 'recall', not 'observe', since the experience to which we turn our attention must necessarily be past by the time our attention is turned to it, and what we regard as a continuation of the same experience is an ingredient in a new complex created by the coexistence of self-examination.

[9] Cf. Bolkestein 156–62, and Hands 26–9 and 44 on how hard it is to draw distinctions between 'self-regarding' and 'altruistic' actions. Hands points out (31) that Greek benevolence did not quite extend to generosity towards those who were incapable of ever returning the favour; but there are many kinds of favour, future reversals of fortune are notoriously unpredictable, and even the recollection of one's own generosity and the happiness created thereby is itself a reward. This last point could be made in connection with a passage of strikingly un-Greek tenor from an ancient Indian play: Kalidasa, *Shakuntala* (tr. A. W. Ryder, London, n.d.), 8: 'We have watered the trees that blossom in the summertime. Now let us sprinkle those whose flowering time is past. That will be a better deed, because we shall not be working for a reward'. (The cynic might comment: She speaks of *trees*; would she say the same of annuals? And would such an idea enter her head if she were not adopting the standpoint of a princess to whom rewards come anyway, without the need to work?)

But the way we talk about them is altered by the extent to which the outlook of our society permits us to acknowledge multiplicity in our own motives, and in this respect the Greeks seem to have been realistic.[10] In Eur. *Or.* 301–10 Orestes urges his sister Elektra to get some rest—because he depends on her to nurse him through his fits of madness; and she says that she must tend him unremittingly—for, if he died, how could she manage alone? Later in the same play Orestes describes his 'sickness' (*nosos*) as *synesis*, 'understanding', 'awareness', of the fearful act of matricide which he has committed, but he adds to this *lȳpē* ('grief', 'distress') and 'insanity'. He does not pretend, and a Greek would not want to pretend, that conscience and repentance *alone* constitute his suffering. In Eur. *El.* 253–61 Elektra praises the *sōphrōn* character of the honest farmer to whom she has been given in marriage, but goes on to speak of his fear of Orestes' vengeance; his *sōphrosynē*, in fact, consists not simply in his ability to restrain his sexual desire, nor simply in his recognition of the true reasons why Elektra has been given to him, but also in his understanding of the evil consequences which may befall him if he fails to treat Elektra with circumspection. Soph. *Oed. Tyr.* 133–41 is an excellent example of multiple motivation. Xen. *Cyr.* viii 2.22 recognizes the expediency of generosity (cf. VI.A.*1*). Iskhomakhos, portrayed in Xen. *Oec.* 7.32, discusses with his wife the education of their children because it is in the interests of them both that they should be well protected and cared for in their old age; that the children will themselves benefit from being regarded as loving protectors of their parents is not mentioned, but may be taken for granted. A fourth-century orator, not content to prove that a measure which he opposes is unjust, illegal and dishonest, may devote at least as much time and effort to proving that it is also inexpedient (cf. Dem. xx 1 and VI.C.*3*); cf. Thuc. iii 56.7, combining argument from utility with argument for 'being seen to be consistent'.

This kind of realism accounts for the omission of anything corresponding to 'conscience' in examples already noted and in the following: Men. fr. 499, greed of gain the greatest of evils, because it so often fails, and even what the greedy man had to start with is lost; Eur. *Iph. Taur.* 484–9, to grieve over misfortune is to superimpose a second ill (grief) on the first (misfortune); Philemon fr. 160, the same dictum; Isok. ix 6, malevolent jealousy does

---

[10] A notable example from an earlier period is Orestes' declaration in Aiskh. *Cho.* 269–305 of his motives for wanting to avenge his father: fear of the awful consequences of disobeying Apollo's command; love of his father and grief at his murder; the need to regain his patrimony; and shame that Argos should be ruled by Klytaimestra and her cowardly lover. He dwells longest on the first of these motives; in a play of the eighteenth or nineteenth century, he might have put only the second into words.

more harm to the man who feels it than to the man against whom it is directed; cf. Men. fr. 537, jealousy a 'self-inflicted misery', and Philemon fr. 131.

## V.B. HONOUR AND SHAME

### 1. Recognition of Goodness

It will have been noticed that in cases where a modern speaker would probably make some reference to good and bad conscience the Athenians tended instead to use expressions such as 'be seen to . . .', 'be regarded as . . .', and these expressions were also used where we would refer neither to conscience nor to reputation, so that an Athenian's 'I wanted to be regarded as honest' is equivalent to our 'I wanted to be honest'. In such cases there was no intention, of course, of drawing a distinction between disguise and reality; it was rather that goodness divorced from a reputation for goodness was of limited interest.

Eur. *Hipp.* 321: Never may I be seen to treat *him* badly!

Dem. xxxiv 30: You all know that men borrow money with a few witnesses, but when they pay it back they have many witnesses present, so that they may be regarded as honest in their business dealings.

Dem. lvi 14: We thought it best to put up with a certain disadvantage and come to an agreement, so as not to be regarded as litigious.

Is. xi 38: I would admit to being the worst of men if I were shown . . . to be neglectful of Stratokles' children . . . 39: For preserving their estate and augmenting it I would justly be praised.

Isok. xvii 1: The issue at stake for me is not simply the recovery of a large sum of money, but the avoidance of being thought to have coveted dishonestly what is not mine; and that is the most important consideration for me.

Cf. Dem. lii 11; Is. ii 29; ibid. 36, 'I gave him as splendid a funeral as I could, so that all the members of the deme praised me'; ibid. 43; Isok. xvi 3, xviii 63; Lys. xxxii 3. The formula 'Someone will say . . .', spoken by a person considering alternative courses of action, occurs in Homer and is common in drama.

Eur. *Supp.* 314-19: Someone will say, 'Through unmanly weakness you were afraid to compel the Thebans . . .'

Cf. ibid. 343f., 'What will my enemies say of me . . .?'; Ar. *Wasps* 542f., 'We shall be laughed at in the streets and called . . .'; Eur. *El.* 900-4, Elektra hesitates to insult the corpse of Aigisthos in case she arouses resentment ('our city is hard to please and quick to criticise') for *hybris* towards the dead; Eur. *Hel.* 841, Helen's concern that she and Menelaos should die in such a way as to acquire (*sc.* good) reputation; Eur. *Iph. Taur.* 502–4, Orestes, believing that he is to be sacrificed, will not reveal his name, for 'If I die nameless, I cannot be mocked'; *GVI* 287.3, '. . . in return for which I am worthy to be well spoken of and praised'; Soph. *El.* 971–85, Elektra's concern for what will be said of her and Khrysothemis if they achieve the feat of killing Aigisthos (to which Khrysothemis in effect asks [1005f.], 'And what good will *that* do us?'); Thuc. vi 9.2, Nikias's affirmation that the honour which he gains by successful command in war will still not make him speak in favour of attacking Sicily against his better judgment; Xenophon (*Anab.* vi 1.20) declares his own motivation by the hope that he will be honoured by those he knows and acquire renown in his city.

The same kind of argument could be used in trying to persuade or dissuade others.

Eur. *Or.* 827–30 (*the chorus describes Klytaimestra crying out to Orestes*): My child, do not put the need to gratify your father above all else and so attach to yourself ill-fame for ever.

Cf. Eur. *Hec.* 313–20, if we refuse to honour the ghost of Achilles, who thereafter will be willing to fight, seeing the good fighter and the bad honoured alike?; Soph. *El.* 970–2, Elektra, trying to persuade Khrysothemis to join in an attempt on the life of Aigisthos, says that her marriage prospects will be improved by so noble a deed; Soph. *Phil.* 119, 'And you yourself would be called both *sophos* and *agathos*' is the argument which wins over Neoptolemos; Xen. *Mem.* ii 1.31, 'And you have never heard that sweetest of all sounds, praise of yourself'.

Juries and national assemblies could be addressed in the same terms as individuals. 'What will be said of you (*sc.* by your fellow-citizens)?', 'How will you be regarded . . .?', 'How will you face . . .?', are questions put to a jury by a speaker as an argument for a particular verdict: Dem. xix 229, 343, xxiii 143, xxv 6f., 100; Isok. xviii 65; Lyk. *Leokr.* 75. This naturally shades into 'What will the Greek world think of Athens . . .?', 'It will be shameful for Athens . . .', etc., equally applicable to political decisions and to judicial decisions with political implications: Dein. i 93, iii 21f.; Dem. xx 20, 46f., 54, 88, 134, xxii 45; Lyk. *Leokr.* 14f.; cf. Thuc. i 144.3, 'From the greatest perils come the highest honours for city and individual alike'. Thucydides' Nikias (vi 11.6) speaks to the Athenians of the need felt by Sparta to put right the 'unseemliness' of her setbacks; his Perikles (i 144.2) advises the assembly to reply to the Spartan ultimatum in terms which will be 'just and befitting this city' (he does not add, advantageous from a practical point of view). Demosthenes claimed that in his own political career he had been primarily concerned with the honour of Athens—not with her security or prosperity, though both were relevant to her capacity to perform what honour demanded of her, but with her reputation, in the world at large and in aftertime, as a power willing to sacrifice herself on behalf of the wronged and oppressed: xviii 63–7, 80 ('praise, good repute, crowns, gratitude' as a result of the expedition to Byzantion), 89, 97–101, 108 ('reputation' and 'honour' coupled with 'resources'), 199–205, 207, 322; xx 10, where it is argued that good repute has always been more important than wealth to Athens. Cf. i 11, vi 8 and xix 83 on the need to avoid national 'ignominy'.

These passages are entirely in keeping with many generalizations to the effect that the hope of praise is a major incentive to virtue and the fear of reproach a major deterrent to wrongdoing.

Dem. iv 10: In my view (sc. the prospect of) shame at what has been done is the greatest compulsion upon free men.

Cf. Dem. i 27, shame 'as great a penalty as any, to right-thinking men'; Dem. viii 51, distinguishing between the free man who dreads adverse opinion and the slave who is motivated only by fear of bodily pain; Dem. xxii 76, no one has ever refused danger when reputation was at stake; Dem. xvi 24, cited in III.A.3; Dem. xxv 93, the majority 'through fear of the courts and the pain inflicted by shaming words and reproaches' take care to do no wrong; Lyk. Leokr. 46, praise 'the only reward which good men expect for the dangers which they accept'; Lys. xxxi 25; Thuc. i 76.2, 'overcome by the greatest forces, (sc. love of) honour, fear and (sc. recognition of) advantage';[1] Xen. Cyr. i 5.12, whoever passionately desires praise must for that reason face every toil and peril; ibid. iii 3.51; Xen. Hiero 7.1. Eur. fr. 21 presents the interesting notion that rich and poor need each other, for the rich give to the poor and the poor in return honour the rich (cf. Pl. Smp. 190C on the gods' need to be honoured by men).

The praise or blame which I earn by good or bad conduct affects not only the feelings of my family and friends but also their standing. After the women's coup d'état in Ar. Eccl. Blepyros is proud to think that people will point to him as 'the generaless's husband' (725–7). The chorus in Ar. Thesm.

[1] Cf. Huart 457–61.

832–45, less fantastically, proposes that the mothers of good men should be honoured at festivals by receiving precedence over the mothers of bad men. Kadmos in Eur. *Ba.* 334–6 pleads with Pentheus, even if Dionysos is not after all a god, to fall in with the idea and sustain a fiction that brings great renown to the family.

The most important application of this diffusion of honour was consolation of the bereaved, setting against their sorrow the good reputation won by death in battle: Dem. lx 32; cf. Eur. *Rhesus* 756–8, dying is distressful to him who dies, but can be a source of pride to those who remain; Hyp. v 21, vi 27; Xen. *Hell.* iv 5.10, Spartan joy at the courageous death of kinsmen in battle. The fact that our reputations live on after our bodies have died is also a powerful incentive to virtue and a weapon against fear of death, since it offers us a demonstrably justifiable immortality.[2]

Isok. iv 95: Good men would choose to die honourably rather than live disgracefully.

Isok. v 134: Through being well spoken of and praised and remembered we have a share in immortality, and so . . . should be willing to undergo anything.

Xen. *Mem.* ii 1.33: And when their fated end comes, they do do not lie forgotten and without homour, but they are remembered and flourish eternally in men's praises.

Cf. Dem. xxii 77, Eur. fr. 362.32f.; Eur. fr. 585, justice the only thing of which the good reputation is immortal; *GVI* 930, 'I practised *sōphrosynē* and left behind me faultless good repute'; *GVI* 341.2 (Pherai), 891, 1705, 1706; Hdt. v 111.4, 'to be killed by a worthy adversary halves the misfortune'; Lys. ii 23f., 79–81. *GVI* 1384 (Phokis, s. VI/V) is more down-to-earth: 'No one speaks ill of you even now that you are dead'. Old Pheres in Eur. *Alc.* 726 sounds a robustly discordant note by retorting to Admetos's threat of ill-repute, 'A bad name doesn't matter to me when I'm dead'.


## 2. Ambition and Competition

Public reward for virtue, apart from general good repute, might be commendation formally expressed by the assembly (e.g. Dein. i 13) and recorded in an inscription (cf. Xen. *Vect.* 3.11); the award, in addition, of a crown (e.g. Dem. xviii 118–25); or election to offices (Dein. iii 12, Dem. ii 27, xxiii 197, Lys. xxv 13, xxvi 20) which afforded further opportunity for

[2] Cf. Lattimore 224f.

earning honour.[3] Dem. xxxix 10–12 ~ 19 and xl 34 take it for granted that administrative office is desirable; Ar. *Ach.* 595 hits at people who are 'anxious for command'. Modern convention makes it a little hard for us to tell the difference between 'showing admiration' (*thaumazein*) for a person and 'flattering' him (*kolakeuein*), but the distinction was clear enough to the Greeks (Xen. *Hell.* i 6.7) and lay essentially in the fact that the *kolax*, 'flatterer', 'parasite', hoped for personal, individual gain, whereas admiration was disinterested. Dem. xx 16 emphasizes that to a free man the praise of his equals is much more to be valued than the commendation of a ruler (master) to a faithful subject (servant). Conversely, Dem. xxii 31f., and lx 25f., commend *parrhēsiā*, 'frankness', as characteristic of democracy, and as conducive to virtue, because it makes it impossible for a man who has done wrong to shelter behind powerful friends and escape open reproach from his equals.

The motive force which made a man seek public honour was called *philotīmiā*, 'love of honour' (adjective *philotīmos*, verb *philotīmeisthai*).[4]

Aiskhines i 129: All who are *philotīmos* in their public lives judge that they will gain their reputation from good report.

Aiskhines iii 19: . . . those who have to everyone's knowledge spent their inheritance in *philotīmiā* towards you . . .

Dem. xix 223: I thought, as others among you think, that if I myself were *epieikēs* I should be honoured, and I ought not to exchange for any gain my *philotīmiā* towards you.

Cf. Dem. xx 155, on the *epieikeia* of those who are willing to *philotīmeisthai*.

Dem. xx 103: You deprive the people of (*sc. the services of*) those who might *philotīmeisthai*, by giving clear warning that no one who confers a benefit on the people will gain any advantage at all from it.

The 'advantage' sought by *philotīmiā* was, of course, the reputation which was bought at the price of one's own profit, interests, health and life, the reputation of being a man who sacrifices himself for others. *Philotīmiā* manifested itself in the unsparing discharge of financial obligations to the community (Aiskhines ii 111; Dem. xxviii 22, xlii 25 ['useful and *philotīmos* with property and person'], l 15, li 22; Is. vii 35f.; Lys. xxvi 3)—including horse-breeding, since the cavalry depended on this (Dem. xlii 44, Hyp. i 16) —in disregard of one's safety in battle (Dem. xx 82; Lyk. *Leokr.* 98; Lys. xvi

---

[3] Arist. *Eth. Nic.* 1095[b]23 regards *tīmē*, 'honour', as the end which is nearly always sought in political life; cf. Gernet 279–301.

[4] Cf. Huart 393.

18), in a military or naval commander's subordination of his own advantage
to the city's needs (Dem. xx 69; Isok. xviii 61; Lys. xxix 14), in ransoming
prisoners of war (Dem. xviii 257, xix 40, 173), or in zealous prosecution of
miscreants in the interests of the community (Aiskhines i 196); such a
reputation could not be won by conspicuous private luxury (Dem. xxi 159).[5]
In Dem. xx 5 philotīmeisthai and 'treat the people well' are synonymous. Just
as the state valued its own good reputation in the world at large, it could be
described as motivated by philotīmiā (Dem. xviii 66; cf. xxiv 210, on Athenian
pride [philotīmeisthai] on imitation of Attic laws by other states).

It is not surprising that 'patriotic' is sometimes the appropriate translation
of philotīmos, rather than 'ambitious'.

Lyk. Leokr. 15: You, men of Athens, differ above all from the rest of mankind in
behaving piously towards the gods, dutifully towards your parents, and philotīmōs
towards your fatherland.

Xen. Hell. vii 5.18f. (Epameinondas's motives): Philotīmos men think it an honourable
death to die in the attempt to bequeath dominion over the Peloponnese to their
fatherland.

Cf. Dem. xxiv 91, Lyk. Leokr. 140. The common identification of patriotic
action with virtuous action is reflected in Dem. lii 29, where philotīmos is
contrasted with 'kakos or aiskhros behaviour', and Dem. lx 3, 'well-born,
well brought up, and of philotīmos life'. In Ar. Frogs 678, where the sophiai of
the audience are called 'more philotīmos than Kleophon', the implication
seems to be, 'with higher standards and better ideals and therefore with more
to contribute to the community'; cf. Xen. Oec. 4.24, where philotīmeisthai is
applied to the energy and self-respect which makes a man try to do something really well. Applied to a soldier, the word naturally denotes courage
and energy and good discipline (Xen. Anab. iv 7.12, Hell. vi 4.11). Xen.
Mem. iii 7.1 expresses the view that a man is a contemptible creature if,
having it in him to excel in sport and by that to bring honour to his native
city, he declines to compete.

When someone is honoured, the honour is necessarily withheld from
others who wanted it just as badly; no one can win unless someone else
loses, and an honour shared with everybody is a doubtful honour. Hence the
philotīmiā of individuals within the community as a whole took the form of
a 'contest of good men' (Dem. xx 107, cf. 102).

[5] On honour as a motive for generosity and charity, cf. Bolkestein 152–5; Hands
43, 49–52; M. E. Pfeffer, Einrichtung der sozialen Sicherung in der griechischen und römischen
Antike (Berlin, 1969) 80–3.

Dem. xviii 320: When it was a question of the policy which would be most to the city's advantage, and patriotism was open to unrestricted competition (*literally*, '*goodwill to the fatherland having been put up to be competed for by all alike*'), I clearly emerged as giving better advice than anyone else.

Cf. Theophilos fr. 4, young men vying with one another in the attempt to please their father.

The Greeks tended to judge people not on a 'pass or fail' criterion, but by deliberately imparting a competitive character to as many aspects of life as possible (e.g. plays, songs and dances at festivals), and the wide difference between the treatment of winners and the treatment of losers augmented the incentive to excel.[6]

Dem. lxi 52 (*advice to a boy*): If you are better than those whom you encounter, do not cease trying to excel everyone else too; consider that your aim in life should be to become foremost of *all*, and that it is more to your advantage to be seen to aim at that eminence than to appear outstanding in ordinary company.

Metaphors drawn from competition for prizes were common; Thuc. ii 46, 'Where the greatest prizes for *aretē* are offered, the citizens are better men than anywhere else'; Hdt. viii 26.3, Xenophon seems to have thought that the award of prizes was the answer to everything, e.g. (*Hiero* 9.6, *Vect.* 3) prizes for conspicuously just judicial decisions and arbitrations.

It was inevitable that a conflict should at times arise between the desire to win and the desire to be liked as generous and unselfish. Unrestricted competition is not always or in all circumstances to the advantage of society, and *philotīmiā* could shade into aggression, pride and boastfulness. In Ar. *Frogs* 280–2 Dionysos, deprecating Herakles' warning of strange beasts and other horrors on the journey to the underworld, says that Herakles was 'putting up a show' or 'throwing his weight about'; 'He knew that I have a stout heart, and he was trying to get the better of me' (*philotīmeisthai*). Ar. *Thesm.* 383f., parodying the assembly, represents a speaker as opening with the words, 'It is not through any wish to thrust myself forward (*philotīmiā*) that I have risen to speak'.

Dem. viii 71: Although I could speak of trierarchies . . . and payment of ransoms and other similar *philanthrōpiai*, I would not mention any of these, but rather that . . . I was not motivated by (*sc. hope of*) gain or by *philotīmiā*, but I have steadfastly propounded arguments in consequence of which I am inferior to many others in influence over you, but you, if you do as I say, can become greater.

[6] The terms in which Ar. *Clouds* 518–62 speaks of his defeat in 423, i.e. of the award of third prize out of three to the original presentation of *Clouds*, are noteworthy.

Lys, xix 18: It was my father's way to attend to his own concerns (*ta heautou prāttein*), but Aristophanes . . . spent whatever money he had in a desire to be honoured (*tīmāsthai*).

Cf. ibid. 23, *philotīmos*.

ibid. 56: Forgive me if I recount what my father spent on the city and on his friends; I recount it not for the sake of *philotīmiā* but as proof that one and the same man does not spend generously when he is under no compulsion to do so and also covet what belongs to the city in circumstances highly dangerous to himself . . . 57: My father never wanted to hold office . . .

Cf. Dem. ii 11–18, xi 9, on Philip's *philotīmiā* and consequent disregard of the sufferings of his people, the price of his glory; l 54, denying *philotīmiā* as a motive for recounting expenditure; lix 33, the *philotīmiā* of going about with a beautiful and expensive hetaira in order to show off; ibid. 96, after the Persian Wars the Athenians 'led the Greek world in fact, but' (literally) 'in *philotīmiā* did not oppose the Spartans' (i.e. 'did not dispute with Sparta the honour of formal command') 'in order not to incur the allies' resentment'; Hdt. iii 53.4, '*philotīmiā* is a *skaios* thing', of an obstinate and unrelenting hatred; Lys. xiv 2, 35, 42, on boasting of conduct of which others would be ashamed; ibid. 21, on magistrates showing off their influence; Lys. xvi 20, 'Even I admit that I am rather too *philotīmos*'; 'Lys. xxxv' 232A, 234A, a lover boasting of his conquests; Thuc. ii 65.7, the degeneration of Athenian political life after the death of Perikles, since men acted 'in accordance with their individual *philotīmiai* and individual gain'; Thuc. iii 82.8, coupling *philotīmiā* with greed as a cause of violence, hatred and treachery in politics. This is the ambitious, disruptive *philotīmiā* which Iokaste personifies and contrasts with Equality (Eur. *Phoen.* 531–48) in a vain attempt to reconcile her sons; Polyneikes' sentiment (524f.) is, 'If there is wrong to be done, it is best (*kallistos*) to do it in trying to become a tyrant'. In Eur. *Iph. Aul.* 527 Odysseus is criticized for being possessed by *philotīmiā*, 'a formidable ill'; Men. fr. 620 goes further in including competition, reputation and *philotīmiai* as among the unnecessary troubles which the human species has inflicted on itself.

*Philonīkiā*, 'love of winning', 'anxiety for victory',[7] is treated as a virtue in the earlier part of the fourth century: Lys. ii 16 couples it with *philotīmiā* in praise of Herakles, and Xenophon (as one might have expected from his enthusiasm for competitiveness) speaks in its favour—*Ages.* 2.8, *philonīkiā* implanted by Agesilaos in those whom he commanded; *Lac.* 4.2, 5, on the

[7] Huart 395–7.

efforts of the Lycurgan constitution on instil 'rivalry over *aretē*' into the citizen-body; *Oec.* 21.10, the right kind of master makes his slaves emulate one another in their efforts to please him. But *philonīkiā* is also a derogatory term, denoting a quarrelsome, factious, contentious way of behaving: Dem. xliv 63, family quarrels; Dem. xlv 14, incompatible with sensible action; Dem. lvii 6, coupled with malice and jealousy; Lyk. *Leokr.* 5, 'perversity'; Lys. iii 43, coupled with drunkenness; Lys. xxi 8, synonymous with 'quarrelling and trying to outbid one another'; cf. Dem. xviii 141–3, xxiii 19.

## 3. Conceit

The heroes and heroines of tragedy do not underestimate their own qualities, achievements and deserts, and express themselves accordingly; e.g. Euadne. choosing to die because her husband is dead, claims to outdo all women in *aretē* (Eur. *Supp.* 1063). We do not commonly think of the Athenians themselves as modest people, and there are passages in Demosthenes (e.g. xviii 88, 108–10, 113, 297–9) which offend against modern standards of propriety, not to mention Dem. xxi 5, where he casually attributes the failure of his chorus to win first prize to bribery of the judges by his enemy. Nevertheless, modesty was praised as a virtue, boastfulness in an adversary was reviled, and attention could be drawn to one's own reluctance to boast.[8]

Aiskhines iii 141: If men who are really good, men of whose admirable achievements we know, recite their own praises, we do not tolerate it; and when a man who is a reproach to the city lauds himself, who could endure to hear such an utterance?

Cf. Aiskhines ii 21, 111, Dem. xviii 3f.

Dem. xviii 128: What right have you to speak of 'education'? No man who is actually educated would talk in that way of himself; he would even blush to hear someone else do so.

ibid. 221: I felt certain—possibly I was being rather insensitive, but still, I felt certain —that no one else would . . . act . . . with greater zeal or honesty than I.

Dem. xix 167: When he failed completely (*sc. to bribe us individually*)—it is not for me to speak of myself; the facts will suffice as proof— . . .

Cf. Dem. xviii 10, 206 (refusing to take the credit which is due to the Athenian people), 292, 317; Dem. xxi 69, 'whether you like to call it madness . . . or whether it was through *philotīmiā* that I took on the duties . . .';

[8] Cf. Theophr. *Char.* 23.6 on the boastful man who talks about his generosity and public spirit to people he meets at a party.

ibid. 74, 'good fortune' rather than his own good character the reason why he was able to refrain from violent retaliation against Meidias; Eur. *Iph. Aul.* 979f., the disagreeableness of flattery; Isok. v 82, 'uncouth' to praise oneself; Isok. xvi 35, praising Alkibiades, 'I hesitate' (*aiskhȳnesthai*, 'feel shame') 'to speak of his choregiai at Athens; for he so excelled . . .'.


## 4. Substance and Show

A linguistic phenomenon which may perhaps be regarded as illustrating a certain difference between Greek attitudes and ours is the occasional need to import the words 'reputation for . . .' when translating a Greek abstract noun into English. Those who risk their lives for the community, to our way if thinking, 'exhibit' or 'demonstrate' valour, and the same could be said in Greek (e.g. Lys. xii 86), but it could also be said that they 'acquire *aretē*' (Lyk. *Leokr.* 49) and that they 'leave *aretē* after them' (Hyp. vi 41), as if their goodness were not a quality residing in them but their status in public estimation and tradition.[9]

GVI 20.11f. (*on the Athenians killed at Poteidaia*): Putting their lives into the scale, they received *aretē* in return.

Cf. ibid. 1688, 'if justice and sobriety are reputation and *aretē* for mortals'; ibid. 1690.3 (Amorgos, s. IV/III), 'His reputation has praise and his *sōphrosynē* (*sc. has*) *aretē*'; Lys. ii 33 contrasts '*aretē*, poverty and exile' with 'reproach (*oneidos*) and wealth'; Thuc. i 33.2, the Corcyreans claim that the alliance which they offer Athens (literally) 'brings *aretē* into the many', i.e. 'brings you honour in the eyes of the world'.

Dem. xxxiv 40: It is most unlikely that we should have contributed freely so much money in order to be in good standing with you, and yet should have brought a false accusation against Phormion in order to lose even our existing (*sc. reputation for*) *epieikeia*.

Cf. Eur. *Hel.* 932, 'It will bring me back again to chastity', i.e. '. . . to a (*sc.* correct and deserved) reputation for chastity'; Eur. *Tro.* 976f., 'For what reason could the goddess Hera have got such a desire for beauty?', i.e. '. . . for the prize as the most beautiful of the goddesses'.

[9] Cf Ludwig 37–41; Gernet 281; Eduard Schwartz, *Ethik der Griechen* (Stuttgart, 1951), 19–24. Gerlach 7f. is, I think, on the wrong track in seeing conceptual significance in 'he became an *agathos* man' (cf. IV.A.*3*); the verb 'be' in Greek has no aorist, and 'became' serves as the aorist of both 'become' and 'be'.

*Philotīmiā*, which we should expect from its structure and etymology to denote the desire for honour, can approximate in denotation to *tīmē*, 'honour', or to *doxa*, '(sc. good) reputation'.

Dem. xxii 75f. (*on Androtion's supervision of the conversion of votive crowns into cups*): Crowns testify to *aretē*, but cups and the like to wealth, and even the smallest crown is evidence for (*literally*, '*has*') the same *philotīmiā* as a large one ... Androtion, in destroying the possessions of reputation (*i.e.* '*which bring good reputation*'), has made those of wealth mean and worthless. He does not even realise that the Athenian people has never exerted itself to acquire money, but more than anything to acquire reputation. The proof of this is that although it once had more money than any other Greek state, it spent it all for the sake of *philotīmiā*, and it never yet refused any danger when reputation was at stake, but contributed from the wealth of individuals to the common pool.

Cf. Aiskhines iii 23, 'Do not snatch *philotīmiā*', i.e. 'Do not make an unjustified claim to deserve honour'; Aiskhines iii 255, 'Do not distribute *philotīmiai*, but judge them', i.e. '... judge where honours are deserved'; Dem. ii 3, 'I think that everything ... (*literally*) has *philotīmiā* for him (*i.e.* '*brings him honour*') but has not been done creditably by us'; Dem. lvii 64, dedications which 'brought me *philotīmiā*', i.e. '... honour'; Eur. *Iph. Aul.* 337–42 (cf. 385), Agamemnon solicited all the Greek leaders in the hope of being appointed to supreme command, 'seeking to buy *to philotīmon*'.

A related phenomenon, denotation of behaviour by words which normally denote disposition, is illustrated by: Ar. *Knights* 788, 'You have become patriotic' (literally, 'well-disposed', *sc.* to the city), i.e. 'Demos now regards you as patriotic'; Dem. xli 4, 'They were reconciled on condition that ... Leokrates should not be ill-disposed (*kakonous*) to Polyeuktos', i.e. '... should not act in an ill-disposed way'; Hyp. iii 24, 'he was willing' = 'he expressed a willingness'; Hyp. iv 20, 'you hate' = 'you express hatred'.

## 5. Causes and Effects of Shame

Fear of humiliation, reproach and the withdrawal of affection and respect is a very powerful motive for conforming to the behaviour expected by one's family, friends and fellow-citizens; cf. Agathon fr. 22, 'When I consider that I am doing wrong I am ashamed to look my friends in the face'.[10] Yet

[10] On Greek words for 'shame' and 'modesty' cf. C. E. von Erffa, *ΑΙΔΩΣ und verwandte Begriffe in ihrer Entwicklung von Homer bis Demokrit = Philologus* Supplbd. xxx 2 (1937); Huart 457–61.

in a society as addicted to comparison and competition as Greek society was, this sensibility can have bad consequences. For one thing, issues were very readily translated into terms of 'face'.[11] Thucydides' Alkibiades tells the Spartans (vi 89.2) that he bore them a grudge because they 'dishonoured' him by negotiating for peace in 422/1 through his 'enemies'; we do not have to believe what a speaker says when he has a case to make, but the terms of his argument must be plausible to his audience. Dem. xviii 178 says it would have been 'disgraceful' for Athens to *ask* Thebes for help against Philip rather than *offering* to help Thebes; cf. Lyk. *Leokr.* 42f. on the shame of having to ask island states for help, when Athens had once been effective ruler of the islands.

The fear of being judged inferior is the kind of fear which overrules rational calculation; in Thuc. viii 27.2f., Phrynikhos just succeeds in dissuading his colleagues in command from a disastrous course of action by pointing out that however 'shameful' it might seem to them to withdraw in the face of a Peloponnesian fleet, it would be a great deal more shameful for Athens if she suffered final defeat through their sensitivity. The Athenian envoys at Melos were right to say that fear of being shamed leads nations to take action entirely contrary to their own interests (v 111.2f.). The Athenian force in Sicily was lost largely because Nikias preferred to lose it and die with it rather than order a retreat and possibly be condemned for doing so on his return (Thuc. vii 48.4). Cf. Polyneikes in Soph. *Oed. Col.* 1416–23: he *cannot* now disband his army and abstain from attacking Thebes, for 'to flee is shameful'.

Fictitious characters are portrayed as embracing or contemplating death (cf. IV.A.4) in preference to living with the shameful knowledge that others blame or despise them for what they have done, even if their intention was innocent: Soph. *Trach.* 719–32, Deianeira; Eur. *Her. Fur.* 1151f., 1286–90, Herakles, after recovering from his murderous fit of madness; Eur. *Iph. Taur.* 678–86, Pylades unwilling to return to Greece because it will be said that he deserted Orestes. Cf. Xen. *Cyr.* v 5.9, Kyaxares: 'I would rather die ten times than be seen so humbled and see my own family smirking contemptuously at me'. It is intelligible enough to us that Deianeira and Herakles should wish to die rather than live with the *memory* of what they have done, but that is not what they say. Shame was thought of as diffused, like

---

[11] On the importance of 'face' in Mediterranean cultures at various eras cf. P. Walcot, *Greek Peasants, Ancient and Modern* (Manchester, 1970) 57–93 and J. K. Campbell and J. G. Peristiany in (ed. Peristiany) *Honour and Shame* (London, 1965) 139–70 and 173–190 respectively; Adkins (1) 154–6.

honour in happier circumstances, over the family of the offender; Leda in
Eur. *Hel.* 134–6 is said to have hanged herself in shame at her daughter
Helen's flight with Paris. We do not need to look anywhere but in our own
society to find many examples of unbearable parental shame at the misdeeds
of their children, and this is rational in so far as parents know that they will be
regarded as having failed in the job of bringing up good children; but shame
felt by children at their parents' misdeeds (e.g. Is. vi 24), or even at having a
mad cousin or an uncle who has been to prison, is also common enough in
our own time. Abroad, one may on occasion be ashamed of one's compatriot,
in the sense that one does not want foreigners to draw any conclusions
about oneself from observation of someone else. It seems to us more unusual
when Aiskhines i 26 (cf. 118, 120) alleges that when Timarkhos spoke in the
assembly decent men were embarrassed and ashamed that they should be
addressed by a fellow-citizen who had allowed his figure and muscular
development to deteriorate so shockingly.

Shame at defeat or failure, even if I know perfectly well that I did my best
and was worsted by overwhelming force or by dishonesty so alien to my
character as to be unintelligible and unforeseeable, can still be felt very keenly,
because I am aware that other people cannot know all the circumstances
and may therefore believe that I lacked courage, determination, prudence or
common sense. There are few shaming situations to which this consideration
is inapplicable, and after all, failure *is* commonly the consequence of sloth,
negligence or remediable ignorance. We tend to give the benefit of the
doubt, and the Greeks (for reasons given in III.H.5) tended not to. The
losing side in a war is disgraced by losing even if the logistics of the war
made the victory of the other side inevitable; the man in the street is not
good at logistics, and when Kassandra in Eur. *Tro.* 385–405 tries to prove
that the outcome of the Trojan War reflects more credit on Troy than on
the Greeks she is (like many a Euripidean character) making a case which
was not accepted by general opinion and tradition. If I return alive from
defeat in battle, I 'prove', by the mere fact of being still alive, that I did not
do my utmost (though I may know that I had no opportunity to get myself
killed). If I lose a lawsuit, the verdict shows that the jury thought my
testimony less trustworthy than that of my opponent (cf. Dein. ii 2); at
worst, this means that I am a dishonest man, and at best, that I have not lived
in such a way as to earn an unassailable reputation.[12] Cf. Dem. xxiii 109 on

---

[12] When Daos in Men. *Epitr.* 367 exclaims, on losing the case which he has submitted
to arbitration, that what has happened to him is *aiskhros*, he may be expressing the shame
of defeat, but in 371 he describes the event as *adikos*, 'unjust', which would suggest that

the shame which will be incurred by Athens if she is seen to have less grasp of her own interests than the Olynthians have of theirs; since she has a reputation for intelligent political decision, an unintelligent decision is a negligent failure to do what she could have done.

Poverty (e.g. Eur. fr. 53.16f. [Austin]), even sickness, *can* be one's own fault, in so far as we know of circumstances in which it has been avoided by energetic and intelligent action. Moreover, a certain reluctance on the part of the Greeks to associate with those who may have incurred the displeasure of the gods (cf. IV.D.*1*) must have tended to diminish the expectation of the poor and the sick that they would be treated compassionately, and to increase their desire to hide their misfortune, if need be, by avoiding contacts (cf. Men. *Farmer* 79–89 on the desirability of having as few witnesses of one's misfortune as possible). But we must not exaggerate the difference between modern charitableness and the apparent rigours of life in an ancient 'shame-culture'. It is not so very strange that people should fear the shame of missing a payment though dilatoriness (Ar. *Eccl.* 381f.) or failing in an elaborate trick and being detected (ibid. 484f.), or that Kadmos and Teiresias in Eur. *Ba.* 365 should think it shameful for 'two old men to fall down' through over-exertion and carelessness.

When Helen in Eur. *Hel.* 270–2 finds it even worse to be blamed untruly for what one has not done than truly for what one has done, she expresses just what people who find themselves in that predicament commonly feel, for all that may be said in other circumstances about clear conscience (cf. V.A.*2*); shame combined with indignation at injustice is more painful than shame alone. Similarly, the speaker of Dem. 1 45 quite reasonably resents his financial loss much less than the mockery of the man who has defrauded him and has so far got away with it. Kroisos's son in Hdt. i 37.2f., cannot bear the shame of having to stay at home and not go hunting, even though it is his father's command; how will his friends be *sure* that his father's command is the only reason?

Shame for what is unquestionably beyond one's own control, e.g. illegitimate birth (Eur. *Ion* 591–3, where Ion calls the status of a bastard a 'sickness')[13] is a different matter; cf. III.B.*2*.

moral reproach is directed against his adversary and/or the arbitrator; that is what his modern counterpart would mean by 'I've been shamefully treated' or 'That's a shameful thing to happen!' I suggest that Daos's words express a verbal reaction to both aspects simultaneously.

[13] Eupolis fr. 98, referring to the younger Perikles, illegitimate son of the great Perikles by Aspasia, means '. . . if he were not so excessively afraid of the (*sc. appellation*) "(*sc. son*) of the whore" '.

When the issue of blameworthiness had to be faced, in order to defend oneself, excuse someone else, or distinguish for argumentative purposes between what merits blame and what merits compassion, there could be only one answer: it was judged wrong to reproach a man for misfortune or poverty:[14] Aiskhines i 27; iii 88, misfortune in war not a disaster in itself, but a disaster doubled if the defeat is inflicted by an unworthy enemy; Dem. xviii 252, 256, 275, xxi 58, xxii 62, xxiii 148, lvii 36; Isok, xx 19f. We should be angry, says Is. ii 23, at a man who has children if he makes the misfortune of the childless a reproach against them. At least by 346, the law made it actionable slander to reproach a man or woman for trade or work pursued in the agora (Dem. lvii 30), however 'servile' its character. Equally, it was judged wrong to reproach anyone whose own guilelessness and upright character had made him fall victim to the aggressive dishonesty of others (And. i 146, Dem. xx 6), or when he had done his best but had been cheated of success (Dem. xviii 192f.); the principle, 'Do as you would be done by' is of some relevance in this connection (V.E.2f.).

Ar. *Wealth* 590f.: You're trying to fasten on to him something much more shameful than poverty, if, although rich, he's so illiberal and avaricious.

ibid. 771–81 (*Wealth, his sight restored, is speaking*): I am ashamed (*aiskhȳnesthai*) of my own misfortunes (*symphorai*), (*sc. when I think*) of the kind of men I associated with, all unknowing ... In future I will show all men that it was unintentionally (*ākōn*) that I gave myself to those who were *ponēros*.

He implies that his shame will be removed when it is realized that, since he had been blinded by Zeus, his actions were not of his choosing (he may be wrong, but it is very important to him to persuade himself that his shame will be removed).

Dem. xxxvii 52: 'And', he says, 'Nikoboulos is objectionable, and walks hurriedly, and has a loud voice, and uses a stick, and all these factors', he says, 'are in my favour'.[15] ... 55: So far as concerns my walk or way of talking, I'll be completely frank and tell you the truth. I'm not unaware that in these respects I'm not among the well-endowed by nature ... 56: It's not practicable to fight against the nature one has ... but easy enough to look at someone else and criticise him.

Eur. *Phoen.* 1691f. (*Oedipus to Antigone*): It is shameful for a daughter to go into

[14] Cf. Glotz 423f. on democracy as protector of the 'little man'.

[15] Nikoboulos's opponent probably contrasted his own career and Nikoboulos's at length, suggesting that the contrast told in his own favour, and in the course of this managed to ridicule Nikoboulos's voice and manner. Nikoboulos in turn tries to score by suggesting that his opponent was so mean and ridiculous as to claim judgment in his favour on irrelevant grounds.

exile with a blind father. ANTIGONE: Not if she is right-thinking (*sōphronein*), father; it is honourable (*gennaios*).

Why should Oedipus say not that it is a *hard* life for a girl to go into exile and look after her blind father, but that it is *aiskhros* for her to do so? Partly, no doubt, because she must (as she does in Soph. *Oed. Col.*) face the world of men without adequate protection, discard the modesty which was the outward clothing of chastity, and to that extent resemble a *hetaira*; partly too because, debarred from marriage and motherhood, she will not play that role in society which a daughter is assumed to desire and a father to desire for his daughter, so that other men, seeing her, will be repelled by her situation as by an unpleasant *object* and will say to themselves, 'Thank the gods my daughter is not in that situation, and I pray that she may never be!' Antigone's reply means that a good daughter will not take, and eventually will be recognized as not taking, the opportunities for promiscuity which an unprotected life offers, and also that if she is considered as a moral *subject*, she will be honoured and respected for her self-sacrifice and filial loyalty. Every one of us, whether we like it or not, is an object as well as a subject. Sophokles' description (fr. 598.9f.) of the mare who hides herself away in shame because her once beautiful mane has been shorn is a paradigm of man in society as an object. Unlike the mare, man can argue in his own defence and try to persuade others to see him (and himself to see himself) as a moral subject. In this area of social tolerance and compassion, Christian teaching is greatly superior to pagan practice, but if we are to avoid the mistake of comparing the theory of one culture with the practice of another, we must note not only that the divergence between Christian precept and explicit pagan precept is not so great, but also that the gap between Christian precept and the actual conduct of Christian societies is very great indeed.[16] If we think that in the everyday life of our own society during the last hundred years we have generally behaved towards each other in such a way that victims of misfortune, or their friends and relations, have so little cause for shame that

[16] I was born in 1920 and brought up on the edge of the London area. The society which I remember—most people took secondary education for granted, but had little or no acquaintance with university education—was dominated, to an extent for which I can hardly find adequate analogies in Greek literature, by the fear of humiliation, such as might result from (e.g.) a sister in a mental hospital, an untended garden, a child who had been seen eating an ice-cream in the street, or a situation in which it was impossible to avoid admitting that one could not afford a car. At the local school which I attended a boy was beaten in front of the assembled school because he had worn a school cap while helping a milkman. I knew some boys and parents who were Christians, but the distribution of social tolerance within that category was not significantly different from its distribution in the larger category of ex-Christians.

they can freely allow their condition to be seen as it is, we deceive ourselves sadly. The Greeks were perhaps franker than we are; we tend to feel that if we admit to being repelled by ugliness and suffering we are somehow declaring ourselves incapable of practical compassionate action, whereas the Greeks' readiness to use the word *aiskhros* of what was repellent *for any reason* reflects their capacity for recognizing simultaneously different aspects of the same thing.[17]

'Shameful', 'disgraceful' or 'ignominious' death is a special case. If a man dies in dignity at the end of a long, virtuous and enviable life, or if he chooses to risk his life and is killed in battle, he can be confident of posthumous 'fame'. If he is treacherously murdered, however good a man he has been and however much his murderer may be reviled, the circumstances of his death are such as to confer no merit on him, and recollection of them, let alone celebration, will give no pleasure to his family or his ghost. A man poisoned by his wife died 'godlessly and *akleōs*', i.e. '... ignominiously', without *kleos*, 'fame' (Ant. i 21). When the same man is said (ibid. 26) to have died 'unrighteously and *aiskhrōs*', the shame seems to be attached by the speaker less to the victim than to his murderer; cf. ibid. 23, 'she who did away with him recklessly and godlessly'. Similarly, when Lys. xiii 45 refers to good citizens who 'were forced' (*sc. by the Thirty Tyrants*) 'to perish by a most *aiskhros* and ignominious death', it is impossible that he intends in any sense to reproach the dead; certainly their death was 'ignominious', because it is not the kind of death whose glory consoles the bereaved, but *aiskhros* expresses the revulsion produced in the speaker and like-minded people by contemplation of the murders as events, a revulsion of which the moral component is directed against the murderers. Cf. Eur. *El.* 677–83, where Agamemnon is said to 'dwell unrighteously' beneath the earth, and his murderers are called 'unrighteous'; Eur. *Rhesus* 756–61, 'we have perished *aboulōs* and ignominiously', i.e. through treachery against which we took no precautions and which gave no chance to acquire fame; Hdt. ix 17.4, 'most shameful fate', of men killed treacherously without the opportunity to fight back; Soph. *El.* 486f., 'most shameful mutilations' of the corpse of Agamemnon, which of course made his corpse ugly and were also grounds of reproach against the perpetrators.

[17] Cf. B. E. Perry, 'On the Early Greek Capacity for Viewing Things Separately', *Transactions of the American Philological Association* (lxviii (1937)) 403–27; in general, the Greeks acknowledged that each of us is an object as well as a moral subject, beautiful or ugly (ch. II.C.*3*, IV.E.*3*), admirable or repulsive (V.B.*5*), serious or funny (cf. Jaeger i 359f.) as well as righteous or unrighteous.

## V.C. THE DEAD

A doubt whether the dead perceive what is done and said in the world of the living was often expressed by the Greeks, even in circumstances in which we might have expected a more positive affirmation of faith.

Isok. xix 42: They will perhaps have recourse to the argument that her father Thrasyllos will be indignant at his treatment—if the dead have any perception (*aisthēsis*) of what happens here—when he sees his daughter deprived of his property . . .

In that passage, it is in the speaker's interest to detract from his adversaries' hypothetical argument in every way, but that cannot be said of the following passage.

Lyk. *Leokr.* 136: I think that his dead father, if those below have any perception of what happens here, would judge him more harshly than anyone.

Cf. Soph. *El.* 355f., where Elektra admits as an afterthought a doubt whether her antagonism to her mother and Aigisthos is known to her dead father, much as it would gratify him if he could know of it; Eur. *Her. Fur.* 490f.; Isok. ix 2; Philemon fr. 120 ('If it were true, as some say . . .'); *GVI* 170 (Thessaly, s. IV), where a dead man's family is not sure whether he will know that they have given him a tomb.

These doubts do not preclude strong subjective affirmation when emotion or need prompt it: Soph. *El.* 400 (Khrysothemis speaking), 'Our father, I know, forgives what I am doing'; Eur. *El.* 684, 'Your father, I know, hears this appeal'. Exceptionally, lack of awareness on the part of the dead is assumed.

Aiskhines i 14: After he has died, when what is done for him is done for a beneficiary no longer aware of it, but custom and religion are honoured thereby, then, the legislator says, he should be buried and all the customary rites should be performed.

The contrast between penalties in life and forgiveness after death makes an effective point, which would be vitiated by qualification. Such passages serve as a good illustration of the flexibility of religious belief in the service of rhetoric.

Despite the intellectual honesty which underlies 'If the dead have any perception' (cf. III.F.4 and Dem. lx 34, Hyp. vi 43, Xen. *Cyr.* viii 7.19–22, cited in V.D.4), we can observe a strong tendency to speak *as if* relations between the living and the dead were not unlike relations among the living themselves.[1] The presence of the dead was felt, even though it could not be demonstrated, their goodwill was valued, and their hostility or contempt was feared.

Dem. lx 12: . . . in the belief that this would be acceptable in the highest degree to both (sc. *the recent dead and also their ancestors*).

Is. ix 4: They brought my father to the grave of Astyphilos, knowing that Astyphilos had been fond of him.

Lys. xii 99f.: . . . and on behalf of the dead, whom you should support in death since you were unable to protect them in life. I think that they are listening to me and that they will be aware of your voting; they will regard those who vote for the defendants' acquittal as passing sentence of death upon *them*, and those who make the defendants pay the penalty as having avenged them.

These passages assimilate the dead to gods and heroes ('acceptable . . . to both', as one might speak of a sacrifice or dedication, and 'are listening . . . and will be aware', as is said of the gods [cf. V.D.4]). In the Lysian passage the dead in question have been unlawfully killed, in some cases (xii 18, 96) denied adequate burial rites, and the defendants are charged with responsibility both for the murders and for the denial of rites. There was a traditional belief, exploited by the author of the *Tetralogies* (Ant. ii. α.10, iv. α.3f., β.8, δ.10), that a murdered man becomes an angry ghost,[2] capable of causing sterility in crops and beasts and other misfortunes. There was also a long-standing belief that denial of proper burial, irrespective of the cause of death, angered the soul of the dead man and was productive of misfortunes for the living. The Athenian law of homicide was permeated by belief in the operation of such supernatural mechanisms,[3] though it is hard to say how far in the fourth century this aspect of the law (codified at a much earlier date) corresponded to a systematic eschatology or simply satisfied a strong sense of propriety.

Dem. xxiii 40: Next (sc. *the law says 'the murderer must keep away'*) 'also from Amphiktyonic sanctuaries'. Why did the legislator exclude the (sc. *exiled*) murderer

[1] Cf. Rohde 162–74, Adkins (2) 68–71. On the difficulty of drawing precise inferences from practice to belief and feeling, but the certainty that the living felt some kind of 'reluctance to credit separation from the dead', cf. Donna C. Kurtz and John Boardman, *Greek Burial Customs* (London, 1971) 206.

[2] We know more about Hellenistic ghosts than Classical ghosts; cf. Rohde 593–5.

[3] Lys. xiii 79, 'No one spoke to him, regarding him as accursed (*alitērios*)' ∼ 82, 'No one spoke to him, regarding him as a murderer'. On the whole question of pollution and purification in connection with homicide cf. MacDowell, especially chapters I, XII and XIV.

from these? Whatever was open to the victim in his lifetime, from that the killer is debarred.

Even in the fifth century, the ghost's capacity for direct action on its own initiative and at its own discretion was regarded as limited; it was rather the gods' interest in the rights of the dead which mattered, an interest which extended to funeral procedures as well as to the avenging of homicide (cf. V.D.1).[4] This concern on the part of the gods was independent of the dead man's awareness of the situation, and did not have to be aroused by an appeal from the ghost. Eur. *Phoen.* 1320f., speaks of 'piety towards the god beneath the earth' as manifested by the honours which the living pay to the dead.[5] Aiskhines' reference to 'custom' (in i 14, cited above) points to an element which may have been more significant in the fourth century than any actual fear of the dead: the social value of preserving, within each family and within the total of families which made up the city-state, a consciousness of continuity with forebears, a consciousness of particular importance when ancestral examples can serve as a stimulus to virtue.[6]

Dem. xliii 84: I am coming to the defence of both the dead and the law ... and I implore you ... not to allow either this boy to be insulted by my opponents or his ancestors to be treated with even more contempt than now ... but to defend the law and care for the dead, that their house may not be made empty.

Cf. Is. ii 15, 'to insult him after his death and make his house empty'; Lyk. *Leokr.* 59, 'depriving the dead of traditional observance'; Lys. ii 75, showing gratitude to the dead by caring for their families; Eur. *Hel.* 1165–7, Theoklymenos erected his father's tomb immediately outside his palace, so that he might constantly salute it.

Ant. i 21: The dead man ... who deserves your pity and defence and vengeance ...

Cf. Is. ii 47, 'come to the defence of both us and him who is in the underworld'; Lys. x 28, xii 99.

To admit the absence of evidence for a positive belief that the souls of the dead, once admitted to the underworld after the proper performance of burial rites, could on their own initiative punish the living for (e.g. cowardice, dishonesty or cruelty is not to say that morality was unaffected by an

---

[4] Cf. Hom. *Od.* xi 72f., where the ghost of the unburied Elpenor enjoins performance of his funeral rites on Odysseus, 'lest I become a cause of the gods' wrath against you'.

[5] Cf. Gernet 146. Soph. *El.* 792, 'Hear me, Nemesis of him who died!' the grammatical classification of the genitive case is necessarily a problem in the history of religion.

[6] Cf. Lattimore 220–8 on funeral observances as a tribute to the memory of the dead.

individual's awareness that the eyes of his ancestors *might* be upon him, that he *might* be able to gladden or shame or anger the souls of people whom he had loved and respected when they were alive, and that he *might* himself be welcomed or rejected by them when his own soul passed into the underworld. The dying Herakles threatens Hyllos in Soph. *Trach.* 1201f., 'If you do not obey me, I shall await you, my curse heavy upon you for ever, even in the underworld'; cf. Soph. *Oed. Tyr.* 1371–3, 'How could I ever have looked upon my father or my unhappy mother when I had gone to the world below?' The idea that we may meet after death those whom we knew in life,[7] together with those who had gone before them (an idea linked to the question, 'Do the dead perceive what happens among the living?', but distinguishable from it), has a good psychological foundation: when we behave in ways of which our parents and older relatives strongly disapproved, our attitude to our own behaviour takes on a colouring which would be appropriate if they were still alive and we were risking their disapproval. Consideration should be given to the possibility that an irrational desire to earn the approval of the dead and an irrational fear of their disapproval played a very much larger part in ordinary Athenian morality than could be inferred solely from the surviving literature.

Since living parents (then as now) could have their standing in the community raised or lowered by the virtues and vices of their children, and people long dead could be felicitated (e.g. in encomiastic poetry) on the virtues of their descendants, it was possible to speak of the achievements of the living as 'bringing glory' to their ancestors (e.g. Thuc. ii 11.9, vi 16.1) and of their failures as 'shaming the virtues of their ancestors' (Hyp. vi 3) or 'depriving their families of their ancient glory' (Lyk. *Leokr.* 110).


## V.D. THE GODS

### 1. Piety

It is possible for a man's relations with the gods to differ from his relations with his fellow-men. He may, for example, establish a claim on the gratitude

[7] Cf. Lattimore 247–9. In passages such as Dein. i 66, 'How will each of you dare to look upon your paternal hearth on returning home, if you have acquitted the traitor ...?', the issue is complicated by the tendency to personify (cf. III.G.3) anything which has emotional importance (e.g. the family hearth) and by the assumed interest of gods in any place or institution which serves as a focus of religious procedures. The speaker is not simply saying, 'Your fathers' ghosts will be waiting for you'.

and protection of the gods by generous and punctilious sacrifices while at the same time acquiring a bad reputation among his fellow-citizens as a stickler for his legal rights; or he may incur divine resentment by boasting or blasphemy while serving his city's interests without regard for his person or his property. It was possible to offend gods directly and immediately, e.g. by desecration of their sanctuaries, by violation of what were believed to be the divinely ordained rules of their cults and festivals (cf. Ar. *Thesm.* 672ff.), by omitting to perform a customary rite, or by breaking a vow. One might offend them also by boasts, threats or insults, which would offend one's fellow-men only indirectly, however gravely, in so far as they would fear collective punishment if they failed to get in first by imposing a penalty themselves.[1] Even curiosity about the universe could be regarded as offensive to the gods (it is so described by Xenophon's Socrates in *Mem.* iv 7.6), whether or not it led to scepticism about the existence of personal gods or to neglect of customary observances.

If a Greek was scrupulous in honouring the gods, he was *eusebēs*, 'pious', 'god-fearing' (abstract *eusebeia*, verb *eusebein*); if he offended them, he was *asebēs* or *dyssebēs*, 'impious' (abstract *asebeia* [or *dys-*], verb *asebein* [or *dys-*). In the traditional treatment of the cardinal virtues *eusebeia* and *dikaiosynē* were distinguished, a fact which carries the implication that a man could possess one of these virtues without the other; cf. 'impious towards the gods and disgraceful (*aiskhros*) in his dealings with men' (Xen. *Anab.* ii 5.20), and Thuc. ii 53.4, 'No fear of gods or law of men restrained them'. This separation was facilitated by the tendency to assimilate the relationship between gods and men to that between human benefactors and beneficiaries. Man offered sacrifices and festivities to the gods, and claimed divine help and protection in return, reminding them of their debt in his prayers.

Since the gods are our rulers, they not only exact material tribute from us, their human subjects, but also (as rulers will) make laws for us to obey. Hence it is possible for us to please or offend them in certain ways by our conduct towards each other. The Greek gods' interest in different fields of behaviour was unequal. We find that from the first they were believed to command good treatment of guests, suppliants, heralds and the dead; in this way some basic problems of intercourse between communities (including the realm of the dead)[2] were solved by being removed from the sphere of

---

[1] Cf. J. Rudhardt, 'La Définition du délit d'impiété d'apres la législation attique', *Museum Helveticum* xvii (1966), 87ff.

[2] Eur. *Supp.* 561–3 speaks of the surrender of enemy dead for proper burial as (literally) 'customary usages of the gods', i.e. usage required by the gods.

ineffective human authority. During the classical period divine interest in human activities tended to greater comprehensiveness.

Actions which the gods approved or at least permitted were called *hosios*, 'righteous', and transgression of the divine rules was *anhosios*;[3] a negative aspect of *hosios* is conspicuous in the distinction (important in Attic law and administration) between 'sacred (*hieros*) money', which belonged to the gods, and '*hosios* money', which, since the gods had no claim on it, could be spent for secular purposes.[4] The formal conjunction of *hosios* with *dikaios* was sometimes augmented by reference to '*both* gods *and* men', as if recognizing a distinction between divine law and man-made law (e.g. Ant. i 25, Lys. xiii 3); but, as we shall see, the distinction became of little practical significance in the fourth century. A strong tendency to synonymy of *eusebēs* and *hosios* is observable even earlier, and that should not surprise us. Lyk. *Leokr.* 15, 'piously towards the gods and righteously towards our parents'[5] is unusual and somewhat artificial. Lys. xii 24, where 'impious' is contrasted with 'righteous and pious', and Dem. xix 70, 'nor is it righteous or pious for you to acquit him', are rhetorical pleonasm.

Ant. i 5: I am surprised that my brother . . . thinks it piety (*eusebeia*) not to betray his mother; I regard it as much more unrighteous (*anhosios*) to forgo vengeance on behalf of the dead.

Ant. vi 33: I will prove to you that my accusers are the most perjured and impious (*asebēs*) of men . . . 48: This evidence alone is enough to make you . . . regard them as the most perjured and unrighteous (*anhosios*) of men.

The second passage is an instance of ring-form (cf. II.B.*3*). Cf. also Dem. xxiii 25 ∼ 38, 29, 78; Eur. *Hel.* 1021; Eur. fr. 388; Xen. *Apol.* 19.

We can choose to involve the gods in our actions by swearing an oath.[6] The oath makes them witnesses of the action; this interpretation, given by Dem. xlviii 11, is illustrated by the term *histores*, which means 'witnesses' in several Greek dialects and is applied also to the gods listed at the end of a declaration headed 'oath'.[7] Lykourgos's metaphorical description (*Leokr.* 127) of an oath as a 'hostage' given to the gods is valid only in so far as it suggests that just as an international injustice cannot be perpetrated with impunity when

---

[3] Cf. J. C. Bolkestein, ʽ*Οσιος* en *Εὐσεβής* (Amsterdam 1936); Adkins (1) 132–5; Ferguson 28.

[4] In Ar. *Lys.* 743 'a *hosios* place' is a place where, by contrast with the Akropolis, childbirth is permissible, and in *Wealth* 682 conduct modelled on a priest's in a sanctuary is called *hosios*, implying that the priest should know what is permitted there and what is not.

[5] Cf. Vollgraff 71f.          [6] Cf. Latte 5–47.

[7] M. N. Tod, *Selection of Greek Historical Inscriptions*, vol. ii (Oxford, 1948), no. 204.

the aggressor has previously given hostages to the victim, so perjury invites divine retaliation. The idea that we injure (*adikein*) the gods by perjury (Dem. xlviii 52) departs to a similar extent from a simple equation of gods with witnesses, for in human affairs it is not the witnesses to a contract who punish its breach, but the courts.[8] Perjury injures the gods because they have decided to treat it as wrong, and they were credited with this decision because the oath was of overwhelming importance in a culture which put much less in writing than we do.[9] It seems that in Aristophanes' *Clouds* the creditors of Strepsiades would have found it hard to prove, in a manner which would satisfy a modern court, that they had lent him money; one creditor challenges him to deny on oath, by Zeus, Hermes and Poseidon, at a place of the creditor's choosing, that he had received the loan, and is taken aback at the 'shamelessness' with which the old man gaily agrees to do so (*Clouds* 1232–6). Strepsiades at that point in the play has ceased to believe in the gods; but need, desire and fear were no doubt effective, even in the absence of philosophical atheism, in causing people to treat oaths with contempt. In Ar. *Lys.* 915 Kinesias is so desperate for intercourse with Myrrhine that when she protests that she has taken an oath not to have intercourse he cries impatiently, 'On my head be it!' In Eur. fr. 645 the gods are said to forgive the breach of an oath sworn under duress to save one's life; cf. Pl. *Smp.* 183B, on a popular belief that they were indulgent towards lovers' oaths.

Since the swearing of oaths played so large a part in commercial transactions, it was hard to be fraudulent or dishonest without at the same time being impious; when Hermogenes in Xen. *Smp.* 4.49 defines religious duty as fidelity to oaths and abstention from blasphemy he is going much further towards the equation of religion with morality than we might think, and in Ar. *Wealth* 61 ~ 105 'faithful to his oaths' and 'of good character' seem to be treated as synonymous. Interstate treaties were also sealed by oaths; hence any action which could be regarded as a contravention of such a treaty could also be called impious (e.g. Dem. ix 16), and the gods were expected to be on the side of the injured party (Dem. xi 12).[10] Cf. Xen. *Anab.* ii 4.6, an inevitable 'war with the gods' follows from the breach of an oath, and ibid. iii 1.22, oath-keepers fight oath-breakers with confidence,

---

[8] It might be said, however, that witnesses represent the community as a whole, and to that extent the community both witnesses the contract and, through the courts, punishes its breach; and the gods by whom the oath is sworn similarly represent the supernatural world.

[9] Cf. Radle 7–16.        [10] Cf. Martin 399–412.

the gods presiding over the battle. According to Thuc. vii 18.2 the Spartans attributed their setbacks in the Archidamian War to their condoning of the breach of the Thirty Years' Peace by Thebes, their ally; Isok. xiv 28 treats the Thebans' loss of their citadel to the Spartans in 382 as a 'penalty paid to the gods' for their failure to keep their oath of alliance with Athens and Corinth.

## 2. Extensions of Piety

The jurors in the courts swore to give as honest a verdict as they could. A speaker was therefore able to assert that in returning a verdict in his favour the jurors would 'abide by their oath', and that if they found in favour of his adversary they would be 'impious'.

Dem. xxiii 96: If an unconstitutional proposal . . . is acquitted, that is no reason to say that it is not illegal. Does this mean that the jurors who give such a verdict do not abide by their oath (*euorkein*)? But they do! How? I'll explain. They have sworn to arrive at verdict as honestly as possible, and their opinion is formed by what they hear; so in voting according to that opinion, they act piously (*eusebein*).

Lys. fr. 89: When you are judging a case on which a man's life depends, you should not transgress the law (*paranomein*), but act in piety (*eusebein*).

Cf. Dem. xviii 217, xx 119, xxii 101, xxiii 194 (a wrong verdict impiety), xxiv 34, lvii 17.

Lys. xiii 4: When you have heard my whole exposition in detail, you will give your verdict against Agoratos with greater satisfaction (*literally*, '*more agreeably*') and more righteously (*hosios*).

Here 'righteous' seems to stand for 'just and righteous', jointly distinguishable from the pleasure one feels in condemning to death an enemy of the community.

The most comprehensive oath which an Athenian swore in his life was that which he took on reaching the age of eighteen, swearing, *inter alia*, 'I will not hand on (*sc.* to the next generation) my fatherland less (*sc.* than it was when it was handed on to me), but larger and better'.[11] Any action which could be called unpatriotic could be regarded also as a violation of this comprehensive oath, and therefore as impious (Lyk. *Leokr.* 76, cf. 148).[12] Moreover, any action which adversely affected the worship of gods was simultaneously impious and unpatriotic, because divine protection and

[11] Cf. n. 7 above.          [12] Cf. Latte 87f., 112f.; Gernet 57-9.

goodwill were the return made by the gods when honoured and withdrawn when they were not. So Aiskhines is treated by Dem. xix 86 as having offended the gods, since in consequence (Demosthenes alleges) of his policy it was necessary to evacuate the countryside and celebrate the Herakleia within the city walls; or again (ibid. 256f.), Aiskhines is threatened with divine punishment because the peace-treaty with Philip surrendered places 'where it was appropriate that the gods should be honoured by the Athenians and their allies'. So too Philon is said to have 'abandoned the gods of our fathers' by leaving Attica (Lys. xxxi 31), and Leokrates not only 'deprived the gods of the honours which our fathers paid them' (Lyk. *Leokr.* 97, cf. 129) and showed that he did not care if the sanctuaries of Attica were ravaged (147), but even damaged Athens' relations with the supernatural world by transferring his family cult to Megara (25f., 56). Cf. Eur. fr. 53.14f. (Austin), we beget children in order to preserve the altars of the gods and our fatherland.

When necessary, a different view could be taken. Lyk. *Leokr.* 139f. treats expenditure on *choregiai* as mere display for personal advantage, ignoring the religious aspect of the festivals at which choruses performed; and it is striking that Dem. xxi 217, indignant at the alleged hybristic behaviour of Meidias at a festival, speaks of the presence of the whole population but says not a word to suggest that the god was 'present' too.

A law which had been taken to Delphi or some other oracular site for the god's approval became in effect a divine prescription, and according to Xen. *Mem.* i 3.1 Delphi gave general approval to the maintenance of existing usage in all cities. In certain ways the Athenian state could be said to have dictated to its deities the rules which they were to enforce. Curses were regularly and formally pronounced against political corruption (Dein. i 46f., ii 16), wilful deceit of courts or assembly (Dem. xxiii 97), and, naturally enough, treasonable activities (cf. the partly parodic adaptation in Ar. *Thesm.* 332–71); and they could be prescribed by decree for particular purposes (e.g. Thuc. viii 97.1). No one could actually know whether or not the gods always accepted the particular form of prayer which we call a curse[13] and would accordingly be willing to implement it, but the formal pronouncement on behalf of the community was treated as an assurance that they would do so. Dem. xix 70f. utilizes this assumption in order to argue that the acquittal of Aiskhines would be unrighteous and impious, because, in Demosthenes' view, the conduct of Aiskhines could properly be subsumed under the categories of action officially cursed. Conversely, when

[13] Cf. Latte 61–88.

the Athenians in 410 took measures designed to prevent the growth of a fresh oligarchic conspiracy, such as had brought about the revolution of 411, they found it desirable to annul certain oaths taken in the course of that conspiracy; they did this by prescribing a fresh oath which included the declaration, 'I hereby dissolve and annul all oaths whatsoever sworn . . . in opposition to the Athenian democracy' (And. i 98), the consent of the gods being taken for granted. This same oath of 410 absolved from the pollution of homicide (And. i 96f.) anyone who should kill an anti-democratic conspirator. Greek communities in general found it necessary, or at least convenient, to traat some kinds of homicide as 'legal' or 'just' (Dem. xx 158, xxiii 74), incurring no pollution or prosecution: killing an adulterer caught in the act (cf. IV.E.*3*), killing a fellow-soldier in the genuinely mistaken belief that he was an enemy (Dem. xxiii 55), or causing the death of a patient by well-meant but incorrect medical treatment (Ant. iv. *γ*.5).

We might compare the readiness with which a character in comedy can use 'impious', 'unholy', etc., as terms of abuse (e.g. Knemon in Men. *Dysk.* 108f., cf. 122f.), as if he himself had the right to decide what and whom the gods should condemn. Comedy also uses *theois ekhthros*, 'enemy to the gods' as an abusive term, e.g. Plato Comicus fr. 74.3, where it is applied to a greedy man who has eaten everything up; in oratory we find an abstract noun *theoisekhthriā*.

The consequence of the tendency towards identification of the patriotic, the law-abiding and the pious is that it becomes difficult to think of any conduct which could attract any kind of 'secular' valuation and yet could not be called 'pious' or 'impious'.

Lyk. *Leokr.* 93: It would be intolerable if the same prophecies were made to the pious and to malefactors (*kakourgoi*).

Sometimes we can discern a positive link, however tenuous, with the religious aspects of an issue, e.g. in Is. iv 19, where *anhosios* seems to mean 'unfair' in connection with the performance of funeral rites, or Dem. lix 13, 44, where the 'impiety' of Stephanos might be explained by reference to certain passages later in the speech (72–7, 109f.). A humorous passage of Menander, *Farmer* 35–9, effectively illustrates the inclusion of *dikaiosynē* in 'piety' by saying of a field that it is pious because (i) it produces wild plants which are used in cult, and (ii) it pays back exactly what is put into it (which, means, of course, that its crop is very poor indeed). Sometimes it is not easy to make any clear connection with religion. *Hosios* seems to mean 'legal' in Dem. xxix 39 and 'procedurally correct' in Ant. v 7, Dem. lvii 58,

Is. ix 34, Lyk. *Leokr.* 34; contrast Lyk. *Leokr.* 141, envisaging that a procedure which would be *hosios* cannot be followed because it is not *nomimos*, 'in accordance with customary procedure'. *Anhosios* or 'not *hosios*' is applied to dishonesty (Dem. xxxiii 10), illegality (Aiskhines iii 91), ingratitude (Dem. liii 3), objectionable character (Aiskhines i 95), political blackmail (Dem. xxv 48), unpatriotic argument (Dem. viii 8), acquittal of a man guilty of *hybris* (Dem. xxi 148), or with a general moral and political connotation (And. i 19, 23, Dem. xix 156); Aiskhines and his supporters are called *asebēs* in Dem. xviii 240, *dyssebēs* ibid. 323. Cf. Dem. xviii 31, 'these *adikos* men' ∼ 240, 'these *asebēs* men', with the same reference.[14]

Lys. xxxii 13: 'And', she said, 'even if you felt no shame before any man, you should fear the gods. When my husband sailed out, you received from him five talents, deposited in your safe keeping'.

(On 'safe keeping' cf. IV.B.*1*).

This convergence of social and political morality with religion is by no means a new phenomenon in the time of the orators.

Aiskh. *Seven* 597–608: Alas for the mischance that brings an honest (*dikaios*) man into the company of the impious (*dyssebēs*) ... A pious (*eusebēs*) man goes on board the same ship as lawless (*literally*, '*hot*') sailors ... and perishes ... or, honest (*dikaios*) among citizens who behave as enemies towards strangers and are unmindful of the gods, ... he falls beneath the scourge with which the god strikes all together.

This passage is interesting in that it immediately precedes the sequence *sōphrōn, dikaios, agathos, eusebēs* (612), where honesty and piety seem to be treated as separable virtues. Cf. synonymy of 'just' with 'pious', antonymy of 'just' and 'impious', etc., in Eupolis fr. 74, Eur. fr. 388; Eur. *Hel.* 903f., 'the god hates violence'; Eur. *Hyps.* fr. 60.58f., Amphiaraos ashamed, as a mortal close to Apollo, to tell a lie; Soph. *El.* 114, adultery persecuted by the Furies; Soph. *Phil.* 1050f.; fr. 103; *GVI* 632.5 (s. III in.), *hosios* = 'chaste'. Comic hyperbole furnishes some good examples. In Alexis fr. 15.1–6 one character is requiring another to account in detail for expenditure on food; as one item is read out, the first character says (literally), 'You do not yet *asebein*', i.e. 'So far, everything's above board'. In Eupolis fr. 52.1 'impiety' seems to refer to culinary innovations of which the speaker disapproves.

One conclusion from the convergence of honesty and piety was that virtue, not the performance of sacrifices, is the way to win the gods' favour.

---

[14] Cf. Gernet 54f.

Men. fr. 683: Anyone who believes that he secures the god's favour by sacrifice . . . is in error. For a man must be useful (cf. VI.B.*3*) by not seducing virgins or committing adultery or stealing or killing for money.

Cf. Isok. ii 20, no offering or worship superior to the effort to live a virtuous life; Xen. *Ages*. 11.2.

The chorus in Aiskh. *Ag*. alludes (750–6) to a widely disseminated belief that good fortune generates disaster; this the chorus rejects (757–62), asserting —as if disagreeing with the general view—that whereas an impious (*dyssebēs*) act leads to disaster, an upright (*euthydikos*) house maintains its prosperity from one generation to the next. The belief which the chorus asserts is the normal Greek belief that *hybris* arouses divine anger (e.g. Soph. *Trach*. 280). It can easily accommodate (e.g.) the story of Pheretime, who took a ferocious revenge on her rebellious subjects and later died of a horrible disease, 'for it seems that excessive human vengeance arouses the resentment of the gods' (Hdt. iv 205); it is also compatible with the maxim, 'The god hates excessive zeal' (Eur. *Or*. 708), assuming that 'zeal' in that context means thoughtless, headstrong action which has disastrous results. Euripides adds, 'and the citizens hate it', and Herodotos might have added to the story of Pheretime that her behaviour was revolting by human standards; in both cases the gods are being credited with human reactions. The belief which the chorus in the *Agamemnon* rejects seems to be the sombre generalization which Hdt. i 32.1 puts into the mouth of Solon (cf. III.A.*2*). Gods who thwart human projects for fun and slap down any man who appears to them to be 'getting above himself' make uncomfortable neighbours, but much more uncomfortable for the ambitious and aggressive than for the little man who minds his own business; to this extent jealous gods can operate as a significant moral sanction. In *Ag*. 950–2 Agamemnon tells Klytaimestra to receive the enslaved Kassandra with affability, since 'the god looks with kindly eye (*eumenōs*) on him who is gentle in victory' (literally, 'who conquers softly'). The idea that harshness towards a captive earns divine disapproval may surprise us, if we have adopted assumptions which exaggerate the difference between ancient and modern attitudes, but it surprises us less when we reflect that cruelty, pride, fraud and perjury, being no more than different ways in which one follows one's own inclinations at the cost of others' suffering, are equally offensive to jealous gods, just gods and nice gods.

## 3. Divine Legislation

The personification and deification of justice or right as Dike appear as early as Hesiod (Op. 256–62), where she is a daughter and minister of Zeus, who 'whenever anyone hurts her . . . sits beside her father and tells him of the wicked heart of men' (cf. ibid. 279–85). This remained a fundamental religious concept in the classical period.[15] Eur. fr. 151, 'child of Zeus'; Ar. Clouds 902f., Dike 'dwells with the gods'; Dem. xxv 11, where the Hesiodic doctrine is ascribed to Orpheus. The province of Dike is the enforcement of law rather than the making of law, and will be examined in section 4 below. Let us first look at the scope of divine legislation.

We have seen (III.A) that general characteristics were sometimes predicated of human nature, and we shall see (V.E.1) that they could also be predicated of human usage and custom; we have also seen (section 1 above) that interstate communications and some usages (e.g. burial of the dead) common to all the Greek states were treated as the special concern of the gods. There was a speculative belief, rationalized ('How ever could all mankind have assembled and reached agreement?') in Xenophon's portrayal of a conversation between Socrates and Hippias (Mem. iv 4.19–21), that the unwritten laws[16] of mankind, together with elements common to many written codes, were explicitly prescribed by gods at some time in the remote past.[17] In one direction, it was a short step from such a notion to the ascription of particular long-standing laws and institutions of individual states to divine prescription: Ant. i 3, the Athenian law of homicide; Dem. xxiii 70, the Areopagus; ibid. 81, the other homicide courts at Athens; Dem. xxv 5 appears to speak of every law as 'invented' by the gods—a strange statement, for a man who must have been present at the making of some laws, but he may have meant

[15] On the great importance of Dike in Aiskhylos cf. Lloyd-Jones 97–103.

[16] On unwritten law cf. Hirzel 359–72 and '"Αγραφος Νόμος" in Abhandlungen der philosophisch-historischen Classe der königlich sächsischen Gesellschaft der Wissenschaften xx 1 (1903); V. Ehrenberg, Sophocles and Pericles (Oxford, 1954) 22–50, 167–72; de Romilly 26–38.

[17] Cf. de Romilly 26–38, 46–9, 121–6; Wolf 111f. Sometimes new laws were submitted to an oracle for approval (cf. de Romilly 124), and if the god approved them they could fairly be treated as if he had actually prescribed them. In Eur. Ba. 895f. the apparent reference of 'what is established in usage over a long period and exists by nature' to the worship of Dionysos is curious, since within the story of the play the worship of Dionysos is just being introduced to the Greek world as a novelty; the antithesis between traditional usage and revolutionary criticism is formulated in terms appropriate to the time of performance.

simply to use the idea that the ancient codes to which later laws were mere additions and amendments were divine in origin. We may compare the treatment of human practices, arts and pastimes as the 'invention' of deities who benevolently communicated them to mankind; so, for example, hunting with hounds is ascribed by [Xen.] *Cyneg.* 1.1 to Apollo and Artemis.

In another direction, it was possible to infer from the ascription of the 'unwritten laws' to the gods the intentions of a divine creator in the natural structure of mankind and its environment[18] (incidentally, the Greeks did not ascribe the creation of mankind to Zeus, but to Prometheus or, more often, to 'the gods' in general or an unidentified creator-god). The gods assigned to the two sexes their characteristically different natures (Xen. *Oec.* 7.22–9); cf. 'that which the gods put into the souls of men' (Xen. *Cyr.* viii 2.20); the grant of our power to 'instruct one another by speech' (Xen. *Eq.* 8.13); 'he who originally created the human race' designed our organs of perception thoughtfully and benevolently (Xen. *Mem.* i 4.5–14); the gods showed great 'love of man' in arranging the universe in a way useful to us (Xen. *Mem.* iv 3.3–18). From this it could be thought to follow that what might appear to be no more than a breach of man-made regulations was in fact something more heinous, the frustration of the divine intention.

Ant. iv. α.2: When the god, wishing to create the human race, generated our first ancestors, he gave them land and sea to nourish and sustain them, that they might not die through lack of necessities before they reached old age. Therefore he who illegally kills one of us, who were deemed by the god to deserve life, is guilty of impiety against the gods as well as breaking the laws of men.

(Note 'illegally'; the speaker would have been surprised if told that he was arguing against war or capital punishment.)

The fact that *nomos*, unlike 'law', covers usage and custom, but not as a rule what we call 'laws of nature', throws into relief the comparatively few passages in which it does approximate to 'law of nature', e.g. Thuc. v 105.2, where the Athenian spokesmen at Melos ascribe human aggression to (literally) 'compelling nature', and add that 'this *nomos*' was not made by Athens but existed of old. They do not mean that a god prescribed it, nor should we see religious colouring in Thuc. i 76.2, 'it has always been the case ...', but we come nearer to religious terminology in Thuc. iii 56.2, 'in accordance with the universally established *nomos* that it is *hosios* to defend oneself against an enemy's attack', and it was certainly possible for what we would call a law of nature to be described as a deliberate decision taken by

[18] Cf. de Romilly 159–73, Hirzel 401–8.

the gods: it is a 'vote', i.e. 'decree', of the gods that all men must die (Eur. *Andr.* 1271f.). The language used of laws of nature does not imply a belief that they were older than, and independent of, the gods; when Soph. *Oed. Col.* 863–72 speaks of 'laws begotten in the heavens, laws of which Olympos alone is the father', we can interpret 'Olympos' as 'the gods', and Soph. fr. 860, (literally) 'It is not lawful (*themis*), except to the gods, to live without ills', means 'It is not permitted to man to live without ills; only the gods do that'.

Two passages of Euripides treat the perceptible order of nature as a paradigm for human morality: Eur. *Hel.* 906–8, since the sky and the earth are common to us all, we should not rob one another; *Phoen.* 543–8, the equal proportion of daylight and darkness in the course of a year should shame a man out of reluctance to share equally with others ('Equality' is personified in that passage, and so is her adversary 'Ambition'; cf. V.B.2). More directly, Xen. *Oec.* 5.12: 'The earth, who is a goddess, ... teaches us *dikaiosynē*' by her response to good cultivation.

## 4. Divine Enforcement of Law

Importance was attached to the place where an oath was sworn or a declaration made (Ar. *Clouds* 1232f., Ant. vi 39, Lys. xxxii 13, Dem. iii 2, xxxvi 16, Is. ii 31), as if one could not otherwise be sure that a god had really heard the utterance, but it is doubtful whether anyone was prepared to assert explicitly that there were limits to the range of divine hearing; the point of taking an oath at an altar or in a sanctuary was to enhance its solemnity and leave no room for doubt that the taker was acting deliberately and in full consciousness of what he was doing. The same point may underlie the comment of Dem. xxi 216 on the fact that the assembly which judged that there was a *prima facie* case against Meidias did so at a meeting held in a sanctuary. It was asserted that 'the gods, though far off in heaven, see all that men do' (Eur. *Ba.* 393–4), that they 'oversee all human acts' (Lyk. *Leokr.* 94), that the sky hears what is said (Eur. *Iph. Aul.* 365), and that 'Justice, close at hand, sees, though unseen, and knows whom to punish' (Eur. fr. 255, cf. fr. 151), for Zeus keeps a record of all human wrongdoing (Eur. *Mel. Sophe* [von Arnim] fr. 7). Moreover, the gods read our thoughts. In Kritias's play *Sisyphos* the impious Sisyphos of legend expounds (B25.20ff.) how some wise man in the remote past invented religion as a moral sanction and persuaded his fellow-men that there exists a superhuman power such that 'even if you plan an evil deed in silence, this will not escape the gods, so keen is their understanding'. The orators utilized this belief in divine omniscience especially in warning a jury that although each juror's vote is secret on the human plane, the gods will know it.

Lyk. *Leokr.* 146: Be assured that each one of you, in casting his vote now in secret, will make his own thought apparent to the gods.

Cf. Dem. xix 239, lix 126, Lys. vi 53.

Silent prayers and vows were therefore possible. Hdt. ii 181.4 relates how a prayer and vow to Aphrodite, made 'in the mind' by the wife of the Egyptian king Amasis, were immediately effective. Two other stories in Herodotos (i 159.4, vi 86. γ.2) concern divine anger against men who contemplated a misdeed but had not yet committed it; in both cases, however, the wrongful intention was revealed by their enquiry of an oracle (in i 159.4 the enquiry was honest, and it was not so much the intention to do wrong as the contemplation of its possibility which angered the god). In the nature of things, we cannot expect to hear much about the punishment of unrevealed intentions. We do, however, find some reference to the acceptability of good intentions without adequate performance. The rich naturally tended to think that good relations with the gods depended essentially on the scale and frequency of offerings, but Antiphanes fr. 164, Eur. frr. 327, 946, and Isok. v 30 recognize the principle that a small offering made in a spirit of piety is acceptable to the gods.[19] (By contrast, the chorus tells Elektra in Eur. *El.* 193–7 that she cannot expect to get the better of her enemies if she spends all her time in lamentation and takes no part in the festivities which please the gods.)

From the omniscience and omnipotence of the gods it follows that although a man can hope to escape detection by human authorities if he breaks human laws, no one can hope to escape punishment if he offends against divine law: Soph. *Oed. Col.* 278–81, Xen. *Mem.* iv 4.20. Rarely, the threat of divine retribution is brushed aside without any attempt at self-justification (cf. V.A.*1*): Menelaos in Eur. *Andr.* 440 says, 'I'll put up with that when it happens; but (*sc. in the meantime*) I'm going to kill *you!*'

Belief in divine justice may have tended to give good men confidence that things would go well for them and to implant in bad men—or in those unavoidably committed to a cause of which the justice was doubtful (cf.

---

[19] Regulations for cult practice sometimes made moral as well as ritual stipulations; cf. F. Sokolowski, *Lois sacrées des cités grecques: Supplément* (Paris, 1962) nos. 86.3, 108.6f. (both Hellenistic).

Eur. *Phoen.* 154f., 'I am afraid that the gods may see the issue straight')[20]—
a fear that things would go ill. At least, the belief could be asserted as an
encouragement or warning: Eur. *El.* 1351–5, the Dioskouroi declare their
own role as saviours of the good, and warn against going on board ship with
perjurers; Eur. fr. 584, 'One just man conquers a host of the unjust, with
Justice and the gods on his side'; Lys. xxxiii 10; Thuc. v 104, the Melians
confronting the Athenians, who are not impressed; Thuc. vii 77.2f., Nikias
drawing assurance from his own virtuous life; Xen. *Cyr.* vii 5.77. It was
easy to speak as if suffering must be caused by a past sin: in Hdt. vi 12.3, the
Ionians groaning under hard training ask, 'What *daimōn* have we offended,
to deserve this expiation?' If it was already known that a man had offended
against the gods, any misfortune which overtook him would be attributed to
the offence: Hdt. iv 205, on Pheretime; vi 75.3, on the insanity of Kleomenes.
There were also stories of miraculous intervention to save good men, e.g.
Lyk. *Leokr.* 95f. (cf. III.G.1). As we have seen, the orators posited direct
intervention by a god in a man's mental processes, and the usual purpose of
this intervention was to lead a sinner into a disastrous predicament[21] from
which punishment at the hands of men would follow: And. i 113, Dem.
xix 257, xxiv 124, Lyk. *Leokr.* 92, Lys. vi 22, 27, 32.

Belief of this kind, however, is hard to reconcile with experience, even
when hedged about with reservations and exceptions.[22] It could be said,
for example, that the gods have '*a certain* care' for good men (Men. fr. 321)
and 'help a just enterprise undertaken with a pious heart' (Men. fr. 494)—
cf. Karkinos Tragicus fr. 4, 'Do your best to be a good man and pray to the
gods for good fortune', Soph. fr. 841, 'Fortune does not help those who lose
heart'—or after one has tried really hard to do something for oneself (Xen.
*Cyr.* i 6.6; cf. Eur. fr. 432), maxims which remind us of the English proverb
'God helps those who help themselves' or of Apollo's promise to the Pelo-
ponnesians in 432 that 'victory would be theirs if they fought with all their

[20] We must always remember—for example, in interpreting the choral passages of
the *Agamemnon*—that an inflexibly just god who punishes severely is welcome to us
when it is our enemies who incur punishment, but when those on our own side are
threatened with divine punishment we do not feel so pious.
[21] A Greek god might tempt a man to commit a religious offence in order to punish
him for it afterwards, e.g. Hdt. i 159.4.
[22] Adkins (1) 255 says that the Athenians in the fourth century 'no longer believed
that the gods punish injustice', but this does not seem to me reconcilable with the use of
the notion by the orators. The difficulty lies in the word 'believe' (cf. III.F.4); an individual from time to time experiences mutually irreconcilable fears and hopes which
preclude any clear and unreserved statement about his 'belief', and when we are speaking
of an entire society or period the reservations and uncertainties become overwhelming.

might' (Thuc. i 118.3). Or again, it could be stressed that *in the end*, if only we will be patient, the gods will ensure the victory of the good (Eur. *Ion* 1619–22), for divine justice does not act swiftly (Eur. fr. 979). But the prosperity of the wicked and the sufferings of the good (a theme of Ar. *Wealth*) evoked the sentiments that the gods did not care, that they were foolish or unjust (Eur. *Her. Fur.* 211f.; Eur. fr. 445; Men. *Misum.* fr. 7.2f., 'Where could one find gods as just as that?' = 'But that's too much to hope for!'; Soph. fr. 103), or that they did not exist (Eur. fr. 286; cf. III.F.4).

Solon (fr. 1.25ff.) enunciated in the early sixth century a doctrine destined to a long and vigorous life both in the dramatists' treatment of legends and in the popular imagination: that divine punishment *might* sometimes fall upon the sinner quickly, but might be deferred for many years and might even fall upon his children or descendants. The great utility of this doctrine was its suppleness. It made sense when the bad suffered, because swift punishment was not precluded, and in such cases the comment, 'The gods are swift to punish' could be made as if it were a general rule (e.g. Ar. *Thesm.* 672–86). If, on the other hand, a very bad man died rich and happy, people could say, 'His descendants will surely pay for his crimes'. If a good man suffered, they could say, 'One of his ancestors must have sinned', rather as Oedipus in Soph. *Oed. Col.* 964f., considers that 'perhaps' his forebears had given the gods cause for anger. The use of the Solonian doctrine by the orators illustrates its adaptability to different circumstances and needs.

Lyk. *Leokr.* 79: A man cannot perjure himself without the gods' knowing of it, nor can he escape punishment at their hands; and if not he himself, then the children and all the descendants of the perjurer fall into great misfortune.

Cf. Dem. xix 240, a juror's 'hope for his children and himself' imperilled by an unjust verdict; Lys. xxxii 13.

Lys. vi 20: The god does not punish at once—that is human justice—but I can conjecture (*sc. the likely fate of Andokides*) on abundant evidence, for I have seen others who had committed impiety and in the course of time paid the penalty, and so did the descendants of impious men, because of the wrong done by their ancestors. In the meantime the god inflicts a host of fears and perils upon wrongdoers ...

Cf. Men. fr. 582, anyone who wants to marry a rich heiress is either expiating a sin (literally, 'paying out a wrath of the gods') or wanting to suffer, for all that he is felicitated.

Lys. fr. 53: The gods have so treated Kinesias ... that his enemies wish him to live, not die, as an example to others, so that all may know that when a man is insolent towards religion the gods do not store up the punishment for his children but inflict suffering on the offender himself, visiting upon him misfortune and illnesses greater and more distressing than upon other men.

Cf. Isok. xviii 3, 'so that ... they should not wait for divine punishment'.

We do not hear much about divine forgiveness, for the legends used by the tragic poets were tragic precisely because they were stories of unforgiven sins, and Herodotos presumably did not find the non-expiation of offences an interesting subject. Nevertheless, people spoke of the forgiveness of the gods as if it were perfectly possible, e.g. Xen. *Mem.* ii 2.14, 'If you are wise, you will ask the gods to forgive you'; cf. the old servant's prayer to Aphrodite in Eur. *Hipp.* 117–20 (cited in III.A.2), and the decision of Kadmos and Teiresias in Eur. *Ba.* 360–3 to ask the forgiveness[23] of Dionysos 'for Pentheus and the whole city'. As often, we may get nearer to ordinary people's feelings through comedy. Strepsiades, repentant, asks pardon of Hermes in Ar. *Clouds* 1476–85, and evidently receives it; and Philokleon in *Wasps* 389f. addresses the hero Lykos with the words, 'Pity me, save me now, your own neighbour—and I'll never piss against your railings again!'

## 5. *The Afterlife*

The morality of the doctrine of deferred punishment was acceptable so long as there was no significant reaction against the general principle of collective punishment. It was, after all, widely asserted in the archaic and classical periods (e.g. Eur. *El.* 1355, Xen. *Cyr.* viii 1.25) that a god might sink a shipload of passengers in order to catch one sinner among them, or inflict a plague upon a city which had failed to detect a sinner and bring him to justice (cf. the opening scene of Soph. *Oed. Tyr.*); cf. Aiskhines ii 158, Ant. ii α.3, iii γ.11, v 82. To punish me for my grandfather's sin is not, at any rate, *more* objectionable than to kill me because I am a member of the same lasting or temporary collectivity as someone else who has sinned. I am nevertheless, in expiating my grandfather's sin, *anaitios*, 'not to blame', 'not the cause (*sc.* of the wrong)', as Solon himself admitted. Theognis 731–52 is an early protest against the injustice of punishing the blameless, but he does not go so far as to question that this is how Zeus works. Yet once civilized reflection had begun to suggest that it was incompatible with any notion of

---

[23] The word used, *exaiteisthai*, is the same word as is used of a man who appears in court on the side of the defendant and asks the jury, by virtue of his own record as a patriotic citizen, to grant him the favour of leniency to the defendant.

justice to hurt an individual because of something which that individual had not himself done, and at the same time the emotional need to believe in the punishment of wrong remained imperious, the notion of inherited punishment was gradually replaced by the notion that the soul of the offending individual himself would be punished after its separation from the body. This notion took many forms, all of which coexisted in the fourth century; they must often have coexisted as alternative hypotheses in the same person, and individuals seem to have differed greatly in their degree of assurance.[24]

In the Homeric portrayal of the afterlife in *Od.* xi the great majority of souls, however virtuous or distinguished or wicked they have been in their lives on earth, are consigned to the same shadowy existence, in which they remain unhappily aware that being dead is not as agreeable as being alive. Punishment is meted out to a very few, such as Tantalos and Ixion, guilty of very unusual offences directly involving the gods in a manner not open to most of us. At the other extreme, we hear elsewhere in the *Odyssey* of a happy afterlife in Elysion conferred upon a small number of heroes who stood in some direct relationship to the gods. This ancient view, which precludes differential treatment for most people, is clearly reflected in some epitaphs of later times (e.g. *SEG* xii 93), even as late as the second and third centuries of the Christian era.

At least by the sixth century the Eleusinian Mysteries were offering a process of initiation designed to ensure a degree of preferential treatment in the afterlife.[25] What proportion of Athenians in classical times were initiated, we do not know, but there are clear signs of a widespread belief that initiation was a desirable precaution against a more positively painful fate than befell the ordinary soul in the Homeric afterlife. This view is expressed in Soph. fr. 753; in Ar. *Peace* 374f. Trygaios, threatened with death by Hermes, cries in mock-panic, 'Let me get initiated first!', but this does not tell us what degree of difference between the initiated and the uninitiated in the under-world is presupposed, nor does Isok. iv 28, where initiation at Eleusis is said to give men 'more agreeable expectations about death'. Polygnotos, how-ever, in the middle of the fifth century, painted the underworld in a manner taken by Pausanias (x 31.9) to show how the uninitiated are condemned to

---

[24] On the general idea of judgment after death in antiquity cf. S. G. F. Brandon, *The Judgment of the Dead* (London, 1967) 76–97. The theory of the transmigration of souls, 'up' or 'down' in the scale of sentient beings, was propounded by some philosophers (Pythagoras, Empedokles, Plato: cf. Dodds 143–56) but seems to have left no mark on popular literature.

[25] Cf. Rohde 238–40.

'carry water in a leaking jar'. Other cults and sects made, or were thought to make, promises comparable with those of Eleusis. Aristophon fr. 12.3–5 refers to the Pythagoreans as the only ones in the underworld who 'because of their piety' dine in the palace of Pluto. Philetairos fr. 18 satirizes this kind of promise: only those who die to the sound of music are permitted to enjoy the pleasures of sex in the underworld, while all the rest 'carry the leaky jar'.

Adeimantos's long speech in Plato *Rep.* 363C–365A, referring to the sacrifices, purifications and initiatory rites prescribed in some poems traditionally ascribed to Mousaios, Eumolpos and Orpheus (363C, 364E), describes a belief that by these quasi-magical means one could cancel a life of sin and escape out of the filth and futile labours to which the souls of sinners are doomed into the endless drunken feasting enjoyed by the righteous (363CD). This introduces us to a new element, the idea that virtue and vice determine the character of our afterlife, and to trace the history of this idea we must go back again to Homer, who in two passages of the *Iliad* (iii 278f., xix 259f.) envisages punishment after death for perjurers.[26] It is not until the first half of the fifth century (Aiskh. *Supp.* 228ff. and Pindar *Ol.* 2.58ff.) that we encounter a belief in a general judgment after death, not confined to perjury and not related to initiation. In the conversation between Kephalos and Socrates at the beginning of Plato's *Republic*, of which the 'dramatic date' falls within the Peloponnesian War, old Kephalos speaks vividly (330DE) of how as a man draws near to death he is troubled by 'stories . . . which he used to ridicule'. (A true Greek, Kephalos acknowledges the possibility that this anxiety belongs to the pathology of old age.)

Dem. xxiv 104: (*Timokrates' proposed law would give immunity to criminals*) . . . In my opinion—and even if what I say is felt to be going too far, I shall not shrink from saying it—it is precisely on this count that we ought to sentence him to death, so that he may make this law of his for the impious in the underworld and leave us, the living, to follow the just and righteous laws that we have.

The assumption here is that pious and impious, mixed together in the world we know, are separated in the underworld; cf. the 'two ways' of Philemon fr. 246.

Dem. xxv 52f. (*Aristogeiton has no friends*) . . . He goes about in company with those beings with whom the impious in the underworld are depicted by painters: Curse,

---

[26] Cf. Lloyd-Jones 87. To treat such Homeric passages as interpolations is greatly to underrate the extent to which different notions can coexist in the same culture, now one, now another, coming into prominence at any given time and place.

Abuse, Resentment, Strife, Contention. A man who is unlikely to find the gods of the underworld well disposed to him, but to be thrust among the impious because of the wickedness of his life—will you not punish this man . . .?

The reference to painters reminds us of Polygnotos's famous picture, which included the great sinners of legend (Paus. x 28.3f.). On the personifications of evil which in this passage play the role of devils under command of the gods of the underworld, cf. III.A.2, III.G.3.

Aristophanes' *Frogs* makes combined use of a belief in the general punishment of sins after death and of the claims made by the Eleusinian cult, in such a way that it is hard to disentangle one from the other. When Dionysos asks Herakles for directions to the palace of Pluto, Herakles tells him:

Ar. *Frogs* 145–63: Then you'll come to a lake of mud and an eternal flow of filth; and lying in it, anyone who ever wronged a guest, or pinched his money back while he was up a boy, or thrashed his mother, or hit his father in the face, or swore a false oath, or copied out a speech from a play of Morsimos . . . After that you'll be encompassed by the sound of pipes, and you'll see light, most beautiful, just as it is on earth, and groves of myrtle and happy companies of men and women, and clapping of hands . . . The initiated . . . who will tell you all you want to know, for they live right by the way, at the very doors of Pluto.

The cheating of a boy-prostitute and the copying of a passage from Morsimos are characteristic comic insertions into a list of traditional sins. If we want to know what happens in the underworld to virtuous men who have not been initiated or to parricides and perjurers who have, we cannot expect a completely lucid answer from a comic poet, nor do we get one.

ibid. 454–8: For we alone (*sc. of those in the underworld*) have sun and holy light, we who have been initiated and have conducted ourselves piously towards guests and ordinary people (*idiōtai*).[27]

This passage seems to imply a double qualification for admission to the company of the blessed—initiation *and* a virtuous life—which would leave those who have only one of the two qualifications somewhere in the shadows but clear of the mud. Possibly, however, the underlying assumptions are that (i) most virtuous Athenians would take the trouble to be initiated at Eleusis, (ii) initiation is an expiation of sins previously committed (note that the nervous man in Theophr. *Char.* 25.2 asks whether any of the passengers

[27] *Idiōtēs* is sometimes 'unskilled', 'lay', sometimes 'not holding office' or 'not active in political life', occasionally 'ordinary', e.g. Aiskhines iii 189, '*idiōtēs* in fortune' = 'not particularly well-off'. The passage in the *Frogs* probably connotes 'towards guests and also towards our fellow-citizens, even those who are not wealthy or distinguished'.

on board with him are uninitiated, not whether they are guilty of perjury), and (iii) initiation sets one on the path to virtue.[28]

It is natural enough that a belief in reward and punishment after death should give rise to an interest in purely ritual means of escaping the consequences of wrongdoing, but it is noteworthy that when epitaphs allude to the afterlife they never mention initiation or purification; they do, however, express the hope that the morality of the dead person's life secures honour in the world below.

GVI 1689: . . . and I so lived that no man had cause to charge me with a wrong; and received by the earth, I was held in honour by the gods below.

Reference to the 'place' (or 'chamber', or 'meadow') 'of the pious' becomes common in the third century B.C.; 'pious' is here a general term for virtue (cf. section 2 above).

The belief that the soul was judged in the underworld seems to have competed with an alternative notion that it went up into the sky.[29] The epitaph on the Athenians killed at Poteidaia speaks (GVI 20.4) of their souls as 'received by the sky' (aithēr, the upper air clear of the mists and fog which keep near the ground), while 'the earth received their bodies', a simple enough analogy with the upward escape and disappearance of breath and steam. But Ar. Peace 832–41 uses for humorous purposes the belief that we all become stars when we die, as some legendary personages did (e.g. the daughters of Erechtheus in Eur. fr. 65 [Austin], 71f.), and we should bear that in mind in interpreting GVI 1755, 'the aithēr has his soul' (cf. Eur. Supp. 532–7, Alexis fr. 158).

GVI 595: . . . [preserving (?)] her unforgettable character, [her body] lies [beneath] the earth, but her soul is on Olympos.

No other epitaph of the classical period speaks of a dead person's soul as going to the abode of the gods on Olympos. It could possibly be a poetic expression for 'sky', but little more than a century later we find clear cases of the soul's being described as going to join the gods (GVI 1176 [s. III, Egypt])[30] or the heroes (GVI 677 [s. III/II, Ephesos]). The two extremes of the

---

[28] A 'holy life' of a very strict kind, in consequence of some kind of initiation, is described in Eur. fr. 472.9–20. In Ar. Peace 277–9 there seems to be an implication that those initiated at Samothrace believed themselves to be able to avert evil by prayer more effectively than other people.

[29] Cf. Lattimore 26–31.

[30] In Xen. Cyr. viii 7.2 the vision which warns Kyros of his impending death says (literally), 'Now you will go away into the gods'. If Xenophon had intended us to believe

archaic underworld, Elysion for selected heroes and torment for the greatest sinners, have gradually encroached on the middle ground (the qualifications for entering each have been substantially lowered), until we are left with an upward way to Heaven for all the good and a downward way to Hell for all the bad.

Just as it was common to express doubts whether there can be any communication between the living and the dead (V.C.), so frank expression of doubt about the afterlife was acceptable in circumstances where we might least have expected it.[31]

*GVI* 747: . . . and I know that even beneath the earth, if the good have any privilege, honours are reserved for you above all, old nurse, in the realm of Persephone and Pluto.

ibid. 1491: . . . and if in the realm of Persephone any return (*kharis*, 'favour', 'gratitude'), is made for piety, Fortune has given you in death a share in that return.

Dem. lx 33f. (*on the Athenians killed at Khaironeia*): It could reasonably be said that they sit beside the gods below, with the same rank on the islands of the blessed as the valiant men of old. No one has actually seen that even the heroes of the past are so treated and brought back report of it; but we entertain the opinion, by a kind of divination, that those whom we, the living, have treated as worthy of honours here on earth receive those same honours in the afterlife also.

Hyp. vi 35ff. (*on the Athenians killed in the Lamian War*): And it is right to consider who in the underworld will greet the commander of these men. Do we not imagine that Leosthenes may see, greeting him with admiration, those who took the field against Troy? . . . 43: And, if there is any perception in the underworld, as we suppose, it is likely that those who saved from abolition the honours paid to the gods are looked after more than anyone by the divine powers.

The Periklean (Thuc. ii 35–46) and Lysian funeral orations say nothing at all about the afterlife, and the latter treats death essentially as the end of suffering for good and bad alike, justifying neither the hope of compensation nor the fear of penalty.

Lys. ii 73: What could be more distressing than that . . . they (*sc. the bereaved parents*) should have been robbed of all their hopes and . . . should now be pitied for those same sons for whom they were once envied, and that death should be more desirable to them than life?

that Kyros became a god, he would have said so, for he dwells long on the death-bed scene; I take him to mean by 'the gods' the realm which is governed solely by the gods, in which mortal man has no more power.

[31] Cf. Earp 11f.

Cf. Lyk. *Leokr.* 60, asserting that for the man who is unfortunate in life death puts an absolute end to his hopes of eventual happiness; Thuc. ii 43.5.

Lys. vi 20: And the god inflicts upon wrongdoers many fears and perils, so that many men before now have desired to die and so be rid of their sufferings.

This passage is noteworthy in that the speaker of Lys. vi makes considerable use of religious beliefs and fears; yet he abstains from threatening a continuation of punishment beyond death. Cf. IV.A.4, on suicide.

Treatment of death as the end of suffering (Soph. *Oed. Col.* 955, *Trach.* 1173, cf. Eur. *Ba.* 1363–6, *Supp.* 86f., 1000–8, Men. fr. 648) is at least as important, if we are concerned with the general character of Greek attitudes, as passages which speak of judgment and differentiation.[32] It is natural that tragedy should have so little to say about judgment after death, for it was much concerned with legends in which people atoned in life for the sins of their forebears, but we should note also that Thuc. ii 53.4, describing how the plague caused many people to do as they pleased, and 'neither fear of gods nor man-made laws restrained them', adds, 'since no one expected to live long enough to pay a penalty', as if fear of punishment after death were of no real importance. The survival of the soul after the death of the body was itself recognized to be a matter of speculation.[33] Xenophon portrays Kyros as saying to his sons on his death-bed (*Cyr.* viii 7.19–23): 'I have never believed that the soul ... dies ... or that it will be bereft of understanding ... *If, however, that is not so, but the soul stays in the body and dies with it,* then at least fear the gods ...'.

Anxiety for proper burial by one's own family and in one's own country, coupled with a desire to be favourably remembered by future generations, may well have been, for most people, a more powerful emotional force than speculation about the afterlife.

Dem. lvi 70: Rather than abandon my relations, if it were not possible for me to be saved by them, I would kill myself, so that at least I should be buried by them in my fatherland.

Hyp. i 20: ... when I am on trial and in danger not merely of death—for that is of least importance, to those who reckon rightly; the issue is whether I am to be cast beyond the borders of Attica and not even buried in my fatherland when I am dead.

Cf. *GVI* 545, on 'faultless good fame' bequeathed to one's grandchildren.

[32] For Greek notions of the soul-body relationship in general cf. Dodds 135–43; Lattimore 21–86.

[33] On the robust and mature attitude of the Greeks towards uncertainty cf. Rohde 242, 544.

Plato (*Laws* 721BC) comments on the intense desire which the human species feels for immortality; the individual, he says, attempts to satisfy this desire by marrying and begetting children, so as not to 'lie nameless when he is dead'. It was, after all, observable that some people could be praised and remembered after their death, whereas others were forgotten; hence Isok. xii 260 speaks of our perpetuation in the memory of posterity as our 'share in immortality'.[34] Speculation about rewards and punishments in accordance with a supernatural judgment after death no doubt appealed more to some moods and temperaments than to others.

## V.E. THE HUMAN CONDITION

### 1. Universal Principles

It was possible, as we have seen (III.A.3), to regard some tendencies of feeling and behaviour as determined by human nature. When the words 'nature' and 'natural' were not used, a given law or convention or pattern of behaviour was often alleged to be 'universal', 'common to all mankind' (e.g. Hdt. vii 136.2, immunity of heralds from violence; Isok. xviii 28, 34, the sanctity of contractual obligation; Lys. xxxi 1f., greater indignation against the rich delinquent than against the poor), or 'common to Greeks and *barbaroi*' (e.g. Dem. xliii 22, sons dearer to a man than nephews; Is. ii 24, adoption of children; Isok. xviii 27, contracts).[1] The implication was either that the accumulated experience of all mankind was superior to the perverse and ignorant ambitions of an individual, or that universality was a proof of divine origin (cf. V.D.3). 'Natural' law might be extended to the animal kingdom.

Lyk. *Leokr.* 132: He alone of all men has disregarded what is fixed within us all by nature and is the most signal characteristic of the brute creation. Do we not see how birds, best endowed of all creatures for speed, are willing (*sc. despite the ease with which they could fly to safety*) to die in defence of their own brood?

Of course, those who spoke so readily of 'Greeks and *barbaroi* alike' or of 'men and animals alike' were not well informed in anthropology or zoology, and the speaker relied on his hearers being no better informed. The appeal

[34] Cf. Lattimore 241–5; Hands 55f.

[1] Cf. Baldry, *Entretiens de la Fondations Hardt* viii (1961) 174–6 on the movement in the fifth century towards a recognition of the elements common to human nature.

to 'nature' might serve to suggest that if one acted in defiance of nature (and the absolute universality of a pattern of behaviour is apt to sound as if it were *in principle* demonstrable, however difficult in practice), one would be led to disaster, unhappiness or insanity by the sheer force of internal contradiction, as surely as a cart constructed in defiance of the rules of mechanics will fall apart or refuse to move.

## 2. Human Limitations

We have seen (III.A.2) that awareness of human ignorance and weakness, the unpredictability of the future and the great and sudden reversals to which our fortunes are subject was a strong current which ran all through Greek civilization and found expression at all levels, sophisticated and popular alike. From this awareness many positive conclusions were drawn.[2]

Occasionally, especially on the lips of comic characters, the conclusion may be, 'Eat, drink and be merry . . .' (e.g. Ameipsias fr. 22.4f., Amphis fr. 21, Philetairos fr. 7),[3] but on the serious plane the lessons are: pity and forgive others, for you too are human; restrain your ambitions, for you do not know what the morrow will bring; abstain from violence and cruelty against others for they are no less human than you; endure suffering, for you are not alone. What the Greeks called 'knowing oneself' is recognition of one's own limitations, and has little to do with 'examination of conscience' as a means of acquiring a conviction of one's own worthlessness. Xen. *Cyr.* vii 2.24f., represents Kroisos as admitting that he attacked the Persian Empire 'in ignorance of myself', but his disaster has taught him self-knowledge. Cf. Antiphanes fr. 289; Eur. fr. 799, the folly of 'undying anger in a mortal body'; Soph. *Aj.* 760f.

Dem. xv 21: Even if anyone is going to say that what has happened serves the Rhodians right, this is no occasion for exultation; the fortunate should always be seen to give the most generous consideration to the unfortunate, since the future is hidden from all men.

Dem. xx 161f.: Since we are human, all our proposals and legislation should be such as to incur no wrath (*literally, 'that no one may* nemesan', *a word particularly associated with divine resentment*); we must hope for good and pray the gods to give it to us, but we must reckon that anything can befall mankind (*literally, 'that everything is human'*) . . . The future is, after all, hidden from all men, and great consequences may proceed

---

[2] Cf. Adkins (2) 85–9.
[3] Similar sentiments are not unknown in epitaphs; cf. Lattimore 260f.

from small events. Therefore we should be moderate in our times of success, and it should be apparent to all that we look ahead to the future.

This is religious language (cf. Dem. xxv 37), but the same moral conclusion could be drawn from observation of human circumstances without explicit religious reference, e.g. Dem. xviii 308 and xxxix 14, literally 'many are the human things', i.e. 'anything can happen' (cf. Men. *Epitr.* 912, fr. 46, fr. 395; Xen. *Anab.* vii 6.11). Lys. xxiv 10, where a cripple complains of his prosecutor, 'He was neither afraid of fortune nor ashamed before you', poses the familiar question whether 'fortune' in translation should be personified and given a capital letter.

Dem. xxiii 42: It is reasonable that the unfortunate (*sc. those compelled by the guilt of homicide to go into exile*) should be pardoned by those who have no charge to make against them; no one can know who will one day have need of this pardon (*literally, 'for whom of all men one day it has been stored up'*), given that no individual knows beforehand what mischance will befall him.

Dem. xxiii 76: It is unholy and monstrous to allow an accused man, to whom fortune has given a share in the nature which is ours also, to be handed over (*sc. for punishment*) without trial.

Cf. Dem. xxii 62, the unfairness of making misfortune a reproach against anyone, since 'each of us fares in many ways otherwise than as he wishes'; Dem. xxiii 70, the adverb *anthrōpinōs*, 'humanly', used in connection with what the speaker regards as a humane provision of the law; Dem. lix 57, defending a course of action as 'human and reasonable calculation';[4] Demokritos B107a, 'It is right, since we are men, that we should not laugh at the mishaps of men but lament them'; Eur. *Hipp.* 615, 'Forgive me; it is to be expected that men should err'; Eur. *Supp.* 269f.; Eur. fr. 130, he never insulted the unfortunate, 'fearing to suffer himself'; *GVI* 1227 (s. VI), asking for an offering at the tomb, 'since death awaits you too'; Men. *Phasma* 27–32, the rich man should be distressed when grain is dear, for rich and poor alike are men;[5] Men. fr. 250.8f., 'However well-off you are, put no trust in that, and don't look down on us paupers'; Men. fr. 637; Soph. *Phil.* 501–6, Philoktetes explicitly using the instability of human fortunes as grounds of his appeal for pity ('When a man is enjoying a good life, *then* above all he should consider . . .'). Kyros in Hdt. i 86.6 is moved by

---

[4] Cf. Bolkestein 126–8. In Thuc. vii 77.4, literally 'having committed *anthrōpeios* acts, they suffered a punishment which was bearable', the point seems to be, 'They committed wrongs, which human beings normally do commit, but the gods did not punish them to an unbearable degree'.

[5] Cf. Hands 78–81.

reflection on the insecurity of all human rulers to repent that 'he, a man, is burning another man alive', and tries to save Kroisos from the fire. In Eur. *Supp.* 760–8 Adrastos has expressed surprise that Theseus himself washed the bodies of the heroes who had fallen before Thebes, a task which, says Adrastos, 'had *aiskhȳnē*', i.e. was of such a kind as to create in the performer a feeling of inferior status; but the messenger replies that there can be no disgrace in the performance of a task by one human being for another in misfortune, literally, 'In what way are one another's ills a disgrace for men?'

The theoretical defence of democracy also owed something to the emphasis laid on the common limitations of humanity; in Herodotos's narrative of events at Samos in the sixth century Maiandrios is made to say (iii 142.3), 'I did not approve of Polykrates when he acted as master over men like himself', i.e. '. . . fellow human beings' (cf. Eur. fr. 172).

Clear recognition that death is ultimately inescapable can be an incentive to courage in battle, and in fact improves the soldier's chances of simultaneous victory and personal survival (Xen. *Anab.* iii 1.43). The common injunction, 'Endure misfortune *bravely*', is accompanied by 'Endure misfortune because all men have endured it': Alexis fr. 150; Eur. *Hyps.* fr. 60.90–6, excessive grief over a lost child wrong because 'the generations of mortal men follow one another as do the crops'; Eur. *Iph. Aul.* 31f., advice to Agamemnon from an old servant that one must reckon on sorrows as well as joys; Eur. fr. 454, Merope reflects that innumerable women have lost husband and child; Men. fr. 650, 'Misfortune must be borne humanly'.

Awareness that so many others suffer is more than a consolation, it is a source of contentment to those who reach 'our common lot' (*GVI* 546, 931) and have to obey 'the law that is common to all' (*GVI* 1653) in tranquil old age, free from greater pain or sickness than the common run of mankind, and secure in the knowledge that there are grandchildren to carry on the family (*GVI* 498, 499, 545, 546, 1117, 1687, 1987).[7]

## 3. Identification with Others

Neither sharply defined boundaries nor clear lines of logical deduction are to be found within the complex of ideas which includes (i) a fear that the gods take pleasure in casting down the individual who has competed for power and wealth successfully against his fellows, (ii) a faith that the gods punish those who, in the pursuit of justice or vengeance, exact too much,

[6] Cf. Dihle 96      [7] Cf. Lattimore 211–13, 217f., 251–7.

(iii) a suspicion that there exists some kind of superhuman mechanism (personified as [e.g.] Adrasteia and Nemesis [Men. fr. 366], or impersonal) which ensures the downfall of the arrogant and vainglorious, (iv) a feeling that it is actually unjust not to 'do as you would be done by', (v) a spontaneous warmth of feeling for one's fellow-humans, generated by the recognition of our common suffering,[8] and (vi) a conviction that a good individual is able to restrain his appetites and express his sympathies in his interaction with others because he 'puts himself in their place' and sees the situation through their eyes.

Isok. xvi 12f., xix 51, Lys. i 1, xx 36, are all appeals by a speaker to the jurors to put themselves in his place, exploiting the argument, 'How would *you* feel if . . .?' Such an appeal does not always or necessarily have any discernible relation to the theme of mortal solidarity, but a speaker could make the connection.

And. i 57: For one should arrive at a rational conclusion about the case in a human way (*anthrōpinōs*), as if one were oneself involved in the disaster (*sc. in question*).

Cf. And. ii 6f.; and on 'disaster' cf. III.H.3.

Emphasis could be laid on an experience remembered or in prospect.

Aiskhines i 24: The legislator teaches younger men to respect their elders . . . and to honour old age, to which we shall all come, if we survive.

Eur. fr. 951: If fathers recognise that they were once young, they will be kindly and tolerant of the love-affairs of young men.

Theseus in Soph. *Oed. Col.* 560–7 pities Oedipus, 'since I too was brought up in a foreign land', and explicitly acknowledges the unpredictability of his own fortunes. Deianeira in Soph. *Trach.* 441–8 declares that from her own experience of the power of Eros she cannot blame her husband if he has fallen in love with Iole; that same Deianeira (303–6) was struck with fear on seeing the captives from Trachis and was moved to pray that no child of hers should ever be enslaved.

The speaker could also emphasize a particular analogy between his situation and someone else's.

Eur. *Hec.* 340f. (*Hekabe to her daughter*): Try to persuade Odysseus—and you have a case to make; for he too has children—to take pity on your fate.

Cf. Eur. *Iph. Taur.* 1401f., Orestes' prayer to Artenis that she should understand his love for his sister since she loves her brother Apollo; Eur. *Supp.* 54–9 (the chorus to Aithra), 'You too have borne a son'.

[8] Cf. Arist. *Rhet.* 1362b38f., 'It is said' that community of suffering unites people.

# VI
## PRIORITIES

### VI.A. INEQUALITY

*1. Relations and Friends*

All the moral attitudes discussed in Chapter IV can be regarded as attitudes to the relation between oneself and others. But which others? Given the structure of Greek society, it would be surprising if identical moral judgments were passed on the same dishonest, selfish or aggressive act irrespective of whether it was committed against a relative or a stranger, a man or a woman, a citizen or a foreigner, a freeborn man or a slave.[1] The Greeks might not always have agreed with us in calling two acts 'the same'; they would have been inclined to feel that our description stopped short of the complete act if it did not take into account the limits of the victim's expectations and the extent to which the act could affect his status in the eyes of others. Their tendency to classify people in terms of capacity and function made it easier for them to say, e.g., that a family can bear the loss of a woman more easily than the loss of a man (Eur. *Iph. Taur.* 1005f.).

It may be said in broad terms—but, as we shall see, refinement of the statement intoduces complications—that an Athenian felt that his first duty was to his parents (who merited 'honours on a par with the gods', Aiskhines i 28; cf. Antiphanes fr. 262, Men. fr. 600), his second to his kinsmen, and his third to his friends and benefactors; after that, in descending order, to his fellow-citizens, to citizens of other Greek states, to *barbaroi* and to slaves. It may be observed that his wife and children cannot easily be fitted into this hierarchy; on that question more will be said in VI.C.*1*.

Maltreatment of one's parents was regarded as a worse offence than maltreatment of anyone else: Dem. xxiv 60, 102, classify it with treason and

[1] Cf. Earp 31–3 on the 'concentric fortifications' around the individual in Greek society, and Pearson 136.

with some types of conduct which were punishable by execution or disenfranchisement, and Lys. xiii 91 speaks of it as meriting execution;[2] cf. Lys. xxxi 20–3. Many passages praise filial obedience.

Antiphanes fr. 263: To get the better of one's father is shameful; yield to him, and you have the honour of victory.

Lys. xix 55: I am now thirty years old, but I have never yet gainsaid my father in anything.

Cf. Antiphanes fr. 261, 'A man who at his age can still blush before his parents is not a bad man'; Dem. xl 13, 'While my father was alive I thought it wrong to oppose any of his wishes'; Dem. lviii 2, 58, prosecution undertaken in obedience to the wishes of the speaker's father; Eur. fr. 110, the special claim of a father upon his son; Eur. fr. 1064, the debt of gratitude owed to one's mother; Hdt. i 31, the story of Kleobis and Biton, who acted as draught animals in order that their mother should get to Delphi; Hdt. iii 52.5, implying that a man's anger against his father is shocking; Men. fr. 598, 'I can deal with anything else, but I can't look my father in the face if I'm doing wrong'; Men. fr. 601, the 'madness' of prosecuting one's father; Soph. fr. 850, 'Where parents yield to their children, that is not a city of *sōphrōn* men' (cf. Philemon fr. 139); Xen. *Mem.* ii 2.14, the gods' need to be asked for pardon if you have neglected your mother. Herakles in Soph. *Trach.* treats his son Hyllos as an object at his disposal, telling him to 'come near to me, even if it means that you die with me' (797f.) and—a 'small request' in Herakles' eyes, but horrifying to Hyllos—commanding him (1221–9) to marry Iole. Herakles, too, is imagined by Megara (Eur. *Her. Fur.* 290–3) as unwilling to save his children at the cost of their reputation (a matter on which they would not be consulted), and (ibid. 322–5) Amphitryon asks that he and Megara, if they must die, should at least be killed first, so that they might be spared the 'unholy sight' of the children's execution (again, no question of sparing the children an unholy sight).

Sympathetic characters in New Comedy take a more flexible view of the obedience owed to parents; Pamphile tells her father (Men. *Epitr.* 714f.) that if he tries to command her without persuading her (cf. Men. fr. 609) he will be 'no more a father, but a master', and Men. frr. 388 and 603f., recognize the reality of affection underlying a father's admonitions. Antigone in Soph. *Oed. Col.* 1439–43 sounds a note unusual for the fifth century in telling Oedipus that it is wrong of him to do any harm to his own son Polyneikes, no matter how great the provocation. Respect for parents merged into respect

---

[2] On the legal aspect of the matter cf. Harrison i 78.

for the older generation as a whole (e.g. Ant. iv a.6), but Greek society did not carry such respect to the point of serious irrationality; Xen. *Apol.* 20 observes that in matters of health we take the advice of doctors, not of our parents.

Injustice committed against a relation incurred greater reproach that the same injustice committed against a stranger, and litigation within the family was a matter of great embarrassment.

Ant. i 1: I am in a position of extraordinary difficulty ... because it is unavoidable that in bringing this prosecution I find myself at odds with those with whom it is least appropriate (*sc. to be at odds*), my step-brothers and their mother.

For the stock phrase '... whom it is least appropriate' cf. Eur. *Ba.* 26, *El* 1012, *Iph. Aul.* 487, all of strife or violence within the family, and Dem. xlviii 1.

Is. i 6: I do not regard the fact that I am unjustly put into peril as the greatest of the ills with which I have to deal, but rather that I am engaged in a contest against members of the family, whom it is not creditable even to requite; for I would regard the infliction of harm upon them in requital as no less a misfortune, seeing that they are related to me, than to suffer harm at their hands in the first place.

Is. v 29f.: Subsequently, not under compulsion (*sc. by court order*), but of our own accord, we gave him the town house ... And we made Dikaiogenes this gift not because of any virtue on his part, but to make it clear that we do not value material wealth more highly than we value our relations, even if they are of very bad character. For on the earlier occasion, when we had the opportunity to punish Dikaiogenes and deprive him of what he had in his possession, we had no desire to acquire anything of his, but were content to recover simply what belonged to us.

Cf. Is. ix 25, 'My opponent rates profit much higher than kinship'.

Lys. xxxii 2: My wife is their sister, Diogeiton's niece. I implored them both—at first, with success—to take the issue to the arbitration of our friends, for I thought it important that no one else should know of what they had done.

Cf. Aiskhines ii 93, iii 51, criticizing Demosthenes for bringing a trumped-up charge against his own cousin; Dem. xxix 2, deprecating a possible reproach that he had acted 'cruelly and harshly' dispossessing (in accordance with a court's verdict) his dishonest cousin; Dem. xlviii 2, 8, expressing sorrow and distaste at being 'forced' into litigation against relatives and (58) a pious hope that the verdict which the speaker desires will prove to be in the best interest of his crazy brother-in-law.

In Ar. *Thesm.* 209–12 the old man who is related by marriage to Euripides feels that it is up to him to volunteer, in order to save Euripides, for a mission fraught with danger and humiliation; what may seem to us abrupt and inadequately motivated would have been more easily understood, perhaps, by Aristophanes' audience (but we should note that Euripides, so far from taking the old man's help for granted, has originally approached someone else). On obligation to help relatives cf. Ar. *Lys.* 1130, Isok. xix 31, Soph. *El.* 322; also Thuc. ii 82.6, where priority given to political association over kinship is deplored as one of the evils of stasis. A speaker in Xen. *Smp.* 4.51 complains of those who 'genealogise' to prove themselves related to him when they want help. Oedipus in Soph. *Oed. Tyr.* 1430f., seems to suggest that it is *eusebēs* that one should see and hear the ills that have befallen one's own kin, but not *eusebēs* that everyone should know of them (he means, I think, that there is an obligation on a relative, but not on others). A modern reader may be struck by the fact that Antigone in Soph. *Oed. Col.* 1439–43 worries about the impending doom of her brother, but gives not a thought to the host of others whom he will lead to defeat and death.

In many of the passages cited in Chapter IV as illustrating types of virtuous action, the beneficiaries of the action were *philoi*, 'dear', to the agent; that is to say, they were relations or 'close to him', because he and they inherited this relationship from their fathers or because they had done things for him which made him grateful and affectionate towards them.[3] In the former case, self-sacrifice in the interests of a friend acquired the flavour of family obligation, and in the latter it was classifiable as justice. When the chorus in Eur. *Or.* 680f., urges Menelaos to help those who implore him for help, it might sound, if we detached the passage entirely from its context, as if they were recommending him to grant a request simply because the petitioner needs it; but Orestes, who is that petitioner, has made it plain in the preceding speech (665f.) that 'it is right for *philoi* to help *philoi* in time of trouble'. Menelaos's pity for Agamemnon (Eur. *Iph. Aul.* 477–92) and for the fate which threatens Iphigeneia, although it remains a striking instance of pity overriding an initial insistence on justice, is prompted in part by reflection on the tie of kinship. The magnanimity of Satyros at Philip's banquet (Dem. xix 193–5) in asking for the release of the daughters of his friend, Apollophanes of Pydna, is certainly to be admired, since Philip was in the mood to grant

[3] Cf. Bolkestein 119–21; Hands 33 observes that *philiā* does not necessarily imply affection. On some aspects of the relation between archaic and philosophical notions of *philiā* cf. A. W. H. Adkins, ' "Friendship" and "Self-Sufficiency" in Homer and Aristotle', *Classical Quarterly* N.S. xiii (1963) 30–45. It should be noted that some curiosities in Aristotle's treatment of *philiā* may be due to the fact that he is attempting to analyse philosophically a phenomenon to which philosophy may not have much to contribute.

him a purely selfish request, yet he pitied the girls not simply because their fate was pitiable, but because they were his friend's daughters. It may often be the case that what appears to be a commendation of generalized benevolence and generosity in fact refers to conduct towards *philoi*. Equally, we must recognize that the motivation of such conduct was often a regard for its possible consequences. When the creditor in Ar. *Clouds* 1218f., grumbles that by demanding his money back from Strepsiades he will 'become an enemy of a fellow-demesman' he is not obeying an absolute command, 'Thou shalt not quarrel with a fellow-demesman', but thinking of the embarrassment occasioned by ill-feeling between people who are thrown into frequent contact. If I say 'It's a bad thing to quarrel with a colleague', I *might* imply that one has a special obligation towards colleagues, but I do not think that that would be the thought uppermost in my mind.

There are some interesting passages in which it is suggested that one may take the initiative in creating a bond of affection by generosity, without any sense of fulfilling an existing obligation.

Men. *Dysk.* 805–12: For that reason, father, I think that as long as you have possession of money, you should use it generously (*gennaiōs*) yourself and come to the help of everyone else, and make as many people as possible secure through your agency. For that is something that lives on for ever; if at any time you meet with misfortune, that same help will come back to you from them. A friend who is there before your eyes is much better than money which you keep tucked away and buried.

The passage is introduced with a reminder that wealth is a matter of luck, attending some today, others tomorrow (cf. IV.B.*1*), even though the man to whom it is addressed is an 'unsurpassable farmer' (ibid. 774f.) who presumably does not owe everything to mere luck. The reason offered for generosity is prudential: 'Create friends, so that there will always be someone to help you if you need help'; but that is not a bad reason, especially when material gifts are viewed as a species of virtuous action in general. The same reason is given in a famous passage of the Periklean funeral speech, but somewhat overlaid by the greater emphasis on magnanimity.

Thuc. ii 40.4f.: When it comes to acting for others (*aretē*),[4] we are different from most nations, for we acquire friends not in consequence of what others do for us, but by doing it for them. He who takes the initiative is a firmer friend . . ., whereas he who is under an obligation to repay is slow to do so . . . We alone confer benefits not after calculation of our own interest but boldly, in the confidence inspired by freedom.

[4] Here, as in ii 51.5 and v 105.4, Thucydides treats the good man as the man who accepts danger and suffering in order to help those to whom he is under an obligation.

(The argument is sophisticated, and the words omitted before 'He who . . .' in the translation present grammatical difficulty, but their tenor is clear.)

Positive assertion that a good man should give help where it is needed, even if no claim can be based on kinship—and, presumably, even where there is no calculation of future advantage—is uncommon, but it occurs in Eur. *Iph. Aul.* 983f.; cf. the rejection of the claim of friendship in favour of the claims of merit in Eur. *Hipp.* 614, 'No dishonest man is *philos* to me'. In Eur. *Supp.* 291f., Theseus is surprised at his mother's pity for the suppliants, and says 'They are nothing to do with you'; but she makes him change his mind.

## 2. Merit

The speaker of Lys. x, prosecuting on enemy for slander, draws a distinction, perhaps initially in a jocular rather than an indignant tone, which would sound unusual in a modern court.

> Lys. x 1–3: In the course of that trial he said that I had murdered my own father. Now, if he'd said that I'd murdered *his* father, I wouldn't mind, because I thought his father a worthless person . . . But as things are, I think it would be shameful if I did not exact satisfaction from a man who has said such a thing about my father, who was of great value to you and to the city.

In Attic law, as in modern law, a murderer was a murderer whether the person whom he killed was 'valuable' or 'worthless'; no legal code can afford to give a potential lawbreaker encouragement to assess the relative value of those whom he contemplates harming or to argue in court about the point on the scale between good and bad at which his victim should be placed. Christian religious teaching has also discouraged us from sticking price-tickets on people, even from entertaining opinions about the destiny of their souls. Our ordinary habits of thought, however, do not seem to be deeply affected either by constitutional insistence on equality under the law or by religious insistence on our equality in the sight of God. One man's death saddens us for years, another's brings us nothing but relief and satisfaction. It is never easy to feel as sorry about a crime committed against a bad person or a misfortune which befalls him, as when the same thing happens to a good person.[5]

[5] Aristotle, in the passage cited in IV.D.*1* n. 3, is concerned with how one ought to act; I am speaking of how one actually feels, which on any given occasion may be very far, in one direction or another, for the Aristotelian mean.

Equality under the law was a essential feature of democracy.[6] Explicit criticism of equality as 'unjust' if it treats good and bad people alike is found in writers of anti-democratic sentiment, e.g. Isok. vii 21, Xen. *Cyr.* ii 2.18; forensic oratory composed from a democratic standpoint agrees in effect, but does not criticize equality explicitly, and it means by 'good' 'loyal to the democratic state'.

Lyk. *Leokr.* 93: It would be intolerable if the same prophecies were made to the pious and to malefactors.

Cf. Lys. xxxi 18f., enunciating the principle not that it is wrong to maltreat the poor and old, but that it is wrong to maltreat good citizens when they have become poor and old.

As we might expect in the light of considerations mentioned in V.B.5, the merit of a human being could be assessed by appraisal of his or her status as an object rather than as a moral agent: Hdt. i 38.2, Kroisos does not regard his deaf and dumb son as a real son; Hdt. iii 73.1, the indignation of the Persians at being ruled by a man whose ears have been cut off; Hdt. iii 125.2, Polykrates, a man of such proud achievement and ambition, did not deserve so miserable a death. On the other hand, Dem. xix 283, xlv 58–60, 81 deploy to good effect indignation against adult male citizens who have allegedly maltreated old women or children, and the offence is made to rest on the cowardice and arrogance of such behaviour (cf. IV.A.5), not on the merit or status of the victims. To our way of thinking the young man in Ar. *Wealth* 1042–96, who, as soon as he becomes financially independent, jettisons and mocks the old woman who has kept him as her lover, behaves very badly, but the other characters in the play do not seem to think so (1084f., is no more than a whimsical admonition); presumably an ugly old woman who bought means of continuing her enjoyment of sex was not treated with the same respect as an ugly old man who bought a concubine.

## 3. Foreigners

Commendations of the dead in epitaphs rarely specify loyalty to relatives and friends, but prefer 'he distressed no one' (IV.D.2), etc. On occasion an expression such as 'a tomb for all mortals to see' (*GVI* 1535.3f.) seems to

---

[6] Cf. G. Vlastos, ''Ἰσονομία πολιτική', in (ed. J. Mau and E. G. Schmidt) *Isonomia* (Berlin, 1964) 1–35.

look beyond the fellow-citizens of the dead person. But 'all men' appears in a rather curious context in one epitaph of the mid-fifth century.

GVI 630 (s. V): This memorial is set over the body of a very good man. Pythion, from Megara, slew seven men and broke off seven spear-points in their bodies . . . This man, who saved three Athenian regiments . . ., having brought sorrow to no one among all men who dwell on earth, went down to the underworld felicitated in the eyes of all . . .

The composer of this epitaph would not have denied that Greek enemies of Athens belonged to the genus 'men who dwell on earth' or that to stab a man to death is to bring distress to him and his family; it simply did not occur to him that there was any incongruity in applying the formula 'brought sorrow to no one' to a distinguished killer. Although no comparable incongruity is furnished by fourth-century inscriptions or literature, we may reasonably suspect that 'everyone' and 'no one' carry the implication 'of the Athenian citizen-body' unless a wider application is specified.

The starvation of the Megarians in consequence of the devastation inflicted annually on their territory by Athens from 431 onwards provided extensive material for comedy. In Ar. *Peace* 481f., the Megarian help in the rescue of Peace is rejected because they were, so to speak, the start of the war, and because their efforts, as they strain on the ropes with the toothy grimace of men who have become all bone and no flesh are useless. In *Ach.* 719–835 Dikaiopolis is quite prepared, for his own advantage, to welcome a Megarian to his private market, but he gets plenty of fun out of Megara's predicament, including the frantic gobbling of the Megarian children to whom he offers figs (797–810). A large part of the explanation of such humour is to be sought in the fact that the Megarians, Athens' neighbours in the direction of the Peloponnese, were despised and hated. It was possible to evoke pro-Spartan sentiment at Athens by eloquent reminders (cf. Ar. *Lys.* 1122–61) of mutual benefactions in the past, but there seems to have been no way of evoking pro-Megarian sentiment. The expression 'Melian hunger' is used in Ar. *Birds* 186, not much more than a year after the end of Melos, as a jocular term for the reduction of a city by starvation; the passage may be a faint reflex of the anger aroused at Athens in 416 by the stubbornness of Melian resistance. A peculiarly distasteful passage of Isokrates (xii 70, cf. 89) argues in defence of the Athenian empire that the victims of acts (such as the massacre of the Melians) with which Athens was reproached were only 'little islands of which most Greeks hardly knew the names'. Xenophon's reference (*Hell.* ii 2.10) to the hybristic behaviour of Athens towards 'citizens of little places' has quite a different ring; Thucydides' horror (vii 29.4–30.3) at the fate of Mykalessos may owe something to the fact that the Mykalessians were Greeks killed by *barbaroi*.

A kind of scale of valuation of those who were not members of the Athenian citizen-body is indicated in the following passage:[7]

Dem. ix 30f.: Whatever the Greek world suffered at your hands or at Sparta's, at any rate its wrongs were inflicted by genuine sons of Greece; one might have regarded this in the same way as if a legitimate son, on inheriting great wealth, managed it in some respect discreditably and wrongly ... But if a slave or a substitute child spoiled what did not belong to him, why! how much more outrageous and unpardonable everyone would have said that was! Yet they do not feel like that about Philip and his present actions, although he is not a Greek, nor does he have any connection with Greece; nor is he even a *barbaros* of a famous nation, but a damned Macedonian—a place from which one used not to be able even to buy a decent slave.

Xenophon's soldiers (Xen. *Anab.* iii 1.30) rejected with contumely the advice of a certain Apollonides, who had passed himself off as a Boeotian, when it was observed that he had pierced ears like a Lydian. Nikias in Thuc. vi 11.7 tries to turn the Athenians against the Sicilian expedition by dismissing the Segstans, who had asked Athens for help, as mere *barbaroi*; in Xen. *Anab.* i 3.5, v 5.8f., v 6.1, vii 1.29, the duty of Greek to help Greek against *barbaros* is taken for granted. But we must be very cautious in speaking of Greek belief in 'natural' enmity towards *barbaroi* (despite Pl. *Rep.* 470C); Alkibiades in Thuc. vi 18.2 rejects Nikias's disparagement of Segesta, arguing that it is not in Athens' interest to trouble about the racial classification of those who ask her for help, and Hdt. i 1–4, Isok. iv 183f., Xen. *Ages.* 7.7 view the relation between Greeks and *barbaroi* in terms of a long history of grievance and retaliation rather than in terms of a 'natural' antagonism in our sense of the word.

However panhellenic sentiment might be exploited for political or philosophical purposes,[8] Attic law put the foreigner, whether Greek or not, at a serious disadvantage *vis-à-vis* the citizen.[9] A citizen could not be subjected to examination under torture (Lys. xiii 27), and the proposal made in 415 to suspend this rule in order to investigate the mutilation of the herms (And. i 43) is a good indication of the unusual mood induced by that

[7] It is very important that this passage should not be mistaken for a historian's judicious assessment of Greek sentiment at any period.

[8] Cf. F. W. Walbank, 'The Problem of Greek Nationality', *Phoenix v* (1951) 41–60.

[9] Cf. MacDowell 20–2, 69, 126f., on the problem of the penalties for murdering a foreigner or slave.

mysterious sacrilege. Foreigners, however, could be tortured: Aiskhines iii 223f., Ant. v 29, 49f., and Lys. xiii 54 provide examples.[10] A foreigner, male or female, was forbidden to enter into a contract of marriage with an Athenian, on pain of being sold into slavery (Dem. lix 17); the law (cited in §16) provided a fine for the Athenian man who married a foreign woman, and disenfranchisement for the man who gave her in marriage.[11]

The citizen may have felt that the general tenor of the law was behind him if he wanted to intimidate or oppress a foreigner, and that neither the courts of law nor public opinion in general would be likely to treat citizen and foreigner as if they had the same value. Indeed, in Ar. *Knights* 347, 'winning a piddling little lawsuit against a resident alien' contains two contemptuous elements, contrasting not only with a more important lawsuit but also with a lawsuit against a citizen. The attitude of Dem. 1 26 towards freedmen and foreigners newly enfranchised suggests that they too might fare ill in the courts. Aiskhines i 43 represents the young Timarkhos as 'rescued' by Misgolas and Phaidros (their interest in him was not platonic) from the company of some foreigners who were apparently very frightened that they might be accused of corrupting an Athenian youth.[12] In the same speech (i 195) Aiskhines recommends Athenian pederasts to 'turn to visiting and resident foreigners', so that they can indulge their tastes 'without harm to the city'.

Isok. xvii 34: Considering that he was willing to take such a risk for trivial gain . . . it is hardly surprising that with so great a profit in prospect they falsified a document deposited with a foreigner.

In this passage the term 'foreign *anthrōpos*', almost 'a mere foreigner', is noticeable; cf. Dem. lii 3 (a native of Herakleia) and 29 (a metic), but contrast, in the same speech (Isok. xvii) the neutral *anēr* in §20, 'a man of Pherai', and §42, 'a man of Delos'. The contrast appears with perfect clarity in Aiskhines iii 168 ∽ 233, passages which speak respectively of 'the democratic *anēr*' and 'the oligarchic *anthrōpos*'.

Categorization of people and the placing of different categories at different points on a scale of moral claim was counteracted (cf. section 2 and

---

[10] In torturing an Argive suspected of complicity in the murder of Phrynikhos (Thuc. viii 92.2) the obligarchy of 411 was not acting contrary to democratic practice.

[11] Cf. Lacey.

[12] Aiskhines says 'a freeborn youth', but since the foreigners could not have been charged with any offence if he too proved to be foreign (cf. i 195), I assume that 'Athenian' is taken for granted in the context, which is not difficult, since Timarkhos was in fact an Athenian.

IV.A.5) by the feeling that it was shameful, cowardly, arrogant or insensitive to exploit the strength of one's own position in order to triumph over the weak. It was possible for Diodoros (Dem. xxii 54) to arouse indignation against Androtion for ruthlessness in exacting arrears of levy from 'the unhappy resident foreigners', whom you have treated more high-handedly than your own slaves'. The prosecutor of Aristogeiton describes with considerable pathos (Dem. xxv 56f.) how Aristogeiton struck, threatened and persecuted a foreign woman resident at Athens who had formerly been his concubine and had sheltered and helped him when he was trying to escape from the city. She was his benefactress, and his treatment of her showed cruel ingratitude; their difference of status is irrelevant to the point which the speaker is making.

Cosmopolitan sentiment appears occasionally.

Eur. fr. 902: I reckon the good man *philos*—however far away in the world he lives, and even if I have never set eyes on him.

Cf. Eur. *Phaethon* fr. 163 (Diggle); Men. fr. 475, 'No one is alien to me if he is good'; Xen. *Mem.* ii 1.13, the philosopher Aristippos 'a visitor everywhere' (*sc.* and a citizen of no city).[13] Perhaps the nearest that an orator comes to recognizing sentiment of this kind is Lyk. *Leokr.* 39, 'Even a foreigner would pity Athens . . .'.

## 4. Slaves and Freedmen

With the derogatory use of *anthrōpos*, rather than *anēr*, in referring to foreigners we may compare And. ii 23, 'I see that you grant citizenship to slaves' ('slave *anthrōpoi*') 'and foreigners from all over the place', where the implication is '*A fortiori*, you should honour men like me, citizens of citizen family, who have deserved well of you'; for similar argument, *a fortiori* cf. Ar. *Frogs* 692–4, Lyk. *Leokr.* 41, Lys. xx 19, xxxiv 3. The derogatory *anthrōpos* is conspicuous also in Lys. iv, where the speaker is prosecuted for wounding with homicidal intent in a quarrel over a slave-prostitute, and he makes good use of the difference in status between a citizen and such a person; §9, 'My adversary has no shame . . . in pretending to have been seriously injured because of a wretched prostitute' ('prostitute *anthrōpos*') and §19, 'I resent it very much that I am endangered on a most serious charge through' a

[13] Cf. Baldry on the negative aspects of Cynic cosmopolitanism.

(*literally*) 'prostitute and slave *anthrōpos*'. We may recall Menelaos's indignation in Eur. *Andr.* 648f., that Peleus should be at odds with him' because of a
*barbaros* woman' (i.e. the captive princess Andromakhe). Even a slave highly
regarded by his master is *anthrōpos* (Dem. lv 34), not *anēr*. In Eur. *Mel.
Desm.* 38 (von Arnim) some slaves escape because the heroes Boiotos and
Aiolos are unwilling to kill them with 'free swords', i.e. swords used in
fighting between freeborn warriors.

The institution of slavery was common to Greeks and *barbaroi*, and in
respect of shame, indignation and moral reactions in general the distinction
between freeborn people and slaves was the most profound (cf. III.E.3).[14]
One of its manifestations is the indignation which Lys. xiii 64 tries to arouse
against Agoratos, indignation that the Athenian people should have been so
injured by a man of servile birth. In everyday life it seems that a master
could vilify, strike or beat his slave with impunity. Dem. viii 51 makes the
general point that the free man is deterred from wrongdoing above all by
the fear of reproach and shame, but the slave only by the fear of bodily
pain. The essence of hybris was 'treating free men as slaves' (Dem. xxi 180,
cf. 71f.). Old Comedy extracted a good deal of rough humour from the
flogging and bullying of slaves, and although Aristophanes criticized (*Peace*
743–7) the insipidity of the witticisms associated therewith, he himself makes
a slave battered by the drunken Philokleon in *Wasps* 1292–6 felicitate tortoises
on their thick shells; cf. the harassing, bullying and pecking of Peisetairos's
slave in *Birds* 1323–9, and the inattentive slave remains a comic cliché for a
very long period (Ar. *Lys.* 184, 426f.; Theokritos 2.18–20, 15.27–31, Herodas
4.41–51). A curious scene in Ar. *Lys.* 1216–24 appears to base its humorous
appeal entirely on the grossest bullying of slaves by drunken citizens.[15]

In later comedy a master's bark tends to be worse than his bite, but Men.
*Perinthia* 1ff., evidently shows us a slave, who has sought refuge at an altar,
about to be forced to leave it by the building of a fire close to him.

Extraction of testimony from slaves under torture and offers and challenges
to exchange slaves for such examination were a normal part of Athenian
litigation.[16] As sometimes happens, a comic treatment of this subject reveals
by exaggeration an underlying attitude distinguishable from the main comic
point of the passage.

[14] On the whole question of attitudes to slavery at Athens cf. Ehrenberg 165–91;
W. L. Westermann, *The Slave Systems of Greek and Roman Antiquity* (Philadelphia,
1955) 22–7; Finley, I.F.3 n. 14, and R. Schlaifer, 'Greek Theories of Slavery from
Homer to Aristotle', in (ed. M. I. Finley) *Slavery in Classical Antiquity: Views and Con-
troversies* (Cambridge, 1960) 93–132.
[15] Cf. Dover (2) 10–12.                          [16] Cf. Harrison ii 147–50.

Ar. *Frogs* 615–24. XANTHIAS: And I'll make you a really generous offer. Take my slave here and put him to the torture; and if you find me guilty of any crime, you can arrest me and execute me. AIAKOS: How am I to torture him? XANTHIAS: Any way. Tie him to a ladder, hang him up, flog him with a whip, flay him, rack him, and pour vinegar up his nose, too; load bricks on to him, anything else you like ... AIAKOS: That's fair. And I can tell you, if I maim him by beating him, you'll get a sum in compensation. XANTHIAS: No, no, that's quite all right! Just take him off and torture him!

Despite assertions in the orators (e.g. Dem. xxx 37; cf. I.B.*3*) that torturing slaves was an exceptionally reliable way of getting at the truth, Antiphon had pointed out in the fifth century (v 31) that a slave was likely to say whatever seemed likely to please his interrogators and so end his torture; it would also seem obvious that he might take the opportunity to incriminate his master in revenge for past maltreatment. This seems to be assumed by the speaker of Lys. vii, who regards slaves as 'by nature implacably hostile to their masters' (35; cf. Dem. xxi 45f., III.B.*2*), and the same man argues that he would not have dared to commit an offence with the connivance of his slaves, for this would have given them a hold over him ever after (16). Some characters in Menander resented a slave who 'got above himself', or thought that it was necessary for the good ordering of a household that its slaves should be at odds with one another; but what kind of characters, the citations (frr. 562, 784) do not reveal. Xen. *Hiero* 4.3, 10.4, speak as if a state of perpetual war existed between masters and slaves, the masters (many of whom, says Xenophon, have been murdered by their slaves) 'serving as an unpaid bodyguard to one another'.

Both Aiskhines i 17 and Demosthenes xxi 46 state that the law prohibited hybris against slaves (cf. Hyp. fr. 120, Lyk. fr. 74). Neither Aiskhines nor Demosthenes expects the jury to be familiar with this legal fact or to hear of it without surprise; what exactly constituted hybris against a slave, we do not know, and no doubt it would have been difficult to consider assault on a slave even as prima facie hybris unless he belonged to someone else (cf. the grumble of [Xen.] *Ath.* 1.10 that the Athenian citizen, unlike the Spartan, is not feared by foreigners or by other citizens' slaves). But Aiskhines' exposition of the reason for the law is interesting.

The legislator was not concerned to protect slaves, but through a desire to accustom you to abstaining entirely from hybris against free persons he added a prohibition of hybris against slaves.

Demosthenes' explanation is similar—the legislator was concerned with the disposition and habituation of the agent, without regard for the status of the victim—but he omits Aiskhines' revealing disclaimer, 'He wasn't concerned to protect slaves, of course'. Some light is thrown on the matter by a brief allusion in Dein. i 23 to an Athenian citizen condemned to death because he 'committed hybris against the Rhodian lyre-girl at the Eleusinia', and another because he established an Olynthian girl in a brothel. The former of these two cases presumably involved, or was made to seem to involve, a religious offence, and the political sympathy of the Athenians for the Olynthians sold into slavery by Philip obviously had something to do with the second case. Demosthenes' horrific story (xix 196–8) of how Aiskhines at a drunken party had tried to force an Olynthian captive woman to sing and ordered her to be flogged when she could not obey depends for its effect in part upon her being a freeborn woman who had become a slave through her city's defeat in war; cf. Demosthenes' allegation (xix 209) that Philokrates brought back to Athens freeborn Olynthian women for his pleasure. *Eleutheros*, 'free', 'freeborn', carries a strong emotional charge whenever it is desired to arouse indignation; Aiskhines i 107, on how Timarkhos during his period of office on Andros 'displayed unheard-of licentiousness towards the wives of freeborn men'; Dein. i 19, on the feelings of the Thebans towards Macedonian rule; Lys. iii 23, 'knocking down the door and coming in, by night, upon freeborn women'.[17] A slave born into captivity, or belonging to a *barbaros* nation in which what the Greeks regarded as freedom was not recognized, could not benefit from the restraint which regard for free birth must often have imposed on Athenians who had power over foreigners and captives. Nevertheless, it is interesting to see the terms in which Aiskhines rebuts Demosthenes' charge concerning his outrageous behaviour towards the Olynthian woman.

Aiskhines ii 5: If anyone . . . believes that I have done such a thing to the person of *anybody*, let alone a freeborn person (*literally, 'not only to a free body, but even to any body you like'*), I do not think the rest of my life worth living, and if . . . I do not show that this charge too is false . . ., even if I am shown innocent on every other charge, I consent to execution as my appropriate penalty.

Careful and solicitous treatment of slaves was probably as common as careful maintenance and handling of a car nowadays, and similarly motivated (e.g. Xen. *Oec.* 7.37, 9.5),[18] but gratitude to a loyal slave was a respectable motive for releasing him or her from slavery.

[17] In Theophr. *Char.* 11.2 the 'disgusting' man likes to expose his genitals to freeborn women; presumably it is less objectionable if the women are slaves.

[18] Demokritos B270 expresses the opinion that a master employs slaves as he employs different parts of his own body, for different purposes; but this applies, of course, only

Dem. xlvii 55f.: With my wife was an old woman who had been my nurse. She was a loyal and faithful person, and my father had set her free. When she was freed, she married; but since her husband died, and she was an old woman with no one to look after her, she came back to us. I could not possibly see my former nurse, any more than the slave who had looked after me when I was a boy, living in want . . .

Cf. Lys. v 5, a generalization which assumes that slaves hope for freedom as a reward for loyal service; Dem. xxxvi 14, a particular case, 'They set them free in return for their great good services'; Aristophon fr. 14; Men. *Epitr.* 538f., Onesimos reminds Habrotonon that if Kharisios believes her to be the mother of his child he will set her free;[19] Men. *Perik.* 982f., Polemon promises Doris freedom in return for her loyalty and good advice. We do not know half as much as we would like to know about the circumstances, methods and scale of manumission in classical Athens,[20] but the fact of manumission, which constitutes the really important difference between a slave-stem and a caste-system, tells us something about attitudes to slaves and slavery. Casual allusions tell us by implication quite a lot more, e.g. Dem. xlix 55, 'I asked if Aiskhrion was still a slave', and the formula of entreaty by one slave to another, 'So (*sc. may you be*) free!' (Men. *Epitr.* 266f.). Aiskhines iii 41 speaks of citizens who made the freeing of some of their slaves the subject of public proclamation at the Dionysia, on a level with honours paid to themselves by their phylai or demes, as if manumission were something of which a master would boast in order to be commended for his generosity.

Not surprisingly, a freedman might try to conceal the fact that he had been a slave; cf. Dem. xxiv 124, 'When bad and ungrateful slaves are freed, they feel no gratitude to their master for their freedom, but hate him more than anyone, because he knows that they were slaves'. Prejudice could be excited against a freedman, to judge from Apollodoros's attempt to do so (Dem. xlv 73f.), and a freedman would naturally be nervous of involvement of litigation against a citizen.

All things considered—particularly the exploitation of violence against slaves in Old Comedy—what may strike us most in the comic portrayal of the relation between master and slave is the extent to which the master

---

to purposes which the master could not accomplish without tedium, fatigue or practical difficulty.

[19] It is an interesting aspect of Habrotonon's character that she needs to be reminded; there is no doubt (372f.) of her passionate wish to be free, which finds expression once it has been encouraged.

[20] Cf. Rädle 16–26 and Harrison i 181f.

confides in his slave and the freedom of speech which he tolerates.[21] This portrayal receives a certain confirmation from Dem. ix 3, 'You can find plenty of slaves here at Athens who have more freedom to speak their minds than citizens have in some other states'. Resentment of outspokenness is not common; in Men. *Epitr.* 1101 Smikrines is indignant at the sermon preached to him by Onesimos, but Smikrines is not the most sympathetic of characters.

Ar. *Wealth* 18–27. KARION: I just can't keep quiet, you must tell me why we'r following this man, master; I'll keep on bothering you till you do. You can't hit me while I'm wearing a crown (*They are on their way back from consultation of an oracle*). KHREMYLOS: I know, but if you make a nuisance of yourself I'll take your crown off, to hurt you more. KARION: Rubbish! I'm not going to stop until you tell me who this man is. I know very well I'm as loyal a slave to you as you can have. KHREMYLOS: Well, I won't keep it from you. I regard you as the loyallest of my slaves—and the biggest rogue!

The conversation between Myrrhine and her old slave Philinna in Menander's *Farmer* is a striking example of an affectionate and confiding relationship; Myrrhine calls Philinna *philē* (87), and Philinna calls her 'child'.[22] Recognition of the fact that the boundary between freeborn and servile does not always coincide with the boundary between virtue and vice (cf. III.E.3), and— even more important, perhaps, in the later fourth century—reflection on the mutability and impartiality of fortune (e.g. Men. fr. 681, 'The god is the same for all, bond and free alike') may well have disposed public opinion in favour of humane relationships with slaves to an extent which the letter of the law cannot, in the nature of things, disclose.


## VI.B. THE STATE AND THE INDIVIDUAL


*1. Democracy and Law*

We tend nowadays to associate democracy with tolerance, forgetting that a majority is quite capable of making and enforcing much more repressive laws than an easy-going autocrat. We also tend to imagine that democracies are by nature lenient in punishment and reluctant to take the lives of their

---

[21] Cf. Dover (2) 204–8 on slaves in Old Comedy, particularly Aristophanes' later plays.

[22] So in tragedy (e.g. Aiskh. *Cho.* 323) a slave-chorus may address a prince as 'child'.

own citizens. If we have made this assumption, the conduct of the classical Athenian democracy will sometimes surprise us. Certainly, speakers like to contrast Athenian mildness and leniency with the alleged cruelty and severity of oligarchic states; cf. Dem. xxii 64 on 'imitating the *ēthos* of the city'. Dem. xxiv 192f., expresses the view that the laws of a democracy should be 'mild and kindly' in the field of private litigation, but 'severe and harsh' towards the conduct of those who engage actively in politics; there is an obvious analogy with the military principle of leniency to the private soldier and severity towards officers (cf. Xen. *Ages.* 11.5). The words *dēmotikos* and *dēmokratikos*, 'democratic', imply generous treatment of the ordinary individual. In comedy there is a good deal of humorous play with these words: Antiphanes fr. 192.9, 'not democratic' = 'unfair'; Ar. *Frogs* 952, the claim of 'Euripides' that it was democratic of him to write parts for women and slaves in the portrayal of tragic legends; Ar. *Eccl.* 411, of a speech proposing that tailors should be required to give away cloaks to the poor; Euboulos fr. 72.1f., of parasites; Philemon fr. 4.3, of brothels (the establishment of which is attributed to Solon).

There does not seem to have been any limit, however, to the community's rights over the property and lives of the individuals who composed it. The death penalty was, naturally enough, paid by traitors (Lyk. *Leokr.* 130), but it was also prescribed by law for burglars caught in the act (Aiskhines i 91), for the theft of anything consecrated to a deity (Dem. xiii 14, Isok. xx 6), for conveying a cargo of grain to any destination but Athens (Lyk. *Leokr.* 27, cf. Dem. lvi 41), and for tampering with the sealed urns containing the names of men proposed as judges at a festival (Isok. xvii 34); cf. Lyk. *Leokr.* 64–7. We hear in the fourth century of sentence of death passed upon those who bribed a juror or accepted a bribe while acting as jurors (Aiskhines i 87f.), made a deliberately misleading promise to the assembly (Dem. xx 135; cf. Ar. *Frogs* 1068, 1086), struck a fellow-citizen hybristically (Dem. xxi 180, 182, Lys. fr. 44), or—without offending against the specific wording of any existing law—'wronged the people', as Socrates did (Xen. *Mem.* i 1.1) by allegedly 'corrupting the young' and rejecting the religious usage of the community.[1] It was common for the prosecutor in any serious indictment

[1] It is normal for military codes of law to define at least one offence in such terms that it can be held to cover all undesirable acts which are not easily classifiable under other articles of the code, and the same phenomenon is likely to occur (with varying degrees of explicitness) in the codes of totalitarian states or of liberal states at war. Something like it may take shape even in English law in peacetime. *The Times* (5 May 1961, p. 21) reports Lord Simonds, giving judgment in the Court of King's Bench on an (unsuccessful) appeal by a man who held that he had been sentenced for an action which was not

to demand the death penalty for his adversary, and to describe as 'deserving to die' categories of people of whose political or administrative conduct he disapproved. When the oligarch Phrynikhos had been assassinated in 411 and his killers had been released by the restored democracy, it was decreed (according to Lyk. *Leokr.* 114) that if it should be decided that Phrynikhos's intentions had been treasonable anyone who tried to argue that they were not should himself be executed as a traitor (cf. ibid. 135). A man who escaped the death penalty might be required to pay a fine so heavy that either his family and friends would be ruined in paying it or he would be indefinitely excluded, as a debtor to the state, from exercise of his civic rights; Hyp. v 27 (cf. fr. 47) mentions the case of a certain Konon, who was fined 6000 drakhmai because he had fraudulently claimed the 'festival allowance' on behalf of his son, who was actually abroad.

In practice a father was free to determine the extent and duration of his sons' education, within the limits set by social and cultural pressures and prejudices; it does not seem likely that he could have convinced his critics that in enjoying such freedom as the law allowed he was exercising an 'inalienable right'.

Aiskhines i 11: The clerk will read these laws out to you, so that you may see that the legislator considered that the boy who has been well brought up will be useful to the city when he is a grown man.

Cf. Ant. iii β.3, 'educating my son in pursuits from which the common interest benefits most'; ibid. γ.9 (plainly referring back to β.3), 'practising good (*khrēstos*) < skills >'. If a good education is one which makes a young man useful, and if a community has unlimited rights over the lives and behaviour of its members, we need to enquire into the possibility of what we would regard as a conflict between the morally good and the socially useful; there is much to suggest that in an Athenian context social utility tended to emerge the victor of such a conflict.

At Athens the assembly of the citizens was the sovereign power.

And. ii 19: There is no one else by whom you (*sc. the assembly*) can be accused. It is

an offence, as saying that 'in the sphere of criminal law there remained in the courts of law a residual power to enforce the supreme and fundamental purpose of the law, to conserve not only the safety and order but also the moral welfare of the state . . . There was (*sc. in the Court of King's Bench*) a residual power . . . to superintend those offences which were prejudicial to the public welfare. Such occasions would be rare, for Parliament had not been slow to legislate when attention had been sufficiently aroused. But gaps would remain, since no one could foresee every way in which the wickedness of man might disrupt the order of society'.

in your power, rightly, to dispose of what belongs to you—well, or, if you so wish, ill.

Cf. Dem. lix 88, 'absolute master of everything in the city, and able to do whatever it wishes'. In moments of excitement the assertion could be made that a majority of those present on a single occasion had a right to contravene the laws which governed the assembly's own procedure: Xen. *Hell.* i 7.12, 'The majority cried that it was monstrous that the assembly should be prevented from acting as it wished', at the debate on Arginoussai in 406. This was an uncommon moment of excitement, but there was no denying that the assembly was the ultimate source of law, although the revision and annulment of laws involved an elaborate procedure in the fourth century (Dem. xxiv 19–38), and it was common to indict the proposer of any measure which could be held to contravene existing laws.[2]

The most important theoretical defence of democracy (put into the mouth of the Syracusan demagogue Athenagoras by Thuc. vi 38.5–39.2) was that it ensured that decisions on issues (above all) of peace and war were not taken by a minority which stood to gain at the expense of the majority. This argument is well founded (cf. Thuc. ii 44.3, Perikles' declaration that a fair decision on an issue of state cannot easily be taken by those who have no sons to lose), but it carries no guarantee (nothing can) that a majority always perceives where its own interest, even its short-term interest, actually lies. The most important of the practical ill-effects of the assembly's power and attitude to its own power may have been the reluctance of patriotic individuals to face the opprobrium of being called unpatriotic and undemocratic if they disagreed with the majority, at a given moment, about the right means of ensuring the security and prosperity of the city. Thucydides' Nikias (vi 24.4) exhorts the older men in the assembly to vote against the Sicilian expedition without being intimidated by enthusiastic younger men sitting near them; cf. Diodotos's emphasis (Thuc. iii 42.5) on the importance of allowing the free expression of honest opinion. Demosthenes makes shameless use—shameless, because he himself swam against the current when he thought it right to do so—of the idea that disagreement with the majority is unpatriotic: xv 25, suggesting that it is not for a good citizen to consider the possible arguments against Athenian policy; xv 33, those politicians are trustworthy who 'have the same friends and enemies as the city'; xxi 201.

---

[2] Cf. H. J. Wolff, ' "Normenkontrolle" und Gesetzesbegriff in der attischen Demokratie' (= *Sitzungsberichte d. Heidelberger Akademie* etc., 1970.2) 22–8, 79, on indictment for illegal proposals as a measure designed by the Athenian people as a restraint upon itself.

the good citizen should be 'pleased or distressed by the same things' as the majority.

## 2. Judicial Decisions

An Athenian jury was in some ways like a committee of the assembly, but, unlike a normal committee, it did not have to report to its parent body. There was no appeal against its verdicts; jurors, unlike the council and the magistrates and officers appointed by lot or election, could not be called to account for their actions, and their verdicts could be treated as precedents in the interpretation of the law (Dem. xliii 15, Isok. xx 22, xxi 18, Lys. xiv 4).[3] Sovereign power was in fact divided, according to the nature of the issues to be settled, between the citizens (over eighteen years of age) meeting as an assembly and those same citizens (excluding the under-thirties) meeting in smaller numbers as juries. Hence, although it was perfectly possible for a speaker in court to draw a distinction between the people as a whole and the jury which he was addressing on that occasion (e.g. Aiskhines iii 8, Dein. i 3), it was commoner to identify jury and people, so that in a forensic speech the second person plural can often be translated 'Athens', 'the Athenian people', 'our city', etc. In Aiskhines i 176 the jury which tried the prosecution of Timarkhos is explicitly identified with the assembly in its legislative capacity (cf. Lys. vii 25, 'You send inspectors every year . . .'), and when Dem. xxi 167 says 'You sailed back from Styra to Athens' he means 'The infantry force, which may well have included some of you jurors, sailed . . .'. A fortiori, any given jury could be treated as identical with past (Dein. i 14, Dem. xxi 130) and future (Ant. v 90) juries, or as the general public, when any reference was made to events witnessed by many people (e.g. Dem. xxi 18, Lys. xxii 12) or to common gossip; Aiskhines i 92f. urges the jury to decide the case against Timarkhos not on the evidence presented in court, but on the basis of all the gossip they have ever heard about him.

Since the Athenian people was the source of the law, the people, as sovereign, could forgive its breach. Thus the question before a jury, as representing the people, was not exactly, 'Has this man, or has he not, committed the act with which he is charged?' but rather, 'What should be done about this man, who has been charged with this offence?' (cf. III.H.5). Occasional references to punishment without trial (Lys. vi 54, xxii 2) make

---

[3] Cf. Gernet 62f.; Gernet, Droit et société dans la Grèce ancienne (Paris, 1964) 61–81; H. J. Wolff in Wege der Forschung xlv (1968) 113f.

it sound almost as if a trial were not a method of discovering the truth but either a privilege granted to a man who might wish to plead for leniency or a way of giving publicity to a severe sentence. This fact partly accounts for a feature of Greek forensic oratory which reads strangely nowadays: the defendant's recital of his services to the community in a military or financial capacity and his generosity to his fellow-citizens, as if to say, 'Never mind the charge; let me off because I have been a good friend to you and deserve your gratitude'. Occasionally this motive might be made explicit.

Lys. xvi 17: I did this not because I was unaware of the perils of a battle against Spartans, but so that if I ever stood unjustly in danger (*sc. in the courts*), I would be thought a good man by you and would get my rights.

Lys. xx 30: Our benefactions to you were not intended to make financial gain for ourselves, but to ensure that if we were ever in danger we might ask from you the gratitude we deserved and receive it.

Lys. xxv 13: I spent more than was required of me by the city, with the intention that you should have a good opinion of me and that if any misfortune befell me I might stand a better chance in court.

Cf. And. i 147, ii 22, Lys. xviii 23, 26f., xx 33, xxi 17, 25, all using the word *kharis*; Is. v 35, vii 40 (cf. 38), Isok. xviii 67, private lawsuits in which service to the community appears to be used in an attempt to influence the jury's decision between the litigants; Dem. xxi 208, on the demand for *kharis* by eminent men speaking on behalf of the defendant; And. i 141–3, Lys. xviii 21, xxx 1, 27, on the services of the defendant's father and fore-bears; Thuc. vii 15.2, Nikias's request to the assembly that he should be forgiven, because of his past services, his poor performance as a commander in Sicily.

When these passages are taken in conjunction with others in which a litigant or defendant seems to be offering the community a bribe—e.g. And. i 144f., 149f., Dem. xxviii 24 ('If I recover my patrimony, I shall gladly perform my financial obligations to the state'), Lys. xix 61 ('It is greatly to your advantage to acquit us, for you will profit greatly from our possession of our estate'); cf. Is. vi 61, Lys. xxi 12, 14, xxx 27—it is tempting to believe that an Athenian jury was normally concerned less with the facts of the case than with calculation of communal profit and loss. Such a conclusion, how-ever, would not do justice to the complexity of the issue, which in fact affords an excellent illustration both of the way in which different attitudes could be adopted for different purposes and of the difficulty of demonstrating a single cause for any one phenomenon in the moral field. In the first place, it should be noted that none of the passages cited actually says that a defendant who is in the wrong should have judgment given in his favour or that past service to the state should be allowed to outweigh proof of present anti-democratic intent; the speaker of Lys. xvi 17 (cited above) regards his military reputation as protecting him against *wrongful* prosecution; cf. Lys. xix 2, 'Grant a favour which is both just and easy' (*sc.* for you to grant). In a culture in which documentation was rudimentary, effective techniques for the detection of crime virtually unknown, and the use of forensic evidence hamstrung by the absence of cross-examination and bedevilled by suspicion of organized perjury, the question, 'Which of the two parties is likely to be in the right?' was of the highest importance, and the character of each party, as revealed by his past record as a patriotic and generous citizen, was crucial to this question.[4]

Isok. xviii 58: I will say nothing of all my other financial services, but there is one which is not only a just claim on your gratitude but also evidence bearing upon this whole case. When the fleet was lost in the Hellespont . . .

Cf. Ant. ii β. 12 (cited on p. 177), 'You will see from all that I have done . . . that I am not a man who has designs on others'. Dem. xxxvi 55, Phormion's record of honesty and generosity as showing how unlikely he is to have defrauded Apollodoros; Dem. l 3, 'Tell your fellow-jurors about my zeal . . . so that you may all know what kind of man I am . . .'; Dem. lii 26, financial services to the state show that he was not *aiskhrokerdēs* (cf. IV.B.*1*); Dem. xxi 136 ('Who ever saw *me* . . .?'), xxxiv 40 (V.B.*4*), liv 38, lviii 27; Hyp. i 14, Isok. xvii 57f., Lys. xix 56 (cf. V.B.*2*), xxvi 21–4, all using the character and record of the speaker and his adversary in order to suggest which side is offering trustworthy evidence. Gorgias B11a 15 employs the same type of argument in the rhetorical exercise composed as the self-defence of the legendary Palamedes.

Secondly, it was possible to deny the relevance of recitals of public service. Dein. i 14 (≃ iii 17) congratulates the jury (that is to say, a much earlier jury than the one he was actually addressing) for having refused to take into account the dazzling career of Timotheos when it was a question of punishing him on a charge of receiving bribes from Chios and Rhodes; Dem. xlv 85 denied (not very convincingly, when we look at the context) any desire to

---

[4] This is an aspect of the matter to which I do not think Adkins (1) 201–10 and (3) 119–26 pay enough attention.

claim gratitude for past services; Dem. lii 1 warns against trusting a litigant simply because he has a good reputation; Lyk. *Leokr.* 139f. even speaks scornfully of some conventionally respected forms of public service as mere ostentation for self-advantage; Lys. xiv 16f. argues that even if Alkibiades had deserved well of Athens, it would still be improper to feel that his son could not be convicted of cowardice. Since the jury system was designed to eliminate 'favours' (*kharites*, Lys. xxvii 14) from political life, and democracy was held to give protection against the arbitrary power of 'those in command' (Aiskhines i 4),[5] it is ironic that jurors are ridiculed in Aristophanes' *Wasps* precisely for their arbitrary expression of collective malice and prejudice, and that juries should on occasion be asked to give a verdict which will 'grant a favour' to the people (e.g. Dem. xxi 227) or to allies of Athens (Lys. xxviii 17).

Thirdly, it must be remembered that whereas in our own courts the function of the jury is to return a verdict on a question of fact, and the verdict is supposed to be founded on evidence which we limit by very strict rules, the character and record of the defendant are taken into account in sentencing him if he is found guilty; judges make full use of the latitude which they are allowed, and it cannot be pretended that in so doing they are indifferent to the guilty man's value to society or the probable consequences to society of a severe sentence or a conditional discharge.[6] The only latitude allowed to the Athenian jury—and even that was confined to certain types of case—was a choice between the sentence proposed by the prosecutor and a counter-proposal made by the defendant. Since the jury represented the sovereign people, it was not necessarily unjust or unreasonable that a vote of acquittal should be taken to cover not simply, 'You did not do what you are accused of doing', but also, 'We forgive you', and, 'No further action should be taken on this case'.[7] The phenomenon was not exclusively democratic; cf. Xen. *Hell.* v 4.32, 'It is hard to execute such a man; Sparta has need of men like him'.

[5] Cf. de Romilly 138–54.

[6] In 1972 a Mr. —— was accused of murder but found guilty of manslaughter. His counsel is reported by *The Times* (8 July 1972) as saying that 'there were facts in this case which could enable the court substantially to reduce the sentence which would normally be imposed in an unlawful killing of this kind. Mr. —— had been of real service to Britain. During the war . . . "I would ask the court to say that once in a life-time a man is entitled to credit for his past good works and this is such an occasion. The provocation he underwent might have caused any reasonable man to lose his self-control" '.

[7] Cf. Wolf 191.

## 3. Usefulness

Somewhat confusingly, the antonym of *khrēsimos*, 'useful', is normally *akhrēstos*, 'useless' (cf. Dem. xix 135, which brings out the antonymy clearly), whereas the antonym of *khrēstos*, 'good', is most commonly *ponēros* (e.g. Ar. *Frogs* 1455f., Aiskhines i 30, Dem. xiii 36, Hyp. i 8, Lys. iii 9), sometimes one or other of a wide range of derogatory terms (e.g. And. ii 25f., Ar. *Knights* 191f., Dem. ii 26). *Khrēsimos* forms a regular comparative and superlative, whereas the degrees of comparison for *khrēstos* are supplied by *beltīōn* and *beltistos*: e.g. Dem. xx 14, 'For however *khrēstos* he is, . . . he is not *beltīōn* in character than the city'. The abstract noun *khrēstotēs* is uncommon (in oratory, only Is. ii 7, v 30). There does not seem to me to be any passage in which it is really necessary, in order to produce intelligible English and to do justice to the writer's intention, to translate *khrēstos* as 'useful',[8] though there is undeniably a degree of convergence with *khrēsimos*, especially in association with 'advise', 'propose', 'instruct', 'learn', etc.; Ar. *Birds* 1448, 'good arguments' = 'useful advice', *Knights* 86, 'make a good plan', *Clouds* 793, 'give good advice', 841, 'learn something good' = '. . . useful', *Lys.* 639 ∼ 648, 'begin an exposition useful to the city' ∼ 'give the city some good advice', *Frogs* 686f., 'give good advice and instruction to the city'. In Dem. xx 7, 114 ∼ 116 and in Hdt. i 170.1 ∼ 3 *khrēsimos* and *khrēstos* are used in stylistic variation; cf. Lys. xiv 43, where 'good to you' (literally, 'good in-behaviour towards [*peri*] you') and 'useful to you') denote the same conduct; cf. also 'good to/for the city' in Ar. *Thesm.* 832 and variant readings *khrēsimos/khrēstos* in Hdt. iii 78.3, picking up *khrēstos* in 78.2.[9]

Analysis of a hypothetical 'original meaning' of *khrēstos*, whether as 'usable' or as 'dealable-with', will not necessarily tell us anything about the application of the word in the period with which we are concerned. In Hyp. iv 37 a good (*khrēstos*) citizen is described as a man who cares (*phrontizein*) for the city's interests and for the *homonoia*, 'harmony', 'like-mindedness', of the citizens, to such an extent that he is in all circumstances prepared to subordinate his own advantage *vis-à-vis* other citizens to the advantage of the city *vis-à-vis* other cities. The expression 'care for the city' is used by Dem. xviii 190 in describing the characteristic behaviour of the *dikaios* citizen, and ibid. 292 on the 'loyal (*eunous*) and *dikaios* citizen'. In two passages

---

[8] Despite North 139 and Adkins (1) 215 n. 6.

[9] Cf. G. Redard, *Recherches sur XPH, XPHΣΘAI: étude sémantique* (Paris, 1953) 98–101.

Demosthenes applies 'useful to the city' or simply 'useful' to conduct indistinguishable from that which he and Hypereides attribute to the 'good' citizen. In the first of these two passages, xviii 311f., introduced by the statement that the recent past has provided many opportunities for a man to show that he is 'good' (*kalos kāgathos*), he asks Aiskhines in what way he (Aiskhines) has been 'useful', and he goes on to list possibilities which include the promotion of measures calculated to increase not only the international standing and military security of Athens but also the economic prosperity of her population. In the second passage, xix 281f., he declares that neither Aiskhines nor his father has ever been 'useful to the city' in any respect. The list of rhetorical questions which he puts ('What horse, what trireme . . .?') brings into the category of usefulness: service in the cavalry, service on expeditions, maintenance of a trireme, payment for a chorus, contribution to a capital levy, displaying loyalty and readiness to incur dangers. Cf. Aiskhines i 105, 'a most unprofitable (*alȳsitelēs*) citizen', Dem. iv 7, 'make oneself useful to the city', Is. vii 41, xi 50.

Is. iv 27: Nor are they useless to the city, but they serve in expeditionary forces, pay their capital levies, obey orders, and behave themselves.

There is, so far as I can see, only one occasion on which an explicit distinction appears to be drawn between *khrēstos* and *khrēsimos* (in Eupolis fr. 118, 'When one is *agathos* and a *khrēsimos* citizen and surpasses all in being *khrēstos* . . .', there may well be an element of tautology).

Hyp. ii 10: On what grounds could you acquit Philippides? Because he is democratic? Why, you know that he chose to bow to the tyrants . . . Well, then, because he is *khrēstos*? Why, no; you have twice convicted him of wrongdoing (*adikiā*). Yes, but suppose that he is *khrēsimos*? Why, if you are going to use (*khrēsthai*) a man whom, indisputably, you have twice convicted of crime (*litterally*, 'who has been judged *ponēros* . . .'), you will be regarded either as unable to give a correct verdict (*literally*, as judging *kakōs*') or to want bad (*ponēros*) men (*i.e. deliberately to make use of men whom you know to be bad*).

The first thing we should observe about this passage is that it is not a genuine set of pleas by a speaker defending Philippides, but a set imagined, for the purposes of his own argument, by the prosecutor. The second thing is that Hypereides does not necessarily, or even probably, envisage three successive pleas, of which any one could stand even if the other two were rebutted. 'Democratic', 'good' and 'useful' are alternative and substantially overlapping terms in which Philippides might be commended to the jury. Thirdly, Hypereides does not explicitly say that a bad man cannot be useful to the city in any respect, but he comes close to it in saying that the conclusion to be drawn from the acquittal of Philippides on grounds of utility would be that his two previous convictions were wrong verdicts; I am inclined to take the alternative conclusion, that 'You want bad men', as intended to be self-evidently absurd because self-contradictory. Dem. xxv 40–2 considers the possible plea that Aristogeiton should be acquitted, despite his objectionable conduct, because he is useful. Here again the distinction between virtue and utility—this time, implicit only—is not actually made by the defendant (we do not know what the defendant said) but foisted upon him by his prosecutor, who proceeds to deny the utility of Aristogeiton's behaviour; cf. also Dem. lviii 64.

Dem. xix 277 (*referring to events of fifty years earlier*): You condemned those envoys to death. One of them was Epikrates, a first-rate (*spoudaios*) man, as I hear from my elders, and in many respects useful to the city, and . . . a good democrat. But none of this saved him, and rightly so; for a man who aspires to such high office must not be (*sc. only*) half good nor . . . abuse (*sc. your trust*), but must not injure (*adikein*) you in any way that he can help.

The implication here is that Epikrates lost his title to goodness from the moment that he ceased to act in a way advantageous to the city, i.e. when he ceased to be useful.

The confluence of goodness and usefulness was in part due to the normal valuation in terms of function (III.H.5), but it was facilitated by an absence of distinction between generosity to other individual citizens and generosity to the citizen-body as a collective entity (IV.B.2). The type of man who is lavish in private charity but will go to any length to avoid paying his taxes does not seem to be recognized by the Athenian orators, though that is no proof that he did not exist. Athenian law prescribed that a man should be disqualified from holding public office if he had committed an offence of a category which to our way of thinking embraces both 'private morality' and breach of law: maltreatment or neglect of his parents, dissipation of his inheritance, desertion in battle or avoidance of call-up, and homosexual prostitution of his person (Aiskhines i 28–30; cf. Dein. ii 17). The legislator, says Aiskhines (ibid.), considered that it was 'impossible that one and the same person should be bad in his private life but good in public life' (cf. iii 78). A rationalization of this view could be offered: Aiskhines i 188, 'If he took money for the abuse of his body, what would he not sell?'; Dem. xxiv 201, if Timokrates allows his own father to remain disenfranchised through debt, 'is there anything from which he would not abstain?'; Lys. xxxi 22f.,

'If a man commits such crimes against his own family, how would he treat people who are not related to him?'[10] Everyday experience suggests that these rhetorical questions admit of sensible answers other than the answers suggested by the speakers, and they have rather the same character as the sweeping generalizations (some necessarily untrue, because mutually contradictory) which a speaker occasionally tries to impose upon a jury.[11]

## 4. Fantasy

In I.E.5 I suggested that political, forensic and epideictic oratory, together with the comic parabasis, may have been governed by conventions which delimited the moral stance of the speaker vis-à-vis the hearer. Examination of the orators, undertaken with a view to answering a variety of questions about Athenian popular morality, has by now indicated that a substantial number of closely interrelated moral attitudes were repeatedly adopted by speakers addressing large audiences throughout the period which we have been considering, while on the periphery of this homogeneous area fragments of idiosyncratic and divergent views might from time to time find expression —simple or sophistic, earnest or cynical, ruthless or compassionate. It has often been possible to illustrate the broad central strand of Athenian morality from comedy. Yet it must have struck any reader familiar with Old Comedy that the salient features of that central strand, the highminded insistence on self-sacrifice, self-subordination to the community and meticulous observance of the law, distaste for violence and puritanical disapproval of consumption and promiscuity, are unlike much of the behaviour of characters who triumph in Aristophanes' plays and endear themselves to us in the course of their triumph.

In one respect Aristophanes' 'heroes' play the same game as the orators, and by the same rules: they are democrats who respect no individual master, and they do not suggest (any more than the choruses suggest in the parabases) that Athens would be a better, stronger, or wiser city if the power of political decision were restricted to men of noble lineage or of property above a certain level. But in some other respects they reject the fundamental presuppositions of the public speaker. Dikaiopolis in Acharnians, determined to make peace and enjoy its benefits, is not in the least concerned that the assembly (a meeting of which is caricatured in the first scene of the play) does

[10] Conversely, Lyk. Leokr. 138 argues that a man who does not repay his fatherland for what it has given him must be a faithless friend.
[11] Cf. Dover (1) 25f.

not listen to any talk of peace. By employing a supernatural messenger who claims to have been sent down by the gods to put an end to the war, Dikaio-polis secures a magical private peace-treaty for himself and his family, in consequence of which he is able to welcome to his market people from the nations who were actually at war with Athens, and thus to enjoy imported delicacies of which his fellow-citizens were deprived. He refuses to share any of the benefit except with a newly-married girl who, being a woman and thus excluded from the process of political decision, does not, in his view, deserve to suffer from the war (*Ach*. 1061f.). Nothing could be less like the 'good citizen' who in Dem. xviii 280, 292 is characterized by making the same choice as the majority' or 'grieving when the majority grieve and re-joicing when they rejoice'. Dikaiopolis does not care what the majority choose or wish or think. He does not even care whether they are right or wrong. He knows what he wants, and he pursues the object of his wishes with unswerving and ruthless selfishness. He is willing to argue, to save himself from the angry Acharnians, that the war was unnecessary in the first place (496–556), and we are meant, I suppose, to think of him as assuming that the making of peace would not harm Athens; but these considerations are not his *reasons* for making peace.

The diplomatic and military practicability of making peace is not allowed to become an issue in *Acharnians*. In *Lysistrata*, fourteen years later, when Athens' position in relation to her enemies was much less favourable (though better than anyone, including the Athenians themselves, could have expected it to be two years after the disaster in Sicily), lip-service is paid to the idea of a negotiated peace, but the scene in which the citizens of the warring states are brought (as it were) to the conference table by the sexual strike of their wives bears little relation to the issues (and none to what the Pelo-ponnesians called 'the freedom of the Greeks' from Athenian rule) around which the possibilities of peace actually revolved; the localities which they agree to hand back—a hasty and perfunctory agreement, because both sides are anxious above all to resume satisfaction of their sexual needs—are all selected for the sexual punning which their names permit (*Lys*. 1162–75). *Lysistrata* is fundamentally a fantastic play, in which most of the factors which would become important in a sex-strike of wives are ignored, and the peace in which it culminates belongs to the realm of 'Wouldn't it be nice if only . . .?'

*Acharnians*, *Lysistrata*, and to a lesser extent, *Peace* (lesser, because it was performed after the decision to make peace had been taken and the last formalities were about to be concluded), all served one important moral and social purpose: they enabled the spectator vicariously to reject participation in the communal pursuit of international power and respect, the pursuit which earns posthumous renown at the expense of pain and privation, and to satisfy instead his demand for food, drink, sex, sleep, song and dance, all the things whose indulgence is often incompatible (and explicitly contrasted) with realization of the values of the good citizen and the great nation. People sometimes need to be bad citizens, and the licence of Old Comedy was a mechanism which gave the Athenians a chance to be bad citizens at least in their imagination. In a state which penalized *hybris* so severely that it was possible for a citizen to find himself on a capital charge as the price of the pleasure of hitting an objectionable acquaintance in the face, the comic character was able to strike out with stick or whip or fist as the fancy took him, and laugh off threats of prosecution for *hybris*; the play ends, the fantasy is cut off, before the indictments are drawn up. The glimpse of an attractive woman, especially a personified and deified abstraction, aroused in him strong sexual desire to which he gave immediate expression in coarse words. Peisetairos in *Birds* and Trygaios in *Peace* complete their trumph by marrying beautiful deities; we are not told what they do with their existing human wives, if any, nor are the sexual adventures of Dikaiopolis in *Ach.* 1198–221 or of Philokleon in *Wasps* 1342–78 complicated by any mention of the wife which each of them apparently possesses (*Ach.* 262, *Wasps* 610). The total shamelessness of Philokleon (cf. I.D.*1*) is a rebellion not only against the law and the conventions of public utterance but even against the normal moral standards of his society. The stages by which the Aristophanic conception of comic character turned into the Menandrean are obscure, since we know comedy between the last play of Aristophanes and the first play of Menander only by citations from lost plays; the reasons why comedy ceased to perform the function of rebellion in fantasy against the publicly accepted ideal of good citizenship are necessarily speculative, and must not be sought solely in political and social history without reference to the autonomous development of comedy as an artistic genre.

## VI.C. THE STATE AS A MORAL AGENT

### 1. Conflict of Obligations

While there was no doubt that a good citizen was bound to put public interests above his private interests in general (Isok. xviii 60, Lys. xxxi 5–7), occasions could arise on which service to the community conflicted with obedience to one's parents, protection of guests and supplicants, fidelity to an oath exacted by a friend of business associate, or some other observance of those 'laws' which transcended the nation and were universally believed to be of special concern to the gods.[1] Dem. xviii 205, as part of an exhortation to unhesitating self-sacrifice in the nation's defence, tells the jurors that among their ancestors 'everyone considered that he was born not to his father and mother alone but to his country';[2] cf. Eur. *Erechtheus*, cited below, and *Iph. Aul.* 1374–1401 (Iphigeneia speaking), 'You bore me, mother, for all Greece, not for yourself alone'. The implication is that no one could expect commendation for filial piety if he obeyed his father's injunction to shirk military service. Yet Aiskhines uses against Demosthenes (iii 224f.) the allegation that Demosthenes had personally tortured the suspected spy Anaxines, by whom he had been entertained at Oreos, and had caused an outcry in the assembly by saying that he 'rated the city's salt above the table of hospitality'. Whether this was true or false, the fact that the story, complete with the 'outcry in the assembly', was judged by Aiskhines a good weapon against Demosthenes is important; no one would have expected an Athenian citizen to make positive efforts to save a former host from interrogation under torture, if such interrogation seemed desirable for national security, but a silent withdrawal would have been respected. Even more striking is Aiskhines iii 77f., an attack on Demosthenes for offering a joyful sacrifice of thanksgiving on hearing of the death of Philip, although his only daughter had died a few days before. In so acting, Demosthenes (says Aiskhines) violated custom in respect of mourning for the dead; and Aiskhines goes on to extract both pathos and political argument from this.

Wretch! When he had lost her who first and alone called him father! I am not reproaching him with his misfortune; it is his character that I am considering. A man who hates his own children, a bad father, could never be a good politician.

Cf. Timokles fr. 34, the man who fears and respects his father makes a good citizen and a good soldier.

As a rule, a man's obligation to his wife and children, an obligation which we nowadays rate very highly, was not treated as comparable with his

[1] Cf. de Romilly 40–3. Suicide was not among these offences (cf. IV.A.4), but Aristotle *Eth. Nic.* 1138ᵃ9–14 concludes that it is an injury to one's city.

[2] A father, however, retained his right to expose his children at birth if it seemed to him that it would be (for any reason) difficult or disadvantageous to rear them; cf. Pataikos's explanation of his own action in Men. *Perik.* 810-2.

obligation to his parents and senior relatives, as if his dependants, even his freeborn sons, were a part of his property (cf. A.1). It was inexcusable to put responsibility for dependants above the needs of the community. Lyk. *Leokr.* 101, having recited the speech of Praxithea from Euripides' *Erechtheus* (fr. 50 [Austin] applauds her heroic sentiments and her readiness to sacrifice her child's life for the sake of her city. 'My daughter', says Praxithea, 'is not mine except by birth', and as it seems to her obvious that the city must take precedence over a single family, she professes contempt for any woman who would rather see her son safe without honour than honourably dead.

Lys. ii 71: They (*sc. the war-dead*), subordinating everything to *aretē*, robbed themselves of life, widowed their wives, orphaned their own children, and left their brothers, fathers and mothers bereaved.

This is high praise of the dead. Similarly, the speaker of Lys. xxi 24 boasts, 'Faced with the prospect of danger in the war at sea, I never felt pity or grief or gave a thought to my wife or my own children'; cf. Lys. xx 22–5. Lyk. *Leokr.* 53 expatiates on the fate of a certain Autolykos, who was condemned and punished (whether actually executed, is not clear) because he dared, when danger threatened Athens in 338, to spare a thought for his wife and children and send them out of Attica to safety.

Just as disenfranchisement was automatically extended to a man's children and descendants, and a gift of citizenship by a foreign community had a similar extension, so severe punishment for an exceptional offence committed by one person might fall upon the whole family:[3] Dem. xxv 79, a case in which a foreign woman and 'all her family' were executed for her crimes; Lys. xiv 7, alleging that the young Alkibiades narrowly escaped execution for his father's sacrilege. Dem. xviii 204, speaking of the Persian invasion of 480, says that the man who gave his opinion in favour of yielding to Xerxes was stoned to death, 'and not he alone, but your wives too stoned his wife to death'. Hdt. ix 5.1–3 tells the same story about the man who brought Mardonios's demands to the assembly in 479. These stories (and it must be remembered that Demosthenes was speaking in 330) emphasize the strength of Athenian feeling against surrender, and it was evidently not felt that the murder of the wives was discreditable enough to detract from the paradigmatic character of the stories. It was, after all, normal practice to include a man's wife, children and descendants in a curse uttered against the man himself (e.g. Soph. *Oed. Col.* 868–70) or invoked by him as part of a

[3] On the subject as a whole cf. Glotz *passim* (on the killing of dependants, 457–74).

solemn declaration (Dem. xlvii 70, 73, Lys. xii 70). Dem. xxv 84, in saying that Aristogeiton (unlike some of Aristogeiton's victims) does not deserve that his children should be pitied by the jury, is treating them solely as a means of hurting Aristogeiton, not as people in their own right. Nevertheless, notions of individual responsibility had begun to make an impression long before Demosthenes; clemency was shown in 403 to the sons of the Thirty Tyrants (Dem. xl 32; cf. IV.C.4), and this can be matched by Pausanias's clemency (Hdt. ix 88) to the sons of the Theban Attaginos on the grounds that 'children cannot be guilty of treason'. No doubt children could be treated either as objects or as persons undeserving of punishment according to whether the speaker was attacking their father or (as in Lys. xix 8) defending him. The maturing of the concept of individual responsibility perhaps brought with it a greater recognition of the equality of men and women as moral agents. In one of the most striking scenes in Menander (*Epitr.* 878ff.) Kharisios reproaches himself for his own conduct in treating his wife harshly (by contrast with her magnanimity and loyalty) for bearing an illegitimate child when he himself has begotten one ('I had no compassion on her . . . I'm a merciless *barbaros*').

A man's obligations to family, friends and benefactors included the obligation to help them whenever they were involved in litigation or indicted for offences against the community; Hyp. i 10 calls this *dikaios*, and Lyk. fr. XV.1 limits the obligation only by warning that one must 'stop short of perjury' (cf. Dem. lii 20, Lys. xxvi 15). Euryptolemos in Xen. *Hell.* i 7.21 introduces his plea for just treatment of the generals in 406 by disclaiming any intention (which, he says, would be *aiskhros*) to put the interests of his kinsman Perikles (the younger) above those of the city. Conflict between personal obligation and patriotic duty was obviously a genuine issue (cf. Dem. lviii 30, 'He will claim that he loves you' [*sc.* the Athenian people] 'next after his family'). Whichever way an individual resolved the conflict for himself, he was likely to be blamed in one quarter and praised in another.[4] We have already seen that there were some chinks in the armour of self-righteous patriotism. When Aiskhines iii 194–6, on the familiar theme of ancestral virtue, declares that in the good old days men would indict even their own friends for illegal procedures, and offers evidence in support of this claim, it may be a fair inference that this high-minded disregard for personal loyalties was not common in the late fourth century. As it happens, we have some relevant evidence from the beginning

---

[4] On the political issues involved in the fifth century in the conflict between the obligation to friends and the obligation to the city cf. Connor 47–53, 91–3.

of the century. Andokides does not seem to have earned respect, however he may have relieved the city of anxiety, by giving information against his 'companions' (*hetairoi*), i.e. the members of his club (And. i 54, 'That is the report my enemies spread abroad in their wish to slander me'), and he was no doubt making the best of his situation in saying (i 67) that he opposed his companions' illegal and impious project until they had actually carried it out, and then collaborated with them in concealing their guilt. Some passages of oratory seem to exaggerate the obligations of friendship peculiarly, as when the speaker of Lys. iv 3 implies that his present adversary demonstrated an absence of enmity on a previous occasion by voting in favour of the award of a prize to the chorus of his (the speaker's phyle: other passages play it down by insisting on one's duty to bring information and indictments against lawbreakers (Dem. xxiii 5, lviii 12, Lyk. *Leokr.* 5). Xen. *Hell.* i 7.18 judges that the generals Perikles and Diomedes acted with *philanthrōpiā* in persuading their colleagues to keep quiet about the failure of Theramenes and Thrasyllos to pick up the dead and wounded after the battle of Arginoussai; this judgment may be fair, but the rights and wrongs of the issue are not easily determined. Demosthenes states one aspect of the conflict of loyalties in a manner to which it would be difficult to take exception.

Dem. xxiii 134: Good friends do not requite affection by going along with anything which will result in harm to both parties, but only with what will benefit both; when a man can see further ahead than his friend, he should try to ensure that everything turns out for the best, and not regard temporary gratification as more important than the whole future.

Although it was possible for a speaker to attack indiscriminately all those who dared to speak on his adversary's side, it is noteworthy that Demosthenes for all his contemptuous vilification of Aiskhines' brothers, concedes (xix 239) that it is their business to put fraternal loyalty first, while it is the jury's business to give more weight to the law and the city's interest.[5] In Dem. xlv 56 a certain Deinias, who refused to give evidence which might be used against his own relations, seems to have carried his refusal to the point of falsehood ('I was not there' rather than 'I decline to say whether I was there or not'). Relations of Timotheos, who would not testify in respect of Apollodoros's claims on him, are not blamed by Apollodoros for

[5] The Greeks do not seem to have found it hard to see that the admission that my adversary's conduct is just and admirable does not necessarily impose on me any obligation to yield to him, any more than I am obliged to lay down my arms if my country is invaded by the courageous and idealistic soldiers of a foreign power. Cf. Thuc. iii 46.5 on the *natural* desire of Athens' subjects to revolt.

withholding evidence which might have been highly relevant to the case, but commended for at least not committing perjury on Timotheos's behalf (Dem. xlix 37f.). According to Dein. i 58, a certain Polyeuktos, who had associated with the exiles at Megara, was acquitted when he confessed to the charge but pleaded that he had gone to Megara to look after his stepfather, who was old and 'unfortunate' (i.e. exiled and impoverished). Such a verdict implied no sympathy with the stepfather's politics, but a recognition that the claims of one's mother's husband are not to be brushed aside.

> Dem. xxiv 67: It is not open to Timokrates to admit that his proposal is wrong but at the same time to claim pardon; for it is quite plain that he has proposed his new laws not in ignorance of what he was doing nor on behalf of unfortunate people nor on behalf of close relatives, but with deliberate intent, on behalf of men who have done you great wrong and have no connection with him—unless he claims to regard as kindred those who hire him.

The novelty in this passage is that an intention to relieve distress, as distinct from an obligation to help one's family, is fleetingly envisaged ('nor ... unfortunate ..., nor ... relatives') as a possible excuse for wronging the community. It is not impossible that a defence resting on a plea of susceptibility to compassion as a natural human weakness, supported by reminders of the mutability of fortune in the mortal life which we all share, would have fared better in an Athenian court (especially if the jurors had read or seen Sophokles' *Philoktetes*, in which Neoptolemos must either override his generous compassion or else damage the interests of the Greeks besieging Troy) than a claim (such as Antigone's in Sophokles' *Antigone*; cf. Eur. *Phoen.* 1648f.) that in disobeying the law or acting against the city's interest the defendant had obeyed one of the 'unwritten laws' which all Greek states professed to observe and regarded as divine in origin. Since the state had in effect assumed the right to define religious obligation, and since the ephebic oath and the official curse were so comprehensive in character that they could be held relevant to any act whatsoever (cf. V.D.2), an attempt by a defendant to present an issue in terms of divine versus man-made law could easily have been thwarted by the prosecutor's elevation of the whole issue to the religious plane.


## 2. Criticism of the Law

The extension of *dikaios/adikos* beyond 'just'/'unjust' and 'honest'/'dishonest' to 'legal'/'illegal' and 'fair'/'unfair', even to 'normal'/'abnormal' (cf. IV.C.2), prompts us to ask whether it was possible in fourth-century Athens, as it is certainly possible in our own civilization, to argue that the law itself was in some respects wrong, unjust or immoral. There was certainly no objection (cf. I.E.1) to saying that a particular verdict had been mistaken, that juries tend in certain circumstances to give incorrect verdicts, or that wrong decisisions on matters of policy had been taken by the assembly, provided that whenever a particular case was specified the blame was put upon those who had 'misled' the majority and the man in the street was not accused of any delinquency more serious than insouciance or softheartedness.[6] Wrong decisions, even wrong policies, do not in themselves suffice to prove the possibility of bad laws, for laws outlast the consequences attributable to decrees and verdicts, and mere length of time may be treated as evidence of a law's acceptability to the deep moral sense of the community at large. Ant. v 14 praises the Athenian law of homicide on the grounds that it has remained unchanged since early times, standing the test of 'time and experience', which 'teach men what is not satisfactory'. In calling the homicide law 'the most pious' and in generalizing about 'laws made well or ill', the speaker implies that some laws are better than others; equally, there would seem to be little point in calling an existing law *dikaios* (e.g. Dem. xxiv 34, Hyp. iii 22) unless some laws are less so than others. Dem. xxiii 64 considers the hypothetical possibility that one might make a case against the homicide laws as 'worthless and unjust', but gives no indication of what such a case might be. If a man argues against a prosposed new law, calling it 'bad', 'unjust' and 'shameful'—which is precisely what Demosthenes does in xx 10, 125 ('establishing a bad practice'), 155–7 ('bequeathing the city a most shameful reputation for illegality'), xxiv 205 ('disgraceful, a reproach to the city')—he would seem to be logically committed, if his argument fails, to saying, 'We now have a bad and shameful law'. When allusion was made in general terms to the laws of other states there was no difficulty in contrasting bad laws with good.

Dem. xx 49: Bad (*ponēros*) laws harm even those cities which are confident of their own soundness.

If a law can be bad anywhere, why should not a law made and accepted by

[6] Lys. xxx 22f. asserts that the council 'does wrong' (*exhamartanein*) in prescribing unjustified sequestrations when public funds are low; but he puts the blame on those officials through whose delinquency funds are depleted; and in any case, the council is not a sovereign body, but subordinate to the assembly. There was no objection to calling action by magistrates 'wrongful' or 'unjust' (e.g. Lys. ix 6, 10, 20), for all magistrates were accountable to the assembly and could be punished.

one's own city be bad? The law could be protected from criticism only by the assertion (which is by no means without force) that a community in which the laws, good or bad, are scrupulously and unquestioningly obeyed is stronger and more enduring than a community in which individuals feel free to pass moral judgment upon the laws and obey or disobey according to the dictates of conscience. Thucydides attributes this assertion to Kleon in the course of the Mytilene debate (iii 37.3f.; cf. III.F.*1*), and both Aiskhines (i 6) and Demosthenes make a similar point in terms which could reasonably be applied to any body of people in which decisions are taken by majority agreement after discussion.

Dem. xxi 34: When you are making the laws, it is right to examine what sort of laws they are; but when you have made them, it is right then to guard and obey them.

He goes on, in a slightly different direction, to suggest that the fact of a law's existence is adequate proof of its rightness.

If it had been sufficient that those who committed an assault at the Dionysia should be liable to punishment in accordance with the laws which already existed on assault, there would have been no need for the addition of the present law. But it was not sufficient; and the proof of that is that you made a religious law on the conduct of the festival.

Plainly, obedience to the law as it stands at a given time is compatible with a belief that the law is inadequate and needs supplementation or revision. And since a machinery for repeal existed as one element in a comprehensive machinery for law reform, it should have been unobjectionable in principle to urge the repeal of a law on the grounds that it was a wrong, unjust or shameful law, provided that no attempt was made to secure its annulment without going through the procedures which were themselves prescribed by law. When Dem. iii 10f., recommends the assembly to repeal the laws governing the theoric fund, on the grounds that these laws 'do you much harm at the present time', he was coming as near as makes little matter, given xx 49 (cited above), to calling the theoric laws bad laws.

What made the Athenians circumspect in criticizing their own laws and disinclined to accept pretexts for law-breaking was in the first place their comprehension under the single term *nomos*, 'law', of what we divide into separate categories, 'constitutional', 'legal', 'religious', 'moral' and 'conventional', with the consequence that open defiance of usage could be exploited as grounds for allegations of treason and conspiracy; cf. Thuc. vi 15.4, on Alkibiades, and Isok. xx 10, a generalization (not necessarily correct) about the oligarchic revolutionaries of 411 and 404. A second reason is that the wide range of ideals, eccentricities and obsessions which we nowadays amalgamate under the name of 'conscience' did not seem to Greeks to be good reasons for defying the law.


## 3. Justice and Interest

In respect of an individual's conduct, the contrast between justice and interest is fundamental, and the same contrast can be made in dealings between nations. We should therefore ask whether it can also be drawn with reference to the community as a whole, expressing its will through the law, political decisions and judicial verdicts, and the individuals composing the community. In theory, it could certainly be drawn.

Dem. xx 112 (*on an argument in favour of a proposed law*): I regard his argument as being in many respects disadvantageous to the city and, what is more, unjust.

Lys. xxi 12: If you do as I ask, you will be giving a just verdict and will also be choosing what is profitable to yourselves.

Cf. Dem. xxiii 11, 'to discover what was both just and advantageous to the people'; Soph. *Phil.* 925f., 'Justice and interest make me obey those who are in authority'.

Unfortunately, 'just and advantageous' became a cliché which by no means implied that both the justice and the advantage of the action so commended could be demonstrated independently: Aiskhines i 6, 'Consider how to make laws which will be good (*kalōs ekhein*) and advantageous to the democracy'; i 178, 'In making the laws . . . you consider solely what is just and advantageous'; i 196, 'when you have done what is just and advantageous', i.e. '. . . have given your verdict against the defendant' (cf. Isok. xviii 68); Dem. xviii 308, 'a restraint which is just and advantageous to the city'; xxv 75, 'when vice is honoured and virtue spurned, when justice and interest take second place to malice'. When expressions such as 'a just verdict' were used, without mention of interest, it was presumably taken for granted that the taking of just decisions must always be of advantage to the community, for 'Observance of the oath', i.e. of the jurors' oath to give a just verdict, 'is of the highest importance for everyone' (Dem. xxiii 101).[7] On the other hand, when reference is made to interest alone,[8] without mention of justice, we may

---

[7] The issue here, as in §18 of the same speech, is not, strictly speaking, justice *vs.* advantage, but whether it can ever be advantageous to condone a breach of the procedure laid down by law for the proposal of new laws.

[8] Lys. xxxi 34 speaks only of advantage to the city, but the case is a scrutiny of an archon-elect, not a lawsuit.

often feel that justice is not being taken for granted but rather pushed to one side.

Lys. xiv 4 (*on the establishment of predecent by a verdict*): I consider that it is the business of a good citizen and a just juror to interpret the law in the way which is likely to be to the city's advantage in the future.

Lys. xviii 20: If we could see that the property of which our opponents demand the sequestration was being kept intact for the city, we would forgive (*sc. the demand*). As it is, you know that they are making away with some of it . . . If you do as I ask, you will derive no less benefit from it than we as its possessors, since we . . . pay capital levies to you from it.

'We would forgive the demand', given the context, implies, 'We would treat the city's interest as the only relevant consideration, and would no longer insist that it would be just to restore the property to us'; it is not really quite equivalent to, 'We would forgive you for putting your own interest above justice'. Cf. also Lys. xix 61f., xxi 25; Dem. xxiii 100, 'simple-minded, or rather, shameless', to argue that an illegal proposal may be in the city's interest, 'and yet there is a certain logic in this shamelessness . . .'; lviii 36f., 'possibly it is not *dikaios*' to argue about how much a certain violation of the law would matter, 'but, all the same, . . .'.


*4. Interstate Relations*

The essential features of Greek attitudes to interstate morality can be very simply stated.

First, no one seems ever to have hesitated to apply to any sovereign nation, in respect of its dealings with other sovereign nations, the same array of evaluative words as were applied to an individual in his dealings with other individuals: 'just' or 'unjust', 'honest' or 'dishonest', 'generous', 'magnani-mous', 'cruel', 'selfish', 'ungrateful', and so on.

Dem. iii 26: They (*sc. your ancestors*) acquired, as one would expect, great prosperity by good faith in international dealings, piety towards the gods, and equity within the city.

Cf. (among many passages cited in earlier chapters, especially IV) Dem. vi 8–10, xviii 93f., xxii 76; also Dem. x 53, 'No one likes or trusts or fears us'; Isok. xii 48, on Athens and Sparta; Lys. xxv 31, Athens 'unreliable in the eyes of Greece'; Xen. *Hell.* v 3.13, Sparta regards the behaviour of Phleious as hybristic. Such evaluations might be reinforced by drawing quite explicit analogies between states and individuals: Dem. viii 66f.; Isok. xiv 52, unreasonable that a whole city should not be pitied when it suffers unjust treatment, since an individual is pitied in similar circumstances; Thuc. iii 45.6, the effects of sudden good fortune on states and on individuals. Inter-state agreements, like business contracts, loans, etc., were *synthēkai*, sealed by oaths (Isok. xviii 29f.), and violation of an oath by a nation was no less impious, and no less liable to incur divine punishment, than its violation by an individual (cf. V.D.*1*).

Secondly, everyone was aware that although the content of a moral judg-ment passed on a nation did not differ from the content of a similar judgment passed on a fellow-citizen, the act of passing it differed in one extremely important way: a nation which earned moral disapproval could not be deterred from further wrongdoing or forced to pay a penalty (despite the existence of some elementary mechanisms for recourse to arbitration and a widespread and deep-seated respect for usages concerning the burial of the dead, the sanctity of heralds, etc.)[9] except by acts of war, the threat of war, or the prospect of international alignments in which the ultimate exercise of force against the offender was implicit.

Dem. xiv 3: I think it is advantageous to you to ensure that your grounds for going to war are equitable and just.

'Advantageous', that is, because of the consequences for Athens' relations with other states[10] (or with the gods) and for the morale of the individual citizen.

Dem. xv 28f.: If everyone (*sc. else*) has set out to do what is right, it is shameful if we alone are unwilling to do it; but when everyone else is bent on doing wrong, I do not think it is justice, but unmanliness, for us alone to put up a screen of talk about rights and take no action; for I observe that any nation is accorded its rights in pro-portion to its strength at the time ... The rights of individuals within a state are impartially guaranteed by the law to weak and strong alike; but on the international plane the strong lay down what rights the weak are to enjoy.

Dem. xvi 10: We should also consider what is right, and do it, but take care at the same time that it is to our advantage.

The most important point in these passages is neither the prudential advice to gain a reputation for justice while pursuing advantage nor the recognition that strong nations determine the course of events, but the assumption that in thinking and talking about international relations it is perfectly possible to

[9] Cf. Pearson 214 and de Romilly 40–3.

[10] Cf. J. de Romilly, 'Eunoia in Isocrates', *Journal of Hellenic Studies* lxxviii (1958) 92–101, on the practical importance of attracting international goodwill.

draw a distinction between justice and advantage; cf. Dem. xvii 9, 'Now, when justice, opportunity and interest have coincided . . .'. As in internal affairs (cf. section 3), so in external 'just and advantageous' could be used as a formula (e.g. Dem. vii 46).

The demands of national interest could be insisted on by a speaker advocating a course of action which was deprecated by others as unjust: Dem. viii 1, 'It is your business, setting aside all other considerations, to decree and carry out whatever you believe to be in the city's interest'; ibid. 16, on help for the 'foolish people of Byzantion; Dem. xv 15, 'I would not have argued in this way if it were merely in the interests of the Rhodians; I am not their representative'; Dem. xix 55, to make a treaty 'for ever' deprives the Athenians of the chance to exploit 'the benefactions of fortune'; ibid. 75, the traditional Athenian policy to 'save' any nation whose salvation was in Athens' own interest, irrespective of its virtue or desert (this argument is directed against the view that the Phokians did not deserve support).

Awareness of the difficulty of enforcing law on the international level and the ease of taking action in the national interest combined to produce the notion, exploited very plainly by the Athenian speakers at Melos (Thuc. v 89), that the aggressive behaviour of nations is determined by some sort of 'natural' or 'universal' law or is at least in accord with principles accepted by 'all men': cf. Thuc. vi 18.2, a generalization about 'all those who have ever yet ruled others', and the implication of Thuc. vi 82.3, literally, 'and with regard to precise speaking', (i.e. 'if we are to go into questions of right and wrong') 'our subjection of the Ionians . . . was not unjust'. The Athenian speaker in Thuc. i 75.5 (cf. Euphemos at Kamarina, Thuc. vi 83.2) declares that it is 'unobjectionable' for a nation in danger to take such steps as may be to its advantage (cf. IV.C.1); so Hermokrates (Thuc. iv 61.5, cf. 62.1f.) condemns not a nation which seeks to rule others but those who do not resist aggression by such a nation. Xen. *Cyr.* vii 5.73 calls it an 'eternal law among all men' that a city captured in war is at the absolute disposal of its captors, who are *philanthrōpos* if they leave the defeated anything and cannot be called *adikos* if they leave them nothing.

Aiskhines iii 66: He who bought these (*sc. advantages*) did no wrong, for before he took the oath and made the agreement no objection could be raised against his pursuit of his own interest.

So far as fourth-century oratory is concerned, this passage could fairly be called 'the exception that proves the rule'; it was necessary, as part of his case, that Aiskhines should speak so of Philip.

By contrast, help and aggression were normally described and evaluated in the same terms on the international plane as *dikaios* or *adikos* action between citizens.

Hdt. iii 21.2 (the Ethiopian king to the Persian envoys): If your master were *dikaios* he would not have conceived a desire for a country other than his own, nor would he be attempting to enslave others who have done him no wrong.

Cf. Dem. xvi 25, 'honourable and *dikaios* not to allow ancient cities to be uprooted'; Dem. xxiii 109, Macedonian friendship with Athens *patrikos*, i.e. inherited from previous generations (cf. IV.C.1); Hdt. iv 119.2–4, un-provoked aggression treated as injustice;[11] Hdt. viii 22.1, Themistokles tells the Ionians that in taking part in an expedition 'against their fathers' (i.e. against Athens, since the Greeks of Ionia had originally emigrated from Attica) they are acting in a way which is not *dikaios*; Hdt. v 49.2f., Arista-goras asks Sparta to rescue the Ionians from servitude since they are 'of the same blood', i.e. Greeks; Isok. xii 177, Lys. ii 17, the Dorians 'unjust' in having (once upon a time) invaded and seized the Peloponnese, whereas the Athenians are 'just' in that they sprang from the soil of Attica and did not dispossess others; Xen. *Vect.* 5.6, Athens was deprived of her empire because she was regarded as having exercised her leadership 'cruelly'.

The disruptive ingredients in relations between citizens—ambition, rivalry, pride, jealousy, indignation, shame—are naturally more conspicuous in international relations, because of the absence or ineffectiveness of the forces which within a city can counteract them and tend towards social cohesion: Dem. ii 2, the disgrace of neglecting an opportunity to recover places which Athens once ruled; Dem. viii 60, Athens never willing to be subject to others, for 'you are accustomed to rule'; Dem. xiii 34, the taunt that Athens seems to be aiming no higher than miserable little nations like Siphnos or Kythnos; Dem. xviii 68, Philip's 'greatness of soul' in conceiving the ambition to rule the whole Greek world; Eur. *Iph. Aul.* 102–4, *aiskhros* to allow an enemy to get away with an injury; Thuc. ii 62.3, Perikles' pride in the acquisition of the Athenian empire through *ponoi* (cf. IV.A.2); Thuc. ii 63.1, 'the honours paid to this city, in which you all exult'; Xen. *Hell.* v 1.16, a Spartan commander tells his troops that nothing is more enjoyable or more honourable than to be dependent on no one and to live on booty taken from an enemy, which provides 'sustenance and renown'; Xen. *Hell.* vii 5.18f., Epameinondas's belief that, as a *philptimos*

---

[11] Cf. Pearson 142.

man, he could not die more gloriously than in trying to secure for his own city rule over the whole Peloponnese.

The miseries of war could be denounced, and there was no lack of sentiment in favour of the settlement of international disagreements by debate and arbitration rather than war: Ar. *Peace passim*, and especially 935f. ('so that we shall be lambs towards one another in character'), 997f. (a prayer to bring the Greeks together and 'impart kindly forbearance to their minds'); Dem. xix 88; Eur. *Hel.* 1151–60, on the pointless folly of war; Eur. *Supp.* 119; ibid. 476–93, bad men embark readily on war (this sentiment is designed to serve a very clear argumentative purpose by someone who is in fact in the wrong); ibid. 745–9, the folly of cities in trying to settle issues by slaughter instead of by discourse; ibid. 949–54, when life is so short, mortals should live quietly and cease from *ponoi* (contrast 323–5, 342, on the achievement of honour by *ponoi*!); Hdt. i 68.4, iron invented 'for man's bane'; Hdt. viii 3.1, faction is as much worse than concord as war is worse than peace; Xen. *Vect.* 5.2, 'Those cities are reputed most fortunate which continue longest at peace'.

Against such sentiments we must set: first, the widespread belief that wars against *barbaroi* were reasonable and desirable, especially if (or because) it was easy to win them and to profit by them (Dem. iii 4, xiv 6, xviii 99–101, 109; Isok. iv 182, 'more like sightseeing than campaigning'; cf. Xen. *Anab.* v 6.15; III.B.*1*, VI.A.*3*);[12] secondly, the feeling that it is only in war that the highest virtues can be displayed (Isok. iv 84, the Trojan war caused by a god so that the quality of those who fought in it should not remain unknown); thirdly, the sheer delight of 'routing, pursuing and killing' an enemy (Xen. *Hiero* 2.15); and fourthly, the inescapable fact that a nation gains materially by a war in which it is successful (Isok. vi 49–51, on the 'usefulness' of war as a means of rehabilitating a nation's fortunes; Thuc. iv 59.2, war is unpleasant, but 'no one is deterred by fear of it if he thinks he is going to gain from it'), and so do individuals (Xen. *Oec.* 1.15, estates both of tyrants and of private citizens increased by war). This fourth consideration is relevant to the interpretation of passages which assert not that peace is always and necessarily better than war, but that, *other things being equal*, peace is better than war, for different cultures may differ greatly in their assessment of the equality of other things:

[12] On the question of the 'unity of mankind' cf. W. W. Tarn, 'Alexander the Great and the Unity of Mankind', in (ed. G. T. Griffith) *Alexander the Great: the Main Problems* (Cambridge 1966) 243–86, and the demolition of Tarn's argument by Badian, ibid, 287–306.

Xen. *Hell.* vi 3.6 (*an Athenian envoy, to the Spartans*): If it is fated by the gods that there should be wars among men, we should exercise very great caution over beginning a war, and, when a state of war has come about, we should make peace as soon as we can.

Cf. Thuc. i 124.2, the need to fight a war to establish a lasting and secure peace; Thuc. ii 61.1, the folly of going to war when a nation is prosperous and has a choice between war and peace; Thuc. iv 59.4, we will resume war if we cannot get an equitable settlement; Thuc. iv 92.5, the propriety of a pre-emptive strike against a menacing neighbour; Xen. *Hell.* vi 3.5, *sōphrōn* men avoid embarking on war; Xen. *Vect.* 5.13, of course a city should not stay at peace if it is wronged. In Thuc. vi the two antagonistic speakers at Syracuse during the debate on the news of Athenian preparations for invasion are both attracted by the prospect of a 'creditable achievement' in defeating Athens: Hermokrates (Thuc. vi 33.4), who propounds a plan which, in his view, will make this achievement possible, and Athenagoras (36.1), who is so sure of victory that he says, 'Whoever does not hope that the Athenians are so ill-advised as to attack us . . . is either a coward or no patriot'. It being taken for granted that there must be wars (Xen. *Hell.* vi 3.15),[13] just as there must always be bad weather, the practical problem was always a problem of when, where and how.

One of the reasons (not the only reason) why the Athenian empire in the fifth century held together was that any city which may have wished to secede knew that the Athenians would make war on her to force her back into subordinate status, and that they would probably win. In Athens at the time there was little significant opposition to empire; even the extremists among the oligarchic revolutionaries of 411 wished, if they possibly could, to retain rule over the subject-cities (Thuc. viii 91.3), and the standpoint of Aristophanic comedy, despite its attacks on certain aspects of the style of Athenian rule, was fundamentally as imperialistic as that of Perikles; the rejuvenated Demos at the end of Ar. *Knights* (1329f., 1333f.) is 'monarch of Greece', and in Ar. *Peace* 1082 it is an argument for making peace that Sparta and Athens can then 'rule Greece together'. In retrospect, moral justification was offered, either by focusing attention on the original approach of the Greek states to Athens in the immediate aftermath of the Persian Wars (Isok. xvi 27, 'Your ancestors acquired so high a reputation for

---

[13] Cf. Ehrenberg 312–17, Martin 393–9, and E. A. Havelock, 'War as a Way of Life in Classical Cultures', in (ed. F. Gareau) *Valeurs antiques et temps modernes* (Ottawa, 1972) 19–78. Note also that in Theophr. *Char.* 8.4 the characteristic 'hot' news of the gossipy man is news of a battle.

justice that the Greek cities gladly entrusted them with command at sea') or by stressing the security of those subjects of Athens who obeyed her and trusted to her protection (Isok. iv 101, 'even if some of those who fought against us', e.g. Melos and Skione, 'received a punishment which was regarded as severe' . . .).[14]

[14] Cf. Russell Meiggs, *The Athenian Empire* (Oxford, 1972).

# INDEXES

## I. GREEK AUTHORS AND WORKS CITED

This index contains:

(1) The names of the authors and works mentioned in this book.

(2) The date of each author, expressed as a century B.C. (e.g. 'IV') and the quarters of that century (e.g. 'ii–iii'). This date indicates the limits within which the works of the author in question are known or reasonably believed to have been written.

(3) In the case of fragmentary works and isolated citations, the edition whose numeration is used in this book.

Diels–Kranz = *Die Fragmente der Vorsokratiker*, ed. H. Diels, revd. W. Kranz (Berlin, ed. 6, 1951).

Edmonds = *The Fragments of Attic Comedy*, ed. J. M. Edmonds (Leyden, 1957–61).

Kock = *Comicorum Atticorum Fragmenta*, ed. T. Kock (Leipzig, 1880–88); Edmonds adds some new material not available to Kock, but also adds much confusion and error.

Nauck = *Tragicorum Graecorum Fragmenta*, ed. A. Nauck (repr. with supplement by B. Snell, Hildesheim, 1964).

(4) The page-references to the passages which are translated and printed in small type in this book.

Note:

(a) The printing of an author's name in square brackets, e.g. '[Xen.]', means that the work in question has been transmitted under the name of that author but is demonstrably not by him. The distinction is made throughout the book, but not in the index.

(b) Traditional numbering is not in itself a guarantee of authenticity. Thus e.g. 'Dem. vii' does not mean 'the seventh speech written by Demosthenes', but 'the speech which in modern editions occupies seventh place in the corpus of work transmitted to us under the name of Demosthenes'.

DIONYSIOS of Halikarnassos ('Dion. Hal.'), historian and literary critic, I.iii–iv.

DIPHILOS (-lus), comic dramatist, IV.iii–III.ii. Fragments: Kock, Edmonds.

DISSOI LOGOI, anonymous sophistic work, IV.i (?). Diels-Kranz.

EMPEDOKLES (-cles), philosophical poet, V.ii–iii. Fragments: Diels-Kranz.

## II. GREEK WORDS

## III. GENERAL